WWI MEMORIES OF
GENERAL VON EBERHARDT

WWI MEMORIES OF
GENERAL VON EBERHARDT

GEORGE VON WURMB

WWI MEMORIES OF GENERAL VON EBERHARDT

iUniverse books may be ordered through booksellers or by contacting:

iUniverse
1663 Liberty Drive
Bloomington, IN 47403
www.iuniverse.com
1-800-Authors (1-800-288-4677)

ISBN: 978-1-4917-9384-8 (sc)
ISBN: 978-1-4917-9434-0 (hc)
ISBN: 978-1-4917-9435-7 (e)

Library of Congress Control Number: 2016905610

Print information available on the last page.

iUniverse rev. date: 04/13/2016

Contents

Biography

I, George von Wurmb was born on March 11. 1928 in Porstendorf in the Manor of my Father in Thuringia Hans von Wurmb and his Wife Erika nee von Eberhardt. I attended the Gymnasium (High school) in Jena. 1943 drafted to the Flak 1945 after losing everything through the Russians I lived and worked in W. Germany. In 1955 I went to Canada and in 1968 to USA where I live today.

Abbreviations

A.A.	Artillery Detachment
AHQu.	Army Main Quarter
A.K.	Army Core
A.O.K.	Army Main Command
A.F.D.	Army Field Telegraph Detachment
Art. Kdr.	Artillery Commander
A.	Artillery
Battl.	Battalion
Bad. Ers. Br.	Baden Reserve Brigade
Bahn	Train
cm.	Centimeter
Drag. R.	Dragoner Regiment
Dst. Qu.	Division Staff Quarter
Ers. Abt.	Reserve Detachment
Ers. Battl.	Reserve Battalion
Ers. D.	Reserve Division
Ers. Br.	Reserve Brigade
Esk.	Sqadron
F. A. R.	Field Army Reserve
Fest. MG. A.	Fortress Machine Gun Detachment
F. A. B.	Field Artillery Battery
F. H.	Forest House
Fest. MG. Comp.	Fortress Machine Gun Company
Feld. A. R.	Field Artillery Regiment
Fl. Abt.	Flight Detachment
Fest. San. Comp.	Fortress Ambulance Company
G. O. / GenOb.	Colonel General
G. K. / Gen. Kdo.	General Command
G.M. / GenMaj.	Major General
Genlt.	Lieutenant General
G. F. M.	General Field Marshall
Gen.	General
G. D.	Garde Division

Gru.Fl.	Flight Group
G. J. Br.	Garde Jaeger Brigade
Gren.	Grenadier
G. Fues. R.	Garde Fuesilier Regiment
G. R. K.	Garde Reserve Core
G. Ers. Br.	Garde Reserve Brigade
G. R. zF.	Garde Regiment on Foot
G. Kav. Sch. D.	Garde Kavallery Rifle Division
Kdfr.	Commando Berlin
H. G. R.	Army Group
H. J. R.	Horse Jaeger Regiment
Hus. R.	Husar Regiment
Hus.	Husar
Hptm. / Capt.	Captain
Inf.	Infantry
I. R.	Infantry Regiment
Ia	First Staff Officer
Ib	second Staff Officer
Jaeg. R. zPf.	Jaeger Regiment on Horseback
Jaeg. Battl.	Jaeger Battalion
Jaeg. zPf.	Jaeger on Horseback
K. u. K.	Kaiser and King
Kav.	Cavalry
K. D.	Cavalry Division
Km.	Kilometer
KHQu.	Core Main Quarter
Kdr.	Commander
KWII.	Kaiser Wilhelm II.
Landw. I. Br.	Militia Infantry Brigade
Lt.	Lieutenant
Ldst.	Militia
L. G.	Lieutenant General
Ldw. I. R.	Militia Infantry Regiment
M. W. Comp.	Mine Thrower Company
Mrs.	Mortar
MG.C	Machine Gun Company
M. / m.	Meter

MG. D.	Machine Gun Detachment
Mun. Col.	Munition Column
N. O.	News Officer
Nr.	Number
Oblt.	First Lieutenant
Oberstlt.	Lieutenant Colonel
O. H. L.	Upper Army Command
Pi.	Pioneer
Pi. Battl.	Pioneer Battalion
R. Mun. Kol.	Reserve Munition Column
Res. Pi.	Reserve Pioneer
R. I. B.	Reserve Infantry Battalion
R. I. R.	Reserve Infantry Regiment
R. K.	Reserve Core
Radf. Komp.	Bicycle Company
R. J. R.	Reserve Jaeger Regiment
R. J. Br.	Reserve Jaeger Brigade
R. D.	Reserve Division
R. MG.	Reserve Machine Gun
R. Foot AR	Reserve Foot Artillery
R. F. A. B.	Reserve Field Artillery Battery
R. Jaeg. B.	Reserve Jaeger Battalion
R. Br.	Reserve Brigade
R. Stab.	Reserve Staff
R. I. Br.	Reserve Infantry Brigade
R. Hus. R.	Reserve Husar Regiment
S. M. S.	His Majesty Ship
San. Kraftw. Kol.	Ambulance Car Company
Wuert.	Wuertemberg
X	10
V	5
I	1

Foreword

I wish to thank my Stepson Ronald Fisher and my Step-Grandson Jacob Fisher for encouraging me in writing this Book and also my lovely Wife Edeltraud von Wurmb for supporting me.

World War I Memories of General von Eberhardt

He was born under the Administration of King Friedrich Wilhelm IV on December 6. 1855 in Berlin Germany.

His Father was Premier-Lieutenant in the Garde Fuselier Regiment. The Name was changed in 1860 to Garde Fuselier Regiment. His Mother's Name was von Reuss, also aristocratic background like his Father. The Family was also involved in Military high Commands and Wars, like his Great Grandfather Friedrich Wilhelm Magnus von Eberhardt, who as Major and Commander of Infantry Regiment von Gravert, died in Action near Jena October 14. 1806 and Heinrich von Reuss who as Colonel and Commander of Elb Militia Infantry Regiment (it was later I.R. 26) and was Knight of the Pour le me rite and died in Action on June 17. 1815 at an Attack at Namur. His Grandfather Wilhelm von Eberhardt, who was real"Portepeefaehnrich"(Flag Carrier with Sergeant Rang) in the Infantry Regiment von Sanitz. He was as Orderly Officer ordered to the Command of the Prince Hohenlohe on October 14. 1806, where he near Jena as a 15 Year old, received the Pour le me rite. Then he lost his left Leg near Leipzig, he was active in the Cadet Core and was promoted up to Genlt. His Grandfather, Heinrich Adolf von Reuss, received as Lieutenant in the Regiment that his Father commanded, the Iron Cross 1st. Class and was severely wounded near Ligny. Also the Brothers of his Grandfather had fought in Wars and where severely wounded.

This History left him with strong Impressions.

The Death of the King, who loved Art and Science, but did not enough for Military Development, remained in his Mind. The King died on January 2. 1861. My Grandfather was allowed to go to Potsdam for the Viewing. In Sanssouci he saw G. F. M. Count von Wrangel at the Head of the Casket in the Uniform of the 3rd. Cuirassiers with the German Flag in Hand.

On January 18. 1861. 160 Years after the Establishment of the Kingdom of Prussia, on the Monument of the King in Berlin, where new Flags presented under the new King Wilhelm, to the Troops. It was fantastic to see, when the Bodyguard Company of the first Garde Regiment on Foot, marched on with 142 Flags.

His Parents had also 2 more Sons. Both fought in the War as Genlts. And Troop Commanders and were highly decorated. Also the Husband of his Sister fought as Genlt. On the Front.

On the first Memorial Day of the toppling of the Dueppeler Entrenchments, April 18. 1865 begun work of the Foundation of a Victory Monument, on the Kings Place in Berlin. It was not finished because of the Wars of 1866 and 1870/71. Instead it became a Victory Column.

His Father became Battalion Commander of the 3rd. Posensche Infantry Regiment in Glogau. There he went to School with Alfred von Larisch (General of the Infantry, Knight of the Pour le me rite), Adalbert Falk (later General of the Infantry), Heinrich von Vietinghoff von Scheel (later died as Genlt. in 1917), Hermann von Francois (later General of the Infantry also Knight of the Pour le me rite) and Georg von Glasenapp (later Commander in Southwest Africa died as Genlt. and Commander of the 25th Land Division 1914).

His Father brought his Jung Brother Gaspard and him, after the Battle of Koeniggraetz, to the Battlefields in Bohemia. There they never forgot the Impressions that they became.

He became Cadet in Walstatt in 1870. The seriousness 0f the War times engraved they're thoughts. The Cadets came more together since most of them had Fathers, Brothers, Uncles and Cousins who were either dead or wounded and where awarded Iron-Crosses. Victory News brought happiness.

His Father became Commander of the Infantry Regiment 46 on August 24. 1870. His Regiment fought among others at the Battle of Sedan. He was later wounded and came Home with the Iron-Cross 1st. Class.

My Grandfather saw the victorious Troops as Cadet March into Berlin. He stood near the first German Kaiser, G. F. M. Count von Moltke, G. F. M. Count von Roon, Prince Bismark and Army Leaders.

He met the Kaiser for the first time in 1873. In the round Hall of the old Kaiser Palace stood the Cadets who were permitted to the Officers Exam. The Kaiser came in the Uniform of the Cadet Core, Helm in Hand. Genlt. von Wartenberg, Commander of the Cadet Core, gave the report.

Every Cadet had to come before the Kaiser and state Name and Rank of his Father. The Kaiser spoke to my Grandfather:

> "Your Grandfather was a Jung Hero near Jena and Leipzig.
> Your Father was in the Garde Reserve Regiment.
> "To order your Majesty! And still when the Regiment became Garde Fusilier Regiment."
> "I know, your Father was excellent in the last War."

The Kings of Prussia knew everything about they're Officers and Sons.

After my Grandfather finished his Exam he came in the Selecta of the Garde Core. He had the Honor to become Page of the Princess Friedrich-Karl von Prussia, born Princess Maria-Anna von Anhalt. Prince Friedrich-Karl spoke to him:

> "Become like your Grandfather, he was not only a Hero Officer but also a very good Man, whom I have much to thank."

On Memorial Day of the Battle of Sedan, September 2. 1873 was the Victory Column uncovered and the Band of the Cadet Core played "Hail to the Victory Crown."

The most fantastic Moment for him was when the Cadets formed a Column for the Parade March on the Victory Avenue. Suddenly a Command: "Stop, attention eyes left. "The Kaiser rode with all his Officers through the Column to the Grandstand where the wounded sat. My Grandfather stood only a few paces next to the Kaisers Horse. The Kaiser called to the cheering wounded, with Tears in his Eyes::"This is thanks to you. "This inspired the Cadets to give Life and Blood to the Kaiser and Fatherland.

On the next Day did the old Kaiser install the Foundation Stone to the main Cadet Institute near Grosslichterfelde in a Pine Forest in the Maerkischen Sand with the Berlin Cadets. In this Place were Prussian Officers trained from 1879 until 1920. Many of those became highly honored and died as Hero's.

He became second Lieutenant on April 23. 1874 in the Anhalt Infantry Regiment 93. Superiors and some of the Sergeants had experience with

War and were good Teachers. In the next Year he became Adjutant at Fusilier Infantry Regiment 93 in Zerbst and was from 1878 until 1881 commanded to the War Academy.

His Father took in 1876 as GenMaj. and Commander of the 38st. Infantry Brigade his Discharge.

In 1881 he married Klara von Kalitsch. They had 3 Boys and 2 Girls.

In 1882 he was transferred to the 3rd. Garde Regiment on Foot and became quick Regiments Adjutant and then Brigade Adjutant of the 4st. G. I. Br.

In the sorrowful Year of 1888 did he attend the Funeral Parade for Kaiser Wilhelm I. in ice-cold Weather and Kaiser Friedrich in summer.

The Commander of the General Staff of the Garde Core Baron von Falkenhausen and my Grandfather visited the Battlefields near Jena and Auerstaedt. He was Captain and Company Leader of the 9st. Company and was transferred to the 3rd. Garde Regiment on Foot and in 1890 to the General Staff of the Army. He was placed in the Main General Staff. There he came to the War Historical Detachment. There he was told friendly words by the old G. F. M. Count von Moltke. He was able to celebrate the Counts 90st. Birthday. He stood Death Watch on April 28. 1891 on his Coffin. Kaiser Franz-Josef was in 1890 also at the Kaiser Maneuver. There my Grandfather was commanded to General von Beck, the Leader of the Austrian General Staff. That important Post of the Prussian German Army was in 1891 handed to Count von Schlieffen.

Only a few Men can meet so many important People as he was able to. He always thought it a great Honor to say;" I saw Kaiser Wilhelm I., Bismarck and Moltke."He had this Luck already as a Jung Officer many times. All the words that the Kaiser, or von Moltke or Bismarck said to him, where forever imprinted in his Heart. His Military Work and his simple Life and his Family Devotion that he and his Wife had, brought on that they only sparingly met People of Art and Science. He considered it a Fortune to have met G. F. M. Count von Schlieffen in his Work.

In 1891 was Count von Waldersee Commander General of the IXst. Army Core and his Successor Count von Schlieffen. So my Grandfather had occasion to meet him. He was retaining and hard to get to know. He was big and thin, distinguished especially with his Monocle. His Glance was sharp when you spoke to him.

My Grandfather was told in August 1891 that in the fall he will be transferred to the General Staff of the 8ˢᵗ. Division in Erfurt, but before that he was to attend the Kaiser Maneuver between the IVst. (Commanding General of the Cavalry von Haenisch) and the XIst. Army Core (Commanding General of the Infantry von Grolman). To the jet to be build 4ˢᵗ. R.D. as General Staff Officer. On the Occasion of a Drill of the Queen Augusta Garde Grenadier Regiment 4. That to the Maneuver of the Garde Core from Koblenz to Berlin came, under the Commander Baron von Falkenhausen, his former Teacher, on the Tempelhofer Field exercised. Count von Schlieffen spoke long with my Grandfather:

> "I ordered you to the Reserve Division of the IVst. Army
> Core and I hope you live up to. We build such a Division for
> the first time and hope to learn for the Mobilization. It will not
> be without difficulties since such Formations need time for the
> Leaders. The Mobilization Preparation at the IVst. Army Core
> is good. You will be commanded to Magdeburg 8 Days before
> Commencement. There you can find out all the Essentials at
> the General Command and you can set up your Office."

The Regiment Augusta did at that time a tactical Task and by still speaking to him did Count von Schlieffen further tell him:

> "You will not have it easy with your Commanding General
> von Moeller. He is an excitable Man, but a smart and proficient
> Soldier. They call him "flying Dog" stay calm and everything
> will be all right. I have all the Trust in you."

Then he shook his Hand. My Grandfather was proud of the Trust in him. So with Anticipation he started his Job. It was in the War History Department. He had to collect all important Papers of the dead Count von Moltke.

During this time he was Captain of the General Staff and later as Major and Reporter of the Army Division in the War Ministry. He had no Opportunity to come closer to the Chief of the General Staff of the Army. He had much work in the General Staff. It was not astonishing that both Chiefs of the 2 Departments of the main General Staff Colonel von Heeringen and his Successor von Wittgen had talks in his Office. His wiser Department Chief, Colonel Beseler, was also in the General Staff.

Even so my Grandfather was in close touch with the General Staff. He was in summer 1897 with the General Staff on a Tour (Leader Chief of the General Staff of the XIVst. Army Core Colonel Baron Vietinghoff-Scheel) in Elsa's. When his age Group was considered to become Department Chief in the main General Staff or Chief in an Army Core, it was not decided. In 1898 he became Battalion Commander in the Grenadier Regiment Count Karl von Prussia (2nd. Brandenburgisches) # 12 in Frankfurt on the Oder. There he enjoyed work and private happy times. Because of the kind Words from his Division Commander Genlt. Koepke, commanding General of the IIIrd. Army Core and General of the Infantry von Liegnitz, at the War Ministry and General of the Infantry von Gossler and Chief of the Military Cabinets Gen.Ob. von Hahnke and at Count von Schlieffen, was he placed immediately in the General Staff. At the Parade Diner of the Garde Core spoke Count von Schlieffen to my Grandfather with good words, about his Work at the War Ministry. After the Kaiser Maneuver on October 13. 1900 was he transferred as Department Chief to the General Staff of the Army.

"I gave you the 7st. Division, those are the Russian Fortresses. I hear you do not speak Russian?"" No your Excellence, I do not know Russian Letters and was never on the Fortresses."

"Now this will not be necessary but you will have to read Russian maps."

My Grandfather promised and in not very long time was able to read Russian and later Chinese Maps. At this time did the East Asian Expedition under G. F. M. Count von Waldersee take place.

Even so he took part in a Fortress General Staff Trip (in Strasburg and the Area) and he had good Knowledge of Russian Fortresses, he was happy when he was promoted in the Spring of 1901 to Chief of the 6st. Department. He attributed the promotion to the kind words of Count von Schlieffen, who told him April 19. The Work was to prepare and give reports about the Kaiser Maneuver and report from the General Staff Trips witch where commanded from the Chief of the General Staff of the Army.

The 2 Years he was the Leader of this Department where happy times. In the first Days after take over they took an inquiry Trip through the Area between Dirschau and Danzig west of the Weichsel River. In the fall they had planned a Kaiser Maneuver between the Ist. and the XVIIst. Army Core. Both were to be reinforced by Infantry and Cavalry and also Navy. Count von Schlieffen and my Grandfather took 3 Days to look over the Maneuver Area. After they arrived at the Night Quarters late, they ate the joint Meals, at which they talked about the Daily News. They both travelled in civilian close and where instantly recognized at the Restaurant. The People of the Area looked forward to the Maneuver. Everybody wanted to know if the Kaiser would come.

Count von Schlieffen attended before the Maneuver, Navy Maneuvers in the Baltic Sea and was on Board the Kaisers Yacht "Hohenzollern" together with the Kaiser and Czar Nicolaus IInd. In the last Days before the Maneuver were important details to discuss. In Koenigsberg at the Parade of the 200 Year Celebration of the Kingdom of Prussia was not everything discussed. Count von Schlieffen gave my Grandfather Power of Attorney to handle everything and send most important Decisions by Boat to him. He worked hard in Danzig at the Headquarters of the Maneuver. In the Evening he drove to see the Navy Parade before the Czar in the Danzig Bay near Hela. With him where Officers of his Department on Board "SMS Weissenburg" . He then went with a Patrol Boat to the "Hohenzollern", Count von Schlieffen received him in his Cabin and took his report. He was very grateful.

The Maneuver did not go as planned. After the big Cavalry attack it started to rain and all was cancelled. They had Trouble with the new Motor Vehicles. The Car with Count von Schlieffen, my Grandfather, Major von Heydebreck and Captain Count von Lambsdorf had Luck and mastered all Obstacles with Patience. The other Car with the Officers got stuck. They made it to Danzig with much Trouble.

It was hard for the Count von Schlieffen to get the Commanding General of the XVIIst. Army Core, General of the Infantry von Lentze, who we met with his Staff at forward March to get to rest. His mild Composure won. He kept his Composure also with jammed Roads, collided Wagon Columns and destroyed Bridges. They trusted the Car too much and missed they're Horses. They could not overlook all the

Maneuver Area and so could not reach Troops of the first Army Core under General of the Infantry Count von Finkenstein. They heard that the Cavalry Divisions where put in temporary Quarters on an empty Rest place near Swarotschin and the Commander went back to Danzig. So they hurried back to Danzig. In Danzig came the order from the Kaiser that the Maneuver on the next Day was cancelled. They had to find Accommodation for 6 Infantry and 2 Cavalry Divisions south and east of Danzig witch took long Marches. It was a big Job to change everything for the next 2 Days. My Grandfather and his Officers worked tireless.

On the next Day after the Maneuver begun the big Fall General Staff Trip. My Grandfather met Count von Schlieffen and the Adjutant of Count von Lambsdorf in the Train to Riesenburg in West Prussia. The Count was very happy and told Tales that he heard on the "Hohenzollern". Especially about the Russians.

My Grandfather was Chief of the 6st.Department and was a Confidant of the Count. He was as such included in the main General Staff Trips. The Summer Trip was in the west and the fall in the east. There were always 25 to 30 Officers. Count von Schlieffen wanted to be ready in case of Mobilization and train Officers, for the newly to be formed Army and Cores. He chooses Frontier Territories and Maps.

My Grandfathers Work was hard. They started at 7 or 7.30 in the Morning riding. In the Beginning all rode together, later they split. The Count rode with his Quarter Master and some older Officers and on the Way to the next Quarters they looked at important Areas, Border Fortifications, Bridges also private Establishments such as Horse Farms and Factory's.

After a 6 or 7 hour ride, with sometimes Gallop over Pastures, they arrived at Lodging and ate Breakfast. My Grandfather changed and went to the Count to report. He received new orders. Then they all came to a Meeting about a War Situation. He found the Count looking at Maps. Instead of his Monocle he used big Horn Spectacles. It was amazing how he knew all Maps, Places and Military Columns.

It was hard work but my Grandfather liked it. It was difficult because the Count gave 2 Officers orders to plan. He then worked on both Plans together. In this Way begun one Mobilization Day on the 30th and the other on the 38th. This gave Misinterpretations and my Grandfather had to straighten this out at the report. The one Plan begun at Plancenoit south of Bruessel with the XXVIIst Reserve Core. The other Plan crossed the Mosel at Sierck. The Count had no confusion and knew every Place.

At these Trips by Horse in West and East did my Grandfather see the most beautiful Areas of the Fatherland. In both Years was good Weather. He saw the Eifel and the Vogesen and the Area near Metz and Diedenhofen in the West. Also the West and East Prussian Border near Thorn up to the East Prussian Lakes and Insterburg.

The Kaiser Maneuver 1902 between Infantry and Cavalry of the 3ʳᵈ. Army Core under the Commanding General of the Infantry von Liegnitz and the Vth. Army Core under General of the Infantry von Stuelpnagel between Meseritz and Zuellichau, had difficulties for the Leaders. The main Quarters in the Town of Sonnenburg, where the Kaiser took Quarter in the Johanniter Castle, had enough room for the General Staff. The Maneuver Leadership had to go every Morning and Evening with Cars to Drossen and from there with a special Train to Meseritz or Train Station Tempel. There they got on to the Horses. That took a lot of time. The orders of the Commanding Generals came in the Evening by Telegraph. The Work then for the Maneuver Leaders begun at Night. The Officers of my Grandfather had a lot of work to do. The People there were astonished that Officers had to work so late and hard.

At the Preparation for the Kaiser Maneuver 1903 did my Grandfather with Count von Schlieffen check out the Area near Naumburg. He was transferred in February 1903 as Chief of the General Staff of the Xst. Army Core to Hannover. The Count was always a friendly Boss. On February 25.1906 he retired from the General Staff.

As Chief of the General Staff of the 10ˢᵗ. Army Core, under the Command of General of the Cavalry von Stuenzner, did my Grandfather have a happy time. For the General Staff Trip under his Command he used a Ship from Emden to Wilhelmshafen. He took several Sea Officers along. From there they rode Horses to Verden on the River Aller. He wanted to check out an Enemy Landing at the Coast near Borkum.

He was promoted 1904 to Regiments Commander of the Garde Fusilier Regiment. He was proud of this because his Father was there many Years. Those Years were the happiest of his Life. The People called that Regiment "Maikaefer" (Maybugs). It was the most popular Regiment of the Old Prussian Army. They attained they're Glory in 1866 and 1870/71 at the Battlefields. The Enemy was especially afraid of them.

After he led the Regiment for 3 Years he was promoted to Chief of the General Staff of the Garde Core and in the same Year to Major General. Under the Commanding Generals of this Core, GO. von Kessel and General of the Infantry Genlt. von Loewenfield he had Fun to work and to help training the Troops for the Fall Maneuver. At the General Staff Trip 1907 was also the Kaiser Highness the Crown prince and in 1909 Highness King Prince Eitel Friedrich.

My Grandfather had occasion in1909 for a learning Trip to the Austrian Balkan Provinces. At his report in Vienna at the Chief of the General Staff, General of the Infantry Conrad von Hoetzendorf, he was heartily welcomed. They talked at a long time about the German and Austrian Maneuvers and the General was impressed with the training and performance of the German Troops. He appreciated the help Germany gave Austria and promised to never forget. He said to my Grandfather:

"There be no secrets between us, I will make sure that you get all Military Interests."

My Grandfather was promoted to Genlt. Between 1911 and 1913 and was Commander of the 19st. Infantry Division in Hannover. It was an Honor to train the Troops under the Commanding General of the Infantry von Emmich.

Governor of Strasburg

My Grandfather became Governor of Strasburg in Elsa's on March 22.1913 because of the Kaisers Trust. So he did not train the Troops anymore. He recognized the excellent training of the XVst. Army Core, that under the Command of General von Deimling in German Southwest Africa, at the crush of the Herero Revolt, much Glory earned.

The Kaiser visited Elsa's in April and ordered a Combat Exercise. It was held near Dreiaehren west of Colmar. A red Party occupied Place and Rochette. A blue Party was to attack near Zell and Evaur. My Grandfather was with the Generals von Eben, Ludendorf and Altrock at a high Place south of Henzell to watch. A lot of local People, many French, assembled to watch and nobody knew that a half Year later War would break out.

The Kaiser asked him after the Exercise to come to him. He talked about Fortifications in Strasburg. My Grandfather asked him to see to further completion of the Fortress Kaiser Wilhelm II near Mutzig. The Kaiser answered:

"You can be sure that a Gun Battery will be installed at Scharrach Mountain, I will see to that."

The Kaiser shook his Hand. His Interest in such Fortifications was big, but often there was not enough Money.

The Capital Strasburg was the second biggest Fortress in Germany. It had 200,000 Inhabitants. The Rheine Harbor, Commerce and Industry flourished. German Youth enjoyed the University. A big Garrison brought Money. Business and Trades People were mostly German oriented also the Country People. Industry Workers learned French. Also the small Towns like Hagenau, Zabern, Schlettstadt and Neubreisach had advantage from the Garrison. In all Protestant were German and Catholic People were French in thought. The German speaking Country People in the Rheine Area up to the Vogesen and a big part of the Workers did not want to become French.

In Peace time was the Governor under the Commanding General. My Grandfather thought this was wrong. The Government and the Commanders of the big Fortresses should have been under the Chief of the General Staff of the Army. Only he could see the importance of the Fortress in War. In case of Mobilization became the Governor the Leader. General von Deimling and my Grandfather had some different Ideas.

The most important Border Fortress like Strasburg should have been reinforced in Peace time, but it was not.

Strasburg became a Ring of Fortifications after Elsa's became German. In the Technic of Artillery and Fortifications at that time it was Brick Building with lots of Ground on Top. Also deep steep Ditches.

Strasburg had on the left Rheine Shore 10 Fortifications and on the right 3 big Fortifications and 2 big Bases. All the Fortifications where build similar as the French like Lille and Reims.

Strasburg had on modern Buildings of the Fortification Art only one armored Battery in northwest of the Fortress and one on the left of the Rheine Shore. Also the modern Fortifications on the Molsheimer Hill near Mutzig. The Fortress Kaiser Wilhelm II belonged already in Peace time to the Area of the Governor.

The in 1870 originated Fortifications, because of age, where not adequate and had to be renewed with new Battery's. When the War started that was not finished.

The Task of the Fortress Strasburg was in War to stop the Advance of the French in the Vogesen, the Rheine Area and the Passes over the Donon, Col du Hantz and over Saales and trough the Breusch and Weiler Valley. It flanked an Enemy Offensive into Lothringia and the Pfalz. Also out of the southern Vogesen Passes into upper Elsa's. It would have forced the Enemy to besiege or to branch of Forces. Because of this was a Completion of the Breusch Fortification between Fortress Kaiser Wilhelm II and the Fortifications Ring in Planning.

Strasburg cut the Power together with the Fortress Neubreisach and the Fortifications on the upper Rheine at Mulheim.

This big Weapon Area with its Military and Technic was a big Bridgehead for the German Troops to cross the River.

In spite of many requests to build a few armored Battery's and Fortified Bunkers in Peace time. In spring of 1914 begun the building of a Battery on a high Place between Kolbsheim and Hangenbieten. The building at these Places and the digging at the Dangolsheimer Hill at direct joining the west Front to the Fortress Kaiser Wilhelm IInd had by begin of the War not begun. Likewise was an extension of the Fortification to the north in Mind. For that came by my Grandfathers Reconnaissance a Line at Marle and Stephan's Mountain east of Wasselnheim and the Hills at Ittlenheim, Behlenheim and Griesheim into Consideration.

For the extensive Groundworks where 40,000 Man necessary at the Start of Mobilization.They should come after the 4st. Mobilization Day from Strasburg and surrounding Area up to the Colmar District. The Engineer Officer had his Hands full with all these People but he managed.

The General Command did not have to determine the Plans for the Defense Line. The immense work to arm a not finished Border Fortress and to provide Funds, with big help from his Staff, was a big Challenge for my Grandfather. By the Start of the War and on the most important Places on the Border, the Donon Pass, the Col du Hantz and the Saales Pass, were the Peace time Troops knew all the Roads, where not under the Governor from Strasburg. Instead on the fifth Day of Mobilization was a new formed R. I. R., they were new to the Area, ordered.

It was also bad that German Toll Officials had no training. On the other Hand the French trained they're Toll and Forest People. The French Garrison Troops where well trained and superior and had Mountain Artillery, that the German Troops not had.

June and July 1914

Sunday June 28th. Was a sunny Day. Strasburg People came out in festive Dress to the Rheine Harbor to watch a rowing Regatta between Elsa's and Baden Clubs. Nothing pointed to the Fact that at that time the Stone begun to roll that plunged the World in Chaos.

A Government Official came to my Grandfather and said:

> "I just now got News from the Ministry, that the Arc-Duke from Austria and his Wife were killed in Sarajevo."

The News spread quickly. Now came the significant July weeks with the daily War Rumors. From high up came order to take any precaution for the Security of the Fortress. The only thing that the Government ordered, against the Will of the General Staff, was that the 40,000 Fortress Workers had to have white Armbands. It was utmost important to show that they belonged to the Army.

As the Weather Clouds formed on the political Sky became my Grandfather and his Chief Oberstlt. von Boeckmann the conviction that the Fortress Kaiser Wilhelm II was not safe. On the Fortress were new and reconstruction work in Progress. Among the Workers were People whose reliability was questionable. Many Italians. Only a few Officials and Artillerists and Pioneers that belonged to the Gun Crews where there. A Guard Commando with 2 Officers and 78 Man had to watch over the Fortress and the Area. There was an about 30 Feet wide Wire Obstacle for Protection. In front were in many Places Thickets and Forest. In Front of south and east Barrier were Vineyards. An Asphalt Street ran through the Fortress from Sulzbad to Mutzig for the public Traffic. To step on the Area next to the Street was only permitted to People with a Permit from the Commander. My Grandfather was uneasy, before the Border Guard started, if French People with high Explosives in Cars came. It was possible for resolute People to come through the Obstacles and blow up the, on the west Line build, Armor Guns. All requests where denied for lack of Funds.

So came the hot Days of the last July Week. My Grandfather listened with tension to the News from West and East. The Commander of the IIIrd./ Infantry Regiment 143 in Mutzig, Major von Kuehn, who commanded the Guard Troops at the Fortress Kaiser Wilhelm IInd, informed the Government that, because of News that Russia had Mobilization, he had ordered extra Guard Duty. The Government telegraphed that extra Guard Duty was not necessary but welcomed. My Grandfather drove before Noon to the Fortress and talked about Security Measures, but officially they were not allowed.

The War Ministry ordered on July 29 that all Airplane and Zeppelin Hangers had to be watched with live Ammunition.

The War Ministry ordered on July 30 that all Armor Fortifications of the Fortress Strasburg had to be finished for training the Troops. The Forest in Front of the Fortress at Northwest and South Area had to be cleared. 11 Companies of the Infantry Regiment 126, 136 and 143 also 13 Platoons of the Pioneer Battalion 15 and 19, where ordered for this Work. For the Guard Duty in Strasburg became the Government the Staff IInd./ Infantry Regiment 105, 3 Infantry and 1 M. G. Company and the 10st./ Infantry Regiment 136. Also the Government had Balloon Defense Canons for the Fortress.

My Grandfather became an order from the War Ministry that commanded to start with completion of the Fortress Kaiser Wilhelm II at the Dangolsheimer Hill. The Fortress became temporary Troops that Major von Kuehn already ordered. The Government sends on the Morning of July 30. General Staff Officer Major Mohs to the Fortress. He and Major von Kuehn and an Engineer Officer Oberstlt. Karbe talked about Security Measures.

The Crew at the Kehler Rheine Bridge was ordered to put Machine Guns at the Towers of the Bridge at the right Shore. Also sharp Control of Traffic was ordered of the IInd. / Infantry Regiment 105. The Railroad Crossing at Kehl Appenweier and Kehl Auenheim became at 1.45 in the afternoon a Balloon Defense Gun.

At 7.25 in the afternoon came a Telegram from the General Inspection from Berlin.

"Start with completion of Breusch Position."

Then the Government ordered that the Command Mutzig do the same for Position Scharrach and Sulzberg.

The Political Climate became more and more sharp. My Grandfather wanted to order quite a few changes but did not want to go against the Government. State and Town Officials had a Meeting about Food Supply in case of Mobilization. At the Meeting were Under Secretary of State, Count von Roedern, von Stein and Lord Mayor Schwander. For the Government was my Grandfather, his Chief Oberstlt. von Boeckmann and the Director Schaeffer. Immediate Action of State and Towns evidenced that there was enough Food for the Population. Lord Mayor Schwander was at the Meeting practical and prominent.

On July 31 at 2 in the afternoon came an order from Berlin to construct the Armor Bridge IV over the Rheine. At 2.30 in the afternoon came a Telegram from the War Ministry:

"Imminent War Danger."

My Grandfather could now order all that was necessary. The Forest Master from the Ringgold Valley asked permission at 4.50 in the afternoon to cut Trees in the Forest Haslach. It was important and the Government thought about it in Peace time. They needed Strips of clearing through the Forest so the Artillery could hit the incoming Streets. On August 1st. at 6 in the Evening came the Mobilization order for all Army, Land and Water Troops. The exact trained Mobilization begun. The Vanguard Border Troops where by Evening in Place to watch over important Bridges and Railroad Trak's.

A patriotic Rally was held in the Evening. Old and Jung Soldiers, Workers and Students and Pupils where in the Street and sang "Die Wacht am Rhein."(A German Song " the Watch on the Rheine.) The Masses stopped in front of the General Command and my Grandfather came out and held a Speech and everybody called "Hurrah" and all wanted to shake his Hand. A part of the Population had French Sympathy but in this moment it did not matter.

The War starts

August 2 was the first Mobilization Day. During the Day came many reports of French Troop Formations and also placement of Guard Troops

It was important to inspect the Fortress Kaiser Wilhelm IInd since the Commander Bavarian Genlt. Ipfelkofer could only come August 3 in the Evening. My Grandfather drove with his first General Staff Officer at 12 Noon to Molsheim. The Population was very friendly and did not know the seriousness of the Situation. The Substitute Commander Oberstlt. Karbe and his Troop Officers where ordered for a Meeting. There they became a bad Surprise. Even so the public Road from Sulzbad to Nutzig was, according to Regulation, with Obstacles and Barb Wire blocked by a Guard Sergeant. All the Troops where there but other than that nobody worked. When he asked they said: "Today is Sunday."

"Mobilization was ordered! You do not know if in the next few hours a French Patrol comes close to the Fortress! Immediately reinforce all Obstacles, put the Vineyard into an Obstacle!"

The answer was; "I have no Armor Workers".

"Immediately get the Mayor from Mutzig on the Telephone and order him to come in an hour with all People that can still work. By Morning I want a report that the Forest by Dinsheim is down, the Obstacles between the west Front and the Dangolsheimer Mount reinforced, the Vineyards on the south Front become a big Obstacle. "The Substitute Commander was ordered likewise. The Spirit of the Man in the Fortress, the Musketeers, Foot Artillerists and Pioneers made a good Impression on my Grandfather.

The French had not come across the Border. Brisk Truck Traffic was observed because of incoming Reservists. They heard from the French side Detonations but did not know what they were. Then they observed that the French exploded Trees to block the Roads.

Meanwhile was the Government Office in the Blauwolkengasse changed into a Field Office. They had to put Obstacles in the Street to stop the many People that wanted to work. The Guards had lots of work. The Courtyard was many times filled with Officers and Men to get orders. In between came People that wanted to talk to my Grandfather.

The Chief of the General Staff of the Army G. O. von Moltke gave the Government a War Arrangement for the German Army. It said the Government Strasburg with the XIVst. Army Core (Commanding General of the Infantry Baron Hoiningen called von Huehne) XVst. Army Core (Commanding General of the Infantry von Deimling) and the one to be established in the Grand Dukedom Baden XIVst Reserve Core (Commanding General of the Artillery von Schubert) also the 7st. Cavalry Division (Commander Genlt. von Heydebreck) to the 7st. Army under the Commander GenO. von Heeringen. 2 Italian Cavalry Divisions were in time to come by Train. They were to be a Cavalry Core. The Commander of this Core was supposed to be General of the Cavalry Knight von Frommel who was already in Strasburg but left after 3 days to find on other Assignment.

G. F. M. Count von Schlieffen did as his General Staff Trips in the Years 1901 and 1902 in Elsa's Lothringia, said that he did not believe that we could count on Italian Armors Help.

On August 3 became the Government many reports of French Troops on the Border.

The Armoring of the Fortress and the Mobilization went forward. A wireless Message came from the General Head Quarters in Berlin at 6.15 in the evening and ordered that from 6 in the Evening Germany and France were at War.

Genlt. Ipfelkofer was from this Day on Commander of the Fortress. He hurried the Armoring Work and laying of new Obstacles on the west Front of the Fortress up to the Scharrach Hill. So my Grandfather could be calm.

On August 4 came reports of movements of the French on the Border. Even so the Enemy was probably informed about the Fortress, they did not do anything.

The Fortress was divided into 5 Sections. (North, Northwest, West, South and East) for various Fronts. The Troops of the Government where divided in the Positions in the Breusch Valley, on the Scharrach and Sulzberg, Train and Bridge Defense in Strasburg and Khel, Border Defense, Fortress Kaiser Wilhelm IInd and inclusive Dangolsheimer Hill, Armoring Commandos, Guard and Safety of the Town of Strasburg. A General took over Command of the Positions. On August 3 came the Generals to take over the Command of these Positions. Genlt. von Ferling, GenMaj. Rasch and Neuber, von Gynz Rekowski, Nikolai and as Commander, who had to build the main Reserve of the Fortress 30st. Reserve Division Genlt. von Knoerzer. They all had a lot of work to get the newly build Militia ready for War.

On August 5 were in the Positions of the Fortress only substitute, Reserve and Garrison Company's. Most had jet to be trained for War. Several Militia Battalions arrived with not enough Officers. At 10 in the Morning became the arriving Infantry Regiment 60 (Commander Oberstlt. Zechlin from Infantry Regiment 17) order to be Garrison of the Fortress. From the News, which the Government trough the General Command of the 15 Army Core, also from the Border Security Detachment obtained, was learned that Enemy Troops where in the Plaine Valley near Celle's also in St. Die near Ban de Sap and south near Wisembach, Plainfaing and Fraize. The Enemy had Anould, the Gore Pass, and the Hohneck (1361 m. high) and Geradmer occupied. Lieutenant Wrede from Jaeger Regiment of the Pfalz 3 gave a report that he with a Patrol found the Plaine Valley near Celles void of anybody and also the Street Bionville – Badonviller.

The main Commander of the 7. Army G. O. von Heeringen came on August 5 to Strasburg. My Grandfather gave report and found him amiable. The General Staff Chief of the 7st. Army was Genlt. von Haenisch.

In the Evening of this Day was the devil loose in the Town. Exited People thought they seen a Man on the Roofs cutting electric Wires. Everybody screamed and the Soldiers got their Guns and shot up on the Roofs. A lot of People came to the Government Building and said the Spy was there. A total Search proved not so.

The Application of the heavy Battery's was almost done. So from August 7 on could the 10-13 and 15 cm.Guns defend the outer Lines. The Army upper Command 7 announced that the French marched before Noon in the upper Elsa's. These where not light Patrols but heavy Units. They marched from Belford on several Streets fore. They also marched through the Mountains. Forest People and Customs Officers were expelled west of Grandfontaine. From the Jaeger Battalion 14 came a report that near Markirch heavy Troops were west of the Town. In this critical time came the relief of the Border Security in the Breusch Valley. A bad Mobilization decision. The local trained I. R. 143 was relieved by the Garrison Troops new and not jet trained R. I. R. 99. The Commander Oberstlt. Rayle reported at 5 in the afternoon that his Regiment was in Place. The Border Security Detachment was from then on under the Government.

The Army upper Command ordered on August 8 to build a Detachment from the main Reserve of the Fortress witch was to take Quarters near Oberehnheim. Then used from the incoming Troops: Genlt. von Knoerzer with his Staff Ist. IInd. And IIIrd. / Bavarian R. I. R. 60 and 99, Fortress M. G. Core 2 and R. M. G. Detachment 3, 1 Group H. J. R. 3, one Reserve F. A. R. 80, Staff and III. (2 Battery's 15 cm.) R. Foot A. R. 14 (10 cm.) and 2 Groups A. F. D.

At the National Hill near Oberehnheim was with a Light Signal Group a connection between Detachment Knoerzer and the Government established. At the Fortress was left: I. / R. I. R. 60 and at the Breusch Position IV. / R. I. R. 99. The Regiments Staff and IInd. / R. I. R. 60 were at the Scharrach Hill positioned.

In the afternoon came G. O. von Heeringen to my Grandfather and informed him about his Intention, the VIIst. French Core, that near Muelhausen in advance was, to attack. He gave him the order, the right side of the 7st. Army to defend and gave him for that all Border Security Troops from Donon to Markircher Valley.

General von Deimling left Strasburg in the Evening of that Day with the XVst. Army Core. My Grandfather did not see him again. He could never understand why a good Soldier and Troop Leader, that loved Kaiser and Fatherland, later turned into a Pacifist.

The Army order for the XVst. Army Core was given in that Night was to tenaciously defend Train Transport near Colmar and the Vogesen Passes. The XIVst. Army Core was to stand by near Breisach and Neuenburg. The XIVst. Reserve Core was to place the on August 9 incoming Troops at the Rheine Bridges near Schoenau and Markolsheim. The Government Strasburg was ordered to close the Breusch Valley and on August 9 to assemble Troops near Oberehnheim for Border Security. My Grandfather had now the Task to combine all Border Security Forces under his Command. Adjacent at the R. I. R. 99, who had Fest. M. G. A. 9 under Captain von Meyer and a R. F. A. B. was Jaeger Batl. 8 in the Weiler Valley, with Outpost at Hang east of Saales, Climont, Urbeis and Pass Chaume de Lusse. Adjacent was north and south of Markirch the R. J. B. 8 and the Jaeger Battalion 14. Behind was in the Leber Valley a Battalion of the I. R. 172 and several F. A. B. as Reserve. The Troops at Markirch were under Maj. von Schaeffer from the Jaeger Battalion 14.

It was clear that these week Detachments could do only little Defense if the Enemy came with heavy Forces trough the Vogesen.

My Grandfather was informed from the Army Main Command 6 that the Ist. Bavarian Army Core would be moving forward south. He gave the order to Oberstlt. Rayle in Luetzelhausen to move his Troops fore to Schirmeck, to secure against Raon sur Plaine, and to occupy St.Blaise with 1 Company where the Streets to Col du Hantz, Saales and in the Weiler Valley intersecting. Next Morning came the IIIrd. / R. I. R. 99 by Train to Schirmeck. 1 Company from the Jaeger Battalion 8 had to move to Trimbach, Weiler and Grube. The German Positions where at the Climont (966 m.) and the Hallemont (822 m.) east of the Climont. Urbeis was free of the Enemy.

In Strasburg was on this Day, because of the good Work of the Pioneers of the IInd. / Battalion 15 under Commander Captain Hartmann, the War Bridge near the Kehler Bridge completed. The Artillery Armoring was so far advanced that at this Day 2 Batteries were finished with Guns and Ammunition. The 10 cm. Battery at the Scharrach Hill was finished.

The French had on August 8 with the VIIst. Core and parts of the Main Reserve to the Fortress Belford and the Line Sennheim, Illfurt and Altkirch and defense at Wattweiler, Wittelsheim and Muehlhausen advanced. The 8th. French K. D. was between Altkirch and Pfirt. In the Area southeast of Muehlhausen were Patrols were ordered.

The order from G. O. von Heeringen from August 8 at 9.50 in the Evening placed, the XVst. A. K. at 7 in the Morning, with the Infantry Point, at the Line Rufach, Enzen passing to Sennheim, Wittensheim. The right Division from the XIVst. A. K. was to advance from Hirtzfelden in direction of Ensisheim and the left according to the order also.

Right after the order to attack, came the order from the Government that the Detachment Knoerzer had to march in the Area of Dambach. It was there to help with the planed attacks in the upper Elsa's and to protect the right Flank of the 7. Army in Leber and Weiler Valley.

At the Government came a report that August 8 in the Evening the French Jaeger Battalion 31 had crossed the Border at Markirch and was with heavy Casualty's repelled. As of early Morning August 8 and 9 was Combat at Col du Bonhomme.

The A. O. K. 7 said telegraphically that the Battle at Muehlhausen require all active Infantry from Strasburg and they are to be transported with two 10 cm. Battery's and light Ammunitions Column by Train past Colmar to Rufach better to Bollweiler. The Government ordered LG. Mueller (Commander of the 3rd. Bavarian R. I. B.) with the IIIrd. / R. I. R. 99 and 4 Battalions of the Bavarian R. I. B. 4 and two 10 cm. Canon Battery's and a light Ammunitions Column to go by Train south and move against Sennheim.

So was a big reinforcement for the 7st. Army arranged. This detachment did not come to be deployed. The G. K. of the XVst. A. K. asked and got in the Evening for his Troops at Markirch and for the Battery two R. F. A. 80 in the Leber Valley an Ammunition supply.

At the then present War Situation on August 10 it was decided the Area at Blaesheim to dry up. Colonel Fritsch of the Engineers and Pioneers was ordered at 6 in the Morning:" The Swamp at Blaesheim has to be dried up fast and the one at the Breusch Position next" The work went quite fast.

The A. O. K. 7 informed at 10.30 in the Morning the Government that the XIVst. And XVst. A. K. where south of the Line Sennheim— Muehlhausen. The French where marching back to Belfort. Short there after came an order to stop the Transports. But the Trains were already on the Way and partly offloaded. Also the Detachment Knoerzer was left in March. It reached at 6 in the Evening Kestenholz and Schlettstadt and went into Quarters. It took connection with the right Column of the XIVst. R. K. witch marched over the Rheine at Illhaeuser. It was the Intention of the A. O. K. 7 to use them in the case the Enemy came east of the Vogesen from the Leber and Rappoltsweiler Valley.

The result of the Battle at Muehlhausen was not what the A. O. K. had in Mind. They thought that the frontal attack would envelope the French left Wing, but in the Vogesen were no Streets in the north-south Direction. The XVst. A. K. lacked in the Morning of August 9 a right Squadron so they could not push the Enemy towards the Swiss Border. Nevertheless a Success was obtained. The French VIIth. Core, after heavy Combat, left in the Night there Position and in dissolve went back to Belfort. The upper Elsa's was free of the Enemy.

At the Border Security in the Breusch Valley occurred this on August 10: In the Night did the Radf.Comp. Of the Jaeger Battalion 8 under Captain von Cossel and one Company Jaeg.z.Pf. 3 march from the Border Security Area through Lupine and came early in the Morning in the Area of Provencheres in contact with French Jaeger and Artillery. They became Fire and went back. Oberstlt. Rayle arrived with the main Body of the R. J. R. 99 at 11 in the morning in St. Blaise.

The Ist. Bavarian A. K. (Commander General of the Infantry Knight von Xylander) had planned to thrust in the Plaine Valley and north on the Street to St.Die with all available Force to divert the French from further attacks in upper Elsa's. On that Day came reports that Detachments of the Ist.Bavarian A. K. could not advance towards St.Die and were short of Ammunition and that the 7. K. D. at Badonviller stopped because of exhaustion of the Horses. My Grandfather called by Telephone at 8 in the Evening the A. O. K. and asked:

> "Enemy Jaeger and Artillery are positioned against our Border Security at Saales in the Area of Provencheres. Intend in the Morning to advance with Detachment Knoerzer and Border Security to St.Die. Ask permission to use Jaeger 8 and Border Security Markirch."

For his regret came 20 Minutes later the answer:

> "Intended advance to St.Die not allowed."

The important Task of the Flank Security of the 7th. Army against the attacking French in the Vogesen Passes gave him the Obligation to check Leaders and Troops himself. So he drove on August 11 at 4 in the Morning with his Chief, the first General Staff Officer and his Adjutant, Captain von Glasenapp, over Schlettstadt to Markirch. In Front of the Hotel was the Staff of the Battalion of the I. R. 172 that told them about the Battle that Major von Schaeffer with his small Border Security Detachment had for 3 Days. The losses were high especially Officers. The French had dashingly attacked. They left in one Place near Markirch 400 Dead. They were still standing in the Street, when the French opened Artillery Fire from a Hill south of Col de St.Marie at a German Battery witch was near south of the Town. He had ordered to place the Battery there from the Ers.Apt. 80. They drove up towards it as much as the steep Hill aloud. They took as Guide a Jaeger named Scheele who told them of the Battles of August 9 and 10. The Road went steep up the Hill 600. The exploding Splinters flew over the Road in a valley left of them. They were not visible in the Forest. The Battery Leader called as they came near to the Battery, which was out of the Forest. That they were in the Line of the French and a Grenade exploded behind them. After they talked to the Leader they drove back. They visited wounded Soldiers in the Hospital in Markirch.

At the return Trip from Markirch came from Strasburg a report of a heavy Battle with many casualty's at Provencheres. The Border Security Detachment in the Breusch Valley under Oberstlt. Rayle attacked in the Night of August 10-11. 1914 the French Jaeger Battalion 3 and Heavy

Artillery. German losses were Officers and 40 Man and 150 wounded. Oberstlt. Rayle had order not to attack. But he did it because he thought he could do it. My Grandfather thought that in the first Mobilization Days Troop Detachments used for the Border Security were not trained well. The French were in this superior. He thought it was wrong that the German Army did not have Mountain Artillery on Mules.

When he in 1909 came back from a Trip to Bosnia and Herzegovina he told the War Ministry and the General Staff that the Austrian Troops had such and it would be very helpful in the Vogesen. They thought it not necessary.

Oberstlt. Rayle leads his Troops back over Saales in the Area of Bourg-Broche and had them dig Trenches. The French followed onto Saales and they're Artillery fired on to Bourg-Broche. When my Grandfather arrived again in Strasburg before Noon on August 11, he ordered the present Bavarian R. I. R. 15 to Schirmeck by Train as Support for the Border Security in the Breusch Valley. The I. Battalion of this Regiment under Maj. Stapf arrived at 8 in the Evening in Fouday where 2 Company;s took Quarter the other 2 went to St.Blaise.

The big Baggage was left in Schirmeck. Am Col du Hantz was a Field Watch from the R. J. R. The Commander of the R. J. Br. 60, Genlt. von Hopfgarten was send to the Breusch Valley, with its Streets from France into the Rheine Area, with the order to take over the Border Security Detachment. The Genlt. Went to Schirmeck, with his attached Captain Dittler from the I. R. 143 who knew the Border Security Remedies from the XVst. A. K. from Peace training in this Area. The A. O. K. 7 on order from the O. H. L. under the Command of the A. O. K. 6 who's Leader was GO. Crown prince Rupprecht von Bavaria had ordered Detachment Knoerzer the Area near Schlettstaddt for the XIVst. R. K. to clear and to get to the Area near Oberehnheim. That would free the Troops in the upper Elsa's for Operations in Lothringia. Genlt. von Knoerzer reported that he marched to the Area Barr Eichhofen and Epfig and was going to stay there. He had a Battalion and a Field Artillery Battery that he had left at the Border Security Detachment Markirch. He established a Connection with the Jaeg. Batl. 8 in the Weiler Valley, also with the R. I. R. 99 in the Breusch Valley. In the Night came the first Troop Transport from the upper Elsa's to Strasburg and then marched toward Northwest.

The A. O. K. 6 demanded in the Evening August 11 to hand over the heavy Artillery to the Army. The Army order from August 12 at 3 in the Morning ordered the Government Strasburg:

> "Keep the Border Security in the Breusch Valley and form with his main Reserve as the backup for the Border Security so far south as this is then taken over by the XIVst. R. K."

And also:

> "The Responsibility for the Security of the Rheine Valley in the Vogesen has in the Breusch Valley and in the Area of the Jaeg. Batl. 8 the Government Strasburg and in the other Area inclusive Muenster Valley the Commanding General of the XIVst. R. K."

It was clear from the News from August 12 from the Border Security in the Breusch Valley and the smart lead Radf. Comp. from the Jaeg. Batl. 8 that the French followed the German Troops slowly.

L.G. von Hopfgarten reported his Establishment at 11.15 before Noon with Ist. and IInd. / R. J. R. 99 Northwest of Diespach the IVst. Batl. Right behind spread out. East of Diespach was the Ist. / Bav. R. J. R. 15 with 2 Battery's. They fortified the Position. Also the Regiments Staff and the IInd. And IIIrd. / R. J. R. 15 where in the Afternoon in Strasburg put on a Train and taken to Schirmeck. The Fortress M. G. Comp. 9 under Captain von Meyer was marching to Schirmeck

The Government sends an order at 1 Noon to the 30. R. D. in Epfig:

1. Heavy Enemy Infantry in March over Saales to Diespach-Fouday, there Detachment Hopfgarten in Position.
2. Border has to be held.
3. Detachment Knoerzer (without a 15 cm. Battery.) move today to Triembach there Border Defense Jaeger 8 under orders General von Knoerzer.
4. Border Security Detachment Markirch remains, is under Command XIVst. R. K. Markolsheim. The 30st. R. D. was by Train on August 12 from Barr Eichhofen Epfig to Triembach

transported. The Government became on August 12 from the A. O. K. 7 one more order:

"The Border Security is by all means to be held. The A banded Posts at the Hill are again to be taken with Reinforcement. Big Undertakings into France are strictly forbidden. The Government Strasburg is responsible for the execution in the Area Breusch Valley, in the other Areas the Gen. Kdo. XIVst R. K. (Markolsheim).

The constant change of the Command Structure over the Border Security Troops was disturbing and had bad Results. The Governor remained the Leader at Markirch and had to help with Troops, Artillery and Munition. Maj. von Schaeffer and his Detachment fought a heavy Battle against French from Col de St. Marie and needed often help. The 30st. R. D. from Weiler reported 8.20 in the Evening they were in the Area Erlenbach Meisengott Lach Gereuth Hohwarth.

The Government ordered at 11.15 in the Evening that Gen. Knoerzer must not advance over the Area Triembach Weiler.

August 13 was very busy because of many contradictory reports. The at Saales ascertained French knew how to hide their Intentions. The Gens. von Hopfgarten and von Knoerzer thought because of Patrols that the Main Body of the French fell back to the Urbeis and Weiler Valley. Gen. von Knoerzer occupied in the Afternoon a Position at the Hills between Triembach and Neukirch.

Gen. von Hopfgarten presumed after reports that opposite at Saulrures was only a week Force. Gen. von Knoerzer reported 7.30 in the Evening that the Enemy marched over Bourg Bruche and Steige. The French had spread this News and the German Gendarme heard it from so called confidence People and the German reconnaissance was slow in the Mountains. Gen. von Knoerzer thought the next Day would bring an attack and requested the Detachment Hopfgarten for help. Detachment Knoerzer reported at 10.35 in the Evening from Weiler that the Enemy did not get to Urbeis and Steige and everything is quiet. The 30st. R. D. did occupy the Hills east of Triembach and Neukirch and blocked both Valleys.

In the Evening came G.O. von Heeringen to the Government and thanked them for the help at the Battle of Muehlhausen. He gave direction in case the Enemy attacked again in the upper Elsa's from Belfort.

The A. O. K. 7 wanted to stop the Enemy trough a south from Strasburg positioned Flank and had fore that devised the Area between Colmar and Neubreisach.

They brought fore that the Wuertemberg L. D. W. I. R. 120 (3 Batls.) from Kehl, the Park Company III. / R. Foot A. R. from Genzau and the Park Company II. / R. Foot A. R. 14 from Khel to Colmar.

The Armoring of the Fortress required almost daily movements of various Troops. Because of this moved the L. D. W. I. R. to the west Segment Avenheim and Handschuhheim, the R. I. R. 70 to Huertigheim. The Regiments tere where under the Command of GenMaj. von Gynz-Rekowski and defended in the Evening the Line Huertigheim Fuerdenheim and the Road Fork north of Osthofen. The ready to march parts of the Reserve Battery of the Field Army Regiment 51 and 84 came under the Detachment. The Regiment Hus. R. 9 were transferred from Ittlenheim to Marlenheim with Field Guards at the Line Obersteigen Wangenburg Pandurenplatz F. H. Eichelberg Oberhaslach. Patrols in the Breusch Valley Luetzelhausen, Relay Posts at Romansweiler, F. H. Zimmerkoepfel, Still, Rosheim, Wangen and Westhofen.

Because of Heat and Drought it was to expect that the overflow at the Southfront would be slow. So my Grandfather gave the order 7.30 Mornings to the General of the Pioneers Colonel Fritsch to start flooding. Because of this was the whole Area before the Southfront a Swamp.

The A. O. K. 7 gave Information on August 14 at 5 in the Morning that a lot of Troops of the 7st. Army where in March from the upper Elsa's to the North Vogesen.

My Grandfather had talked to Gen. von Knoerzer and von Hopfgarten about the movements of the French. He thought that both would act together and with reports he could help. It was emphasized, at the talks with the Generals, that the French most likely attacked in the Breusch Valley to get to Schirmeck where the Donon Street enters the Valley. In this case was the Detachment Knoerzer to attack over Steige to hit the Enemy in Flank and Back. If the French marched in the Weiler Valley then the Detachment Hopfgarten had to act. Gen. von Hopfgarten asked on August 14 at 6.45 in the Morning if his Brigade had free movements. It was permitted with the following order:

> "It can only move with agreement of the Weiler Valley Troops under Gen. von Knoerzer. A single advance against a superior Force is not permitted."

At 8 in the Morning came a report from the Post Office Fouday:

> "Since a half hour is a heavy Battle in progress. Artillery and Infantry. Gen. von Hopfgarten wounded. Commander of Bavarian R. I. R. 15 took Command."

The French had attacked but from Weiler Valley came no reports of French Troops. Gen. von Knoerzer should move to Steige and take all Troops to help in the Battle. So the Government ordered at 8.50 in the Morning to move the 30st. R. D. to St. Qu in Hohwarth:

1. "Border Security by Fouday in heavy Battle.
2. Detachment Knoerzer should take the Border Security in the Breusch Valley to march over Steige, relief with securing to Urbeis."

To the General Command of the XIVst. R. K. in Schlettstadt was also an order send, to take all Troops in the Weiler Valley fore defense of Urbeis, to help in the attack at Steige.

At 9 in the Morning was the IIIrd. / R. I. R. 99 still in Strasburg, ordered to move by Train to the Border Detachment Luetzelhausen. The reports about the Battle were until 11 before Noon contradicting but my Grandfather thought the Position in the Breusch Valley where good. The wounded Gen. von Hopfgarten, with a Grenade Splinter in the under Thigh, came at this time by Car to Strasburg. At 10.30 in the Morning came a report from Gen. von Knoerzer:

> "The Core is in March to Steige. 2 Batls. Of the R. J. R. 180 (XIVst. R. K.) March over Laach to Salcee. Brigade Hammerstein 6 Batls., 3 Batterys, March for Security of the left Flank of Detachment Knoerzer."

From Fouday came a report that the Battle became stronger. They were told that Gen. von Knoerzer would over Steige intervene in the battle. Genlt. Mueller, Commander of the 3rd. Bavarian R. Br. Became order to take over the Command of the Troops from Gen. von Hopfgarten. He became Reconnaissance of the Situation and went with the IIIrd. / R. I. R. 99 at 1 in the afternoon to Luetzelhausen. Also Captain Schurig from the General Staff of the Government was send to get order in the Breusch Valley. From self-Initiative did the Horse review Commissar in Strasburg, Oberstlt. Kumme, go to the Breusch Valley as a Correspondent for the Government. From him came many reports about the Battle that became more serious for the Troops. At 12 Noon came a report from Detachment Knoerzer from Hohwarth that the Brigade Hammerstein (XIVst. R. K.) at Neukirch Thannweiler was prepared. Oberstlt. Kumme reported at 12.15 in the afternoon that French Artillery smashed the German Field Battery's with a Flank attack. An attack at the Infantry at the left Wing did not happen. The German right Wing was attacking.

My Grandfather found the Battle Situation not unfavorable. The more the French right Wing advanced and got stuck the more favorable was the intervene of Detachment Knoerzer, that could attack the Flank and Back of the Enemy. For the Battle were available at Diespach under the Command of the Commander of the Bavarian R. I. R. 15 Oberstlt. Grassmann: R. Staff I. II. IV. / R. I. R. 99; R. Staff I. II. III. / Bavarian R. I. R. 15; Fest. M. G. Comp. 9. 2 Ers. Battr. / Field A. R. 15; 1 Battery heavy Howitzers.

In the afternoon came the IIIrd. / R. I. R. 99 to Luetzelhausen. At 1.15 in the afternoon called the Government again Gen. von Knoerzer and demanded advance to Steige. Then became my Grandfather the following answer:

> "The XIVst. R. K. is answering the call of the Government witch took Command of the 30st. R. D. Advancing over Meisengott cannot happen today. Unity Command for Troops in the Breusch Valley and Troops in Steige and Urbeis Valley's for the XIVst. R. K. and the 30st. R. D. very important to guarantee the uniform handling in the Breusch and Steige Valley."

That hit my Grandfather and his Chief like a Thunderclap. Immediately he drove with the Captain of the General Staff Hosse to the Weiler Valley and met in Thannweiler the General Command of the XIVst. R. K. the Commanding General of the Artillery von Schubert and asked him how he could order over his Head the his subordinate 30st. R. D. The main Reserve of the Fortress which could cause loss in a Battle. He became as answer that the A. O. K. 7 made already the Detachment Knoerzer available to the XIVst. R. K. Late in the afternoon became the Government the Confirmation of this from the 7. Army. So he could be calm especially since Gen. von Schubert told him he would draw the Detachment Knoerzer forward over Steige. So he drove to Gen. von Knoerzer at St. Martin. He just ordered rest for his Troops. The Troops where at this heat and the back and fore marches in the Mountains tired so a continuing march to Battle and St. Blaise and also to Fouday was not possible. With a heavy Heart he returned to Strasburg and had to admit that his Leadership failed him.

The Decision at Diespach Fouday was, when he arrived in Strasburg at 4 in the afternoon, already done. The German Troops pulled back to Rothau and from there, because of active intervene from both the Regiments Commanders and a few Officers, orderly to Schirmeck.

His Chief in Strasburg did at 2.30 in the afternoon give an order that the 10cm. Battery place itself at the Scharrach Mountain.

At 5 in the afternoon came a report from Genlt. Mueller:

> "Take Position at Luetzelhausen and Grendelbruch with 60st. R. I. Br. There first parts arrive at 7 in the Evening. Ammunition Detachment stops in Urmatt and need Ammunition."

Ammunition was given, except the 10cm. Munition, which was send back to Molsheim. In Luetzelhausen arrived also in good order, the Border Security Detachment from they're Position by Fouday backed, heavy Field Howitzer Battery. She drove to the Area from Urmatt and Munition was send there.

The French, it was the 13st. and 14st. Division from the XXIst Core that occupied the Donon. They advanced at Col du Hantz and over Saales, Bourg Broche, but did not follow on this Day further then Diespach.

South was parts of the French XIVst Core advanced over Passes at Urbeis and Saales and contacted the XXIst Core.

In the Evening at 7.15 reported Captain Schurig that Fouday was free of French. A German Airplane reported Fire in Fouday, Diespach and Plaine. Also Enemy Wagon Columns at Gemaingoutte 4km. west of Wisembach and on the Street Provencheres Saales. On the Street to Markirch was a Wagon Column 600m. Long, the Streets south of St. Die and 1km. south of Saales where free. Oberstlt. Kumme found out that in the Evening Jaeger on Horseback went forward; Rothau was at 8 in the Evening still free of the Enemy. German Forest Houses where burned.

The course of the Battle at the Diespacher Hills was from the French done only with Artillery. The Diespacher Peak blocked north of St. Blaise and Plaine the Breusch Valley. My Grandfathers K. H. Qu. Was from end of September 1914 until October 1916 in St.Blaise in the Breusch Valley. He really learned the Battle Field.

On August 13 where at the Diespacher Hill Trenches appropriated. Even so French Troops where found out at the Hill south of Saulrures, good hidden. A Reconnaissance and Defense over Champenay to Col du Hantz was not ordered. There were only week side Defenses in the Forest. A good Street lead on the Slope of the "Lange Wand" (Long Wall) along, mostly hidden by Trees, also the high Forest could be easily penetrated. So the Enemy could attack in wide Formation.

On not so good Routes was it possible to get to St. Blaise over steep Hills southwest and east.

There were not enough Security Troops placed there. The whole Detachment, was from description of Participants, massively secured by terraced south Slopes of the Diespacher Hill and by Dugout and occupied Trenches in depressions at Village Diespach. All 12 MGs'. Were on a Hill west of Diespach, that lay in a Depression and you could see only a few Roofs, under light Cover installed. They had Range towards south especially Plaine.

Both Reserve Battery's Field Army Reserve 15 where Northwest of Diespach. The 15cm. Howitzers stood at the North Slope of the Hill. The Terrain was like a Trap for the Enemy. As the French at 8 in the Morning from good hidden Positions with a few Battery's opened Fire it hit the German Trenches and the Observation Post of Gen. von Hopfgarten. He was wounded and had to give up his Command. His Substitute, Oberstlt. Grassmann, Kdr. Of the Bavarian R. I. R. 15, had a hard time to take over Command of the Detachment since Orientation in the difficult terrain and under heavy Artillery Fire was almost impossible. French Infantry, which was thought to come, did not come. Soon hit the French Artillery Fire the MGs. Also the Infantry of the right Wing came under French Mountain MGs. And French Mountain Artillery from the "Lange Wand" (long Wall) gave in the Flank heavy Fire. Then came from the Hill of Sapinot, in the left Flank of the Detachment, French Artillery under Protection of Infantry. That eliminated both Field Battery's. Since the Munition Carts where placed at the Canons, came one Explosion after on other. There were very many Casuality's. Maybe a vigorous attack with the Bavarian Battalions at the right Flank from 2km. North of Plaine situated private Forest Les Evreur, from the R. I. R. 99 might have helped. Since Oberstlt. Grassmann waited for a decisive Intervention of the 30st. R. D. over Steige, it did not come. They were used to secure the Retreat. The Border Security Detachment lost 33 Officers and 1700 Man. The eleven Field Guns and 11 destroyed MG's. Were left. The French found the Flag of the IVst. / I. R. 132 under a Pile of Dead Soldiers.

The A. O. K. 7 gave order at 8 in the Evening to install the heavy Rheine Bridge Trains at Rheingau. By Morning they were put in March from there Quarters. A Pioneer Company was ordered from Neubreisach.

In the Night from 14. To 15. August ordered the A. O. K. a Regulation of the Command Regulations in the Elsa's and upper Rheine. The Substitution General Command of the XIVst. A. K. (General of the Infantry Gaede) had to take over the Security of the upper Elsa's and the Security of the Rheine Line between the Command Area Strasburg and the Swiss Border. The Governor of Strasburg had on Top of his Deploy, orders to take over the south Flank and the backwards alliances of the 7st. Army. In its Command Sphere (Core Area of the XVst. A. K. from the Command Area of the Fortress to south of the Border), to secure. He had under him the Fortress Strasburg and Neubreisach, the 1st. and 2nd. Bavarian Militia Brigade (with exception of the Bridge Heads of Markolsheim and Schoenau) and the Border Security in the Vogesen, and the in connection to Breisach from General von Mertens to build Position Colmar Neubreisach and the heavy Rheine Bridge Train.

This Command Regulation was soon changed.

The A. O. K. 6 had ordered that the following should stay in Strasburg:

1. The provided Formations: Airplanes, heavy movable Searchlights, Fortress MG's.., Transport Unit 12 and all fly and departure ready.
2. The heavy Field Howitzer Regiment Bansi and the Steamplowpark in the Quarters from 13 August.

In the Night from 14.to 15. August were, on order from the A. O. K. 7, several Detachments of the XIVst. A. K. in the Area of the Fortress K. W. IInd, moved forward. GenMaj. Freyer and parts of his reinforced 56th. I. Br. (XIVst. A. K.) Was to move from Gressweiler (west of Mutzig) to the Area of Wasselnheim and to secure the Streets west and southwest leading. Near Romansweiler stood on Top of the Duerrenberg, Hill 305, and the R. Hus. R. 9 in there on August 14 advanced Positions. Besides French Infantry and Cavalry Patrols west of Heiligenberg and one French Cavalry Patrol south of Zabern, it was reported, that the French in the Breusch Valley slowly advanced were and at Midnight at the Donon and in Grandfontaine where 2 Infantry Company's and Cuirassiers.

Under the Security of the Reconnaissance Detachment at Luetzelhausen did the Border Security Detachment of the 60st. R. I. Br. back up to Molsheim. They left Outposts in Dinsheim 1km. west of Mutzig and Gressweiler. South from there came before Noon the 60st. I. Br. under GenMaj. von Altrock (XVst. A. K.) at the Nationalberg near Oberehnheim and build Entrenchments. The Government ordered him at 7.25 in the Morning:

> "A. O. K. 7 wants to make clear not to give the Breusch Valley easily to the Enemy. The Enemy is to prevent to become insight of our Troop distribution by advancing of Company's in the Forests on both sides of the Valley."

The Government ordered at 9.50 in the Morning, to strengthen the Breusch Position, to overflow the Area south of Kolbsheim Hangenbieten. The Troops of this Area under GenMaj. Rasch became as Reinforcement 2 Battalions of the Wuert. Ldw. I. R. 120. The Bavarian R. I. R. 4, that came back from the upper Elsa's, went to Osthofen.

On August 15 drove my Grandfather to Molsheim and Mutzig and inspected the Fortress. He saluted both Regiments that fought at the Diespacher Hills. In spite of the Defeat was the Attitude of the Troops good. He spoke with many Soldiers about they're Experience. All said that the French Artillery fired well but they're Infantry was good for nothing. He took the Officers together and discussed the necessary Measures. He consoled the valiant Oberstlt. Rayle, who was distressed. He delighted about the State of Mind of the Commander of the Bavarian R. I. R. 15. Oberstlt. Grassmann, who with his Bavarians wanted to wipe out the Disgrace.

The Gendarme, Forest and Customs People in the Area of the Breusch Valley came under Oberstlt. Kumme. They were to do Patrols and because they knew the Land and People they were to get News. The Border Security Troops went on August 15 in the Afternoon near Diedolshausen back to Schnierlach. Maj. von Schaeffer had in the Evening, after a heavy Battle with a superior Enemy, to vacate Markirch and pull back to Rappoltsweiler. German Troops held Drei Aehren, Muenster and Stossweier.

The temporary Gen.Kdo. Of the XIVst. A. K. moved on that Day his Place from Karlsruhe to Freiburg in the Breisgau.

The freed Troops in the upper Elsa's came now in the Area of the Government. It was to prevent shooting on our Troops and it was announced to the sector Commanders and to the Commander of the Fortress K. W. IInd:

> "XVst. A. K. went over Markolsheim Friesenheim Plobsheim and over Benfeld Hindisheim Kolbsheim on August 16 and 17 in March over Strasburg and to the Breusch Position."

From the Breusch Valley came Reports on August 16 that the Enemy maybe planed no more forward Movements. Also Gen. von Altrock reported, that he thought heavy French Troops would not come over the Vogesen. The report from Gen. von Altrock went immediately to the A. O. K. 7 and at 9.15 in the Morning they gave the order to send the Border Security from Dinsheim again in the Breusch Valley and to get in touch with the Enemy. Thereupon became Genlt. Mueller at 9.30 in the Morning in Molsheim the order:

1. "Enemy did not follow in the Breusch Valley over Schirmeck.
2. IIIrd. / R. I. R. 99 Maj. Hahn with all Bicyclers of the Regiment moves to Luetzelhausen and place outposts and establish touch with the Enemy.
3. Ist./ I. R. 142 remain as security in their Position at Gressweiler.
4. Connection with 60st I. Br. at Oberehnheim (Nationalberg) over Fortress K. W. IInd with Light Signal.
5. In case Enemy attacks move back to Mutzig.
6. Security of the Flanks important."

In this way could the Outposts with smart Advantage of the Valley Dams in the Breusch Valley delay the Enemy and to entice them to come forward to the Position of Mueller and von Altrock witch where under the security of the Fortress.

From the F. H. Meierei on the Street Donon Alberschweiler came by Telephone a report that the Donon is occupied since August 15 with French Infantry and one French Infantry Company turned west before the F. H. on the Street to St. Quirin Loerchingen and kept marching.

The R. Hus. R. 9 witch was still in the Area Romansweiler, Singrist was commanded to reconnoiter until the Line Dagsburg Donon Fouday.

After a report from Genlt. Ipfelkofer where in the Breusch Valley and Area at the retreat 12 Bridges destroyed. The immediate Reconstruction was ordered from the Government so German Troops could advance in the Breusch Valley.

The main Post office Command in Strasburg was ordered to repair all Telephone Cables that were destroyed in the Demolition of the Bridges in the Breusch Valley to Luetzelhausen.

Then came a Telegram from the O. H. L. to the A. O. K. 7:

> "The Army gets 3 mobile Ers. D. incoming in Strasburg Presumable August 17."

The A. O. K. 7 did add to that:

> "The Bavarian mobile Ers. D. is under the Governor of Strasburg. Coming: 5th. Bavarian Ers. Br. Strasburg, 1st Bavarian Ers. Br. Appenweier, 9st. Bavarian Ers. Br. Achem, 19st.

Mobile Ers. D. Accommodation in Pfettisheim, Behlenheim, Pfugriesheim, Offenheim, Stuetzheim, Dingsheim. Mobile G. Ers. Br. 1. Mobile G. Ers. Br. Geudertheim, Bietlenheim, Weyersheim, Hoerdt."

This order from the O. H. L. will always be ground to critic. These 3 Ers. Ds. Witch came from Home, where put on the left Army Wing instead to the right. That's why knowledgeable People thought the Marne Battle had to be broke up.

My Grandfather thought it important to form the 30st. R. D. in 2 Brigades. He had to change himself the War Arrangement and did this more often. So are the Troops under the Government not the Way they were and the Generals not at the Point they were ordered. First he gave Genlt. Mueller, who was the Commander of the 3rd. Bavarian R. I. Br., the 10st. Bavarian R. I. Br. He intended from the Mobil Bavarian Ers. D. the first arriving 5th. Bavarian Ers. Br. to give to the 30st. R. D. This seemed possible since the Bavarian Ers. D. was formed in 3 Brigades. Gen. von Knoerzer needed in the Weiler Valley, to do his Task, Reinforcement. Especially an offensive Task. So the first Transport, Bavarian Ers. Batl. 6, 20 Officers, 911 Men, 44 Horses and 21 Wagons, where send on to Benfeld.

After the Staff from the 10st. Bavarian R. I. Br. came to Strasburg. Genlt. Mueller drove with the Staff on that Afternoon to Baar and reported to Commander of the 30st. R. D. This exchange led often to confusement until the Bavarian War Ministry gave it's OK to the Measure.

Commander of the 10st. Bavarian Ers. Br. was Genlt. Ipfelkofer who was also Commander of Fortress K. W. IInd but could not get away from there. To this Brigade belonged Bavarian R. I. R. 4 and 15. My Grandfather ordered those 2 to the Commander in the Breusch Position, were he thought they were necessary for Reserve. The Command over the Troops of the Fortress Strasburg in the Breusch Valley took Oberstlt. Rayle. The IIIrd. / R. I. R. 60 came from Detachment Knoerzer by Train back to Molsheim. That and Ist. / R. I. R. 70 where both ordered as Garrison to the Fortress K. W. IInd. The IIIrd. / Ldw. I. R. 80 was ordered to Behlenheim.

From the Troops at the XIVst. Army Core, who was still in the Area of the Fortress, came by order of the A. O. K. 7 the Ist. / I. R. 142 and a Squadron of the Jaeg. R. z. Pf. On August 16 from Gressweiler to Wasselheim so they could follow the Brigade Freyer over Maursmuenster to Dagsburg. All the Troops under his Command where now at order.

The over Urmatt advancing IVst. / R. I. R. 99 reported at 5.20 in the afternoon that it had put Outposts near Luetzelhausen and Enemy Infantry and Cavalry Patrols where from Luetzelhausen expelled. It confirmed the Occupation of Schirmeck of French Patrols at the Hills north and east of the Breusch. The from Weiler Valley incoming reports gave no clearness from there. The Enemy was supposed to be repulsed from Steige, the Detachment Knoerzer marched back to Baar from the Position at Triembach and left Hohwarth weekly occupied. This was done by order from the XIVst. R. K. but not told to the Government. Near Lach where light Enemy Troops. Schirrgut and Hohwald were with German Bicycle Troops occupied.

The Commander of the Bridgehead at Gerstheim reported that the preliminary work for the Cut through the III Speise Canal was done. So it was ordered to do the Cut through when the Enemy came. The local Traffic Officer, Maj. Lindow, reported that because of Flood at Blaesheim, the Narrow Gauge Railroad Strasburg Markolsheim between Grafenstaden and Eschau, was flooded and the Traffic stopped. Because of this it was not possible to get the Railroad Material; which became free because of removal of the Stretch Ostwald Eschau. So the completion of the Fortress Railroad Net would be delayed.

The IVst. / R. I. R. was in the Night of August 17 positioned with Outposts in the Breusch Valley in the Forest south of Muehlbach. It was opposite of a French Company that did nothing. So the German Light Signal Detachment stayed in Luetzelhausen. At 6.30 in the morning came 2 French Companies with a Squadron from Schirmeck towards the Battalion. It pulled back on the left Breusch Bank to the Area near Heiligenberg. It left Outposts and took Position near Gressweiler. The Ist. / R. I. R. 99 were positioned at Still, the IIIrd. / R. I. R. 99 on the Hill northeast of Rosenweiler, the IInd. / R. I. R. 99 as Reserve in Molsheim.

The R. Hus. R. 9 became order from the A. O. K. 7 to stay, until there relief, near Singrist in front of the Line of the XIVst. A. K. Then to leave Outposts and move back to Still. Second Lieutenant von Michelmann reported that the Enemy occupied the Hills west and south from Grendelbruch. He thought they would move towards Odilienberg. Schwarzbach where occupied from the Enemy.

The 5ᵗʰ. Bavarian Ers.Br. under GenMaj. Count von Zech arrived with the first parts in the Night of August 18 near Benfeld. It marched over Epfig to the Battlefield to help Detachment Knoerzer. They reported on Afternoon of August 18 that the French at 5 in the Afternoon reached Triembach from Weiler with 12 to 14 Companies. Gendarme from Kestenholz brought News that at 3 in the Afternoon 2 French Regiments where in March from Leberau to Wanzel. It seemed to be, that the Enemy wanted to move through the Weiler and Leber Valley into the Rheine Area. This would have been threatening for the 7ˢᵗ. Army, especially for the advancing XIVst. R. K. in the Breusch Valley.

An advance of the Detachment Knoerzer with the 2ⁿᵈ. Bavarian Ldw. Br. near Schlettstadt into the Weiler Valley was in order.

The A. O. K. 7 needed for the Operation in Lothringia reinforcement with heavy Artillery. In the Afternoon came the order from the Government to transport on the 17ˢᵗ. and 18ˢᵗ. from the Train Station Hausbergen:

Oberst Pohl with Staff R. Foot A. R. 10
IIIrd. / R. Foot A. R. 10 with light R. Mun. Kol.
Ist. / R. Foot A. R. 13 and 1 Battery 10cm.
Foot A. R. 14 with 1 light Mun.Kol.

In the Night gave the Government also a 10cm. Battery to the XVst. A. K. They ordered replacement from the War Ministry.

The XIVst. R. K. was positioned before Noon on August 18 with the 26ᵗʰ. R. D. in the Mountains near Grendelbruch, the 28ᵗʰ. R. D. did move with the first parts right next to it in the Breusch Valley fore and came to Heiligenberg with the R. I. R. 110. The R. I. R. 111 was ordered to march to that Place.

The Gen. Kdo. Of the 14ˢᵗ. R. K. did inform at 12.15 in the Afternoon:

"In the Breusch Valley many Enemy Troops. Government Strasburg ordered R. I. R. 99 to lightly fight but back up.

Fortress K.W.IInd does not take part in. everywhere attacking, with parts also north of the Breusch."

The French did not go into the Trap. They occupied at Noon Luetzelhausen and moved to Urmatt. In the Afternoon hours started with the Rifleman of the R. I. R. 111; witch where advanced to Heiligenberg and the Enemy occupation Troops of Urmatt, a Battle. The Commander of the 28st. R. D. Genlt. von Pavel requested the Artillery of the Fortress K. W. IInd. In the Evening stood the 28st. R. D. with they're first parts north of the Breusch in Upper and Under Haslach and wanted to attack on August 19 at 4 in the Morning at Luetzelhausen and Muehlbach. The 26st. R. D., under Gen. of the Infantry Baron von Soden, stood near Grendelbruch with they're advance Troops the R. I. R. 119 opposite of Enemy Infantry. On August 19 was also there to be an attack. On order of the Divisions Commander was the IIIrd. / R. I. R. 99 from Rosenweiler to Mollkirch, 3km. west of Rosenweiler, advanced.

On the other Hand did Gen. von Knoerzer march in the Morning of August 18 with the 10th. Bavarian R. I. Br. on order from the Gen. Kdo. Of the XIVst. R. K. from the Area at Hohwarth to Triembach. He wanted to reoccupy the prepared Positions on the Hills northeast of the Village. He led the 5th. Bavarian Ers. Br.,

Witch came from Benfeld over Epfig, follow and started a Battle on the 28th. At 8 in the Morning against the French Troops that came over Weiler and Neukirch.

The Government learned of this because the 30st. R. D. asked at 1.30 in the Afternoon for Ammunition, which came in the Evening. In this Battle in the Weiler Valley was on both sides also other Troops used. From the 27st. French Division, which came over Markirch in the Leber Valley, was alleged a Regiment with Artillery to Gereuth used. That was a Danger to the left Flank of the 30st. R. D. Against this did Gen. von Knoerzer asked the from Schlettstadt to Kestenholz Train Station Weiler Valley oncoming 2nd. Bavarian Ldw. Br. under GenMaj. Lachemeyer to help. At 4 in the Afternoon did German Forest People guide the Bavarian Ldw. I. R. through the Forest at Gereuth witch hit the French in the back. In the Evening at 9.35 reported Gen. von Knoerzer:

"After 12 hour Battle Victory at the whole Line Weiler Neukirch Gereuth."

This Victory was because of the fast Decisions of the Generals and the 10st. Bavarian R. I. Br. under Commander Genlt. Mueller, who already had in Mind to attack.

Because of the long Night March could the 5th. Bavarian Ers. Br. only later intervenes. The Men where tired but went with the same Bravery like the Bavarian R. I. R. 11 and 15 fore. Since late in the Afternoon a decision was not had, did Gen. von Knoerzer give Signal to storm. Then the whole Division attacked and the French could not withstand. They pulled back with heavy losses to Steige and Urbeis. The 30st. R. D. followed to the Line Erlenbach Weiler Gereuth and installed Security Posts at the west leading Streets.

The 2nd.Bavarian Ldw. Br. marched back in the Evening of August 18, after the Battle at Gereuth, with Ldw. I. R. 3 to Scherweiler. The Rest was at Kestenholz. It was noticeable that the Bavarian Militia after victorious Battles pulled back into they're Quarters and because of that lost Touch with the Enemy. My Grandfather learned after several Days that these Regiments where without a Field Kitchen so they had to be within a Village or Town.

The Gen.Kdo. XIVst. A.K. reported, from the upper Elsa's, that the Detachment Mathy at 6 in the Morning would move forward to Muehlhausen.

The Gen. of the Infantry Knight von Benzino, Commander of the Bavarian Ers. D. reported to the Government at Noon. He got the order to march to Kestenholz with 2 Brigades and to observe the Leber Valley.

The A. O. K. 7 left on August 19 Strasburg and moved to Zabern. Since the last Troops of the XVst. A. K. (60st Brigade on the National Mountain) moved through the straight at Wasselheim ordered the A. O. K. at 8.40 before Noon:

"Government has to place a Reserve near Wasselheim after the XVst. A. K. left, who has to secure the backwards Connections of the XVst. A. K. against the from Upper Haslach and the from the upper Breusch Valley to Wasselheim leading Streets."

After that became at 9.20 in the Morning Oberstlt. Stadthagen, Kdr. Of the R. I. R. 70, the order:

> Detachment Stadthagen assembled in the Area Romansweiler, Secured the backwards Connections of the 15st. A. K. against the Streets that lead from Upper Haslach, Upper Breusch Valley and Upper Hasselbach Valley. Instead of the missing Cavalry, utilize Bicyclers. A Platoon R. Hus. R. 9 have to be brought from Gressweiler. One Ers. Battr. Will be send from Romansweiler."

In the Breusch Valley moved the XIVst. A. K. while fighting forward. The Enemy gave Way in heavy Fog slowly on the Hills south of Schirmeck. The 28st. R. D. marched forward over Wish Hersbach. The 26st. R. D. in 2 Columns with the 52nd. R. Br. Commander GenMaj. von Auwaerter, reached Barenbach, the 51st. R. Br. Commander GenMaj. Wundt, was moved at 9.30 before Noon to Natzweiler. The R. I. R. 99 was dragged along in the Breusch Valley and occupied late in the Afternoon with the IIIrd. And IVth. Batl. Schirmeck and Barenbach, Hersbach, Russ, Wish, Schwarzbach and Luetzelhausen where occupied from the advanced Battalions. The Government had to give up from the 15st. A. K. the R. Hus. R. 9 (without 1 Squadron). It went as Vanguard of this Core over Obersteigen Dagsburg and was there at the Battle at Saarburg. Later it went back to the Troops of the Fortress and came to the 30st. R. D. With a proposal did the A. O. K. 7 allow that the Ldw. Squadron of the 60st Ldw. Br. came under the Government. On August 19 was the 30st. R. D. in the Area south of the Breusch Valley (Weiler Valley). Steige and Urbeis where occupied by the Enemy. The Bavarian Ers. D. got to Kestenholz. The News from the upper Elsa's was not good. The Detachments Mathy, Dame and von Bodingen were at Muehlhausen Altkirch, the 1st. Bavarian Ldw. Br. met west of Colmar a strong Enemy. With valiant fighting against a superior Enemy moved the Militia back into Rheine Area at Neuenburg back to Hueningen. The Enemy occupied Muehlhausen. The 1st. Bavarian Ldw. Br. was attacked by strong Enemy Troops and moved back out of the Mountains to west of Colmar.

Replacements for the on August 19 lost heavy Guns came to Strasburg on August 19 from the Artillery Depot Rastatt 11 Guns 96 new design.

As on the right Wing of the German Army, the Army's where in advance, now could the 6ˢᵗ. And the 7ˢᵗ. Armies together attack the French Troops in Lothringia and Vogesen. The 7ˢᵗ. Army was supposed to encircle the right French Army Wing. It was thought that the 1ˢᵗ. French Army was under Gen. Dubai, because our XVst. Army Core and the XIVst. R. K. forward March, could be attacked in the Flank. Since the French had on the right heavy defenses and the resistance in the Vogesen could not be fast broken, started on August 20 a big Front fight Battle in Lothringia. The more the German of the left Wing were entangled and the further to west the over the Vogesen advancing Divisions won Areas, all the more precarious became the backwards Contact with the left Flank of the 7ˢᵗ. Army. The Army d'Alsace, under Gen. Pau, which broke back into Germany from Belford, was still in the Upper Elsa's. Also where parts of this French Army Group in the Vogesen Passes up to the Area from Colmar. My Grandfathers work became from Day to Day harder and independent. Because of the victorious Movements of the 6ˢᵗ. And 7ˢᵗ. Army was the Government liberated from the anxiety in the Breusch Valley and later also in the Weiler Valley. It could now use all of the War Garrison from Strasburg for the Field Army. The security of the Fortress became now the Militia and Reserve Formations.

The Troops in the Breusch Valley were first available. The Bavarian Ers. D. met in Leber Valley the Enemy. Gen. of the Infantry Knight von Benzino reported at 9.45 before Noon:

> "One Battalion of the 1ˢᵗ. Bavarian Ers. Br. had advanced to Leberau was attacked from the Enemy at Night and pushed back to Train Station Weiler Valley. The 1ˢᵗ. Bavarian Ers. Br. did this Morning follow the Enemy to Hurst and pushed them back to Leberau and continued the March to Markirch. The 9ˢᵗ. Bavarian Ers. Br. with the main part of the Artillery, March under my Leadership over Rappoltsweiler to Markirch. The 2ⁿᵈ.Bavarian Ldw. Br. is no more under my order, occupied Mountain
>
> Positions at Schlettstadt. Gave them 1 Battery 30ˢᵗ. R. D. in Steige." Because of this was the concentration of the at Kolbsheim and Area quartered Bavarian I. R. 14 and 15 and later other Infantry Troop parts, Artillery and Pioneers,

ordered. They were to move to Schlettstadt with the Train. My Grandfather ordered as Leader of this Detachment Genlt. von Ferling, at the time Commander of the south Area of the Fortress. And then he ordered at 12 Noon:

"Detachment Ferling to reach today and early Morning of August 21 with Train Schlettstadt. The Detachment secured in the Area from Schlettstadt the left Flank and the backward Connections of the Army. Food and Ammunition send later to Schlettstadt by train."

From Noon on arrived at the Government the following Reports:

From the 30ˢᵗ. R. D. at 12.35 from St. Martin:
"The Division moved Yesterday Afternoon towards the Steiger Valley, Lach and Grube. Enemy moved back on whole line towards Climont and Hills North of there. Our Infantry at Hills North of Steige moves towards St. Blaise. Forward movement slows because of steep Area. French dug Trenches but left without Fight. From reports did French Troops march this Morning to Leberau and there deviate to North."

From the Bavarian Ers. D. at 1 in the Afternoon from Rappoltsweiler:

"The 1ˢᵗ. Bavarian Ldw. Br. that stood in Colmar moves back over Andolsheim And Neubreisach. Reason not known. Post Station Colmar empty. Gen. von Benzino did ask Permission for the XIVst. R. K. if needed towards South to intervene."

It became known from further Reports that the 1ˢᵗ. Bavarian Ers. Br. Commander GenMaj. Krieger, were the Division Commander was, went to Rappoltsweiler and wanted to take Quarter. The Division became from Colmar a Report that the Enemy moved back to Schnierlach, but in 2 Columns with superior Force advanced towards Drei Aehren and in the Muenster Valley.

At 3.52 in the Afternoon came this Report:

"Strong French Cavalry in Verrweiler. On August 19 were 2000 Men French Infantry in Lautenbach Zell. On August 20 Enemy Infantry with MGs. in Rufach. Strong Enemy of all Weaponry advancing over Tuerkheim and Drei Aehren towards Colmar, at 12 Noon in Tuerkheim, Ingersheim and Drei Aehren. Train Bridge Colmar demolished from garrison Company."

At 4.30 in the Afternoon came a Report from the Command Neubreisach, Kdr. GenMaj. von Beck.

"At Markolsheim are 2 Bavarian Ldw. Pioneer Company's without Weapons on August 20 was a Batl. Ldw. I. R. 40 from Breisach to Markolsheim ordered for Security of the Bridge. The Bridges at Schoenau and Markolsheim are not to be demolished when Enemy arrived; instead they are to back up. At inquiry how strong the Enemy near Colmar is, it is reported, unknown since there is no Connection with the Brigade since 12 Noon. Right Wing of the Brigade crushed because of strong Artillery Fire from Drei Aehren and the Old Guns could not withstand. One Gun destroyed."

Later was reported that the Area Command was moved back from Colmar to Neubreisach. My Grandfather and his Staff had thought that a new Menace would come to the left Flank from fresh French Army Troops. North was the Situation good for the German Army.

The A. O. K. 7 reported at 4.30 in the Afternoon:

"The Enemy moved back destroyed from the 6st. and 7st. Army. The South Wing still holding. The XIVst. R. K. in Combat at the Donon. More French Troops and Jaeger Battls. With MGs. are in the Rheine Valley advancing. They can get to the Area south of Colmar with they're point today. The Division Benzino has to engage near Schlettstadt."

This Victory News brought in Strasburg Jubilation. The Government reported to the A. O. K. 7 at 4.50 in the afternoon:

"The 2nd. Bavarian Ldw. Br. will be reinforced at Schlettstadt in the Night of 20 to 21st. August. Ask assumption of the 2nd. Bavarian Ldw. Br. Under Genlt. von Ferling."

The A. O. K. 7 gave order to pass to Gen. of the Infantry Knight von Benzino:

"Enemy moves back defeated from 6st. And 7st. Army. Orders from here are not possible. Evading of the 2nd. Bavarian Ldw. Br. with touch with the Enemy has to happen in portions of Schoenau and Markolsheim.

Unite they're Divisions north of Schlettstadt to secure Flank towards Colmar and Markirch. Division Knoerzer is to inform to hold the Area near Weiler."

As result of further Discussion with the A. O. K. 7 was the Gen. Kdo. XIVst. R. K. informed from the Government at 6.30 in the Afternoon:

"30st. R. D. has with first Point the Climont attained. Bavarian Ers. D. positioned with a part at Rappoldsweiler. The 2nd. Bavarian Ldw. Br. is backing up to Neubreisach. Government Strasburg send by Train a Detachment (My Grandfather ordered additional 1 Battl. R. I. R. 60 and 2 Battl. R. I. R. 70) and 2 strong Battery's to Schlettstadt, to block the Rheine Valley and to defend the Back of the 3rd. R. D. The Unload should be finished in the Morning of August 21. The A. O. K. 7 want to make Shure that the Fortress Detachments and the Bavarian Ers. D. work together. Von Schubert has to take the upper Command."

Thereafter learned the Government, in Consultation with the Chief of that Core, Oberstlt. Bronsart von Schellendorf, that the Detachment Ferling came under Gen. von Benzino.

All these Commands and orders gave a Picture of the obscurity of the Command Structure. Since direct Telephone and Telegraph Connection between the A. O. K. and the Gen.Kdo. Of the XIVst. R. K. with the 30st. R. D. and the Bavarian Ers. D. and the other Detachments where not available, had the Government to be the Mediator.

The 30st. R. D. reported at 7.30 in the Evening from St. Martin:

"The Division came to the Line, after a 12 hour Battle, Ranrupt Salcee Climont."

The Situation in the Breusch Valley moved forward. To that came, that on Command of the XIVst. R.K., the 19st. Ers. D. Commander Genlt. Mueller, should come on the Morning of August 20. At 7 to Hohwald. He was to join the Battle either right or left according to the Situation.

Also on this Day did Gen. von Knoerzer find out, even so him and Bavarian Genlt. Mueller intervened vigorously, that in the Evening the Troops of the ordered Trenches, break up the Battle and move back to the Villages to get to rest. Therefore the French occupied the Trenches again. Because of that came the German Troops in a bad Situation. They had to storm the steep Hill again. On Top of that it was very hot and it was hard to get Water and Food.

The 19st. Ers. D. could not fulfill they're order. They were tired because of long marches on the previous Day. They were supposed to move forward on August 20 over Hohwald to Schirrgut. But they're Main Core branched off to Hochfeld. A false Report about the further use of the XIVst. R. K. and the unfavorable Position of the Outpost, that are at Bellefosse in Battle with the French, made the Divisions Commander to order the Division to march back. With further large March Casualty's, they came in early Morning in the Rheine Area near Barr. Because of this was the right Wing of the 30st. R. D. not decided, since the French still stood at Schirrgut and westerly and the 26st. R. D. in the Breusch Valley had not moved fore over Schirmeck.

Gen. von Benzino reported at 9.30 in the Morning from Rappoltsweiler:

"On the Hills south and southwest at Markirch did the North Brigade of the Bavarian Ers. D. got into heavy Battle. The Battle is still on."

Towards Evening incoming Reports from upper Elsa's said the Position is good. The 1st. Bavarian Ldw. Br. reinforced with 3 Wuertemberg Battalions and heavy Artillery stood in the Area of Colmar and occupied it. They wanted to go back, from the Enemy forced, to Neubreisach.

The French had on the Hills and in the east Valley Exits of the Vogesen, opposite of Colmar, installed more Battery's and in the Afternoon occupied with Infantry Winzenheim, Wettoldsheim and Egisheim. The result of the Day was good, even so the Position of the right Wing of the 30st. R. D. was not so good.

After a Report from Gen. von Ferling on August 21 at 7.40 in the Morning, wanted Gen. von Benzino combine the Detachment Ferling, which was at his disposal, at Rohrschweier south of Schlettstadt. From the Brigades of his Division was the 1st. (Grueber) reinforced with 2 Battalions from Detachment Ferling, they moved forward fighting in the Leber Valley. They had at Noon occupied St. Kreuz. The 9st. Bavarian Ers. Br. (Krieger) came with they're 4 Battalions and 3 Battery's from Rappoltsweiler over F.H. Iberg at 9 in the Morning about 3km. south of St. Kreuz into Battle. They attacked French Artillery in the back and moved then forward to Markirch. The Staff of the Division stayed in Rappoltsweiler. From the Detachment Ferling were the Villages of Gemar, Bergheim, Rohrschweier, St. Pilt and Kinzheim occupied.

The advancement of the XIVst. A. K. was different then what the A. O. K. 7 wanted. The 28st. R. D. did on August 20 occupy the little Donon but left by mistake in the Night. They had to storm the steep Mountain Peak again. After heavy losses was the Line Herrgottshoehe little Donon at 11 in the Morning again in German Hand. The French still occupied the Slopes of the big Donon. The left Flank of the 28st. R. D. could not break the resistance of the Enemy at Grandfontaine. The to the Division attached R. I. R. 99 was in the Morning from the Enemy in Frecomrupt attacked and with heavy losses pushed back, the Commander wounded. This Regiment was taken back and put under the Government. The 26st. R. D. from whom parts in the Battle on the Donon were, stayed in their Positions south of Schirmeck and averted French attacks. The Intervention of the 19st. Ers. D. that from the Gen. Kdo. XIVst. R. K. over Hochfeld Schirrgut demanded was did on August 21 not happen. The Divisions Commander thought they needed Rest and they stayed in Barr. The 30st. R. D. did come forward, without this help, after a Battle with heavy losses over the Line Hill 763 La Guiche (1 km. east of Ranrupt) to les Bas.

From the Bavarian Ers. D. came Reports to the Government that came over the Command from Neubreisach. The 1st. Bavarian Ldw. Br. Stand on the right Shore of the Ill between Holzweier and Andolsheim. Brigade Staff in Bischweier. They were supposed to move forward on the next Day to Kaversberg, Ammerschweier and Ingersheim. The detachment of the Fortress had moved Security's forward to Appenweier in west to Herlichsheim. It wanted to march there on the next Day early in the Morning. The Enemy in Front of the Brigade was supposed to be Cavalry and various Regiments of Alpen jaeger with MGs. The strengths of the Enemy were not known. Gen. Mathy, Kdr. Of the 55th. Ldw. I. R. that occupied the Bridge Heads at Markolsheim, Schoenau and Gerstheim. He had one Battl. Ldw. I. R. 40, one Battl. From the Bavarian 2nd and one from the 3rd Ldw. I. R. and 3 Platoons Pioneers.

The Reports from the Bavarian Ers. D. about the Battles at Markirch was good. After my Grandfather spoke to the Gens. von Benzino and von Ferling, he thought that there were no more Danger in the Rheine Valley. Gen.von Benzino wanted to move further forward and he gave his ok. From the A. O. K. 7 came a Report that the Enemy moved back to Luneville Blamont. The Gen. Kdo. of the XIVst. R. K. reported:

"Tomorrow will be an attack on the heavy occupied Northwest Donon Peak. R. I. R. 99 is from Troops of the Core at Frecomrupt relieved and is moved back to Schirmeck. 19st. Ers. D. move forward tomorrow from Area Hohwald. Gen. von Knoerzer moves tomorrow from Line Ranrupt Climont further fore. Since the whole XIVst. R. K. is very thin will the Core welcome if the Fortress would send Troops to Schirmeck."

Because of that was in the Evening an order sends to Gen. von Gynz Rekowski to send Ldw. I. R. 80 in the Breusch Valley, that in Luetzelhausen had to help XIVst. R. K.

The 30st. R. D. reported at 9.40 in the Evening that the Division was victorious after 12 hour Battle and had caused many losses to the Enemy. They would stay in the Position at Ranrupt because the Troops, after 4 Days of Battle, needed Rest. Next Day in the Afternoon is forward move to St. Blaise planed.

The main Job for my Grandfather was to end the Armoring of the Fortress. Every drive to the Breusch Valley was used to check on the Fortress K. W. IInd. Every drive to Schlettstadt to check the south Front of the Fortress. The Commanders of the Artillery and Pioneers reported daily and he had to make Decisions.

He and his Chief wanted to talk personally with the Gen. Kdo. Of the XIVst. R. K. They drove in to the Breusch Valley and used the Streets that the fighting Troops past Schirmeck used. They stayed in telephone contact with the Government since in the Villages the Field and regular Lines where ok.

As they approached the Outskirts of Schirmeck, they met the stopped Cars from the Gen. Kdo. XIVst. R. K. and the 26th. R. D. in Front of the Hotel at the Stone builds undestroyed Bridge. Inside was the Telephone connection with the Troops that were in the Battle. Also to the 28st. R. D. who battled heavy at the Donon and to the Government Strasburg. At the Hills on both sides of the Valley south of Schirmeck were Wuertemberg R. Field Artillery Battery's in Battle with the French who occupied the Hills south of Rothau. The Gun and Infantry Fire was heavy. The Chief of the XIVst. R. K. told them about the Situation. The Commanding General. Had rode on Horseback forward to the Troops. The Situation at the XIVst. R. K. was this:

> "Enemy pushed back. 28st. R. D. moves from the big Donon to Raon sur Plaine, 26st. R. D. in direction of Salm. 30st. R. D. fighting victoriously in Line Ranrupt Climont then to St. Blaise attacking Saales. From the 19st. Ers. D. was thought that they are again March fore over Hohwald.

At Markirch and at the Rheine Valley, where Gen. von Benzino has the Command, started the Battles in the Leber Valley again. French Alpen Jaeger had occupied Reichenweier. From the A. O. K. 7 came a Command on this Day at 9.25 before Noon:

> "Main Job of the 1st and 2nd Bavarian Ldw. Br. is the Security of the Rheine Valley at Schoenau and Markolsheim. For this, they are under the delegated Gen. Kdo. Of the XIVst. Army Core, which can lead to combine with Benzino Division. The Governor of Strasburg, whom the Benzino Division, with main parts at Bergheim, subordinate becomes, secures the left Flank of the Army. It is not the Intention in the Rheine Area

with minority Troops to fight against superior Troops, since the result at Saarburg and at the Donon is in our Favor. Connection with the Division Knoerzer, which is near Ranrupt, has to be demanded for the Security at the Area near Weiler."

From Schirmeck gave my Grandfather the order to the Gens. von Benzino and von Ferling.

"You have a definite order, under no circumstance to move forward over the yesterday occupied Line Gemar Bergheim instead to give strong Resistance if the Enemy moves forward in the Rheine Valley."

The Chief of the XIVst. R. K. asked my Grandfather if he could occupy all Villages in the Breusch Valley, also the Streets Grendelbruch Schirmeck and from the Donon, for Security of the Streets to Alberschweiler St. Quirin Raon sur Plaine, with Troops of the Fortress. Before they left the Gen. Kdo. Of the XIVst. A. K. did my Grandfather gave an order that the Gen. von Gynz Rekowski became the Command of the R. I. 99 and Ist. / R. I. R. 60. He and his Staff had to go to Luetzelhausen.

He drove with Maj. Mohs at 4 in the Afternoon to Schlettstadt and Bergheim so he could talk to the Leaders of the Troops there. From the Rheine Valley came several Reports that the Enemy moved forward with many Troops to Colmar and Muehlhausen.

The 1st. Bavarian Ldw. Br. had left Colmar. It started an Artillery Battle at witch Logelbach and west parts from Colmar became in Flame. In the Evening stood the 1st. Bavarian Ldw. Br. Commander Genlt. Eichhorn, reinforced with IInd. / Wuertemberg Ldw. I. R. 123 and IIIrd. / Wuertemberg Ldw. I. R. 121 east of Colmar in the Villages Holzweiler, Fortschweier and Andolsheim with Security on the Ill. They reported at 11.30 in the Evening that they would stay.

My Grandfather looked at the produced security measures at Bergheim and spoke with the Staff of the Bavarian Ers. D. at Rappoltsweiler. There they found out of the victorious result of the Battle at Markirch. 2 Battl. Of the Bavarian R. I. R. 15 and reinforced Brigades Grueber and Krieger attacked in the difficult Mountain Area with Bravery and forced the

Enemy to withdraw. They stormed a French Battery in the main Position on a high Pass, and there a French Commander died.

The A. O. K. 7 at Loerchingen became a Report:

> "The Division Benzino took today the Col de St. Marie after bloody Battle. They have an order to not go further west. Detachment Ferling is in Armored Position at Bergheim with Front to south. They have connection with 1st and 2nd Bavarian Ldw. Br."

The 30st. R. D. became the same Report. At 10 in the Evening they came back to Strasburg. In the Night from 22 to 23 ordered the A. O. K. 7 to move from Finstingen 3 Fortress MGs. with Ammunition and Crew and a heavy movable Searchlight over Saarburg if possible to Avricourt. The R. I. R. 99 became the new formed MG. Company.

The 30st. R. D. had this Day a very heavy Battle, since the Enemy had not backed up, but at Night got reinforced. The Bavarian Battl. Suffered very much under the Fire of the French Artillery. The losses became more and the Enemy encircle attempt against the left Wing of the 30st. R. D. had to be repulsed with Bayonet. Since the 19st Ers. D. deviated towards Bellefosse were they unable to help in this Battle.

Gen. von Knoerzer moved by Night to the Area at Weiler back. The Reason for that Movement back of the Division was that it was not possible in they're hard to reach Position to bring Food. Only half of the Infantry had Field Kitchens. Alone and in small Groups they went into the Valley to the Field Kitchen. So daily one or more Company had to bring back the Men that got lost in the heavy forested Mountain. Because of that and the many Battles in the Forest Mountain brought a mix up in the Troops. At Report from both Brigade Commanders and the Commanders of the 2nd Bavarian Regiments, they thought that this Situation, if the Enemy attacked, would be a Catastrophe. They had to either move forward or move back. The Infantry was tired and Artillery help for a Battle was not possible because it was high in the Forest. Also the Telephone Wires between the Observation Posts and the Infantry Line was hard to install. When they knew that the 19st. R.D. moved back did the Divisions Commander also moved his Troops back. He wanted to create order and provide Food and then over Urbeis again attack.

This News came to the Government on August 23 at 9.35 in the Morning over the Post Station Weiler.

The Division had for observation in the Urbeis Valley only 1 Company and a few Bicyclers. The Government knew that and was alarmed that an encircling movement of the French at Markirch over Urbeis would be possible. Because of that did the Division Benzino receive at 8.45 in the Morning an Order:

> "After your Excellence brave Troops yesterday stormed Col de St. Marie you will use these points as your Measure.

1. Fortify and occupy Col de St. Marie towards west Streets to Wisembach and Laveline and towards south and southwest Streets to Diedolshausen and Eckerich. Reconnaissance also over the Border.
2. Prepare parts of the Division to intervene in the Flank at an attack at the Detachment Ferling.
3. Secure and cleanup of the Street Markirch Schlettstadt
4. Connection with Division Knoerzer who is as Security in Urbeis and Weiler Valley."

Because of that, came at 9.30 in the Morning from the Bavarian Ers. D. a Report:

> Enemy across Col du St. Marie collecting Troops. Observation to Altweier and Diedolshausen started. The Division asked for Bicyclers, since there are no more Riders, for Construction of the Train from Leberau to Markirch, to send the 2 Battery's from the Detachment Ferling."

The Requests from the Division where send without the 2 Battery's. The Batteries could not be taken away from Detachment Ferling because of News. It was necessary to build a mixed Detachment that could be a reserve in the Weiler and Leber Valley. At 10.20 in the Morning was Gen. von Ferling ordered to send an Infantry Regiment and 1 Field Battery to the Train Station Weiler Valley. It was to be there for use of the Government.

The Bavarian R. I. R. 4 with 3 Battl. and 1 Battery went there. The rest of the Detachment Ferling stood at 11 in the Morning at Bergheim.

At 1.45 in the Afternoon, came from Gen. Kdo. XIVst. R. K. a Report with an order to Division Benzino:

> "Immediately move forward from Markirch to St. Die. There occupy Cotton Factory. The Division Knoerzer and the 26ˢᵗ. R. D. also moves forward. It is all about to attack the Enemy in the Area Bourg Bruche from all sides."

It was clear that the Division Benzino could not move forward at this time without the 2 Battery's, that came from there, where given back. The Detachment Ferling became 2 Wuertemberg Reserve Battery's from Strasburg. On Afternoon started on the high Pass Col de St. Marie a Battle. The French attacked in the front and through the dense Forest north of the Col to the right Flank of the Bavarians and they had to give up the Position. The 3ʳᵈ Battl. That stood at the Train Station Weiler Valley came to the Bavarian R. I. R. 4. The Division reported at 9.35 in the Evening that they were positioned west of Markirch and wanted with the Bavarian R. I. R. 4 to conquer the high Pass again

In the Night to August 23 did the substitute Gen. Kdo. XIV. Army Core report to the Government:

> "1ˢᵗ. And 2ⁿᵈ. Bavarian Ldw. Br. comes under one Command of the oldest Brigade Commander. 1ˢᵗ.Br. now east of the Ill and behind the Line Holzweier Horburg Andolsheim. 2ⁿᵈ. Br. united all they're Troops except of 1 Company of the Bridge Head Schoenau at 9 in the Morning at Eisenheim. Task: Prevent the French from crossing the Ill west of Colmar in partner with Neubreisach. 1ˢᵗ. Br. moved today from Colmar back because no help from Bergheim."

At 10.35 in the Morning reported the Commander Neubreisach that 1 French Division moved forward from Logelbach to Colmar. The 1ˢᵗ. Bavarian Ldw. Br. would stop the Enemy behind the Ill, and the Detachment Ferling would be asked to move forward against the Enemy Flank. This Wish was in no manner like the Command of the A. O. K. 7

of the previous Day. It was surrendered by a report at 11.20 before Noon from the Waterworks Inspection in Colmar:

> "In Colmar this Morning French Patrols. Enemy probably forward Logelbach, probably only Cavalry, in Ingersheim Infantry."

They were sure that there was no Enemy in Colmar and this came true at 12.30 in the Afternoon as there came a Report from the Command Center Colmar:

> "The Enemy had moved out of the Muenster Valley in 2 Columns. They had not until 11 in the Morning moved over the Line Ingersheim Wizenheim and were there digging Trenches."

Because of that ordered the substitute Gen. Kdo. Of the XIVst.A. K.

> "If Enemy moves forward with superior Troops, move 2nd Bavarian Ldw. Br. to Schoenau and Markolsheim, the 1st Bavarian Ldw. Br. with the Fortress Detachment back to Neubreisach."

Because of the Situation did my Grandfather again made Contact with the substitute Gen. Kdo. Of the XIVst. A. K. and told them again of his Order, which it already knew from the Order of the A. O. K. 7.

The pursuit of the at Saarburg defeated French Troops, because of the 6th. And on the right Wing the 7th. Army had to be hard for the Enemy, who still fought in the Vogesen. A long stop could mean Detriment. The smart moves of the French rear Guard slowed down the German advance in the Mountain Area. So the French main Troops could avoid encirclement. The A. O. K. 7 had ordered the Core on August 24 to reach the left Shore of the Meurthe. The XIVst. R. K. was according to the Order to pursue with the 28st. R. D. to branch off south to Senones, the 26st. R. D. over Saales to Ban de Sapt, the 30st. R. D. over Urbeis to Provencheres, the Bavarian Ers. D. over the Col de St. Marie to St. Die. Gen. von Knoerzer started over Urbeis and moved with his right Wing against the Vineyard and with his left against the Col d'Urbeis and southward. The

Bavarians could only slowly break the stubborn resistance of the French. The Enemy was pushed back over the Climont Peak and the Urbeis Pass to Provencheres and Lubine. Near Markirch had the Division Benzino learned, from found Papers, that the French wanted to encircle the left Wing of the Division from Wisembach at Markirch. Because of that did the Division send from St. Kreuz an encircle detachment in the Forest Area north of Markirch and now expelled the Enemy in a dash attack from the Border Peak. At Noon moved the Division in the Front to retake Col de St. Marie. Wisembach was taken by the Division.

On the left Wing of the XIVst.R. K. was good success; even so St. Die could not be taken from any of the Columns. The Hardship of the Mountain War and the tough resistance of the French have to be emphasized. The performance of the German Reserve and Militia Troops was outstanding.

At the Government came on August 24 Reports from the Rheine Valley that where not clear. Gen. Gaede gave on August 23 a Core Command that he changed because of the reports. An Airplane reported many Troop assemblies and vivid Traffic by the Enemy near Muehlhausen.

At 1.45 in the Afternoon received the Division Benzino an order, in the pursued of the Enemy to St. Die, the Col de St. Marie heavy to armoire and to occupy. To allow connection with the Detachment Ferling at Bergheim and in the Leber Valley with Schlettstadt.

The Division was also to stay in constant connection with the Government. My Grandfather did not want to lose the connection, so he could give orders if necessary. In order to facilitate the mission for the Ers. D. became Oberstlt. Hoffmann from the I. R. 71 with the Ldw. I. R. 71 the Staff and with the light Howitzer Detachment 51 in the Night to August 25 transferred to Schlettstadt. This Detachment was under the Government. The French attacked on August 25 on the whole Front of the 7st. Army. The Divisions of the XIVst. R. K. came on this Day fore to Senones, east of Ban de Sapt, Saales and Bourg Bruche. The 30st. R. D. started in the Morning to pursue over Climont Hill and Lubine towards Colroy la Grande. They bend off, because of a wrong Report that the 26st. R. D. marched to Provencheres, Germans supposed to be in St. Die and Lusse. They came with they're Vanguard to Frapelle in the Valley of the Fave.

A Flank of the Bavarian Ers. D. had in the Morning of this Day a Battle with 2 Company's Alpen Jaeger and pushed them back to Urbach. The Division came west of Wisembach against strong Enemy defense and had to stop. They came; because of Command of the A. O. K. 7 at 1.45 in the Afternoon with they're Troops at Markirch, without Detachment Ferling, under the XIVst. R. K.

The untiring Oberstlt. Count von Holnstein, who was the Leader of the Work Columns, learned from my Grandfathers order, that the R. I. R. 99 took part with bravura at the Battles of the 26st. R. D. and for further forward moves came under the 52nd. R.Br. With that it was no longer under my Grandfathers orders.

For the Security of the connections in the Breusch Valley, where 2 Companies of the IIIrd. / Ldw. I. R. 80 moved from Grendelbruch to Schirmeck.

For the Security of the connections from the Weiler Valley over the Col d'Urbeis, which the 30st. R. D. had crossed, came 2 Companies of the Landst. Battl. Hagenau I with an Armored Train over Schlettstadt to Train Station Weiler Valley

At the Col de St. Marie had the Bavarian Ers. D. left the 2 Batt. Of the Bavarian R. I. R. 15 for Security of the Passes and cleanup of the Battlefield. The Bavarian R. I. R. 4 was supposed to come again under Detachment Ferling. From the Government was moved by Train the Ldw. I. R. 71 (3 Battls.) with the 1st. / Ers. Field A. K. 15 to Kestenholz. 1 Company of this Regiment occupied the armored Train 9 in the Leber Valley and relieved the Company from the Ldw. I. R. 70, which went back to they're Regiment.

The Bavarian Ers. D. asked the Government for an "wound" Platoon, an Ammunition Platoon and 2 Provisions Platoons and Maps of France. Similar Whishes hat the 30st. R. D. There they were short on Field Cables, Telephones and Accessories. All these whishes where taken care off. 1 Request from the 30st. R. D. to quickly help with the heavy losses of Officers, was send to the Bavarian War Ministry.

The French Intentiones were still unclear in the upper Elsa's.

Gen.Oberst von Heeringen became order from Crown Prince Rupprecht on August 26 to continue the attacks with the 7st. Army. The

XVst. And XIVst. A. K. where started in the direction of Etival. The XIVst. R. K. had to move forward in the direction of St. Die and north at the Meurthe.

The A. O. K. 7 ordered at 9.20 in the Morning that the ZIV. R. K. had to attack at St. Die and north from there.

Gen. von Schubert had ordered the 2nd. R. D. of his Core to attack the Enemy first at Ban de Sapt. Then was the 28st. To turn to Etival. The 26st. R. D. and the subordinate 30st. R. D. and Bavarian Ers. D. had to reach from north, east and southeast St. Die. The 19st. Ers. D. was kept back as reserve at Saales.

The 30st. R. D. kicked the Enemy out of Neuviller and Coinches. The Bavarian Ers. D. had kicked the Enemy at Noon from the Hills west of Laveline, who went back over the Meurthe to Taintrux. The Bavarians wanted to pursue but Gen. von Schubert stopped them at Coinches.

The Government became in the Morning a Report from the Bavarian Ers. D. that they took the R. I. R. 4, which was under the Detachment Ferling, (without IV) and 15 (without II) to attack west of the Vogesen Rim. Also the 2nd. / Ers. Field A. R. 51 went forward by mistake with these Troops. They had to look for a new Garrison for Markirch and Col de St. Marie. My Grandfather ordered, that the at Kestenholz positioned Ldw. I. R. 71, moved in that Place. He notified Gen. von Benzino of this. To Kestenholz came a Detachment from the Ldw. I. R. 81, a few Hussars and 1 Field Battery under Gen.Maj. Rash, subordinate Kdr. Of the 59st. I. Br.

The Enemy was thought to have inferior Troops before the Front of Gen. von Ferling. They had Kienzheim and Kaysersberg and further south the Area west from Colmar occupied. It was again taken by the 1st. Bavarian Ldw. Br. It was still the Danger that the French Troops, who were still in the Mountains, came forward against the Valley from Markirch. In this they would have hit the backward Connections of the Bavarian Ers. D. My Grandfather thought it important to move the Security's south of the Col de St. Marie on the Border Rim forward. He hoped that they could expel the in the Mountain positioned French rear Guard over Diedolshausen and Zell and occupy the Col du Bonhomme. He notified the Gen.Kdo. XIVst. A. K. and the Command Center Neubreisach.

After the Report that the French Troops were transported from upper Elsa's to Nancy, ordered the A. O. K. 7 for Security of the right Flank of the 6st. Army, all dispensable Troops from the War Garrison of the Fortress to Chateau Salins.

On August 26 ordered the French Army Leadership to dissolve the Army d'Alsace. They vacated the upper Elsa's. They only left 1 Division of the VIIst. Core at the Schluchtpass.

On August 27 before Noon drove my Grandfather with a few Officers of the Staff to Bergheim for a Meeting. Because of that came at 11.30 in the Morning an order that the Enemy was positioned west of Colmar, get attacked in the Morning of August 28. The 2nd. Bavarian Ldw. Br. was supposed to move forward with her right Wing over Ostheim, the 1st. Bavarian Ldw. Br. with 2 heavy Howitzer Battery's over Colmar, the Fortress Detachment Neubreisach south from there. The Detachment Ferling was supposed to be standing by to attack at 4.30 in the Morning northward of Reichenweier Bebelnheim at the Hill Schwarz Sigolsheim. The Troops in Altweier were to go in the Flank and back of the Enemy. Gen. Rasch had with the Troops under him Ist. Law. IR.71 (3 Company's) the Col de St. Marie to occupy and with the Ldw. IR. 81, 1 MG. Company and 1 Field Battery to march to Urbach and from there at 5 in the Morning go Forward against Flank and Back of the Enemy.

From Bergheim they drove to Kestenholz to talk to Gen. Rasch about the Situation and his Intention. On August 28 at 5 in the Morning, came my Grandfather with his first Gen. Staff Officer and a few Men from his Staff to Reichenweier. There convened the Detachment Ferling to get ready to march to Kienzheim. There he sends with his Car the orderly Officer Oblt. Zimmermann to Urbach to Gen. Rasch to make Shure that he knows the Route for the march to Zell. At 7 in the Morning he went with Maj. Mohs to Kienzheim in the Expectation to see the Battery's from the Detachment Ferling in position to the Siegolsheimer Hills. In and near at Reichenweier stood the Squadron and south of the Village stood the march Column of the Artillery:

> "Why are the Battery's not in Place?"
> "This cannot be done in the midst of the Vineyards!"
> "Why not?"
> "You can't just move in the Vineyards!"

He had to get quite distinct until the Batteries were in Place. Soon thereafter he met Gen. von Ferling who told him that French Artillery stood on the Meiwihr Koepfle, Hill 425, 1000m. Southwest of Ammerschweier. The north Edge of Kienzheim was lightly occupied by Enemy Infantry. The Gen. intended the French Artillery from the Sigolsheimer Hill to shell and then to order the forward move to Ammerschweier. From the south Slope of the Sigolsheimer Hill did they see the Battle. You could by the warm Weather in the Valley see close north of Kienzheim Sigolsheim the Rifleman Line of the IInd. / Bavarian R. I. R. 15 and the IVst. / Bavarian R. I. R. 4 in Battle with French Alpen Jaeger who lay in the north Edges of the Villages. 2 French MGs. shot, the 1 from the Roof of a Building of the Monastery, the other from the Steeple of the Church. The other Troops they could not see. From the south direction they could hear heavy Artillery firing.

About 9 in the Morning started the French Guns at the Meinwihr Koepfle to fire in the Valley of Weissbach.

At 9.15 in the Morning came a Report:

> "Detachment Neubreisach passed with Vanguard at 7.30 in the Morning Herlisheim towards Egisheim."

Because of the Canon Fire, that they could hear was also the 1st Ldw. Br. in touch with the Enemy. Not till 10 in the Morning came a Report that the 2nd. Bavarian Ldw. Br. arrived at the ordered Point Street crossing east of Sigolsheim. They became order to only move forward in the open Area near Sigolsheim after the Enemy Fire there ended. At 12 Noon they went to Kiensheim and there met Gen. von Ferling. From him they learned that the Enemy from Kaysersberg, witch German Troops had stormed, had moved back towards Zell. At 1 in the Afternoon came the orderly Officer back, who was send to Gen. Rasch. He brought a report from Gen. Rasch, for my Grandfather that he was marching according to the order towards Zell. Because of French Patrols was the March difficult. Meanwhile had the 2nd. Bavarian Ldw. Br. pushed Enemy Infantry back towards west and was in connection with Detachment Ferling and the 1st. Bavarian Ldw. Br.

As they came again to the west Exit of Kienzheim they met there Gen. Rasch who reported to my Grandfather that his Detachment had arrived in Kaysersberg.

> "Sir General, I had given you order to march over Hachimette towards Zell, what are you doing here?"
> "I was at the March forward through the Mountain many times hindert by Enemy Infantry and came only slowly forward, because I had always send new Vanguards. When I heard the Canon Fire from The east I marched towards it."

My Grandfathers hope to encircle the Enemy had failed.

He came to the conclusion on the next Day to move forward on the whole Front and to try the Enemy, with pressure to Urbeis, to move towards west.

In the Evening they came back to Reichenweier. There came unpleasant Reports. The Bavarian Ldw. Br. did not stay in there gained Battle Line, but moved, without sending a Report, back to they're Quarters from the previous Day. They stood east of the Street Gemar Colmar. The worst Reports came from Bavarian Ers. D. who was attacked at Anozell and was pushed back to the right Shore of the Meurthe. Also did the French from Mandray attack they're left Flank. My Grandfather understood that the French wanted to use the free Troops from the upper Elsa's for attacks at the German Troops who had advanced over the Meurthe. His Problem: The Security of the left Flank and the backwards connections of the 7st. Army could now no longer be done at the east Slope and in the Mountain. He had immediately more Troops to move forward over and on the Passes for the Security of the connection Streets. He hoped to do the Pursuit towards Zell with the Bavarian Ldw. Br. and the Detachment Ferling on August 29.

He had to abandon his move towards Zell on August 29 because of incoming Reports. He sends a Report with Maj. Mohs to Strasburg. At 6 in the Morning he met Gen. Rasch at the west exit of Kaysesberg and ordered him:

> "Detachment Rasch marched immediately from Saegemuehle west of Kaysersberg over Altweiler to Markirch

and occupied the Col de St. Marie. Reconnoiter to St. Leonard Diedolshausen. Detachment Ferling stays in Area Ammerschweier occupies Kaysersberg and reconnoiters to Diedolshausen Urbeis Zell. Gen. Ferling retains his previous order: Security of the left Flank and backward connections of the Army. I demand from the subordinate Gen. Kdo. XIVst. A. K. in joining the Detachment Ferling to block the Streets over Katzental Niedermorschweier Tuerkheim."

After he had spoken with Gen. Ferling he drove on to visit the Ldw. Br. He met Genlt. Eichhorn, Kdr. of the 1st. Bavarian Ldw. Br. in Colmar. He explained to him that the Bavarian Ldw. Br. we're not suited to attack in the Mountains. Yesterday they had reached the Line Ingersheim Tuerkheim Winzenheim Egisheim. The advance Troops stood still there. Because of this and other reasons he had to give up on the isolated move forward of the Detachment Ferling.

After he came back to Strasburg he found a Report from Gen. Rasch that his Detachment reached, without to be in touch with the Enemy, Altweier at 9.45 in the Morning. French Infantry still occupies Urbeis. The Detachment became as reinforcement the Detachment Staff and the Ers. Battr. / Field A. R. 15 and a Signal Squad. The A. O. K. 7 was informed of the achieved successes at Ammerschweier, the present Position of the Enemy and the orders that where given to Gen. Rasch and Detachment Ferling.

The 30st. R. D. was given to Gen. von Benzino and the Meurthe Area Saulcy Anould was attacked. The Troops of both Divisions became very mixed up and a centralized Leadership could not be obtained and so it could not be achieved to push the Enemy over the River. Gen. von Benzino took the Division back in the Evening of August 30 to a Line east of Saulcy Hill 740 De Behouille to get order in the Formations and to clear up the Position.

As Compensation for the delivery of the Foot Artillery from Strasburg, which was used for the Siege of Maubeuge, became the Government from order of the O. H. L. 2 Bavarian Foot Artillery Battl. With heavy Field Howitzers from the War Garrison Germersheim.

It came an order to finish the Armoring of the Fortress and to give the Workers to the 7st. Army. The Forest Master Johansen from Markirch reported that the Cote de St. Marie (about 6km) south of the Col de St. Marie was occupied from the Enemy and the Street to Markirch totally barricaded and Trenches dug left and right on the Forest Edge.

From the Gen. Kdo. XIVst. R. K. came a report in the Evening of August 30:

> "About at 4 in the Afternoon attacked on all Fronts. At the left Wing from St. Leonard Mandray La Croy, Gen. Kdo. Asked to occupy Wiesembach and make connection with Laveline. At the left Shore of the Meurthe Enemy attacks from Anould Taintrux and from St. Michel. It is asked for Airplane surveillance. Dropping Reports at Provencheres, where the Gen.Kdo. Will move tomorrow. St. Die occupied from us."

The Troops for the Occupation of Wiesembach where prepared. In the Evening at 9.10 became Gen. Rasch in Markich an order:

> "Immediately march to Area Wiesembach. Col de St. Marie remains Occupied with 1 Battl. And 2 MGs. 2 Company's stay in Altweier. The Detachment has to stand tomorrow at Daybreak at the Hills South of Wiesembach so it can help at the left Wing of the Division Benzino. 2 Battl. From the Detachment Ferling will be marching tonight over Rappoltsweiler towards Markirch and will come under your order."

Gen. von Ferling in the Castle Kienzheim became this order:

> "Strong Enemy attacks XIVst. A. K. on the whole Front. Gen. Rasch has order to move forward immediately to Area Wiesembach, Col de St. Marie and Altweiler to keep occupied. Detachment Ferling send on August 31 in the Morning 2 Battl. And 2 Batterys over Rappoltsweiler to Markirch. If your Excellency instead need reinforcement in the Area Kaysersberg Ammerschweier is such to be asked from Bavarian Ldw.Br. (Division Eichhorn) in Colmar."

Gen. Kdo, became a corresponding Report.

In Strasburg came until August 31 more Militia Troops available. Slowly could parts of the Reserve and Militia Formations, who were used for Train Security, go back to they're Regiments. In the Breusch Valley did the Ldst.Battl. Rastatt took over from Luetzelhausen upwards the Security. Therefore was the IInd. / Ldw. I. R. moved by Train to Markirch. The Regiments Staff and the 2 other Battl. Moved there also. From his own Initiative drove Genlt. von Gynz Rekowski with his Regiment to Markirch. At that time he had no Troops under his Command. My Grandfather gave him the Command over parts of the Detachment Rasch that was at the Col de St. Marie and Markirch. This Gen.reported on August 31 before Noon that he:

> "With the Ldw. I. R. 81, the IInd. / R. I. R. 60, the IInd. / Bavarian R. I. R. 15, the IIIrd. / Ldw. I. R. 71 and the Artillery that was given him, according to his order, took Position east of Laveline with Front west and south. Took connection with Division Knoerzer whose left Wing stood at Laveline."

Apparently was the Danger that the French would break through south of the Col de St. Marie gone. From Col was in the Afternoon a Light Signal connection taken up with Division Knoerzer and detachment Rasch. The Reports from the Airplane Detachment 2, Lt.Schlueter gave nothing important about the Enemy Positions.

Gen. von Ferling reported in the Afternoon the Occupation of the French at Schweighausen, Lautenbach and Zell. It was found out that it was the French Jaeg. Battl. 15 with MGs.

The Government had to transport, on order from the A. O. K. 6, on this day a put together Pioneer Battl. Existing of Staff, 2nd. And 4st. / Res. Pi. 15 and the Fortress Airship Squadron 15 to Dieuze to the IIIrd. Bavarian A. K. Also were the Ist. / Ers. Foot A. R. 14 (without Guns) sends to Marvionviller. The Fortress K. W. IInd became Ers. Foot A. R. 10.

So was Strasburg almost empty from all Battle tested Troops. The XVst. A. K. was moving forward to Battle at Muehlhausen and he wanted to give them all dispensable Troops. The right Flank of the 7st. Army was secured because of this main Reserve in the Vogesen Passes as it crossed the French Border. My Grandfather was sad that he could not be there. He wanted to see the Troops under his Command and tell them his Thanks and Appreciations.

It seemed Necessary for him and his Chief, After the Experience from August 28 and 29 that they checked the measures in Person of the Detachment Rasch for the security of the Col de St. Marie and the Connection with the left Wing of the XVst. A. K.

My Grandfather decided with his Chief of the Gen. Staff, Oberstlt. von Boeckmann, to visit the Battle Field on the other side of the Passes at Markirch, were they would meet the Division Benzino and Knoerzer and the Detatchment Rasch.

Into France 1st.Sept. Until 26. Sept. 1914

My Grandfather left on September morning with his Chief and the Chiefs orderly, Oblt. Ihssen (Hus. R. 16) Strasburg. They drove over Markirch to Wiesembach. At the Col de St. Marie he found out his surmise about the Security of the Passes was right. The Battl. There camped on both sides of the Street and did at the Peak have no Security installed against Cote de St. Marie. From the Meurthe Valley roared Cannon Thunder from the Battle Field. After intense explanation of the Situation with the Officers, where the security Measures installed. That also at the Peak resting IInd. / Ldw. I. R. 80 under the Command of Maj. Ulfert from I. R. 138 that was without order became order to move forward to Gemaingoutte and to be under Gen. Rasch. Then they drove over Wiesembach to Gemaingoutte. The Chief wanted to establish Connection with various Detachments. In those Days were the Telephone connections quite bad.

At 10 in the Morning they mounted in Wiesembach they're Horses, witch were brought there, and rode on the Street for to St. Die. German Field Battery's where on the Hills of the Street in the Area of Gemaingoutte and stood in Battle with French Infantry, who was to be seen east of La Croix. Bavarian Infantry and parts of the Wuert. Ldw. I. R. 120 took Position in the Area of Laveline. At the north Slopes of the Tete de Behouille, the Hill 740 northwest of La Behouille you could see were German Battery's and a few Company's were. They thought that the 30st. R. D. who was at the Battle, moved forward over Coinches and Coinchimont, which proved right.

Towards Evening they rode on to Fouchifol were the Divisions Staff was supposed to be. In the west was the Sun and illuminated the Battle Field. In Front of them was the beautiful Meurthe Valley, with its dark Forest Mountains, in them stood the 26th. R. D. in heavy Battle. German Battery's fired nearby west of the burning Fouchiful at heavy French Artillery. At the Village Entrance dictated the Bavarian Genlt. Mueller, Kdr. of the 10th. Bavarian R. I. Br. an order. French Prisoners and wounded Soldiers stood in the Street. My Grandfather gave Gen. von Knoerzer a fresh plucked Oak Twig. He told him that he would give him, the asked for reinforcements. The Gen. notified him that because of a Flank attack of the French from the south the Bavarian Ers. D. did move back to the right Meurthe Shore and took a Position Front towards south. Attacks of the French where repelled. The 30st. R. D. had been removed from St. Die and is since then, on order of Gen.von Schubert, put under Gen. von Benzino. Gen. von Benzino had inserted the Division between the 9st. and 1st. Bavarian Ers. Br. and caused a mix-up in the Formation.

They rode back to Wiesembach and drove from there to Markirch were they got a report from Strasburg:

> "From the A. H. Qu. Cirny came directives:
> "The 6th. And 7th. Army has to attack the Enemy on September 3. The 30th. R. D. who was put under the XIVst. R. K. and the Bavarian Ers. D. and 19st. Ers. D. push the Enemy fore they're front back. They will be reinforced with Troops from Colmar (21 Battl. With Artillery) who were put in March on September 1 to Diedolshausen Schluchtpass. Those Troops should take on the Security, after The Enemy is repelled, on the southern Army Flank towards the Line Epinal Geradmer. Upper Command is under Consideration."

Gen. von Ferling was to attack at Altweier Schnierlach and was ordered to vigorously pursue the Enemy in the Mountains.

On the Morning of September 2 they rode to Germaingoutte. There became Gen. Rasch the order to help at the left Wing of the Division Benzino in the direction towards Tete de Behouille. At 6 in the Morning they were in Coinches were the 30st. R. D. gave out orders. The Street was full of Troops.

On order from Gen.von Schubert was on Srptember 2 the Line to be held and the Bavarian Ers. D. pulled out. Gen. von Knoerzer found this odd since the Division had also many losses in the Battles of the last Days. He was afraid that because of weakening of the Front he could lose hard won Victory's on his right Wing. He explained the Situation to my Grandfather and asked him to intervene. He did and gave Gen. von Schubert a Report.

He promised Gen. von Knoerzer to ride to the battling Troops on the left Wing at the Tete de Behouille since there the Detachment Rasch was send with Reserves. They rode over Coinchimont to Algoutte.

As they rode they past several Farms. One of these Farms had a Well and they saw several Jung Men wash themselves. They did not think them to be French Soldiers. As they were past several 100m. They heard the Bullets fly past them. They galloped over a Pasture towards the Forest.

The Forest which covers the east part on the intense cleated Tete de Behouille was already under heavy Enemy Artillery Fire. The Battle had started on the whole Line. The Gun Fire in the Forest was heavy. They're Horses became hard to handle because of the Noise from the Grenades and breaking Tree Trunks. They walked towards the west Edge of the Forest were they had a good overlook of the Battle Field of the Division. On the way there they met 2 Companies of the Ldw. I. R. 81. They had with they're Front Troops the south and southwest Edge of the Forest occupied and where in a Gun Battle with the Enemy. The Troops made a good Impression. Shortly after they had reached the Forest Edge came 2 Battery's from Fouchiful to the Farms at the west Edge of the Forest and took Position on the Hill west of the Tete de Behouille. While they took Position they lost Men. They did not have Reconnaissance and moved to wide fore. The Men left they're Guns and went back to the Forest Edge to wait for the Enemy Fire to slow down. Later they had no Courage to man the Guns again. In the Evening Infantry had to retrieve them.

My Grandfather had concern about the left Wing of the Detachment Rasch, since he knew that east of the Tete de Behouille was a void in the Valley of the Morte, which was not filled. To make sure if there was a Danger of an encircling from east, they walked at Noon back through the Forest. It was hot and the from Laveline incoming Companies of the IInd.

/ Ldw. I. R. 80 with the Regiments Staff came towards them tired and in bad marching order.

At the southeast Edge of the Forest they could see the French Positions at the Bois de Mandray. At the northeast Slopes of the Grand Rein, a Forested Hill northwest from Ross Berg, stood a French Mountain Battery another Battery was at the Hill 697 north of Le Chipal. They fired into the Forest of the Tete de Behouille. Detachment Rekowski could not be seen. Because of that became Gen. von Knoerzer at 1.45 in the Afternoon a Report:

> "It is desired that the Hill 697 be attacked with heavy Artillery. With the Intention of Gen. Rasch to wait until the encircling detachments attack and then to attack is agreed."

To that Gen. von Knoerzer reported:

> "That he will try to attack the Enemy on Hill 697 from the Area of La Cuche. His Division has no Artillery because Gen. von Schubert gave them other Targets at Anozel."

At this Wing with Connection to the 5th. Bavarian Ers. Br. Kdr. GenMaj. Count von Zech (30. R. D.) Were the Troops like this Positioned:

> 5th. and 8st. / R. I. R. 60, IIIrd. / Ldw. I. R. 80 at Les Planches Pres west of the Tete de Behouille, Ist. and IIIrd. / Ldw. I. R. 81 at Hill 740 under Oberstlt. Vogel, IInd. / R. I. R. 15 at la Behouille at the Hills west of the Morte, IInd. And IIIrd. / Ldw. I. R. 120 under Maj. Wist, Kdr. of the IInd.Battl. Moving forward at the Hills east of the Morte about in the Area Au Voue, IV. / Bavarian R. I. R. 4, the MG. Company of the 9st. Bavarian Ers. Br. and 2nd. / Ers. Field A. R. 13 under Maj. Etzel, Kdr. of the IVst. Battl., following Maj. Wist to le Grand Rein. IInd. / Ldw. I. R. 80 and 2 Battery's under Oberstlt. Petersen from I. R. 143, Kdr. of the Ldw. I. R. 80 in March forward through the Forest of Coinchimont to Tete de Behouille.

They could see the whole Morte Valley from they're Position toward Bois de Mandray. At 5.15 in the Afternoon did my Grandfather look back and did see a driving Column come out of the Forest back towards Algoutte. They looked through they're Field Glasses and seen that they had Canons and also the Staff. They got on they're Horses. At that Moment came Infantry out of the Forest in disarray. All this a few 100m. behind their backs. They galloped towards them. A bunch of several 100 Man, of the in the Forest positioned Militia Troops, hurried down the Hills. They're Leader called to us:

> "All is lost, the French took the Forest. All are dead or wounded!"

My Grandfather called to them:

> "Front! In the Valley you are lost if the French come out of the Forest! Think of the Number on your Sleeves, of the Hero's from Wessenburg and Woerth! Forward back again up on The Hill!"

They jumped from they're Horses, they could not ride up on the steep Hill, pulled they're Sabers. The orderly Officer from Gen. Rasch, Oberlt. Michelmann a big Map roll like a Baton under his Arm, throws himself against the hesitant. So they succeeded to get the man back up the Hill. At any Moment they expected the French to break out of the forest in Front of them.

> "Mount Bayonet! Drummer!"

It was a Hair rising Moment! But it was not heroic, because the French were nowhere to be seen. In the Forest in Front of them were still many brave troops from the Ldw. I. R. 81 and they're Commander guaranteed that the Enemy will not get back. The Panic was caused by wounded Soldiers going back and Cowards. The continues creaking of the Artillery Explosions and splinters of the Trees got on they're nerves. My Grandfather brought order to the Men and ordered the Leader of these Troops to report to Oberstlt. Vogel. On the eastern Forest Edge they met 2 Bavarian Battl.

In good order. He called to the Flag Carrier: "Stop, Front to the Enemy!" The Battl. Kdr. reported:" Since the Prussians on our right move back, I will lead the Battl. Back to those Hills. The Enemy Artillery from the Vogesen Ridges is heavy on the Flank from here."

My Grandfather ordered him to move again forward with the Battl. And take Position with connection on the Ldw. I. R. 81. The Battl. Executed this order faultless.

Since he was here now personally involved did he want to take further Responsibility at this Wing and did send a report to Gen. von Knoerzer:

> "Algoutte, September 2 at 6 in the Afternoon.— Took Command at Left Wing, northwards Mandray Troops pushed the Enemy collected and the south Edge of the Forest at Behouille occupied. German Artillery, probably Batteries of Detachment Etzel (IVst. / Bavarian R. R. 4) Positioned at Hill northeast of Le Chipal and fired towards west."

Meanwhile came, at his order, Gen. Rasch with his Staff to him. They talked about the Situation and that the Hill 740 northwest of La Behouille had to be defended because the 30st. R. D. would otherwise be threatened in their Flank or Back. Panics, which they had just seen, must not happen again.

Gen. Rasch asked him if he knew from an order of the 7st. Army that he was to take the main Command over the Troops of the left Wing of the Army. An orderly on Horseback was looking for him for some time.

The happiest Moment of his Life was here!

On the day of Sedan, on French Ground, at the Battlefield did he take over Command of a Core with more than 3 Divisions! He rode with his Chief immediately to Coinchimont, from there they tried Telephone connection with Gen. von Schubert, since he was to give him more Directions. His Adjutant and orderly Officer went ahead to get the Car and to make Connection with Strasburg. There were not able to get a Connection with the Gen. Kdo. Of the XIVst. R. K. They rode further to Laigoutte and drove, after the car came, to Provencheres. This was not a good Trip in the Darkness. They were afraid to drive into the Enemy as they were not clear about the Situation at the right Wing of the XIVst. A. K.

Gen.von Schubert received him shortly before Midnight. He reproached him because of his interference on the morning at Coinches, my Grandfather responded:

> "Gen. von Knoerzer reported to me, that his Position at the right Wing was critical, since he had no Connection with the 26st. R. D. So that the pulling out and move away of all parts of the Division Benzino would cause Doubt about the continuation of the victorious Battle. Since hurry was necessary, I took the responsibility as a Prussian General to take over. What would your Exellency have done in my Place?"

Gen. von Schubert said: "We will quit talking about it", from then on they were working good with each other.

There he also learned of the Message, which came on September 2 at 12.40 in the Afternoon from the Government in Strasburg from the A. O. K. 7.

> "Governor of Strasburg, Gen.of the Infantry von Eberhardt, takes over Command of the Troops of the left Wing. Core Eberhardt stays in tactical Relation under the XIVst. R. K."

A little later came to the Government an order:

> "A.O.K.7 September 2. 1914 at 1.45 in the Afternoon to Government Strasburg and to subordinate Gen. Kdo. XIVst. A. K. Freiburg. Upper Commander Orders: Gen. von Schubert stays leader of the Divisions at the left Wing. Gen. von Eberhardt takes over under him on September 2 after orders from Gen. von Schubert the Command over the left Wing. Gen. von Eberhardt becomes independent as soon as the XIVst. R. K. according to they're orders, in the Forest Area of the Line St. Michel St. Die advanced. Gen. von Eberhardt forms his Staff from the in Strasburg available Officers that are necessary to run the Business. The Bavarian Ldw. Br. and the Detachment Neubreisach are not under Gen. von Eberhardt but are under the subordinate Gen. Kdo. Of the XIVst. A. K."

My Grandfather thought that the Bavarian Ldw. Br. was not under him was a Mistake. Because of that was a unity Battle Act at the left Wing of the newly build Core Eberhardt not guaranteed. The Importance of the Col du Bonhomme and Diedolshausen was very important for the Security of the left Flank and the backwards Connections. This Area was not in the Zone that was given him from the A. O. K. 7 that was only for Security of the Leber Valley. Because of that he asked and got on August 28 from the subordinate Gen. Kdo. XIVst. A. K. the Bavarian Ldw. Br. and the Detachment Neubreisach.

According to the order from the A. O. K. 7 had Maj. Mohs in Strasburg begun with the building of the Staff for the new Core.

September 3 was early in the Morning sunny and hot. He went with his Staff to the Road crossing St. Die Markirch and Laigoutte Laveline.

The Situation, when he took Command of the left Wing, was not clear to oversee. Later he found out from the Records of the Troops about the mix-up of Troops and various Detachments. The Gen. Kdo. Of the XIVst. A. K. did not notify the Government; from witch a clear Picture was visible about the Battle. On the other Hand he was himself to blame for the building of the Detachments witch often came from Battls. From various Regiments. This could not be avoided because of the Troops that were used wherever they were.

Tactically he seen the Situation of his Troops good and he hoped soon to straighten out the mix-ups. The Division Knoerzer stood still west of the Hill 740 northwest of La Behouille in their Position that they conquered . Only a big part of the subdivision of Detachment Rasch had cleared the Forest and was moved back to the Hills west of Laveline and La Croix aux Mines also in the Mountains east of the Morte. Parts were marched to Markirch. During the Day of September 3 became it known that the Detachment Wist and Etzel had not found the Grand Rein but in the Evening took Quarter in Laveline and Raumont. One Fortress MG. Company was marched back to Markirch under Leadership of an active Captain because on the march forward they came under Artillery Fire. So my Grandfather had to take strong Measures.

The Division Knoerzer had partly rested. She was also with Detachment Rekowski and Ferling ready for insertion. Gen.von Schubert ordered the Core Eberhardt on September 3:

"30st. R. D. keeps Position. Division Benzino moves over ordered Line Hill 740 northwest of La Behouille La Croix au's Mines at Le Chipal. Detachment Rekowski moves forward to Laveline. Detachment Ferling attacks at Rossberg."

During the Day came from Strasburg the ordered Officers and Officials to the Gen. Kdo. And reported to him.

Before Noon came in the Position of his KHQu. The Staff of the Division Benzino. This was a big advantage because he became the Respect of the Bavarian Officers under him. Since the Gen. Kdo. Of the Core Eberhardt did not have Telephone Lines, they used the Lines of the Div. Benzino. His Chief worked hard and they soon had they're own.

At 3 in the Afternoon came an Airplane Report, the Enemy were in assembly at Geradmer and north of the Street only small Detachments.

The difficulty Area and the steep Hills gave many Ldw. and Res. Regiments that came from flat Areas, heavy exertions and breathing Difficulties. Whole Troops marched back from the Front to look for Hospitals who were hard to find because they were located out of the Vogesen. The mix-up of the Troops brought many Difficulties for the Battle Leadership. The Morte Vally was hard to overlook and swampy. In the Morning did my Grandfather send his orderly Officer, Oblt. Ihssen, over Algoutte for to get connection with the Ldw. I. R. 81, who fought in the Forest of the Tete de Behouille, and also with Division Knoerzer. He was to report about the Position of Troops and the Situation. Since he did not come back it was thought he stayed with the 30st. R. D.

Composition of the Staff of the Core Eberhardt September 1914

Service Position	Service Rank	Name	Previous Milit. Unit	To the Staff on
Comd.Gen.	Gen.of the Inf.	von Eberhardt	Gov. Strasburg	Sept. 2. 1914
Chief Gen.Staff	Colonel	von Boeckmann	""	"2. 1914
1. Genst.Offc.	Maj.	Mohs	""	"2. 1914
2. ""	Captain	Kuehn	Fortr.Teleph.Comp.4	"2. 1914
3. ""	sec. Lt.	Winter	Foot A. R. 14	"3. 1914
4. ""	sec. Lt.	Berlin	"" ""	"3. 1914
1. Adjut.	Captain	von Glasenapp	Gov. Strasburg	"2. 1914
2."	Lt.of Res.	Koch	Jaeger Batt. 8	"4. 1914
Orderly Offc.	Sec. Lt. ret.	von Mossner	Gov. Strasburg	"2. 1914
Kdr. of KHQu.	Capt. of Cav.	von Borsig	R. Hus. R. 9	"6. 1914
Kdr. Mun. Col.	Oberstlt.	Fehr	Gen. of Foot Art.	"2. 1914
Adjutant	sec. Lt.	Juelicher	Foot A. R. 14	"2. 1914
Kdr. of Pi.	Captain	Toepfer	Gen. of Ing. +Pi	"6. 1914
Adjutant	Lt.	Simon	Pi. Battl. 19	"6. 1914
Kdr. Staffguard	Lt. of Res.	von Sydow	R. Hus. R. 9	"3. 1914
Field Commiss.	Commiss Secr.	Guenther	Gov. Strasburg	"4. 1914
Core Phys.	Ass. Phys.	Hagenau	I. R. 132	"4. 1914
Field Police	sec. Sergeant	Karcher	Police Br. Elsass	"11. 1914

At 6.45 in the Afternoon came a report from Oberstlt. Vogel, who was substitute for Gen. Rasch, who was sick, in the Forest of the Tete de Behouille, that the Ldw. Br. was deeply shocked and could not hold they're Position. He became the order to dig Trenches and to defend. The Battle was favorable since the French right Wing was threatened. The French would not attack in this Place. The Detachment Rekowski had reached the Area 2km. southeast of Laveline but the Department Ferling had not moved forward.

To send orders was very hard to do. The reports about the strength of the French at Rossberg and Col du Bonhomme were exaggerated. The Enemy had built skilled Trenches like Steps and could oversee the whole

Area. The German Artillery was at this time not experienced with Battle in the Mountains.

Gen. von Schubert gave in the Evening an order. Because of that gave on September 4 at 1.30 in the Afternoon the Core Eberhardt an order:

> "In Front of the 30ˢᵗ. R. D. stays the Enemy at Benifosse, Basse, Haute Mandray, and Hill 697 northwest of Le Chipal. At the Cote de St. Marie Enemy Jaeger with Artillery and MGs. Airplane reports an Enemy Column from Geradmer to Gerbepal and one from Geradmer to Le Valtin moving forward. From the German Troops has the 26ˢᵗ. R. D. reached the Area at Anozel. The from Colmar moving forward Detachments did reach the Line Schnierlach Urbeis Sulzbach and will try to push the Enemy back over Col du Bonhomme and Gorge. The Task for the Core is the reached Line to build up for stubborn Defense and to hold. The Troops west of the Morte are under Gen. von Knoerzer, the Troops east of the Morte are under Gen.von Benzino. His Troops hold, with weaker Detachments, Les Grandes towards southeast of the Mountain Ridges. The Brigade Rekowski stays under Gen. von Benzino, who has to set up heavy Forces behind his left Wing. Reconnaissance of the Streets from Cote de St. Marie Diedolshausen. The Companies in Wiesembach and Germaingoutte of the Ldw. I. R. 81 and 71, the Staff and IInd. / Ldw. I. R. 120 (Detachment Breyer, Kdr. Ldw. I. R. 120) are from 6 in the Morning under The Gen. Kdo. At Germaingoutte. They secure the 15cm. Howitzer Battery at Germaingoutte. The Col de St. Marie stays occupied from the Ist. / Ldw. I. R. 120 and has to secure towards Diedolshausen."

The Night from September 3 to 4 was quiet, the Troops worked on the Reinforcement of the Area.

The Division prepared, with heavy Artillery Fire, the attack against the Bois de Mandray. The heavy Exertions of the last Days in the big Heat caused bloody losses and shortage of Men, because of Exhaustion so the Battl. Of the 30ˢᵗ. R. D. where only 300 to 400 Man strong. Since the Divisions of the XIVst. R. K. because of the difficult Mountain Area could not move forward, had Gen. von Schubert succeeded a Reinforcement for the Troops under him from the A. O. K. 7. He became from the XVst. A. K. the 61st.Infantrie Br. under Oberst von Suter with 3 Battl. Of the I. R. 132, 1 Battl. Of the I. R. 126 and the Field A. K. 80. The Br. arrived during the day at Bertrimoutiers and came under my Grandfathers order. Gen. von Schubert planned to relief the XIVst. R. K. at the west Meurthe Shore with a squeeze from the left Wing. My Grandfather thought that the Division Benzino, reinforced with Br. Rekowski at they're left Wing, would be strong enough to move along the east Slopes of the Mountain and take the Bois de Mandray who like a Wall the Area towards south closed. Because of that he wanted to put the 61st. Br. under the Division Knoerzer and from there to attack the west part of the Forest. Gen. von Schubert arrived on this Day at his Combat Position and agreed with him.

It became apparent during the Day that the scarcity of the Equipment for the Troops Food and Ambulance Core became evident.

Out of the Elsa's came a few voluntary Columns with a Red Cross Flag to the Battle Field. First they were welcomed and did wonderful Work. Like a Professor Roemer from Strasburg with his Family. Later disturbing, because some were Battle Bums. Under the Flag of Samaritan came People with knowledge of the German Positions and Troop Detachments and either careless or willing committed Treason.

His Gen. Staff Officers worked hard to help the Deficiency of those Columns but it took time before these Columns could be put together. Later helped the Bavarian War Ministries for the Bavarian Troops in the Core Eberhardt.

At 10 in the Evening came the Core Command that on September 5 to attack with embrace of the Enemy's right Wing. The 30st. R. D. had to move forward to the Line Benifosse Hill 697 north of Le Chipal, the Bavarian Ers. D. had to attack with the right Wing over the Road crossing at Le Chipal. The order to Fire of the heavy Field Howitzers wanted to give my Grandfather himself and then the other Battery's had to Fire. After 30 Minutes had the Infantry to cross over the Line Entre deux Eaux south Edge of the Forest La Behouille Hill 697 and north of Le Chipal. The Meurthe Valley Bottom was not to be crossed. The Detachment Breyer stayed in Verpelliere under the Core. The Ist. / Ldw. I. R. 120 had to demonstrate against the Cote de St. Marie, the Detachment Ferling had to move forward against the Border Ridge.

On the Morning of September 5 came heavy Enemy Artillery Fire. After the order was given to open Fire for the German Artillery did the Enemy Fire eased off. The Command Position of the Gen. Kdo. Was moved to Laveline, were a Lookout Tower good Observation aloud, to see the Bois de Mandray with his Characteristic Forest Window and to the Hill 740 northwest of La Behouille. The Battle became lively. At 12 Noon came an Airplane report:

"Enemy Columns move back on Street to Gerbepal."

Immediately an order was given to the 2 Divisions:

"Pursuit of the back moving Enemy to the Meurthe Valley. Separation Line between the Divisions La Croix Fraize."

This Report was not for my Grandfathers Side because there the French defended tenaciously.

At 12.20 in the Afternoon they rode to La Croix where Gen. von Benzino was and his Troops were still in heavy Battle at Le Chipal and east of there.

The Battle in the Line Mandray Le Chipal and the Farms east of Les Chaumettes in the Forest further east, Hill 897, at the south Slope of the Grand Rein, continued violently. Futile waited Gen. von Benzino the arrival of the Detachment Rekowski, who came slowly forward in this Heat and bad Mountain Roads.

At 7 in the Evening they came east of Le Chipal to Gen. Krieger who told them of the Situation. Also his 9st. Bavarian Ers. Br. came only slowly forward in the Forest. The French had put clever Obstacles and Trenches. Very bad for the Moral of the Troops were the French Tree Snipers who killed from behind. There came the Adjutant of Gen. von Rekowski, Captain von Oertzen and reported that the Troops were coming and the first detachment had touch with the Enemy.

The more the Sun sank in the west became the French better light for Observation and the French Artillery became more violent, The German Artillery had the Sun in their Face and they could not see the French Battery's towards Fraize, St. Leonhard to attack them. Even so French Infantry did not attack so that the Gun Fire was as result that many Troops moved back to find Security and quiet. In the Front Line were only week security's left.

At the right Wing of the Core was the 30st. R. D. victorious. There did the 61st. I. Br. succeed with advanced left Flank west of Le Chipal over Hill 643 in the Bois de Mandray to penetrate, behind stood at the Hill 740 northwest of La Behouille the Battl. Of the Br. Grueber who was under the 30st. R. D. Further west were the Br. Zech, Rasch and Mueller until the Line Basse Mandray Les Planches and Sauley Entre deux Eaux also at the Hills east of Le Paire, Rememont in Position.

Several French attacks where repelled.

The east of the Morte battling Troops under Gen. von Benzino came with they're right Wing, Br. Krieger, only to north of le Chipal. Br. Rekowski stood still at Grand Rein and in the Forest at Les Chaumettes. Both Divisions had in the Battle Line no direct connection. After the Reports of the Divisions and my Grandfathers understanding of the Situation at this Day, it became necessary to put order in the Detachments and to place them that a centralized acting of the Divisions could be obtained. He thought that the ordered Departure of the 61st. I. Br. from the first Line would create an unfavorable Impression on the troops, since losses at both Divisions where quite high. He asked Gen. von Schubert to see to it that they could stay. So the A. O. K. 7 approved it until September 9.

He ordered the Divisions at 10 in the Evening to hold and to strengthen the Positions that were obtained this Day.

The Night from September 5 to 6 was quiet. Also the French Troops had exerted themselves, according to Prisoners. To bring order in the Detachments, the obtaining of Food and Ammunition gave the Troops little Rest. From the left Wing came the Report that the French had left the Cote de St. Marie and now had a better connection been established between the Division Benzino and the Detachment Ferling. The Ist. / Ldw. I. R. 120 had moving forward from the Col de St. Marie occupied the Cote de St. Marie. The Detachment Ferling did have on the left connection to the Ldw. Br. Lachemair southwest of Altweier from whom they still had 2 Battl. Of the Bavarian Ldw. I. R. 12.

The Division Knoerzer had sent a Patrol in the Bois de Mandray, who found the Forest in the Morning free of the Enemy. Airplane reports said that there were no Enemy Columns in the Meurthe Valley. The heavy

Enemy Artillery Fire continued and became stronger in the Afternoon. The French attacked on the whole Line. They had brought Reinforcements from the Area of Belford and had found out that it was important to not allow Rapture in the German Forces towards Plainfaing Fraize so that they're Troops at the Vogesen Ridge could not be secluded. They succeeded to expel the German Troops who had moved in the Bois de Mandray and easterly parts of the Forest. The Line Village Mandray Hill 643 Le Chipal stayed in German Hand. My Grandfather hoped that the pressure of the Detachment Ferling and the Bavarian Ldw. Br. towards the Rossberg, would bring Victory.

Repeatedly came orders to send Artillery Observers to the Infantry to hinder the Firing into the own Lines. The good Observation that the French Artillery had, from the Bois de Mandray and from other Hills, made it possible to guide the Fire of their Guns from flanked Positions. That was bad for the Moral of the Troops, that where mixed up in the Forest Battle and thought that the incoming Fire came from their own.

In the Evening it was apparent from the Battle Reports a big mix-up. The lower Leaders tried hard to get order, but the older Officers that came from Retirement had a hard time to overcome the Strain of the Battles. They were not fit to climb the steep Hills and encourage the Troops. Because of that they had to give up the victorious won Line and moved back. Only in the backwards Villages could they be brought together.

My Grandfather ordered Lt. von Sydow (Hus. R. 3.) Since Lt.Ihssen had not come back, orderly Officer in his Staff, to look after him. Lt. von Sydow came back after several hours and reported that he had found the Grave of Lt. Ihssen and his Companion. On a Wood Cross near Algoutte hang the Fur Cap of the Officer. The Death of this heroic Man hit all very hard. It came as a big Surprise when the thought of dead Ihssen on September 7 reported from a Hospital at Tannenberg near Saales that on September 3 he was wounded in the Lung. His Companion was deadly hit. He lay many hours in Gunfire from both Sides. His pretty Horse with the Map Container in which the Core orders were was caught by the French.

The Command for September 7 ordered that the Division Benzino again moved forward at the Bois de Mandray, who's south Edge then to be held by both Divisions. The Detachment Ferling had to move forward at the Rossberg (1128m.)And Col du Bonhomme. The 61st. Br. would on September 7 be removed.

A unity attack did not come on September 7. Gen. von Knoerzer reported that he ordered his Troops to dig Trenches and to hold the Position. In the Afternoon it started to rain. The wet Weather lasted several Days. Gen. von Schubert came to my Grandfather and told him that the Divisions of his Core could not come forward in the Mountain Area west of St. Die. The losses where heavy and the Battle Will of the tired Troops became a Problem. It was to expect that the further pressure of his Core, after overcoming the Bois de Mandray in the Meurthe Valley, would bring a Decision in our Advantage. Because of that had Gen. von Schubert succeeded that the 61st. I. Br. stayed under the Core. The French attacked violently from Benifosse against the 30st. R. D. They also attacked more east, after heavy Artillery Fire, the Positions south of Hill 740 northwest of La Behouille.There did Gen. Grueber, Kdr. of the 1st. Bavarian Ers. Br. became a heavy Wound on his Head from a Grenade. This heroic, prudent Gen. gave the Command of the Br. first to Maj. Baron von Ostini, Kdr. Ist. / Bavarian R. I. R. 4. On September 22 took Gen.Michahelles the Command of the Br. until Gen. Grueber came back cured.

In the Evening they considered the French attacks as failed. The Troops of the Core penetrated the Forest in several Places. During the Night the Battle kept on but they could not stay in parts of the south.

After several Reports was the Rossberg on September 7 supposed to be in the Hand of the Ist. / Ldw. I. R. 120 and the IInd. / R. I. R. 60 also the IIIrd. / Bavarian Ldw. I. R. 12 but could not be held because of heavy Enemy Artillery Fire.

The KHQu. Moved on September 8 to Laveline where the Quarters of the Staff were good. The Chief and the Gen.Staff Officers became good work Rooms.

In the Afternoon came an order that the Core Eberhardt was under the AOK. 6.

Crown prince Rupprecht von Bavaria had his AHQu. In Dieuze. The AOK. 7 were to the right Wing of the Army advanced.

The Ldst. Battl. Friedberg moved into Markirch. That fried the 2 Companies of the Ldw. I. R. 80, they had the Train Security in the Leber

Valley and had the Col de St. Marie occupied and could come now to the Detachment Rekowski.

On September 8 continued the Battle on the whole Line. The French had because of the German attacks at the Bois de Mandray heavy losses and Prisoners. The Germans advanced at they're attacks. Enemy attacks failed in German Fire. When in the Afternoon the French Artillery Fire from the heavy Battery's from the Area Anould and west of the Meurthe Valley started, moved the German Troops from the Forest and looked for Security in the Ravines, were they found Cover. This evade without Enemy Infantry was bad since the high Leaders learned from that too late. It was hard to become oversight in this difficult Terrain and hard to intervene in dangerous Positions. Because of that it was ordered that the Division Benzino moved out of the Forest at begin of Darkness and occupies the Hills north and east of Le Chipal. The reports from the Division Knoerzer at the right Wing where better. This and the Conviction that the 4 active Battl. Of the XVst. A. K. would do they're Task and the Detachment Ferling and Lachemair at the Col du Bonhomme and at the Rossberg, let my Grandfather hope, that the Pressure at the Col du Bonhomme would break the Resistance of the French. Gen. von Schubert had at this Position the first parts of the Troops that came by Train to Markirch, 55th. Ers. Br. Kdr. Genlt. Dame, on September 9 inserted.

On September 9 began at 6.30 in the Morning the German Artillery they're Fire. The Bois de Mandray was for 2 hours bombarded with Guns of all Calibers. The French Artillery answered week. When the German Infantry moved in the Forest they found the Enemy Positions empty, the south Edge of the Bois de Mandray became occupied. The Ers. Battl. / Field A. R. 13 drove south of Halle des Iourmaux, 1km. west of Le Chipal, in Position. The 5th. / R. Foot A. R. 10 took Position with they're heavy Howitzers at the Forest Edge west of Hill 643, northwest of Le Chipal. Gen. von Benzino had occupied Le Chipal and moved with the Br. Krieger and Rekowski in the southern Forest Parcels fore. Gen. von Knoerzer was Shure that he could with his Division on this Day move down into the Valley of the Meurthe. Only from the left Wing from the Vogesen came bad Reports. The German attacks came in spite of heavy Artillery against the Fortress like Area defenses of the French not forward.

At 2 in the Afternoon came Gen. von Schubert to my Grandfather in Laveline and my Grandfather informed him of the Situation. Gen. von Schubert told him that from September 10 on my Grandfather would no longer be under him. After detailed Talks he left.

My Grandfather and his Staff proceeded at 4 in the Afternoon on Horseback over Le Chipal to Hill 643. As they came to the heavy Howitzer Battery they were approached by the Battery Leader and a Bavarian Regiments Kdr. and they reported that from Statements of Prisoners an Enemy attack was imminent. The German Infantry where so mixed up in the Forest Battle, that they were afraid that they could not withstand, without fresh Troops. The heavy Battery would be in Danger. In this Moment broke the Sun, which stood low in the west, and illuminated a beautiful View of the Area between the Bois de Mandray and St. Die, bound from the steep dark Forest of the Vogesen. At the same time did the French Artillery open heavy Fire at the Division Knoerzer. The heavy Romello Battery at Anould took at first Target his Staff and the Street Le Chipal Fraize. He ordered the Bavarian Regiments Kdr. to make sure that no Howitzer would get lost, in case of retried. My Grandfather wanted to start a return attack with the Division Knoerzer and the 61st.I. Br. The Regiments Kdr. gave immediately his orders, arranged his in the Forest positioned Battl., and positioned them at the south Edge. To give further orders to Gen. von Knoerzer did he send his Chief to Le Chipal from there by Car to Laveline. He went with Maj. Mohs over the Hill 697 to the 61st. I. Br. to give the attack order.

All Troop parts, so heavy mixed up, where still in the Hands of the Officers. They all believed that they were fired on by their own Artillery. It was hard to explain to them that it was French Artillery Fire from the west Flank. They had to move under the Fire to get to the Bois de Mandray and there to defeat the French. And so it was possible to get several Detachments to the Position west of Le Chipal in the Forest, which was in Danger.

My Grandfather had sent several orderly Officers to find the Leader of the 61st. I. Br. He came from the Direction of Breheville at the North Slope of the Bois de Mandray but not alone. The 4 Battl. Under him followed him in Formation according to the Area. What had happened?

Maj. Wasserfall, Adjutant of the Gen. Kdo. Of the XVst. A.K. who was send from Gen. von Deimling, had asked my Grandfather that the Brigade according to the Wish if his Commanding Gen. would be send back on September 9. He declined because of the Battle Situation and the order from the AOK.6. Which said the Brigade is under the Core Eberhardt until September 9. Without his knowledge did Maj. Wasserfall rode to the Brigade Leader, Oberst von Suter and said the Brigade had to be pulled out and moved back. So the Brigade turned back and left they're Positions. The right moment for a counter attack was missed. The Troops had the steep Slopes and Gorges at the North Slope of the Bois de Mandray in their march back overcome. The Sun was about to go down. He could only order that the Battl. Stopped were they were and make a Front to be as Reserve at a French attack. The Commander of the Battl. Of the Wuertemberg I. R. 126 did follow the order the Forest Parcel at Hill 697 to occupy. My Grandfather had the Reassurance that the valiant Schwaben would be a good Security if there was Danger at the Howitzer Battery. With Maj. Mohs he went to the Wuertemberg Batt. And found everything in order. After dark he rode with his Staff down the steep Slope witch ended at the Street near Le Chipal.

Since the attack of the French only went into the Bois de Mandray and there was brought to stop, could the 61st. I. Br. at 8.30 in the Evening be put to march to Saales. From there they were transported by Train to the XVst. AK. Witch was pulled out of the Front and transported to the right Army Wing. Sadly did lose the Ers. Battr. / Field AR. 13 3 Guns, witch were shot to pieces at the south Edge of the Forest.

The weakening of the Front by 4 active Battl. Made a change in the Division Benzino necessary. The Div. Kdr. took the Brigade Krieger to the south Slope of the Hill 740 northwest of La Behouille back and the Brigade Rekowski to Le Chipal.

It was very important to occupy the Rossberg. Orders to that were given again to Gen. von Ferling. To his Support had one Detachment (1—0—1 MG. Comp.) from the Division Benzino from the north Edge of the Grand Rein, to move forward at the Rossberg. The Core order for September 10 commanded that both Divisions keep their Positions and Patrols should go forward through the Bois de Mandray.

In the Evening came the Iron Crosses 2nd. Class from the AOK. 7 for the Government Strasburg. He could put these on his Chief, Oberstlt. von Boeckmann and a few Officers of his Staff.

The Instruction of the OHL. Because of the unlucky retreat of the German Army at the Marne made it necessary that the 6st. Army pulls the left Wing back. The XIVst. RK. Gave on Sept. 10 at 9 in the Morning in Provencheres orders.

The Command came at 10 in the Morning to the Core Eberhardt:

> "Total change of the Situation—Several Army Cores will be pulled from the Army for other Duty's. Rest of the Army keeps Border occupied. XIVst. RK. With 19th. Ers. D. has to get to Line Bacqueville – Celles by Sept. 11. Then go back further. Core Eberhardt secured left Flank of the XIVst. RK. And blocks the Border Passes in the Area Saales Lubine Col de St. Marie. Most have to get to this Line by 5.30 in the Morning. Rear Guard to the Line Le Paire Coinche south of Germaingoutte. Gen.von Ferling act on his own in connection with Gen. von Lachemair of the 2nd. Bavarian Ldw. Br. from the AA. Gaede."

My Grandfather and his Chief had the Opinion that the withdrawal of the Core would be no good. They could take care of the first Problem, Security of the left Flank of the XIVst. RK. And the 19th. Ers. D. by move back a little at the right Wing. They advised the 19th. Ers. D. only to move back to Badonviller, since they could occupy Celles with a Detachment from the Donon and so they could secure the Plaine Valley. This proposal by Telephone was denied.

The Saxonians of the 19th. Ers. D. had later much Blood to give to gain Area towards Badonviller. They never reached the Village nor could they win back the Street Badonviller Celles witch was important for the Core Eberhardt.

This broad move back and give back occupied French Area was a Mistake in the Mind of my Grandfather. In the following 2 Years that he was Commander in this Area he found out that he was right.

The new Position was not favorable for the Defense and did not shorten the Front Line. In the Sector of the Meurhte was given up Area that had been occupied with German Blood that would have been a good Defense Line and in the Celles, Movenmoutier, Hurbache, St. Die, Entre Deux, 3km. southwest of Coinches, Bois de Mandray south of Le Chipal, Grand Rein, Cote de St. Marie, Haicot, Bressoir would have been a shorter Section to be occupied than the one that he had to choose and that stayed in German Hands until Wars End.

The News of the Result of the Marne Battle came to them much later. Also confidentially did he as Commanding Gen. not become insight in the OHL. Which changed Position lead to a sudden transition to Trench War. Because of that they could not know that according to the order from the AOK.6. By choosing Positions it should be a coherent Frontline. Because of that came Mistakes they could have been avoidable. He thought it would have been better to order him:

"Core Eberhardt secured the left Flank of the XIVst. RK. And prepared the Area at the right Meurthe Shore to the Position between Moyenmoutier, St. Die, Hill 740 northwest of La Behouille, Cote de St. Marie for Defense. The Plaine Valley at Celles is with a Detachment to secure."

He had to take an Inquiry Tour, with a heavy Heart, to look at the Terrain in the Area near Saales, like the order said. Since the Chief and the first Gen. Staff Officer were busy with the orders of the detaching from the Enemy and the move backward. He took Oberstlt. Fehr and for the selection of the Position 2 Soldiers from R. Hus. R. 9 Hussar Wember and Lang von Langen. Oberstlt. Fehr agreed with him that the Hill from Ban de Sapt should be the Key point of the Position. The importance of the high, heavy Forested, Majestic Ormont, was clear to them, should stay in German Hand. Since only a few bad Mountain Paths from the Meurthe and Fave Valley went up he thought that a defense would be easy.

The Donon was occupied with a Detachment from Strasburg. He thought that an immediate Danger in the Rabodeau Valley from an Enemy who did pursue toward Celles was not possible because of the impassable Mountains between Plaine and Rabodeau Valley.

Always thinking that the voluntary move back to the Passes on the Border would be a temporary move that soon would be followed with a new Attack. The Thought that looking for a Position for a 50km. Front and there maybe for Years to be, could not come.

The time was short and he had to order fast that on Sept. 11 the Main Body had to be under concealing move back:

1. The from XIVst. RK. To the Core Eberhardt delivered 55th. Ers. Br. (from the Area of St. Die) Chatas were they was under the Division Knoerzer.
2. The Division Knoerzer the Area south of Saales.
3. The Division Benzino the Area Colroy, Lubine.
4. The Detachment Rekowski the Col de St. Marie.
5. The Detachment Ferling Markirch.
6. Rear Guard, Bavarian R. I. R. 11, Fest. MG. Comp. 3, 2 Squadron R. Hus. R. 9, Radf. Comp. of the 30st. R. D. had still south of the Bois d'Ormont and with few parts south of the Street St. Die, Wiesembach to stay.

The Gen.Command moved in the Afternoon to Bourg Bruche.

The performance of the Troops and Columns at that Day and in the Night to get all Provisions, Ammunitions, Booty of Arms and Equipment to move back, earned the highest Praise. The main Task was to get the wounded from all the Villages in the Battle Area. With that earned Assistant Physician Hagenau and the Pharmacist Braun from the Gen. Kdo. High Praise.

The let go from the Enemy succeeded according to order and without Battle. On Sept. 11 at 5.30 in the Morning separated the Core Eberhardt from the tactical Subordination under Gen. von Schubert and came under the direct Command of the 6th. Army.

The Command of the AOK. 6 (Dieuze Sept.10. 1914 at 12 Noon) was:

> "The Core Eberhardt takes independently over the Defense of the Entrants in the Breusch Valley and west of the Breusch Position and get out from under the XIVst. AK. The Defense of the upper Elsa's and the upper Rheine remains with the substitute Gen. Kdo. Of the XIVst. AK. In cooperation with Core Eberhardt."

With his Chief he drove to Saales were they found a total mix-up of Columns. It was necessary to dedicate time to the Troops. The Mood was down because of the inexplicable move backwards. Repeatedly was he told from the Columns:"But here is not the Way to Paris! "Whenever possible he spoke to Officers and Man.

Remarkable was the total inactivity of the French, who had probably not noticed the moves backward and had not followed. From the rear Guards came Reports that the French Positions had not changed.

At 9 in the Morning was the following Sector occupation commanded:

"1. The Division Knoerzer with the 55th. Ers. Br. becomes Section Chatas, Nayemont near at Ban de Sapt (exclusive).
2. The Division Benzino becomes Section Nayemont, a Village east of The Ban de Sapt (inclusive) Lubine.
3. Orders for the Detachment Ferling also Detachment Rekowski stay the same."

The Detachment Rekowski had to block the Col du St. Marie and look for connection to the Division Benzino at Lubine, the Detachment Ferling has to march to Markirch.

My Grandfather visited the Gens. von Knoerzer, Dame and several Brigade Kdrs. And rode (Horseback) with the Staff to Lubine. There they talked with Gen. von Benzino about the Situation and the occupation of the Sections and Connections.

After they had left, did the People in the Villages south of the Street St. Die, Col de St. Marie tell the French and that enticed Enemy Patrols to come out of they're Positions. In the Afternoon followed the Enemy with heavy Troops to the forenamed Street and sending Patrols to the Line Ban de Sapt, Lusse.

On Sept. 12 did Patrols find out that French Troops south of the Bois d'Ormont concentrated. At 2 in the Afternoon came the Command from the 6th. Army:

"Donon and Col du Hantz absolute hold and enlarge."

It was also ordered:

> Col du Hantz, Oberstlt. Stadthagen, Regiments Staff and
> 1 Battl. R. I. R. 70 and 1 Ers. / Field A. R. 13 to draw by
> Train from Markirch. Foot March to Col du Hantz, there is a
> Defense Position to be build. (This Detachment was on Sept.
> 13 to La Petite Raon moved fore and on Sept.14 moved to the
> Donon.) Donon Detachment Neuber, Ers. Battl. / Ldw. IR.
> 99, Ist. / R. I. R. 70, IIIrd. / Ldw. I. R. 120, IIIrd. / Bavarian
> R. I. R. 4 with 3 MGs., half R. Hus. R. 9, RMG. Comp. 3,
> Radf. Comp. / 60 and 99, eight 9cm. Cannons of the 5th. 9cm.
> Batt. / Foot AR. 14, Staff and 2nd. / Pi. 15, one and two Wuert.
> Ldw. Pi. Comp. 13, Ers. Comp. of the Pi. Br. 9, 14, and 18, an
> extra big Ldw. Pi. Comp. of the XV., 50st Radf. Detachment
> from Government Strasburg, half 2nd. / Fest. San. Comp., 4st
> Wuert. San. Cars. Col."

My Grandfather thought that the French would try to attack between the moving back 6th. Army and the Core Eberhardt. It was of no use to put the Defense Line in the Border Passes. Better to surprise the Enemy with an attack on his Vanguards when he moves forward over Senones

The Resolution to attack came from the 30st. RD. He came in the first Afternoon hours, with the order of the AOK. 6, to the Divisions Staff to Saales and gave more Instructions for the because of the Army Command in the Line Donon, Hantz to taking Measurements. In this Situation hurled the first Adjutant of the Division, Oblt. Isenburg (IR. 143) in his native Slang: "But do we not better attack?" This mention brought the Stone to roll. He and the Divisions Kdr. caught hold of this thought. He went back to the KHQu. To check if this Plan might work. As Gen. von Knoerzer in the Evening drove to the KHQu. In order to recite the attack Plan again, did he find out that it was already set up. Until Evening came more and more Reports that the Enemy on all Fronts moved forward with week Forces, but many Columns marched off toward west.

In the Afternoon did the French attack at the Line Senones, Ban de Sapt against the Hills at Chatas. At 8 in the Evening became the 30st. RD. an order, on Sept. 13 to attack at the Line Senones, Ban de Sapt. The Bavarian Ers. D. to attack over the Line La Petite Fosse 3km. south of La Grande Fosse, Provencheres, to hinder Enemy Forces from moving back.

In the Morning of Sept. 13 was a heavy Storm. In spite of that begun the Battle. At 5.30 in the Morning he went with his Staff to Saales to the 30st. RD. The German Battery's did well because the French had not brought they're heavy Artillery. Especially results had the German far reaching 10cm. Cannons. Gen. Dame reported already at 10 in the Morning the capture of La Petite Raon and Menil. At 11.15 in the Morning was also Senones in the Hand of the brave 55th. Bad. Ers. Br. Left of that moved the Bavarian 1st. And 10st. R. Br. Fore. The Battle between Ban de Sapt and Provencheres was more difficult. The 30st. RD. came to stop approximately in the Line Launois at the south Slope of the Hill from Ban de Sapt Le Fraiteux. The first Bav. Ers. Br. of the Division Benzino battled near La Petite Fosse, the 9st .Bav. Ers. Br. at Provencheres without to come past those Villages. The Bav. RIR. 15 held the Hills north of Luesse to hinder Enemy Forces to move through the Forest between Fave and Wiesembach Valley.

In the Afternoon he rode first to La Grande Fosse where Genlt. Mueller had his Command Post in the Village School. There sat the Br. Leader with his Telephone. Operators, while French Grenades hit Buildings. After a short stop he rode to Nayemont, where he met 100 French Prisoners. And he galloped with his Staff on the Street fore to the Batteries who stood in the Fire on the Forest Edge northeast of La Sausse. Captain Scherer from Ers. Field AR. 51 reported about the Battle Situation. The Battery's had losses but they're Fire made it possible for the Infantry to go against Ban de Sapt, Le Fraiteux.

At 7.30 in the Morning could he report from Saales to the Army, Enemy Vanguards attacked, defeated and the Line Senones, Provencheres in German Hand. 250 French Prisoners from IR. 99, of the Reserve Regiments 299, 52 and 252, the 55th. Br, the 28st. Division of the XIVst. French Core. Also Mountain Jaeger and Soldiers from the IR. 97 where taken.

Since the Staff of the 30st. RD. had moved to the Castle Belval, south of the Col du Hantz on the Street to Senones, was the Gen.Kdo. Moved forward to Saales. There was also the Staff of the Bav. Ers. D.

On Sept. 14 did the Battle mainly on the left Wing of the 30st. RD. continue. The Brigades Zech and Mueller, without that as Core Reserve at Saales moved out Bav. RIR. 11, succeeded Nayemont, Le Fraiteux and

1km. southwest the Village Gemainfaing to take. The Forest Battles in the Bois d'Ormont did not come to a conclusion.

The strange Formation from the Mountain Ridge of the Vogesen from Col du Hantz and Donon towards southwest between the deep cut in Valleys of the Rabodeau and Plaine River and the continues steep and rocky Mountain Ridges divided the battling Troops who had to fight in these Valleys and made connections hard to do.

Since it was not impossible that the French, with tricky Patrols, could make connections impossible, he ordered that the 30st. RD. stretched they're right Wing to the Mountain Ridge between Rabodeau and the Plaine Valley. In the Plaine Valley had a Detachment to move forward that was taken from the Donon Crew to hinder the Enemy from further marching and to secure the Connection with the 19. Ers. D. as Leader of this Detachment gave the 30st. RD. They're Leader from the Columns and Trains, Oberstlt. Kumme, who fought valiantly in the Border security Battles in the Breusch Valley. My Grandfather accepted the proposal from the Division. The Detachment Kumme consisted of Ist. / RIR. 70, half 1st. / R. Hus. R. 9, RMG. Comp. 3, Radf. Comp and Radf. Detachment. It had to move forward on Sept.15 to Celles.

Towards Evening became the Battle heavier. In regard of the Instructions of the AOK. 6, the attained Line not to pass, came this at 10 in the Evening for both Divisions in the Core Command.

The Army commanded the Street St. Quirin, Albertschweiler to demolishing by the Donon Brigade. They had enough Pioneers.

The AOK. 6 had in all Commands, also in the many Telephone. Conversations between the Chiefs and the first Gen. Staff Officers always said, that it was important to hold the Donon. All the more Reason for my Grandfather to bring the Defense of this Pass and Mountain forward. On the other Hand he had to keep in Mind, the Line that was won on Sept. 13 and 14, not to cross. This was acutely ordered.

The Communication from the 6st. Army was highly significant, that said that the XIVst. AK. And the XIVst. RK. And the Staff of the 6st. Army where pulled out of the Vogesen and a new Army Group had been built under the upper Command of Gen. of the Infantry Baron von Falkenhausen and the Core Eberhardt was part of it. The task of the Core stayed the same.

The AOK. Was at that time in Metz and became the Area between the Army Detachment von Strantz in the Mosel Bend east of Pont a Mousson and the Army Detachment Gaede allotted. Chief of the Army Falkenhausen became Oberst Weidner.

The French really tried to become the Ormont in they're Hand. It was a rainy Day on Sept. 17 and on the whole Line was a few important Vanguard Battles. The French attacked in the Forested Area of the Ormont with new and heavy Forces. The 1st. Bav. Ers. Br. that tenaciously resisted, but finally had to abandon the Hill and pull back to the north Edge.

The advance of Oberstlt Kumme in the Plaine Valley, that started from the Molted Lime Tree at the south Slope of the Donon, at the Street over Raon sur Plaine, appeared to have success. Maj. Hoelderlein with 3 Comp. of the IIIrd. / Bav. RIR. 4 cleaned Vexaincourt from French Patrols. Oberstlt. Kumme did put advance Guards there.

The Connection with the, at Cirey, Petitemont positioned 19st. Ers. D. was not established.

Behind of the Detachment Kumme in the Plaine Valley, staggered as Wing of my Grandfathers Core, was Gen. Neuber with a few Battl. At the Donon. Then came:

> Br. Rasch at Moussey, Br. Dame at La Petite Raon, Senones, Chatas, Br. Zech in the Area Laitre, Chatas, Br. Mueller in the Area Le Fraiteux, La Grande Fosse.

From the Bav. Ers. D. became the Br. Michahelles connection to the Br. Mueller at the Ormont and had La Petite Fosse occupied. The Br. Krieger defended southeast from there the Area Provencheres and Frapelle, Lusse and 2km. south Marlusse.

Opposite of the Core Eberhardt stood the French everywhere in touch, only in the wild fissured Forest Mountain between Plaine and Rabodeau Vally was a Gab. In the Bois de la Garde (Forest between Fave and Wiesembach Valley) and in the Forests north of the Col de St. Marie were things not clear about the Line. This was in part of the French Mountain Jaegers Tactic, to be everywhere and quickly disappear.

The Artillery Battles on the Ormont continued on Sept. 18. The 1st. Bav. Ers. Br. moved out of Germainfaing. The superior French Artillery Fire kept the German Battery's down and cost the Infantry heavy losses.

Of Interest was an order from the 1st.French Army, who came in German Hands and who was told to the Troops:

> "1st. AHQu. Sept. 11. 1914.
> Command of Gen. Dubai, Kdr. of the first Army, about the Battle mode witch is to be used against the Germans. The Experience that we learned from the so far fought Battles, show, that we have to change our Tactic and so we give the following Directions:
>
> 1. Our Infantry is to be spared.
> 2. It has to be accomplished with use of our Artillery at less than 5000m.
> 3. It has to be tried to use our Infantry in close Fight, especially with a Blanc Weapon to which she is superior to our Enemy.
> 4. Tiredness of our Troops, which so far was profound. To lessen you can reach an result by following these means, witch several Army Cores already using:

1. When the Battle Situation it allows, start with the Artillery Fire in the afternoon to start the German Howitzers and find out they're Positions. Since we cannot reach a decided Result with our Material, is the Battle at big distance to conduct with little Artillery and few Infantry.
2. In this case is the biggest part of the Infantry all Morning to stay at Rest. During this time are the Troops to feed so that they are ready to march.
3. At beginning of twilight is our Infantry to move forward, since at that time they are safe from Enemy Artillery. They have to win forward Terrain and our Batteries have to follow them, so that in the Evening they are in the right distance from they're Target at Enemy Infantry and Artillery. Then we have to utilize our exceeding Superiority in Material when it can have an effect at less than 4000 to 5000m. If it can have a result with both Weapons. The move forward of the Infantry can happen at Daylight when they use covered Area and large Forests. The Infantry marches in the Forest in small Columns side by side with a Leader at the

Head and a tuff Sergeant at the End, establish the direction and cautious exit.

4. You must not be shy during these Operations to send small Infantry Forces fore to look for Night Battles so the Enemy gets demoralized and disorganized who so far could never withstand a Bayonet Battle. Also the Forest Battle is not to be feared. If a clash in the Forest is to be imminent leave space between the Columns and plant the Bayonet. Battl. Kdrs. Leave in the high Forest in 2nd. Line behind a Wing 1 to 2 Comp.to follow whose attack they order when the first Line starts the Battle.

5. If a Position is taken, entrench, provide for spreading of opposite Trenches, dig deep trenches where you cannot see into, organize to Fire and arrange all Measures for Quarter.

6. All movements, assembly of Troops and Columns to hide from Airplanes for that use Street Trees, Slopes and Forest Edges.

Dubai
General AOK. 1st. Army."

From this and other found French Commands became the Task clear that was given to the battling Troops in the Vogesen."The Reason for the occupation of the Mountain is to keep as many of the Enemy Troops to take part in the decisive Battle, "This was a sentence in an order from a Kdr. from the Mountain Jaeger Br."de la Schlucht", Gen. Gratier. This was lucky for the French; A few more Divisions at the Marne and the Battle would have led to a German Victory and the outcome of the War changed. The Tips in those orders to use this Tactic in the Mountains were excellent. We had felt this on our self!

In the Bois d'Ormont did on Sept. 19 violently fighting going on where the French had established themselves. The Reports from the Plaine Valley were different. Witch he expected after the orders and Reports from the Detachment Kumme. The achieved successes where given up and the Detachment evaded as soon as the Enemy attacked. Because of that were the Moment past, Celles and the Hills at this Place, mainly the Street to Badonviller to occupy. The French occupied now these important Points. An energetic Hand had to intervene there immediately, since the Army

Leader reported that he wanted to move forward to Badonviller with the 19ˢᵗ. Ers. D.

Because of orders of the AOK. Commanded my Grandfather on Sept. 20 Gen. Neuber with his Donon Detachment inclusive the Detachment Kumme, to move forward to Celles, to take up the Connection to the Saxonians. The Donon had to stay occupied. The 30ˢᵗ. RD. was ordered to demonstrate towards Celles. In the Afternoon reported the 19ˢᵗ. Ers. D. that they had, with the left Wing, occupied Petitemont, DStQu. And Blamont.

In the Night from Sept. 20 to 21. Was heavy Train Traffic reported in the Meurthe Valley. From early Morning on raged the Battle at the whole Line. The Enemy attacks failed in the German Artillery Fire. In the Plaine Valley succeeded Gen. Neuber to move forward over Allarmont to Celles and at Night to occupy it. The French stayed in the southwest Farms and at the Hills north and south of the Plaine. It looked like they brought Reserves.

The Battl. from the 30ˢᵗ. RD. that was send to demonstrate, thought it had done its charge, when it seen the Occupation of Celles and went back to they're Position. Gen. Neuber could have really used this Battl. On his left Wing. The Br. Dame did send a Battl. From Senones to the Hill 717, halfway between Senones and Celles, expels the French and created a Connection with the Detachment Neuber. At the left Wing did Gen. von Rekowski took a big move forward from Col de St. Marie, expels an Enemy Comp. from Gemaingoutte and occupied Wiesembach. Never did my Grandfather think it was possible, that with all the German Military Education and the German Correctness that so many Reports could be wrong. The official Reports about the attained Destinations in the Battle, the assertion of occupied Positions and why they were left having to be correct. In this respect did my Grandfather in this War have quite a few Disappointments.

With the big Expansion of the Positions in the Mountain, which had no connections at first and had many spaces, it was impossible for the higher Leaders to be in Person in the first Line and control the Reports of the Positions. But this was what they wanted to attain with the training of Officers, Sergeants and Men: Forgone conclusion and self Confidence for making Decisions. After serious Discussion and without Danger he found himself in French Positions and could so come to the first Line where he could oversee the Positions of the Enemy. It took a lot of time before he seen every Trench and Corner of his 52km. long Front witch led through deep Ravines and high Mountains.

Before Noon came Reports that the 19st. Ers. D. was in Badonviller, but Gen. Neuber left Celles because the French had the Hills occupied and put the Village under heavy Fire. The 30st. RD. had in several Places attacks repulsed.

The Bav. Ers. D. lost the tip of the Spitzemberg on the east Slope of the Ormont and could not win it back. There were still heavy Battles with many losses. Very peculiar was the Report from the Detachment Rekowski,that not only Gemaingoutte and Wiesembach but also the Forest north of the Col de St. Marie was left because of Water, Food and Ammunition Mangle. Since it rained here in the last 2 weeks could there not be a Mangle on Water. This was one of those wrong Reports. Brooks and Springs where full of Water.

On Sept. 22 became my Grandfather and Gen. von Knoerzer the Iron Cross 1st. Class with a personal Letter from the Military Cabinet. He was astonished since he did not have the Iron Cross 2nd. Class. It was very rare that the Kaiser awarded 1st. before 2nd.

In the Afternoon he rode to Castle Belval and gave Gen. von Knoerzer his Iron Cross witch brought a lot of happiness.

On Sept. 23 were on the whole Front heavy Battles. Gen. Neubert reported that he had Celles again occupied. He became a Command on Sept. 24 to hold this Place. The 30st. RD. was supposed to tie the Enemy. The Division Benzino, strengthened with the IInd. / RIR. 60 and IIIrd. / Ldw. IR. 81, was to take the Spitzemberg again. The Detachment Rekowski had to hold the Bois de la Garde. The IInd. / Ldw. IR. 81 was the Core Reserve at Saales.

At the Voyemont, Scheuberg was immediately after the taking of the Position south of Saales an Artillery Observation Post put in Place. The Art. Kdr. of the Bav. Ers. D. Oberst Zimpelmann, took this Point immediately. The Gen.Kdo. Established there also an Observation Post.

The Vogesen are rich on peculiar Mountain Tops which come immediately from the flat either in Form of a Coffin or like the Climont (966m. high) or like a pointed Cone are high over everything. Like this was also the Harcholet, which was in the Area of the 30st. RD. Cote du Mont (720m. high) and the Hortomont (680m. high) which were all good Observation Posts.

In the course of Sept. 24 did the French attack the Position of the Bav. Ers. D. at Lusse but were repulsed with heavy losses. But they succeeded in the Bois de la Garde, the Detachment Rekowski, which was not centralized lead and was week, to push back. Since the move back was started over Chaume de Lusse south of Bucheckerich to Markirch it became a huge Mistake, which cost them the lasting Possession of the Bois de la Garde and helped the French to dominate the Wiesembacher Valley and to move forward to the Hills south of La Parriee to the German Positions. For an opposite attack were not enough Forces, especially Artillery Ammunition.

The Battle on the whole front of the Bav. Ers. D. had an effect in the Battle of the Spitzemberg. The highest Peak of the Berges, which could be seen from the Ormont, stayed in the Hand of the French. The German first Line was about 150m. Below from the Direction Bois Brule, 1km. Southwest of La Petite Fosse to Frapelle.

At 8.15 in the Evening came an order from the AOK. That the left Wing of the Saxonians (19st. Ers. D.) who were in an unfavorable Battle at Badonviller, should be relieved by moving forward with a reinforced Detachment Neuber in the Plaine Valley. For that had my Grandfather not enough Forces. The continuing Battles since beginning of Sept. had also the Battl., who were not in the Battles, weakened. For Gen. Neuber was it possible the Position at Celles to hold, for an attack he was to week. Assisting with parts of other Divisions, was at this Battle Situation, not possible.

So they send a Report to the AOK.

It revenges itself that our Suggestions and Proposals from Sept. 10 where not followed!

On Sept. 25 reported Gen. Neuber that the Saxonians wanted to move back to Cirey. He will stop at Celles. The AOK. Thought it was very dangerous because of the Threat from Badonviller. Also the French had not lost this Place, even so it was reported on Sept. 21 Gen. Neuber moved, because of the Situation, his Detachment to Bionville Allarmont back, were he prepared to block the Valley and build Defenses.

When they talked in the KHQu. In Saales about the Situation did the French Fire with a heavy Battery at the Village. A universal Panic was about to start in this crowded Place. It was full of Carriages in the Street, Train Drivers with Horses that shied. With vigorous Intervention from Officers of his Staff and the Bav. Div. Staff and a few considered People, came quickly order in this Chaos.

The Village Saales is located behind Hill 597. The French wanted to hit the Train Station, the south End of the Breusch Train. There was a Magazine and a Depot for all kinds of War Material. The Depot Manager was hit by a Grenade and lost both Legs. He and his white Horse were the only dead, even so the Artillery Fire lasted until Dark. There was a lot of Damage on Buildings.

It was successful, in spite of the incoming Grenades, to load the piled up Material in the Train and to move it to Safety to Bourg Bruche. Also the Columns and Wagons left in order in the Enemy Fire. The Train Station and the Sheds where demolished. With great concern did they worry about the Church. There were over 80 wounded, some with heavy Wounds. From time to time did Grenades hit the Roof; Stone and Mortar fall on the wounded. With perfect calm and heroisms did the Doctors and Helpers and Nurse Lonny von Versen, she wore the Ribbon of the Rescuer Medallion, held out and told him that they would do all they could, to see about the Transport back Home. At that Moment was a transport impossible; they would have to wait for the Night.

He rode Horseback with his Staff on the Slope of the Hill northwest of Saales, and had a good oversight of the burning Village and could observe the Enemy Artillery Fire.

They formed a Resolution to move the KHQu. Since Quarters in a Place under Enemy Fire were not tolerable. His Chief proposed St. Blaise, they wanted to keep Bourg Bruche free for the Staff of the Division Benzino. From St. Blaise lead Streets in all direction to the 4 Positions of the Core. It was also out of the Enemy Fire and not so far from the first Positions, so he could ride there.

Late in the Evening they arrived at the new KHQu. He did not foresee that he would be there 2 Years and 3 weeks.

The Security of St. Blaise took a Comp. of the Ldst. Battl. Karlsruhe, under the Command of a 70 Year old energetic and able Oberst Weizenegger, over.

On Sept.26 came a Notice from the AOK. That told the difficulty of Ammunition distribution for the Field Army and ordered to use sparingly. How tragic that the many hints of the Chief of the Gen. Staff of the Army for a bigger need of Ammunition in a coming War at the War Ministry received no Notice. The concern to ask from the Parliament large sums of Money and the Thought that it would be quick to change a Factory into a Munitions Factory, lead to this Crisis.

Core Main Quarter St. Blaise (Heilig Blasien) in the Breusch Valley Sept. 27. 1914 until Oct. 15. 1916

Since he had Command of the Core Eberhardt, he was also still Governor of Strasburg. He still used all Material from the Fortress and on Sept. 26 he pulled 2 heavy Field Howitzers for the Front. The interim Governor doubted, because of that, the Defense of the Fortress. My Grandfather told him: "Strasburg is best defended outside of the Fort in the Vogesen."

The AOK. Was notified of this and ordered on Sept. 28 that without asking nothing could be taken from the Fort.

In the Plaine Valley had the Battle of the last Days clarified the Situation. The Detachment Neuber stood near Les Collins right of the Plaine and at the Hill Tete des Herrins northwest of Le Grand Brocart with his Vanguard. Bionville and Allarmont became fortified. Connection with the left Wing of the 30st. RD. was established.

In this part became the Infantry Battle for the next few Days weaker, because the French worked on the Extension of their Defense Positions at Celles and north of there. The Artillery Battle from the French, sometimes heavy, lasted until mid Oct.

At Saales continued Artillery Fire on and they had to tell the People to leave. Only a Village Guard stayed since in the not destroyed west parts were Troops in Rest.

From the AOK. Were again the importance of the Donon accented. There worked 4st Pi. Comp. (IInd. / Pi. 15) under Captain Hartmann, Adjutant Lt. Guth, on a 12km. long Wire Barrier. It became a powerful Buttress who would have withstood most everything. But because of the Knife Stab in the back in Nov. 1918 it came without fighting in the Hands of the French.

(The IInd. / Pi. 15, that was under the Government, was on the first Mobilization Day formed and included: Staff: Captain Hartmann, Kdr.

IInd. / Pi. 15 from Aug. 2. 1914 until Feb. 5. 1915. Captain Toepfer Kdr. IInd. / Pi. 15. from Feb. 5. 1915 until Sept. 10. 1915. Maj. Kordgien, Kdr. IInd. / Pi. 15 from Sept. 10. 1915 until Oct. 10. 1916. Adjutant: Lt. Guth from Aug. 2. 1914 until Jul. 18.1916. 4st Field Pi. Comp: Captain Rentner. 1st R. Pi. Comp. Oblt. Of Reserve Jahn. 2nd R. Pi. Comp. Captain Senftleben.

On Mine Thrower Formations were at the XVst. RK. Following: from Pi. Battl. 15 were the following Troop parts used: MW. Comp. 230; Leader Captain of Reserve Krenker; MW. Comp. 239 Leader Lt. of Reserve Eiermann; MW. Comp. 409 Leader Captain Hausmann; Median Mountain MW. Detachment 128 Leader Lt. of Reserve Velten; Mountain MW. Detachment 173 Leader Captain Tuechert.)

On Oct. 2 were again Battles on the whole Line with opposite Vanguards. With Personal Intervention did he have success, that the Position between the Bav. Ers. D. and the Detachment Ferling did get better and secure. The left Wing of the Bav. And the Detachment Rekowski was moved forward from Chaume de Lusse to La Parriee and a Connection to Detachment Ferling arranged.

The 13cm. Canons from the Fortress Strasburg fired from they're Position at the Hochrein, 1km. west of Saales, the train Station in St. Leonard to Flames. These already outdated long Range Guns proved true all the time in the Vogesen.

At Night on Oct. 3 came a Command to make the Division Benzino ready to transport to the AA. Strantz. Hart and decisive measures had to be taken. First my Grandfather decided not to take the Bav. Ers. D. out, because of the then Battle Structure, it would have caused a hard to close Space and unserviceable Troop movements. Instead to build a new Division from the whole Front, with the same Force as the Division Benzino. Then they had to give up 16 Battl. 1 Esk. 10 Battr. And 1 Pi. Comp. with the necessary Columns and Trains. Availability of Trains was ordered. The Wuert. Ldw. IR. 120 had to depart in the Morning with the Ist. and IInd. Battl. From Markirch and with the IIIrd. Battl. From Schirmeck

At 3 in the Morning was this Resolution send to the AOK. In Metz. The upper Commander Gen. Baron von Falkenhausen ordered my

Grandfather to a Meeting in Rixingen, half way to Metz, in the Staff Quarter of the 19st. Ers. D.

In Rixingen he met the Kdr. of this Division, Genlt. von Tettenborn, Gen. Adjutant of the King from Saxonia. Shortly after he arrived came the upper Commander, who thought that he would be indignant because of the loss of a whole Division and to try to keep a few Battl. Back. When he reported that the preparation for the Transport was on and several Troop parts where already on the Train was he, so he thought, satisfied with his former Pupil in the Gen. Staff and War Ministry. Especially happy was the upper Commander that he had taken 16 Battl. And not the normal number of 12 Battl. He gave to the AA. Strantz the Division with 12 Battl. And kept 4 for his Army Reserve.

From the Formation of the Core Eberhardt were eliminated: Gen. of the Infantry Knight von Benzino with (16— 1 ¼—17). This was: The Ist. Br. Langenhaeuser with the 4st. And 15st. Bav. RIR., the both MG. K. of the 1st. And 9st. Bav. Ers. Br. The Br. Rasch with the Wuert. Ldw. IR. 120 and the IR. von Donop, Genlt. Dame with the Staff of the 55th. Ers. Br. The IR. von Rath; the Bav. Ers. Kav. Abt. The Kav. Abt. Of the 55th Ers. Br. The Bav. Ers. Field A. Abt. The Prussian Ers. Field A. Abt. 15; the 1st. / RPi. 15; the Bav. Ers. San. Comp.; Mun. Col. and Trains.

The pulling out of the delivered Troops went without difficulty. The worry that the Enemy would find out of the weakening of the Front was constant. From the AOK. Became the Gen.Kdo. The Ldst. Battl. Hagenau and the Rest of the Ldst. Battl. Karlsruhe.

The Gen. of the Infantry Knight von Benzino, who my Grandfather a few Days ago gave in Bourg Bruche in the Name of the Kaiser the Iron Cross 1st. Class, was lost reluctantly. He was a wonderful Man with a lot of Soldier Nature in him, quiet, energetic and clear. He died from a Lung Infection on Nov. 28. 1915 in Lothringia.

The Question of his succession in this part of my Grandfathers Front was not easy.

After considerable deliberation and with agreement from his Chief did he give the Command of the new to be build Division to GenMaj. von Gynz Rekowski, who at the Battles beginning of Sept. made the best Impression. At his proposal gave his Majesty the Kaiser his Promotion to Divisions Kdr. and a few Days later to Genlt. Gen. Staff Officer at this

Division was Maj. Baron de la Motte Fouque, a quiet, diligent Officer, who in the Comradeship with his Talent for Music won many Friends.

The Kdr. of the 30st. RD. Genlt. von Knoerzer had shortly before the War retired as Cavalry Inspector. He was fresh and very energetic. His Job as Leader of the Division in the Battle at Weiler and in the Battles at the going over the Vogesen Passes and at the Meurthe were excellent. He was a Man of Action who did not care for Trench War.

Captain von Schaefer was his Gen. Staff Officer. He was capable and trustworthy and had distinguished himself as a Jung Officer in Southwest Africa. In the Staff of the 30th. RD. stood the Art. Kdr. Maj. von Schell from the Field AR. 80 out. He was still Jung but had Experience and practical look for the use of his Weapon.

A self-acting Command in the Section of the Core had GenMaj. Neuber in the Plaine Valley. an always working Man, thinking of the Welfare of his Men and practical. He was assisted from an excellent Adjutant, Captain Schmidt.

At the left Core Wing in Markirch in the important part of the Vogesen Ridge at the Col de St. Marie commanded Genlt. Ferling, the best Companion and always in good Mood.

The Kdrs. Of the Bav. Infantry Br. had stood out in the past Battles as valiant Men. Among them was especially the Bav. GenMaj. Grueber.

The Bav. GenMaj. Krieger was very smart but too old for the Mountain War. My Grandfather had in 1915 asked for a replacement for him. Also left was the Bav. GenMaj. Count von Zech because of Sickness. The always energetic Bav. Genlt. Mueller had his Br. All the time in Shape.

After the Departure of the Division Benzino was the distribution of the Core in the Positions like this: From the right Wing in connection with the 19st. Ers. D. stood: At the Hills north of Les Collins, the outposts of the Donon Br. under Gen. Neuber who had the Bionviller and Allarmont occupied and then over Tete des Herrins, Hill 845 to Le Grand Brocart hat connection to the 5th. Bav. Ers. Br. The Br. Neuber had as Infantry only the RIR. 70 with 2 Battl. And the Ers. Battl. / Ldw. IR. 99.

The 5th. Bav. Ers. Br. was 4 Battl. Strong; they stood with weak posts in the wild Forest Area from Le Grand Brocart, Hills north of Senones which they had occupied to including the Area southwest of Menil.

The 10ˢᵗ. Bav. RBr. With the Bav. RIR. 11 and 14 was 5 Battl. Strong and had the Position from Laitre, Ban de Sapt, Launois to Hill 620 north of Le Fraiteux, were the IInd. / Ldw. IR. 80 stood, that was under the Br. and builds the left Wing of the 30ˢᵗ. RD.

The 1ˢᵗ. Bav. Ers. Br. at the right Wing of the Division Rekowski, stood with 4 Battl. From Le Fraiteux at the West Edge of the Forest between Hermanpaire and La Petite Fosse past to Bois Brule north of Spitzemberg.

There continued the 9ˢᵗ. Bav. Ers. Br. reinforced with 2ⁿᵈ Bav. Ers. Battl. There followed the subordinated Ldw. IR. 81 east of the Fave Grundes over Lusse, La Parriee and towards south bending again 2ⁿᵈ Bav. Ers. Battl. To including Le Mont, 2km. northeast of Wiesembach.

The south from there positioned Portion belong to Detachment Ferling, who had to use in the Forest east of Wiesembach Militia Battl. From Col de St. Marie over the Hill 786, called Bernhardstein, Hill 950, Tete du Violu until the Cote de St. Marie stood the Ist. and IInd. / Ldw. IR. 80.

Because of that they had to hold the Portion of the Core, whose occupation Force was 43 Battl. With only 27. They had additional a few Militia Batt. Who were not supposed to be used in the Front Line. But that changed later and so they could use the Militia Battl. Hagenau and Karlsruhe and the Subordinate of the Core Militia. Battl. Mindelheim, Friedberg, Wasserberg, Dillingen and Kempten in the first Line that was a big help for other Troops.

It should be said that between the Brigades and the Regiments also between both Divisions the Section Borders where often changed.

Since also the Artillery of the Core was weakened by 10 Battr. Was the outlook not so good.

The Formation of the Bav. Ers. Br. with each 3 to 4 Battl. Was not favorable. The building of Regiment Units was recognized. From the 12 Battl. Came 1 to the Bav. RIR. 11 as IIIrd. Battl. Then they build 2 and 1 Regiment with 3 Battl. Who were named Bav. Ersatz Regiments 1 to 5. Since the Bav. War Ministry had only sent 4 older Staff Officers as Regiments Kdrs. Did my Grandfather give the 1 Regiment to the Prussian Oberstlt. Count von Holnstein, who's Family came from Bav. And the War Ministry, at his request, confirmed it.

In the following Days came several Reports that the French had send Patrols for the Front, especially in the Position of Gen. Ferling.

Since Oct.12 was a Civil Commissar send to the Gen.Kdo. In the Person of Government Official Fehr from Weissenburg. This was necessary to oversee the Administration of the occupied Area. This could only be done with the help of a Person who knew what to do in this Situation. The work of this Civil Commissar extended itself also in the German Operations Area. This led often to Friction with the German Administration Official. It was always taken care off because the Governor and the Government Secretary Count von Roedern had full Sympathy.

Unfortunately was on Dec.21. 1914 the Commissar Fehr transferred to Saargemuend. He was an intelligent Man and good with People. His Substitute in the Staff of the Gen.Kdo. Was the upper Forester Dirichsweiler from Rothau, who very soon became indispensable.

On Oct. 14 became my Grandfather through the Bav. War Ministry the Bav." Military me- rite Badge" 1st. Class with Swords" from his Majesty the King of Bav. He had found out that the Bav. Generals. Under him had asked for that. Witch he took as a high Honor.

On Oct. 19 reported at the 30st. RD. a French Officer and 11 Man from the French IR. 140, who stayed from begin of Sept. behind of the German Front. They hid in the Forest and at Farms and wanted to sneak back through the Lines. They did not succeed in that. With German Soldiers everywhere also lonely Farms, cold Nights and no Food they decided it was better to become Prisoners.

Not only Enemy Dodgers where in the Core Area. As they found out that in a Million Army there are also bad Elements. One Day came a Militia Recruit to my Grandfather in St. Blaise and told him that in the House opposite of his, at a Bakers Woman whose Husband was at War, since a few weeks 3 Soldiers where. By Day they were in Bed and only went out at Night. The Woman had told the Recruit in secret. The House was searched and the 3 taken in. Other Dodgers were several Month behind the Front and had lived from stealing and poaching. It was funny that in this sad Situation he himself probably had spoken to 2 of those. As he rode past of the empty Foresters House Salm he thought that the 2 there were fixing the Telephone Wire to the Donon.

On Oct.21 reported the AOK. That according to Spy News the French had planned an Offensive.

On this Day he rode with his Staff to Senones, a pretty French Garrison Town in the Rabodeau Valley. One Quarter of the Houses and the Cathedral where destroyed the other part looked very nice. The People, old and very Jung Man, many well-dressed Woman and many Children, moved about and where in good understanding with the Bav.

On Oct. 25 reported Gen. von Ferling heavy Artillery Fire from the French at the Col de St. Marie.

Sadly he had to give up his Adjutant, Captain von Glasenapp, who he very much liked. But the work in the Staff meant one more Officer. He took from the Government Gen. Staff Officer Captain Hosse and put there Captain Glasenapp.

From Oct. 26 to 30 came more reports that the French on the Border Rim at the left Core Wing serious attacks planed. The Artillery Fire increased and many Patrols from the Cote de St. Marie to Heicot Klein Leberau and the Hill Positions on both sides of the Col took the attention of the Battl. There. Because of Ammunition Mangle could the German Artillery not successful hit the Enemy Battr. Everyday became the AOK. Reports from the Seriousness of the Situation and were asked for Ammunition. The AOK. Had little Sympathy for these reports. The AOK. Intervened often with my Grandfathers orders, even so he thought he had the Responsibility.

On Oct. 27 was he in Markirch and at the Col de St. Marie, Gen. von Ferling hoped with his Battl. The Position, which was heavily wired, to hold if his Artillery would get enough of Ammunition.

On Nov.1 began the French in the Morning to Fire with Artillery at the Town of Markirch and the Area. At the same time moved heavy Forces on both sides of the Col de St. Marie against the positioned Troops. After tenacious Resistance succeeded the French to occupy the German Trenches from the Cote de St. Marie on the Hill 950, the Violu, and from west on the Hill 786, the Bernhartstein, and in the tight Forest only the Pass stayed in German Hand. The result of the weakening of the Core showed now. They're Mood was embitterment, since all they're mentioned warnings were rejected, with the remark that they see the Situation as too serious. Because of the reports from Gen. von Ferling was he forced to report to the AOK. in the Morning at 10.40, that the Situation at Markirch was serious, since he had not enough Reserves. The week Troops, that he could miss in other Positions where put in March to help Gen. von Ferling. And he gave him Captain Hosse as Information Officer to the Gen.Kdo. Also did he send the IInd. / Ldw.

IR. 80 from the 30st. RD. to the Division Rekowski. The Company from the Ldw. IR 80, which was still at Chaume de Lusse, was replaced with parts of the Ldst. Battl. Weilheim, Kdr. Obrstlt. Hegel. The Comp. was send to Col de St. Marie.

Oberstlt. Hegel went with that Comp. from the Ldst. Battl. Weilheim, 2 MGs and 1 Field Canon from north against the Col de St. Marie and cleaned the Forrest Area from the infiltrated Enemy.

(My Grandfather had with the Bav. Ldst. Soldiers a humorous Experience. The Bav. Ldst. Battl. Weilheim was only shortly in the Villages behind of the Front where the troops where hard at work with the Completion of their Positions in the Forrest Mountains. The French People had to be watched they found means and ways to get connection with the French Troops with Signals and personal contact on many secret walks. He rode one Day with his Staff Watch to La Petite Fosse, left the Horses in the Village and walked with the Bav. Br. Kdr. of the Bav. Infantry Regiment who had the Hills at the Village occupied and who lived in the Village, for to the Positions. As they came back in the dark there was a Guard at the Village Entrance. He called at us:" Stop, who are you!"

"The commanding General!"—"I do not know you!"— "Here General Grueber, the Br. Kdr!"He called this in his Bav. speech " I do not know you either! "Came the answer.

"I am the Oberst and local Commander here!"—"I have not heard from you either!"

"This can have a bad end" did he say to the Guard" If you arrest all of us and the French attack then the Battle will be lost because the Leader is in Jail!"—"It will not be so bad! I will let you pass but I have to follow my Instructions and ask who you are!"

At Christmas Eve he sends a Box with a lot of goody's to the Soldier Viktor Christian from the Ldst. Battl. Weilheim for his correct conduct as Guard.

At 3 in the Afternoon gave the AOK. A Detachment of the AA. Gaede (3—0—2—1 MG. Comp.) and a few 9 cm.Canons from Strasburg, under GenMaj. von Dinkelacker, to the Core Eberhardt. The Canons where immediately moved forward to the Kreuzberg, west from the Train Station from Markirch. Then he ordered at 5 in the Afternoon that Gen. Rekowski had to pull out the Ist. / Ldw. IR. 81 out of his Position and to send it to the Col de St. Marie were it came under Gen. von Ferling. In the Evening they were successful to push the French from north of the Col and the Hill 786, the Bernhartstein. South of the Mountain and at the Eckericher Hill they kept they're occupied Positions.

At the Border Crest was heavy Gunfire but it did not come to any attacks on both sides. Neither of the 2 Battl. Of the Ldw. IR. 80 nor the IVst. / Ldw. IR. 99 were able to attack at the Eckericher Hill.

The 30st. RD. had planned an attack to distract the Enemy, which he aloud, to the new northwest from Senones French Position. The Division had Gen. Count von Zech put in charge. In Question was the occupation of a Hill northwest of Hill 670, 2km. north of Senones. From there came Enemy Fire to they're Positions between Hill 670 and the Road crossing north from there. The Command over the attack had the Section Kdr. Oberst Ertl. He became 5 Comp. from the Bav. Ers. Battl. 5,6,7 and 8 and the Radf. Comp. of the 30st. RD. also 2 Platoons of the 2nd. Res. / Pi. 15 and 2 Canons / Ers. Field AR. 31. 3 Comp. of the Bav. Ers. Battl. 8 stood as Reserve at the Road crossing in they're Positions. Apparently was the Preparation for the attack not careful enough planned, especially the approach Area. As they left the Trenches, only 200m. From the Enemy, they had losses. The heroic Bav. Moved forward with dash in the Forest between Cliffs and Rubble. They met wire Obstacles and had losses from hidden Flank Positions left and right. They could not take this Cliff Nest from the Enemy. At dark they moved back and came to they're Positions with 37 dead 99 wounded and 7 missed.

My Grandfather said about the imperfect exploring of the Area was the fault of not enough training during Peace time. He had tried as Regiments and Divisions Kdr. to always stress that Fact. It was never enough time given to that.

The failing of the Operation at Senones was sad because of the losses of the brave Soldiers. Here could have the Danger of an Enemy attack been averted with reinforcement and extension. But the Situation at the Border Crest stayed dangerous. Because of that became the AOK. A Report, that for the continuation of the attack at Markirch, were reinforcement of the Core necessary.

At 12 Midnight informed the AOK. That it had sent as reserve to Markirch the Ers. R. von Rath, Kdr. Oberstlt. von Rath from the IR. 111.

On Nov. 4 did he have a Discussion with Gen.von Ferling in St. Kreuz about the Situation and ascertained that to give up old and partly occupied from the Enemy Positions, would be no good, because it would make the Front Line longer. That had to be avoided because of the weak distribution of Men. It was necessary according to the Area to move the Line for to Le Combe south of Lusse, Le Mont, west Edge of the Forest north from the Col de St. Marie. The French had already near opposite of the German Position Bases build that could not be left in they're Hand. Because of that did my Grandfather at 2.30 in the Afternoon command:

> "This Evening starts the preparation for an attack against the Forest North of the Col de St. Marie. Tomorrow before Noon prepared the Artillery the move forward of the Infantry to that Line."

The Artillery became strict Tasks. In the Afternoon reported the AOK. That big Transports of French Troops from east to west where going on. Also became the 19st. Ers. D. order to move forward and the Br. Neuber in the Plaine Valley had to join.

So he had to give new orders and take new Measures. The preparation for the attack on Nov.5 were hindert because of Fog, witch blocked the Artillery observation. The attack was moved forward east of the Fave towards south and west to Markirch with the Front towards west. The Division Rekowski did move forward to a Line to Herbeaupaire Le Combe and in the Area of Le Mont.

The Detachment Ferling was able, mainly because of the dashing move forward and the expert lead Badisch Ers. R. von Rath, on the right

Wing in the Forest northeast of the Street Col de St. Marie, Wiesembach to south of Le Mont, to expel the Enemy.

At the Hill 786, the Bernhartstein, and the Hill 950, Tete du Violu, was the Enemy expelled, the Eckericher Hill and Klein Leberau occupied.

Parts of the 2nd. Bav. Ldw. I. Br. Kdr. Genlt. von Lachemair were moved forward and 2 Comp. of them occupied the Bludenberg (Haicot at the southwest Slope of the Bressoir). Because of that was the concern for the in the Air hanging left Wing gone.

In the Morning of Nov. 6 had the Troops of the Division Rekowski they're new Positions dug out.

In Front of the Detachment Ferling, had at the right Wing all the way to the Col de St. Marie, the Enemy with little Resistance in the Forest, moved back to the Valley from Wiesembach.

At before Noon was in Markirch a Discussion between Gen. of the Inf. Gaede and my Grandfather. There were also our Chiefs, Genlt. von Ferling and several Gen. Staff Officers. As a Representative of the Army Leader was his Chief Oberst Weidner there.

The Situation at the Front of the Core Eberhardt was serious, since from the Detachment Ferling all Reserves where used. The moving forward of Supply of Ammunition and Food to the first Line was difficult. The French had the east Slope of the high Mountains occupied and so they could take the German Positions on the Border Rim from the south under Flank Fire. So the Supply move could only be done at Night.

Gen. Gaede expected after incoming reports an attack of the French. He demanded to detach that from the Bav. Ldw. Br. Lachemair has given Detachment Dinkelacker (VIst. / Ldw. IR. 99, IInd. / Ldw. IR. 123, Ist. / Bav. Ldw. IR. 3, Ers. Detachment / Field AR. 14, 1 Mun. Col. Mun. Col. Ruedt)

Gen. Gaede and my Grandfather were of one Mind that the French must not again move forward.

Oberst Weidner brought to Markirch a personal Letter from the Top Army Commander to my Grandfather.

The Top Army Commander did not have to worry. My Grandfather had all the Officers and Men under his Command informed to hold out under the Situation.

It was not easy with this big mangle on Ammunition to keep the Artillery Men under Control and to tell the Infantry that they should hold out without this help.

So on Nov. 8 he sends an Answer to the Top Army Commander and he attached the following Letter:

Because of a found Diary from a dead French Officer of the Jaeg. Battl. 13 they found out why the French had so much success. They became on Oct. 28 from 2 Elsaessers, who went to the French, Information of Position and Force of the German Troops at Markirch. Because of that they attacked with the French 66st. RD. Also that Command came in German Hand. The French wanted they're Artillery Observers to move for at the Border Rim. In that they were successful in the last Oct. Days. They used the weakening of the Detachment Ferling at the Cote de St. Marie and north were the weakened occupied Positions gave them a Chance to get the Artillery Observers in the Night to Oct. 31 installed. In the Morning could they're heavy Battr. At Laveline and St. Croix aux Mines open Fire with good Results at Town and Area Markirch. At the same time started the attack of the Infantry to the Flank at Rossberg and Area.

On Nov.7 became the Core Eberhardt from the OHL. 2 Pi. Comps. from Srasburg.

My Grandfather wanted to attack because the French had all the Mountain Tops occupied and the German Trenches where at Places only 50m. Below them.

That's why the addition of 2 Pi. Comp. where very welcomed. They helped the Infantry with building Trenches. They brought Mine Throwers which were new to the Troops. Since there was no training with that Weapon everybody had to learn to put it to good use. It was very soon a very valuable substitute for the Artillery. It was especially useful to destroy Enemy Wire Obstacles.

They were quite accurate and also had a Moral Effect in the Mountains. The explosive and Splinter Effect at the rocky Places and the many Echo's in the Mountains had an Effect on the Enemy. That's why the French Artillery tried to hit them first. Since the Mine was in Flight visible they could tell where they came from.

In spite of that had the Pioneers to stay with their Weapons and make them ready to Fire again. Often came with the first Mine Throwers mishaps like Barrel and early detonation mistakes. So the Crew had to have strong Nerves. Later came modified versions that where good.

The losses were at the Pi. And MWs. In this difficult Trench Battles conciderable.

From the Plaine Valley came bad reports. Gen. Neuber was, according to order, moved forward with 1 Detachment to help the 19st. Ers. D. He had to break up the Battle since the Saxonians had not attacked.

The Top Commander wanted a personal Discussion. My Grandfather proposed the Government Strasburg as Meeting Place. So he drove on Nov. 9 to Strasburg. To the Meeting were among others the Kdr. of the Fortress, Gens. Of the Artillery and Pioneers. He could on the Map demonstrate the Tasks of the Core; such stretched Lines to defend with weak Forces. Especially the difficulty on the left Wing. He assured that the Forces would hold the Positions but could not reach results with the little Ammunition.

Of that came from the upper Quarter Master of the Army on the previous Day, Maj. Baron von Berchem, a hopeless report. The Top Commander could give in this Matter no Hope. They separated with full Agreement about what to do. The French attacked again with heavy Forces in the upper Elsa's. Because of that had the Troops be pulled out that were from the AA. Gaede put into the Detachment Ferling.

He was Shure that the Danger to crush the Front at the left Wing of the Core was eliminated, since the insertion of the Badische Ers. R. von Rath. The Ldw. IR. 80 thought they were secure since at both Wings was support from the Ers. R. von Rath and the Bav.Militia the Enemy Artillery Fire continued with heavy Force and were also directed at the Division Rekowski.

In the Afternoon attacked the French the 19st, Ers. D. Gen. Neuber did send a Detachment to the right Flank. The 30st. RD did secure between Plaine and Rabodeau Valley.

In Nov. 1914 was the Br. Neuber assigned only at the Street over the Donon to Allarmont. A real assist for the Saxonians, who were in the flat Area on the other side of the Mountain Ridge.

He had to go to Gen. Neuber in Luvigny on Nov. 18. There they were worried about the Gen. since at Nov. 16 in the Evening the Br. reported:

"The Gen. and a few Companions since 2 in the Afternoon
on the Way and had not returned. A search Party with Lights
and Light Pistols is on the Way."

The Gen. came back on the next Day. He had lost his Way in the
Forest rocky Mountain Terrain. At the beginning of Night they found
at the Schweinefelsen under Stone and Leafs Shelter. My Grandfather
punished him, because he had disturbed the Night Rest of the Gen.Kdo.
With worry about his Life. He had to pay Repentance Money in to the
Christmas Cashbox for the wounded of the Core. With a nice Poem did
Gen. Neuber send his Money. My Grandfather wrote this little Episode to
show that he always tried the companionable Relation between the older
Officers of the Core to cultivate. He said this especially, because at begin of
the War, were the southern Gens. And Staff Officers under his Command,
quite restrained. From begin on did he try, in spite of sometimes harsh
Commands; to be companionable and win they're Trust. He was very
happy that he succeeded in this and that he had a good relation to the Bav.
Officers and Men in spite of him being a Prussian.

He drove on Nov. 27 with a few of his Staff over Urbeis and the
Border Pass at the Col d'Urbeis to Bucheckerich. From there they walked
6 hours over Chaume de Lusse through the Forest west of there to the
Front Positions of the Bav. Br. to the Regiment of Oberst Ertl. Ab and
down were the Trenches in the rocky Mountain. They were working hard
on completion and reinforcement. So he was satisfied with the Inspection.

The Troops were always happy when he came in the Positions and
proud when they got the Iron Cross from they're Commanding Gen.

He was very concerned to facilitate the work of the Troops by obtaining
Pack Animals. They were working to build a Cable Car from Rumbach
to Chaume de Lusse, 2km. southwest of Bucheckerich at the Border Rim.

The AOK. Expected a heavy Enemy attack since the French, at the
whole Front, Fired Artillery and did many Patrols. It was commanded that
2 Battl. Of the Core would be positioned at the Train Line in the Breusch
and Leber Valley. For that was the Ers. Battl. / Ldw. IR. 99 in Schirmeck
and a put together Battl. With 1 Comp. of the Ldst. Battl. Landshut and
1 Comp. Weilheim positioned in Markirch.

The XVst. Reserve Core

The OHL. and the War Ministry had another Name for the Core. The Regiments under him were named after they're Commanders. The Name "Core Eberhardt" disappeared then.

From Dec. 1. 1914 on did he Command the XVst. RK. The Troops deplored this Measure, because they had fought under him with Honor and he had a good Relation to all under him.

The Division Rekowski became the 39st. RD. The Br. Neuber the 84st. Ldw. Br. and the Detachment Ferling the 52nd. Ldw. Br.

On Dec.2. Was the left Wing of the Core moved more south, the 52nd. Ldw. Br. took over the occupation of the 1228m. High Birschberg in the Bressoir Massive. Because of that was the right Wing of the AA. Gaede relieved. The Daily Battle's and heavy Enemy Artillery Fire at the Front of the XVst. RK. Continued for the next few Month.

The superintendent Backhaus was on Dec. 9 transferred to the east Front. To the Gen. Kdo. Came the Intendant Counsellor Eberhard Busse. This always happy, diligent Man became a true Friend.

On Dec. 17 did the OHL. Partition the 3 Groups on the left Wing of the Army. Because of that was west the Mosel as Border between the AA. Falkenhausen and the AA. Strantz. South was the Partition Line between the AA. Falkenhausen and the AA. Gaede from the Cote de St. Marie south of Altweier south of Leberau. The AOK. Falkenhausen moved at Christmas 1914 they're AHQu. To Strasburg.

On Dec. 21 came to St. Blaise the Foreign Military Attaches of the Neutral Countries to look over his Core Area. There where Representatives from USA, Argentinian, Brazilian, Chile, Romanian, Sweden, Switzerland and Spain. We rode from Belval to the Le Harcholet and the Hortomont. At the Position of the Bav. They were astonished about the carving Art of the Bav. At the Trip back over Le Pult were the German 10cm. Canons were positioned came a few Grenades from the French. The Attaches were happy to have been under Fire.

On the next Day did he go with the foreign Officers to the Haicot. For guidance reported 10 Men. They were former Gardisten and he had immediate accord. One of them was a Garde Fusilier under him when he was Commander of the"Maikaefer". Private Lussy came from Markirch. He was slain in Russia in 1917.

The foreign Officers were impressed that he had such personal touch with those men. Later he could a few of them, including Private Lussy, in presence of the foreign Officers, decorate with the Iron Cross. Later as they had enjoyed the outlook at the Forest Edge at the Haicot Meadow towards the French Positions and the Buchenkopf were they could observe French Detachments train Tiraillements, they went back.

The Jaeg. Battl. 8 with they're Radf. Comp. had arrived in Markirch and came under the 52nd. Ldw. Br. A part of this Battl. Knew the Area. They were the Ist. / Ldw. IR. 81 send back to the 39st. RD. and the IInd. / Ldw. IR. 80 at the Train St. Blaise Rothau came under the AOK.

On Dec. 29 came with an extra Train the War Minister, who was also chief of the Gen. Staff of the Field Army, Gen. of the Inf. von Falkenhayn, into St. Blaise. With him was Oberst Tappen, Oberstlt. Tieschowitz von Tischowa, Maj. von Bartenwerffer and Captain Mewes. My Grandfather drove with Gen. von Falkenhayn over Saales to the 2km. west situated Beau Soleil. From there he told him about the Area and the Positions. They then drove back to St. Blaise were they had a short talk with the2 Divisions Kdrs.

The visit of the Chief of the Gen. Staff at the XVst. RK.was short.

On Dec. 30 was the Cable Car from Rumbach to Chaume de Lusse finished. He drove to the Inauguration Ceremony of the "Eberhardt Cable Car" with his Chief and a few Officers of the Staff. Since the connection to the back of the Positions between La Combe, Le Mont in the Forest west from there Bois de Menaupre deviant les Heraux and Bois du Dansant de la Fete, in the hard accessible Mountain only from St. Kreuz over Klein Rumbach lead. That's why all Material for the Positions had to be transported by Carrier Columns. That's why the War Ministry aloud the building of the Cable Car.

The Material came from the Bleichert Comp. in Leipzig. The building was under Captain Toost with the Fortress Train Construction Comp. 7.

The Cable Car went from Station Rumbach to Chaume de Lusse were on the 800m. high Rim at the Forest Edge the End Station "Eberhardt" was.

In the beginning of 1916 did Captain Wicke transform the "Eberhardt Cable Car" in to a work of Art with the Ldw. Construction. Comp. 4 and 180 Russian Prisoners.

From the End Station did Donkey Columns move the Material to the Positions. At the Cable Station came Gen. von Rekowski and they both had Pictures taken with the Donkeys. The Picture started a humorous conversation: My Grandfather asked one of the Bav. Ldw. Man" what is the Name of the smallest Donkey? " "That is Lulu." "And what is the Name of the biggest Donkey in the Column?" "That I cannot tell your Excellency!" said the Soldier with a light Grin.

At Herbaupaire, 1km. west of Lusse, was at the same Day a dashing Coup accomplished. A Patrol of the 2nd. / Bav. Ers. R. 1 brought, after shelling the French Positions with the Mine Throwers, 19 Prisoners in.

On Dec. 31. He drove to the Forest House Plant School and met with Gen. Baron von Falkenhausen, the Quarter Master of the AA. Maj. Baron von Berchem and Gen. von Ferling. They wanted first to accommodate the Jaeger Battl. 8. Then they walked from Col de St. Marie through the Forest north from there to the Position of the Bav. Ldst. Battl. Weilheim. The Kdr. Oberstlt. Hegel, was a Descendant of the big Philosopher. He was capable, Mind and Body fresh and had a good Relation with his Troops. The nice clear Winter Day and a fantastic long distance sight deep into France made this strenuous Walk through the Positions worthwhile.

At 10.30 in the Evening he rode with a few Companions into the Sylvester Night. A bright Moon and Star Firmament, no Wind everywhere Snow and Ice at the Mountain and Pines. They rode over Saales and Grande Fosse. From the Front came Infantry Fire, but it was in reality crazy shooting from both Outposts.

They greeted in Nayemont shortly before Midnight Oberstlt. Abel and the Officers of his Staff. They were surprised as they recognized him also the Troops where happy when he called a happy New Year to them.

They were in Chatas at the stroke of the Bell 12 Midnight, were he met the Staff of the Bav. RIR. 11 at the Sylvester Punch. There he called the Kdr. Oberstlt. Schoettl and congratulated him to his success.

One Comp. of his Regiment had in the Afternoon at Ban de Sapt the "Buchenwaeldchen"occupied.

The continuing ride through the Mountains at slick and rocky Passes was hard. They had often to lead the Horses. Especially hard was the descent from the Stone Steps from Castle St. Louis to Saulxures. They came back at 3 in the Morning to the KHQu. During that time tried the French to take back the "Buchenwaeldchen" but were defeated.

On Jan.2 came a letter from the AOK:

"From secure News had the French, they're in the Vogesen battling Troops, who were opposite of the XV. RK. In Places very much weakens, so they could use them in other Places to break through. Also with Artillery was the Enemy weaker than the XVst. RK. He thought it be absolutely necessary, in consideration of the whole Situation, that the XVst. RK. The Enemy, who was in Front of them, detained by attacking them. After looking at the Situation it must not be a total frontal attack but here and there were ever the Area, Leaders and Troops have a Guarantee to succeed. He could not give the AOK. Support since all other Forces were used in other Places. The XVst. RK. Is compared to all other parts of the Army on Troops, Munition and Material for the attacks ready. It can take care of this Task with its Battle hard Leaders and Troops. He looked forward to hear from the Kdr. Gen. How he wants to do this Task."

My Grandfather had because of that in St. Blaise with the Gen. Staff Officers of the 30st. And 39st. RD. and the 52nd. Ldw. Br. a Meeting and the result of that he wrote in a Letter to the AOK:

"Because of the orders that I became and the strategic and tactical Situations before my Front, I did not order a total attack but limited myself to detain the opposite Forces.

To detain and harm the Enemy are on the entire Front in many Places small attacks which will allow a gradually move forward on the whole Front of the Core against the heavy Fortified Enemy.

Gen. Neuber attempted with many small attacks with small Detachments to get the attention of the Enemy. A reoccupation of Celles would be desired and with the available Forces possible but only appropriate if the on the right connecting 19st. Ers. D. moves forward to the Hill Badonviller and so the right Flank and back of the Troops at Celles secured.

At the 30st. RD. were lately at Hill 670 north of Senones as at the Hill northwest of Launois Enemy attacks with counter attacks repelled. On both Places was forward Area won.

The left Wing of the Br. of Gen. Grueber did slowly move forward from the Area of Provencheres over le Beuley to Frapelle in order to encircle the Enemy Position at Spitzenberg and to create better Observation for they're Artillery.

The left Wing Br. of the 39st. RD. Did move forward beginning of Nov. from the Line Lusse, the Hill east of La Combe, La Chaige, Le Mont, Gravelle. They are at middle and left Wing in touch with the Enemy and are trying to gain Area with Trench attacks.

The 52nd. Ldw. Br. has the order to attack the heavy Fortified Enemy Position at the Bernhartstein at Hill 786.

The main Emphasis lies at the continuing attack against the Troops that are in Front of the 10st. Bav. RI. Br. and against the Enemy Position in the Bois de la Garde north of Wiesembach and the Hill 786 the Bernhartstein. The attack against both Enemy Positions, were the Trench Work is very hard because of the rocky Ground, has to be taken from the left Wing Br. of the 39st. RD. And the right Wing of the 52nd. Ldw. Br. With each other's Agreement. Without help from the Pioneers and all close Fight means, is a move forward impossible.

For that I ask the AOK Pi. Troops under my Command not to further weaken and to supply me with abundant Munition for MWs. And Hand Grenades.

I also ask that the Army Reserve Ldw. Battl. That is behind my Front, will be at my disposal for the attacks, since all Troops in the front Line at implementation of the attacks need Reserves.

I will always try to oppress the Enemy."

After this Letter came the answer from the Army Leader:

"I am agreeable with your Intention but I have to regretful keep the disposal over the Reserve Battl. But it can be used in an attack at a critical Situation at a proposal of the Core. A switch with another Battl. At the Front Line is aloud."

In personal talk with the upper Kdr. In which my Grandfather recommended a strong Offensive on a Place on his Front with reinforcement of his Troops especially Artillery. His Excellency Count von Falkenhausen agreed to this and to his proposals the Enemy to encircle east of the Fave Grundes up to the Col de St. Marie. But he had regretfully decline to the proposals since they would not fit in the Plans of the OHL.

Always when he was alone or with his Chief he thought about such Proposals, did he think back to the ordered move back in the Border Passes from Sept. 10. 1914 where they gave the French the Bois de la Garde back.

That he followed that order he has regretted all of his Life.

On his Front Sector came now everything to a freeze. The French could now build they're advantageous Positions to big strong Points and far in to they're back Country reinforce the defense Positions so an Offensive in this Section was almost impossible.

The Task "stop the Enemy" could now only be done with small Operations. The heroisms and thirst for Action of Officers and Man brought almost daily Prisoners, Booty and important inquiry's. The French changed very often they're Troops in his Section and was in Artillery and Ammunition far ahead. And so it is the Ingratitude Task to write a Memorial for the Vogesen Guard in the War History.

Almost daily was he and often also his Chief and the other Officers of his Staff in the Front Positions and at they're Battr. The Army Leader inspected, even so he was 70 years old, the Front Positions and was not afraid of the strain witch a hike in the Mountain brought. He could for hours, while talking, March, climb and crawl through the Trenches and dug outs

The under Ground work of the French at the Mountain Ridges gave them a hard time. Who would have thought that a Mine War would have such significance outside of a Fortress. In a Fortress War was by undermining something destroyed or to blow a breach for an attack. Here was after week long work and with much Technic very little won.

Certainly, like everything else, did have this Mine War also a good side. The Men of the Pi. Regiments that were positioned there, had a lot of Pleasure in spite of the hard work. Most of these Men where Miners and where proud to show the French they're superiority and were happy over every success at blasting.

On Jan. 27.1915 they celebrated the first Kaisers Birthday in the Field. In the Afternoon he drove to Saales and gave a few Officers and Man the Iron Cross 1st. Class.

The 30ˢᵗ. RD. reported on that Day that they averted an Enemy attack at the Hill 670 and 521 on both sides of Senones. There had parts of the French IR. 23 and 133 near Senones the Jaeger 7 and the Colonial IR. 37 attacked. At Ban de Sapt were 51 French Prisoners cought. Under the 90 dead, in Front of the Core, was a French Regiments Kdr. Oberstlt. Daylen.

Under the Leadership of the Kdr. of the 10ˢᵗ. Bav. RI. Br. had at the 30ˢᵗ. RD. an Operation to be executed. After blowing Mines under the French Trenches were they to be occupied and made ready for defense. My Grandfather wanted to see this, so he drove in the Afternoon with Lt. Koch, Jaeger Battl. 8, who was as wounded to the Gen. Kdo. Transferred, to Chatas and from there on Foot to Laitre.

At the set hour begun the German Artillery from all Directions heavy Fire witch the French then answered. It was loud crashing and thundering mainly because of the multible Echo's in the Mountains and Forests. At a set time was the Pi. To blow up the Dugout Tunnel under the French Trenches. Then came a report that the ignition cords were destroyed from Enemy Fire and the repair would take a long time.

Genlt. Mueller who lead this Operation from his Quarter in St. Stail near Grandrupt telephoned:

> "Because of this Circumstance cancel the Operation and the Artillery should slowly end they're Fire. The attack will be made on another Day."

This did not sit with my Grandfather. Oberstlt. Schoettl, Kdr. of the Bav. RIR. 11, with whom he was sitting in Laitre became a Command:

> "Captain Bowien (Pi. Battl. 15) Put the wires in 10 Min. together then Detonation. The attack will immediately begin after the Detonation. The Artillery continues its heavy Fire. The Br. is by Telephone to be informed of my order."

15 Min. later was a heavy Detonation and the brave Bav. broke in the Enemy Trenches. After a further 10 Min. came one report after the other:

> "Trench is from several Groups taken."
> "The first assault Column is in the Enemy Trench."

"The second assault Column has losses but also moves in."

"The assault Troops of the Bav. RIR. 14 also move for."

"1 MG. and 2 Grenade Launchers have been taken, 31 Prisoners, 29 from The Line Reg. 23, 2 from the MG. Detachment 133, in our Hand."

"The Position will be enlarged."

The Battle did slow down. Attacks from the French were repelled. German losses were Lt. Schmidt and 2 Corporals and 10 wounded.

They went back to Chatas. Genlt. Mueller was happy about the outcome of this Operation.

The Operation at the 39st. RD. was from the Core to Febr. 18 decided. A few Days before were the necessary Measures in the Division Staff Quarter Bourg Bruche discussed. For the next few Days became the Division the IIIrd. / Ldw. IR. 80. less 1 Comp.

With his Chief and a few Officers of his Staff did he drive on Febr. 18 to the Hill 690 2km. northeast of Lusse. They went to the Leader of the attack Troops, Gen. Krieger, who had on the Forest Edge an Observation Post. Later they stayed at the Hill 690 north of Lordon at the Artillery Kdr. From whose Position they had a good View. From there he could hear the Fire Commands and watch. At 12 Noon begun the Artillery they're preparatory Fire for the attack. Also Battr. Of the 30st. RD. and the 52nd. Ldw. Br. Where involved.

From the north fired 46 from the east about 20 Canons at the Hill La Combe south of Lusse and at the French Stronghold at the highest point in the Bois de la Garde near south of La Chaige.

At 5.45 in the Afternoon begun the attack. The Ldw. IR. 81 took the Hill near La Combe south of Lusse, it was called the Schusterberg. A few Groups moved for over La Combe towards Buisson but had to move back with losses. However they took 2 MGs. 28 Prisoners from IR. 253 and 22 Alpine Jaegers.

The Bav. Ers. R. Ertl could, in spite of heroic attacking not take the fortified Position.

In the Night did the Troops suffer under the Flank Fire of the French Artillery and had 40 dead and 160 wounded.

In order for him to see personally about the success of the Ldw. IR. 81 south of La Combe at the Schusterberg, he went with Maj. Mohs to La Pariee to the Command Post of Colonel Vogel. It was a wooden Barrack and also gathering Place for wounded. In the Evening they planned to prepare for the continuation of the attack. They walked for to the Troops were he told the Man his Appreciation.

The request of the Core for more Ammunition, in order to demolish the fortified Position with Artillery, was from the AOK. Denied. That was sad because now he had to order:

> "The heavy attack is to brake off, the Fortress like attack
> is to be continued."

The Troops found this to be painful because the Bav. Were jealous of the Prussian Ldw. Who had taken the Schusterberg. On Feb. 19 came there heavy Enemy Artillery Fire and the French tried several times the lost trenches again to occupy. The brave 81er repelled those attacks.

On Feb. 20 did he inspect the Battle Field at the Bav. Colonel Ertl was in a down Mood because of the failed outcome of his attack. The assault Troops moved forward with bravery to the wide tangled wire Impediment witch were between the rocky Cliffs which were not destroyed by the Artillery. The calculation of the Artillery that they could destroy these with the Ammunition that they had was wrong. The Men of the Bav. Infantry made a good Impression in spite of heavy losses.

A Command of the French Gen. Serrate, Kdr. of the French 132nd IBR. Witch belonged to the 41st. Division, was found in a dugout in the captured Trenches at the Hill south of Lusse at the Schusterberg. My Grandfather could not understand that in this official Order from a French Gen. the Word "Boshes" was used. You have to treat also your Enemy with Respect. Woe to the Army whose Officers Core sinks that low.

The difficulties of the before Hand attack of the 84st. Ldw. Br. On Feb. 27 was first to overcome the impassible, rocky Forest Area. In spite of Observation with Officers Patrols, they had no real knowledge of the French Positions. They knew about they're Vanguards but had no knowledge about the course or Condition of the main Position.

It would have been desirable if the Streets from Les Collins and from Celles to Badonviller were occupied. The Saxonians should have had this in they're Hand. With the weak Force of the 84st. Ldw. Br. And the impossibility to reinforce, could he only occupy the North Streets.

For the move forward and the Supply Transport for the Battle was in most Places only a difficult Foot Path and in other Places a neglected Wood Transport Road. Ammunition, Food and wounded transport had to be done by Men since in this Place where no Donkey Columns available.

On Feb. 27 at 5 in the Morning he went with Colonel von Boeckmann, Maj. Mohs and Oblt. Winter from Bionviller to the steep Cliff, north of that Village by Name Pig Rock, Roche aux Cochons to the Top. There in a Grotto had Gen. Neuber his Command Station with his Staff and an Artillery Observation Post.

The Moon just went under and the Sun came up and colored the Spruce Trees, heavy with Snow, a tender pink and illuminated the peaceful Plaine Valley and that from the French occupied Celles. Like a Scene were on both Sides of the Valley the Forested Mountains.

The occupants in Celles were harshly alerted from the German Grenades. At 9 in the Morning reported the RIR. 70 that the French Vanguards at the Hill were taken and in they're Hand. With his Escort and the Ski Detachment Berkes, those without Skis, who were no good in the Forest, did he go in the First Line, to see what had been accomplished? At slippery icy Paths they got after an hour to the main Field Dressing Place. Then they soon came through the Forest to the Trench Line were they were almost hit with Rifle Fire from some French in the Trees.

Colonel Stadthagen, Maj. Roerdanssand and Captain von Glasenapp, who at the time lead the IInd. / RIR. 70, reported to him. His Troops had the first Enemy Vanguards in their Positions surprised but the French could under heavy Fire in that harsh Area moves back to backwards Positions.

There were only a few dead French at this part of the Battle Field. They took 4 Prisoners from the RR. 349.

At the Hill 542 and at the Hill Edge witch from there in the direction towards Les Noires Colas leads, came the Battle to a Halt. At the right Wing of the Regiment who in connection with the Saxonians and there added Jaeger Battl. It was still on. The Regiment and the Pi. Comp. lost 6 dead and 60 wounded.

A few Officers and Men in the first Line became from him, still in the Battle, the Iron Cross. Among those, the dashing Vice Corporal Lange from the IInd. / RIR. 70.

The Troops dug in at the arrived Lines. He wanted to include the Hill west of Les Collins in the defense Line since it could be occupied without opposition. His Chief advised him that with the small Force in this Section they could not hold it. Because of the hard backward connections and the incalculable Area and the distance to Bionville he gave in.

After the French had occupied the Hill they could from there reach the Hill 542 from the Flank and could control the North Street to Badonviller. To get this important point back later proved futile and did cost many losses.

Towards Evening did the French several times try to regain the Positions of the RIR. 70 but where repelled.

The Troops were on this Day and in the following Days outstanding. The Br. Kdr. And his Adjutant had earned high Honor. The RIR. 70 and the subordinate Ldst. Pi. Comp. XV. Were heroic and the Artillery done well. The Militia of the Ldst. Battl. Kempten and the Ambulance Core did exert themselves to help the battling Troops. This Day will always be a glorious Day for the XVst. RK.

On Feb. 28 begun the building of a Connection Road from Bionville up to the Hill. The Troops knew the importance of this work.

Also in other Places of the Core Front, were Roads build to the Front. Between Bucheckerich and Chaume de Lusse and at Senones. The building of the almost impassible Foot Path in to a Road to the Position of the RIR. 70 at the Hill 542 several km. In a few weeks was a top performance of the RIR. 70 and there Technical Personnel.

My Grandfather had urgently asked the War Ministry for Carry Animals for the 84st. Ldw. Br.

The new Position of the RIR. 70 made it necessary, the Comp. of this Regiment which was positioned at the left Plaine Shore, to move to the north side of the Valley. Because of that had the 30st. RD. they're right Wing to make longer to the Le Grand Brocart. For that they became from the 39st. RD. the IIIrd. / Ldw. R. 80 witch now had been put at the left Wing of the 30st. RD. at Hill 620 south of Nayemont at Le Fraiteux.

On March 2 did the French attack several times at Hill 542 north of Les Collins but were repelled.

As Proof for often optimistic and also Pessimistic Battle reports did he mention this Incident:

Gen. Neuber reported that after a repelled attack more than 200 dead French were at his Front. My Grandfather went with Maj. Mohs immediately to this Front Section. They could even with Field Glasses count only 10 brave French Soldiers that had valiantly given they're Life.

In the Afternoon of March 4 did the French again attack the Hill 542. With loud Signals and repeated Gunfire did they bring the Line fore. The 9st. Jaeger at the left Wing of the Saxonians and the RIR. 70 at the right Wing brought those brave attackers heavy losses.

The Report of the 84st. Ldw. Br. that more than 1000 dead French were for their Front, did he not trust anymore.

The City Councilor of the German Area, Excellency von Dallwitz came on March 14 with Cavalry Captain Mueller of the 15st Ulanen to St. Kreuz where my Grandfather picked them up and escorted them to the Col de St. Marie to view the Positions.

He had the wish as Reserve Officer (Maj. of Reserve in the Ul. R. 15) to view something from War. He talked with the Men and one could see that he enjoyed this.

On March 18 went my Grandfather to Luvigny in the Plaine Valley where the upper Kdr. wanted personally to see how hard it was to build the Road and Positions. He showed appreciation of the hard work and gave praise to the XVst. RK.

The Royal Bav. Gen.Field Marshall Leopold, Prince of Bav. Came on March 21 to St. Blaise. He greeted my Grandfather as an old Acquaintance since he was years ago in his Army Inspection. He was in spite of his old age mentally and bodily fit. In their Lecture Room he could show him the Position of the XVst. RK. On the Map. Then they drove over Col du Hantz to Belval and from there to Petite Roan. As much as possible were the Bav. Troops pulled together. So could the Prince at radiant Sunshine greet his Countrymen. He also went in the Front Position to greet his Countrymen of the XVst. RK. Who stood direct before the Enemy.

In Schirmeck did my Grandfather invite all Bav. Generals. At his Front and the 2 Divisions Kdrs. After Dinner they drove to the Donon were at the Pass they had a Parade. Then they went back into France to Gen. Neuber who in Luvigny had the Ldst. Battl. Kempten put together. Since for this Battl. With the visit of the Prince, came the Bav. Medals for their heroic conduct in the Battles north of Les Collins, he asks him these personally to give to the Officers and Men. This gave him great pleasure. He knew some of these Men from his hunting and Mountain Tours and could talk to them in they're Bav. Slang.

Because of a high order were on March 31. Lothringian from the French speaking Area of the RIR. 70 approximately 250 Men first to a Reserve Depot transferred. The substitute Gen. Kdo. Of the XXIst. AK. Gave replacement of only German speaking Men. A part of these transferred Men where sad to leave the Regiment they thought themselves to be good Germans and were true to the Oath. If this was necessary will always be questionable. They never had Mass Desertion A few filthy Dogs will always run, no matter what Language they speak. Those Psychologized orders do more bad because they do not eliminate bad Elements but do harm to otherwise good People.

The 52nd. Ldw. Br. became the Name 61st Ldw. Br. In the Afternoon of April 10 did he drove with a few Officers of his Staff to Chatas and went on Foot there to Laitre. The Path and Ditches there were very wet and soft. The 11ers were supposed to take a Trench Position. It was only a small Trench but the French had there worked under Ground and the Germans had that under mined. They were supposed to detonate first. He went to the Command Post of Maj. Bauer (11st. Bav. IR.) Who, as substitute for the vacationing Kdr. was in charge. At 7.30 in the Evening exploded the German Mine and ignited the French Mines. That was the Signal for a heavy Artillery Duel and lively MG. and MW. Fire. Gun Fire and Hand Grenades flew through the Air. The Room where they sat, was a wooden Shack in witch Adjutant Lt. von Waechter attended to the Telephone, and gave reports and handed the Receiver to the Maj. so he could give the orders himself. This Maj. Bauer was a Pearl, a first class Soldier, admirable, quiet, and clear and decided. His order on to the MW: "Bav. Lyon roared! " were then always a Mine flew, will always stay in his Ear. The French replied with they're Fire but no attacks. The Bav. Occupied the demolished Trench and made it ready for defense.

On May 23 reported the AOK. That Italy had declared War on Austria. The French celebrated this with loud Jubilation. They shouted at the whole Front: "Vive la France! Vive l'Italie! A bas les Boshes!"

On May 25 he drove to his left Neighbor to talk about connections and to look at the Position of the Bav. Militia at Schnierlach. They drove at the east Edge of the Vogesen to Kienzheim, there they crossed the Battlefield from Aug.28.1914 and drove for the first time through the strange Barrier who Gen. Gaede from Rheine until the first Trenches had built. It was a high wire Fence between both Army Sections that only on certain Places military guarded Passages had. It went towards the Enemy to the Area between Haicot and Cote de St. Marie.

The Gen.Kdo. Wanted to do a big Operation in the Area from Ban de Sapt and the AOK. Was notified of those proposals. My Grandfather thought to have his whole Area between Ormont and Hortomont (Hill Ridge south of le Puit) were necessary. Certainly he thought this was not enough and he wanted to include also the Section La Vercoste Nayemont (the Forested high Area between Ban de Sapt and the Street Denipaire towards east in order to control the Bottom of the Hurbach.)

The upper Kdr. agreed with these proposals.

The execution of these had a number of Obstacles. Mainly not enough Artillery and Ammunition. The attack at the Ormont made it necessary to also take more connection Positions of the Enemy. For that were not enough Forces at the Division also Infantry and Pioneers.

The execution of this Operation made it necessary to get Reserves.

Ban de Sapt was originally the Name of a Church Play from 7 Villages in the vicinity. Since at the Maps, the Name meant the Hill Ridge north of Launois (near southwest at Ban de Sapt) to south Laitre, so they kept the Name for the Hill, who is in Front of the huge Bois d'Ormont. At the description of the March back in Sept. 1914 did he mention that it was a Mistake to put not more emphasis at the Ormont. The more he thought about it, which causes then the Troops had to not occupy the Forested Mountain, the more he came to the Conviction that next to avoid the Forest Battle, mainly Quarter and provisioning pulled the Troops in the lower Villages. One has to think that the Reserve and Militia Formations in this section had no Field Kitchens. The Battle reports spoke from the "first Line" witch often was already left. That used the French, who were better trained in Mountain War, and moved in those Positions. When the upper Leaders then on the next Day wanted to reoccupy it was costly on Effort and Blood and in spite of that it did often not work. In that was built at End of Sept. the Front Line of the Core. In Front of the

Ormont dominated the Hill Ban de Sapt, 600m. High, the Area. The 10st. Bav. RI. Br. stood in the Villages Laitre, Launois, Nayemont tight against the Enemy. In hard Battle struggled the Bav. Hero's to take from the French, a Trench Section, or to blast a Bunker, or to take Prisoners and Booty. After the tactical Look in which the Leaders and Troops were trained in Peace, it was understood that it was necessary to occupy a Hill in the further course of War came the Belief that at Places that with Enemy Observation the Artillery Fire could be steered at a Hill. The own Position would be better at this side of the Hill, The Infantry Fire at the before Area is limited.

On May 27 was the upper Kdr. with him at the Hill south of Chatas where the 30st. RD. had an Observation Post at Ban de Sapt and could oversee the Positions. The upper Kdr. agreed with the Judgement of my Grandfather and gave the necessary Reserves for the Battle especially Artillery.

It was necessary, before the main Operation, to move the German Position to the Hill south of Laitre north of La Fontenelle, named Fox ground, for, because the French could from there hit them in the Flank.

On May 30. Carried the 30st. RD. this preparatory Operation out and reported that they had reached the east Edge of the lower Fox ground in 500m. Wide.

On June 1st. did he rode with his Officers to the Hill Ridge southwest of the Moulin de la Vaux were the Fox ground Position was. The Landscape was very nice, heavy fissured and with steep ascent, witch from Hill 521 souths of Senones towards Ban de Sapt reached. They shined like all Vogesen Slopes in decoration with the Gorse Flower Bloom. They had to leave the Horses at the Mill brook and from there they had to climb the Hill. First he visited the section Kdr. who showed him the Course of the Battle with the Map. He recognized that the Intention of the Division and Brigade was not reached. The French could still attack them in the Flank. As he walked then through the troublesome Trenches he was even more Shure. The Men worked hard on building the Trenches even so the ordinary Soldiers could see that this Line was bad. His Opinion about the Battle and the building of the Positions that were won and the Command dispenses and the tactical Experience he wrote in a Letter to the 30st. RD. Mainly he said it is the Duty of a higher Leader often and as quickly as possible to look personally at the Condition of the first Line.

The advance on May 30st. was so, that now they could attack at the Hill of Ban de Sapt.

For the Attack on June 22nd. Became the 30st. RD:

From the 39st. RD. 2/3 of the 4st. / Bav. Foot AR. 2 (heavy Field Howitzers). 1 Platoon of the 3rd. / Bav. Foot AR. 2 (heavy Field Howitzers), 1. And 2. Ers. Battr. / Bav. Field AR. 4 (1 Field Howitzer), Staff of the Ers.Abt. Of the Bav. Field AR. 10. From the 19st. Ers. D. Half of the 7st. / Saxonian Foot AR. 12 (Mrs.) and the Bav. Ers. Battl. 11 and the Br. Ers. Batt. 82. The 39st. Became from The Gen.Kdo. The order on June 21 to perform bigger attacks at Lusse and in the Forest north of Wiesembach. The French probably noticed the Intention; because they worked hard on they're Positions. Also was lively Traffic observed in the Area of St. Die. In the Night came the Jaeger Battl. 8 with 3 Comp. and were activated in the Morning as Core Reserve north of Laitre and south of Launois.

On June 22 at 2.45 in the Afternoon did he arrive with his Staff at the Command Post at the Forest Edge east of Nayemont. All of a sudden begun heavy Artillery Fire. The French also started and hit also the Area south of Ban de Sapt so they're Observation Post was in the Fire. They could clearly see the start and the execution of the assault; which was done lively and with dash.

At 9 in the Evening did he go with Maj. Mohs and a few Officers of the Staff to Laitre where over a 100 Prisoners were taken. Sadly were also many heavy wounded of the brave Bav. Troops there. They walked through the Maze of the Trenches up to the Command Post of the Regiments Leader of the Bav. RIR. 11, Maj. Bauer. From him did they learn many details of the attack and he enjoyed the calm of this excellent Soldier.

At the walk back he visited Maj. Schaaf, Kdr. of the IInd. / Bav. RIR. 11. Who was wounded from a Grenade Splinter in the back He was in a lot of Pain and tried to overcome it with a Bottle Champaign.

They were back at 2.30 in the Morning in St. Blaise.

On June 23rd. at 6.30 in the Morning did they drive again to they're Observation Post. At 11 in the Morning did the French attack with break up in the Artillery Fire. The French left 235 Prisoners from the Line IR. 132, Territorial Regiment 43 and Art. R. 4 also 3 MGs. and 1 MW. German losses on dead were considerable, because of the French Artillery Fire. In the Afternoon he went to Launois to the Bav. RIR. 14. On the previous Day did the attack there not go as they hoped. The German Artillery did allegedly not destroy a French Stronghold west of Launois, so the attack Columns, were from left flanked, could not move forward. They had seen from they're view point that parts of the Columns had to move back. On the contrary the good leads Comp.took further north the first French Trench and occupied it. In the Evening came a report from the Bav. RIR. 14 that sounded good. In the Morning came another report that the French in the Night had taken almost the whole Comp. Prisoner. When he went to Launois he found the Troops in a down Mood. He calmed the Men with encouraging words but after finding out what had happened he had to scold the Regiments Kdr. that he had left the forward Comp. without support even so he had enough Forces.

The Day of Ban de Sapt had a morally bad effect on Colonel Abel (6st. Bav. IR.). He called in sick and went on Furlough. He was later promoted to Kdr. of the 15st. Bav. IR. And died on Oct. 23. 1916 in the Brule Gorge at Douaumont as a brave Soldier.

The Situation at the Top of the Ban de Sapt was not good. North was the totally shot to pieces La Fontenelle, south the Positions opposite of Launois in the Hands of the Enemy. Because of that was the German Line a good Target for the French Artillery because they had good observation from the side. His Chief was right, he knew right away the Danger. They both were of one Mind to do the attack at least to the Forest Edge of the Hill. The AOK. Did not approve that Plan, It wanted to take only the Hill Ridge. They also did not allow the right amount of Ammunition and the heavy Howitzers. They both had hesitation about those Measures.

On June 24 did he change the Bav. RIR. 11 with the Bav. Ers. R. 2. The Position building continued. The Bav. RIR. 11 became reinforcement with MG. Platoons.

On June 25 were Prisoners caught from the French Positions. Trench work continued but was interrupted also at Night with Artillery Fire. The Bav. RIR. 14 were relieved with the Bav. Ers. R. 4. The IIIrd. / Ldw. IR. 80 stayed in the section of Launois. On June 26 exchanged both Brigade Staffs they're Sections, so the 30st. RD. Stood now:

> At Senones the 10st. Bav. RI. Br. with the RIR. 11 and 14.
> At Laitre the 5th. Bav. Ers. Br. with the Bav. Ers. R. 2, Jaeg.
> Battl. 8 and Br. Ers. Battl. 82.
> At Launois the Bav. Ers. R. 4 and IIIrd. / Ldw. R. 80.

The AOK. Ordered in the next few Days that the reinforcements which the Core had received had to go back. On June 30. Was the Saxonian MW. Abt. 22 transferred to Saarburg, the RMG. Comp. 3 to Rothau, on July 3 the Jaeg. Battl. 8, without Radf. Comp, back to the 61st. Ldw. Br. This intervention in the Distribution of the Troops in his Section did he find serious. The personally spoke Suggestions to the Army Leader where rejected. My Grandfather seen the Disaster coming when also the heavy Howitzers on July 6 from they're Position at Grandrupt were pulled out and given to the 19st Ers. D. the French Artillery Fire of heavy Caliber became heavier and the Enemy did many Airplane Observation's.

At an Inspection of the first Lines at the Hill Edge of the Ban de Sapt was he accompanied from Maj. Mohs and Captain Toepfer. He spoke with a Jaeger Guard of the Radf. Comp. / Jaeg. Battl. 8 who told him in detail about the Area and the Enemy. He told the Leaders up there to use the Night to cut off the old French Trenches. Towards La Fontenelle and to St. Jean d'Ormont was the Danger near that the French under the cover of a Gunfire attack, would from 2 sides move in the Trench Labyrinth, before the Men could be ready to fight. They became Artillery Fire up there, because every move or a Head shown above the Trench was visible from French Observation Posts at the Ormont.

The attack intention of the French became clear. In spite of that continued, at order of the AOK. The changes of the Troops in his Core Section. On July 6 and 7 transferred the 2nd. / Ldw. R. 99 from the 30st.

RD. back to the 84st. Ldw. Br. The 1st. / Ldst. Battl. Rosenheim came from Markirch to the 30st. RD. Staff and the 2nd. / Ldst. Battl. Passau, 1 Comp. from the Ldst. Batt. Rosenheim, 1 from Wasserburg and 1 from Kempten transferred to the work detail in Lothringia. This caused uneasiness in the Command structure at the Divisions and Brigade Staffs. On July 8 did he drive with his Chief to the 84st. Ldw. Br. Were the upper Commander have gone, to view the Positions at the north Plaine Shore.

In the Morning was reported that the Hill at Ban de Sapt was under heaviest Artillery Fire, even 220mm. Grenades. Also at the 39st. RD and at the Border Rim, were the Positions under heavy Artillery Fire. The Army Leader aloud the reinforcement with Ammunition.

The 30st. RD. reported at 6.15 in the Afternoon that an Enemy attack were imminent at the Ban de Sapt. Excellency Baron von Falkenhausen, with whom he was at that time in Luvigny with Gen. Neuber, admitted that the Situation was more serious than he had thought.

After they got back to St. Blaise did he drive with Maj. Mohs to Chatas. They went to the Command Post where the Staff of the 30st. RD. was.

The French succeeded to break into the German Positions at the Hill at Ban de Sapt and at Launois. They were still fighting. At 9.15 in the Evening was it known that the Battle Position northwest of Launois was taken by the French only further east was the Position still held. The Bav. Ers. R. 4 caught a few Prisoners from the French Line R. 23.

The 39st. RD. became an order to prepare 1 Comp. and 6 MGs. in La Grande Fosse, who then were moved to Chatas.

At 11 in the Evening did my Grandfather report to the AOK. That the Hill at Ban de Sapt was occupied from the Enemy. He asked for reinforcement especially Howitzers. The AOK. Gave the Ist. / RIR. 60 with whom the Hill Position was to be retaken.

Without a Bombardment from heavy Artillery was this not possible. It became known on the next Day, that the Troops in the high Position where completely under Enemy Fire. The French continued on July 9 they're heavy Fire so it was impossible to move forward in the old Positions. The 5th. Bav. Ers. Br. had not enough downward staggered. The Men was in the Bunkers and Trenches tight together. When, after hour long Fire, the

French from the right Flank from La Fontenelle at the backward Slope, broke in, was little resistance done.

After French reports was the conduct of the brave Maj. Michahelles from the Bav. Ers. Battl. 11 exemplary. The Enemy took 5 MGs. one German and one French repeat Canon, who was taken on June 22, 26 Officers and 1192 Men.

On the Enemy side fought: Line Regiment 23, RR. 357, Territorial R. 43 and 115, Jaeg. Battl. 13, much heavy Artillery, also a Battr. 220mm. Howitzers.

He pulled everything possible from his Core Section. The AOK. Gave half of the Howitzer Battr. Of the 19th. Ers. D. to the 30st. RD.

It started now again the asking for reinforcement of Battr. And Ammo. And the decline from the AOK. He knew that the French would not be satisfied with the Top Position of the Ban de Sapt. They probably wanted the connection Trenches to Launois.

The AOK. Transferred on July 13 the Regiments Staff of the RIR.73, the IIIrd. / RIR. 73 and the IIIrd. / RIR. 78 in the Breusch Valley. These Troops could be used from the Core only after proposal from the AOK. And a break through from the Enemy.

The Core could use freely the Ist. / RIR. 60. The 5th. Bav. Ers. Br. was told from him to build up and reinforce the Launois Position.

As the brave Gen. Deppert, who commanded the 5th. Bav. Ers. Br. on July 14 the first Position ascertained, did he die of a Bullet in the Head.

The French Artillery made it impossible to work at Daylight. Behind of the French Front was heavy Traffic by Train and Columns. The German Artillery destroyed a French 12cm. Battr. at Charimont and a Field Battr. At Wiesembach. The French did throw a few Grenades in the Ludwig Church in Markirch.

The 30st. RD. tried in the Evening of July 16, after a Fire attack west of Laitre, a move forward who failed with the loss of 7 Officers and 150 Men.

On July 17 gave the Core a Decree because of the experience of the Battle at Ban de Sapt. They had to build several defense Lines behind each other from which counter attacks could be made. The Comp. Leaders had to create a shock Troop with whom they could immediately, after an Enemy break in, do a counter attack. The loud "Hurrah", a close shot, a Hand Grenade, a Knife or the side Arm always has an effect. The Section

Kdrs. Had not only on the Telephone to move Reserves but they had themselves to be at the Point and lead through the Enemy Fire.

The AOK.Wanted with the Group of Genlt. Fritz von Unger at Leintray northwest of Blamont an Operation initiate. They pulled all available Troops out of the Core Area. The Core became the order to hold the Enemy and to lead they're attention away from the Operation. The XVst. RK. Had to give back the Howitzers, the half 4ˢᵗ. / R. Foot AR. 14, and several 10cm. Canons. My Grandfather asked to leave all this for him, since they're use was necessary for the defense of the expected French attack. In spite of that they were moved on July 22. The Battl. Of the RIR. 73 and 78 were transferred to Weiler and Baar, the Ist. / RIR. 60 to Saarburg. To a new Formation was the rest of the Bav.Ers. Battl. 11 moved to Fouday and in the Area of the Breusch Valley. The Bav. Genlt. Meyer took the Command of the 5ᵗʰ. Bav. Ers. Br.

In the Afternoon of July 24 came lively Enemy Airplane Observation. In witch manner and how the French were informed of the Positions and changes is never made clear. In spite of all Attention was it easy for People to give Signals and in the Mountain Area to leave Signs and in a few Places to sneak between Senones and the Plaine Valley. The French probably knew in time that the Howitzers and the 10cm. Canons where moved back.

At 5 in the Afternoon reported the 30ˢᵗ. RD. that the Launois Position were under heavy Fire. The 30ˢᵗ. RD. became everything that the Gen. Kdo. Could bring. The AOK. moved from the Weiler Valley the IInd. / RIR 73. This far back held Battl. Could not come in time for the Counter Attack. At 6 in the Evening he went with Cavalry Captain Bahls to the Command Post of the 5ᵗʰ. Bav. Ers. Br. An awful pretty sight was in shine of the Evening Sun, the whole back Area from Launois was under Grenade and Shrapnel Fire.

At 7.30 in the Evening came a report that the French had broken into the Position. They were moved for with the help of a then new Fire Roll. The Section Kdr. Colonel Baron von Feilitzsch from the Bav. Ers. R. 2 brought all Men that he had and went to a counter attack. He came to the last defense Lines at the Road Laitre Launois. To push the French from other Ditches was not possible. The Ruins of the Village Launois stayed in German Hands. At 10.50 in the Evening became the AOK. A Report that the Battle in the Launois Section continued and that the adjacent Sections were also under Fire. At 11.20 reported the 30st. RD. that the French had moved for to the Street Launois Fontenelle, the east part of Launois was still in German Hands, the counter attack came to the Street. A further attack was thought hopeless from the 5th. Bav. Ers. Br. under the Gen. Staff Officer of the 30st. RD. Maj. von Schaefer. He reported that the Divs. Kdr. got sick. Because of that did my Grandfather give an order:

> "The Commanding Gen. takes over the lead of the 30st. RD. Position at the East Slope of the Hill at Ban de Sapt, Church Launois and the adjacent Hill 620 Are to be held, no further counter attack to be taken. Artillery disturbing Fire at Enemy's Trench works."

A heavy laden Moment, which he blames for the loss of this Position, is the conduct of the IIIrd. / Ldw. IR. 80 at the Hill 620, 1km. southeast of Launois. At a few Days later he inspected the Position and asked the Leaders right there for they're actions. He found that from the Hill 620, because of its natural hidden Position, the Launois Position could be seen. From there could Infantry and MG. Fire hit the Flank of the Enemy and cause heavy losses by their attack from La Frecoste St. Jean d'Ormont. The Hill 620 was not under Artillery Fire. In spite of that was the Crew not used for Battle.

Later had this Battl. Under Leadership of other Officers at the Hill 786, the Bernhardstein, and the Hill 950, Tete du Violu, done excellent Deeds and with Patrol and Observation service at the Border Ridge west of Markirch acknowledgement earned.

Again the losses were very high. In the 700m. Wide and 300m. Deep Area Strip, who the French took, where at the Battle Day: 13 Officers and 860 Men. From them where missed: 12 Officers and 843 Men. According to French Statements where 11 Officers and 825 Men, from them 70 wounded, taken Prisoners. So 1 Officer and 18 Men must have been dead.

If the French Statements where correct, than the Troops must have been in shock with that heavy Artillery Fire and just gave up. Missing were parts of the 4th./ Bav. Ers. Battl. 3 and 2nd. Bav. Ers. Batt. 6; The 4st./ Jaeg. Battl.8; the 8st.and 10st. / Bav. RIR. 14 and the Fest. MG. Abt. 2.

Sadly did his definitions from July 7 fund no Consideration.

The Enemy did build the taken Area up for defense. At the next Day became the Core from the AOK: The Regiments Staff and the Ist and IIIrd. / RIR. 73 with 1 MG. Comp. and a Motorized MG. Comp. at 8.30 in the Morning came parts of the RIR.73 who were send to the Core, with Trucks over Meisengott and Steige.

The AOK. Ordered to build up the Positions and to hold. Enemy attacks immediately to push back with counter attacks.

The 30st.RD. became from the AOK. Reinforcements on Artillery and Ammunition to attack the Enemy Artillery with the help of Airplane Observation.

Deserters from the French Line R.133 at Launois spoke of big losses through the German Artillery. The 4st. / Jaeg. Battl. 8 were transferred to Markirch for a new Formation and the Bav. 4st. / Ers. Battl. 3 to the 39st. RD. The Bav. Ers. Battl. 6 were as Core Reserve moved to Saulxures, Plaine and Champenay.

The Battles at Ban de Sapt came to an End. The Area loss that came with the reoccupation of the Positions from the French was at the widest Place only 200m. But the Moral Impression on the Troops was tangible.

The brave 11ers were furious, that the Position that they took in month long Battles, were given up from other Troops.

From Aug.17 until 19 was his Majesty King Ludwig from Bav. With his Entourage, for a visit with his Bav. Troops, in the Core Section. At the Inspection Trips were in several Places lectures held for the King about Battles in which in 1914 the 10st. Bav. RI. Br. and the 5th. Bav. Ers. Br. victorious battled. The Bav. Gens. and Staff Officers and possible all Bav. At the XVst. RK. That had the Iron Cross and Bav. War Medals, where introduced to the King. He then spoke at length in his natural manner with them.

On Aug. 19 could my Grandfather give Commendation in a daily Core Order to, Patrols of the 84st. Ldw. Br. who north of the Plaine had ascertained French Troops of the Territorial R. 43 and Patrols of the 30st RD. who had north of Senones took French Prisoners from the IR. 363 and Alpine Jaeger. Especially dashing where Patrols of the 39st. RD. and where also commanded. Under all this brave Patrol Soldiers where especially Corporals Gorad and Ganser, and the Privates First Class Wagner and Fischeneuer and the Infantrist Elner from the 3rd. / Bav. Ers. Battl. 1

who had himself distinguished at Frapelle. Also was the 17 year old MG. Rifleman Frick and the MG. Rifleman Markschiess, Huf and Jost of the Fortress MG. Comp. 7 distinguished themselves at Lusse.

On Aug. 28 was Maj. Mohs transferred as Chief of the Gen. Staff of the Government Brest Litowsk. My Grandfather was happy for him, but it was for him and the Staff a big loss. They all liked his quiet and distinguished Personality. His successor at the Gen.Kdo. Was Maj. Baron de la Motte Fouque from the 39st. RD. were Maj. Baron von Rotberg (Theodor) was promoted to Gen. Staff Officer

On Sept.2. 1915 was the Day the Core Eberhardt was build. He used this Anniversary to remind all that belonged to the Core to think of the victorious Battles and to commemorate all that died on French Soil. It was there at the left Wing that Troops fought from Prussia, Bavaria, Wuertemberg, Baden and Elsa's Lothringia under his Command. They're Bravery is it to thank that the German Soil is freed and defended from the Enemy.

Genlt. Von Knoerzer was on Sept. 10 because of Sickness send on Leaf. The Trench War was not good for him. His fresh Soldier Nature wanted more. He became in 1916 the 7st. Ldw. D. and was promoted to Gen. of the Cav. and in 1918 Leader of the Core Knoerzer in Ukraine.

His Successor in the Vogesen was Genlt. Krause, who was earlier Inspector of the 1st. Pi. Inspection, who my Grandfather knew as Comp. Kdr. in the Garde Pioneer Battl. And from the War Ministry. He was a fresh Personality and filled up his Position well.

On Sept.23 was a Parade in Front of his Majesty the Kaiser and everybody will keep this in good recollection. His Majesty spoke to the Troops his appreciation. He asked his Majesty the Iron Crosses to the Officers and Men, who were named for that, personally to award. Providently he had brought the Medals for the Core along. From a List did he read the Names to the Kaiser and his Majesty gave everybody the Iron Cross personally, with a Hand shake and a friendly Word.

He reported to his Majesty that the Rhinish Jaeg. Battl. 8 on Oct. 3 they're 100 year Anniversary celebrated. The Kaiser went in front of this Battl. Who were still in the Parade and spoke Words of Praise and reminded them of the heroism of the Batt. In the War of 1870/71 at St. Private and with the Nord Army.

Then followed the Parade, the Bav. Band played and the Music of the Jaeg. Battl. 8 played. Everything went good, even the Donkeys of the Mountain Troops were in the March. The Troops positioned themselves after the Parade on both sides of the Street and the Kaiser drove through this Espalier happily greeted by the Soldiers to the Music "Deutschland ueber alles"(Germany over everything). Then they drove to St. Blaise were his Majesty and his Entourage and the Officers of the Gen. Kdo. Were together for some time.

On Sept.25 was a year gone since they moved the KHQu. To St. Blaise. They had a Celebration and the Leaders of the Village invited. The Mayor Galland who had served with the "Maikaefer" in Berlin did sit on my Grandfathers right side on the left his Cousin and Brother in Law and his Quartier Host the Shopkeeper Galland opposite of him was his Chief between the Manufacturer Thormann and the Teacher Adam. They had a few nice hours.

The Government of Germany had resolved to give the French Town Names in Elsa's Lothringia back they're old German Names witch are recorded at the Maps.

The Enemy did not dare to weaken the reinforcement of their Forces during the French attack in North France opposite of the XVst. RK.

The Grand Duke from Baden came on Sept.26 to visit his Soldiers in the Leber Valley. After the Parade which was near the Train Station Wenzel, had the Officers, Corporals and Men who had War Decorations to come to him. He talked with each one and showed an amazing personal knowledge. He knew almost all Names of the Family, Position and Events in the Home place and the Relatives Information. Such a Father and Friend of his Country Men, did they in the November Days 1918 ignominious betrayed.

On Oct. 1 was his Chief, Colonel von Boeckmann, promoted to Kdr. of the Field AR. 9. In his Place came Maj. Hassenstein, who was until then at the Gen. Staff of the Army of Crown Prince Rupprecht.

On Oct. 15 ordered the AOK. the change of the IIIrd. / Ldw. IR. 80 in the Section at Fraiteux with the Rifleman Battl. Of the 7st. KD. He wanted in the Evening to be present at the change and get to know the new Troops. As he got there they were at order from the AOK. Already moving out. So did they interfere with the Command Power of the Commanding Gen.

On Oct.27 came the Chief of the Swiss Gen. Staff, Colonel Egli to the Gen. Kdo. To Heilig Blasien. They drove together to Markirch and walked at snowfall up to the Haicot and Birschberg. There they could see in the Evening Sun the Berners Upper land with the Jungfrau. The Swiss Colonel was an interesting Man, with whom you could nicely talk. He was German friendly and believed in the German Star.

On Nov.2 died in the Field Hospital in Strasburg the Genlt. Von Gynz Rekowski. Kdr. of the 39st. RD. A real Prussian Soldier, who in the Sept. Days 1914 lead his Detachment with bravery at the Battles on the Bois de Mandray and rode on his white Horse in the Enemy Fire.

My Grandfather asked the Bav. War Ministry as the Successor the capable and wise Genlt. Grueber, who knew the Situation in the Sector of the 39st. RD. He was happy that this was done.

On Dec. 1 did he order the Artillery to Fire at the French Positions at the Hill 786, the Bernhardstein, and south from there, with good Result. It was for the Troops incomprehensible that this chance was not taken to break in the Enemy Positions. They could have done so, he thought, the Position west of Markirch was better with a forward move. The AOK. Did not allow such self Determination because of the OHL. They wanted always to check all details before a big Operation. That led to a decrease in self Determination at the local Leaders.

On Dec. 15 was the Ldw. IR. 81 relieved with the Ldw. IR. 15. The 81ner were from beginning of the War under his Command and had everywhere proved true.

On Dec. 17 came Foreign Officers for Observation into his Core Section. After the customary walk through the Positions they spend several hours in the Casino. One of the Officers told him that he had seen in a French Newspaper a Picture of the Eberhardt Cable Car from Rumbach to Chaume de Lusse, Probably send through Switzerland. It was supposed to have been built from the Engineer Eberhardt, who had invented it. From him had it only the Name it had been built by Captain Toost with the Fortress Train Building Comp. 7 and the Captain Wicke and his Ldw. Building Comp. 4 with 180 Russian Prisoners.

The Weather at Christmas was rainy and stormy. The Trenches were full of Water, in parts unusable because of the Mud. Several Dugouts were not livable. He went from Chatas over Laitre to the Fortress Eberhardt, through the Fox ground Position and the Trenches before Le Menil to Senones, he got there at dark. He came as Santa Claus and could cheer up the Mood of the Men by bringing Tobacco, Chocolate, Books and Pocket Watches, that was send to him.

On Dec.27 died the Kdr. of the newly build Bav. Ldw. IR. 15. GenMaj. Hinzler with a Gunshot in the Head. He went for the first time in his Section Trenches and had observed from an MG. Stand. The Bullet fired from long Distance went through the see slit. He died with a joke on his Lips. With the first Lt. von Sydow and von Waechter did he ride to the Forest Chapel south of Merlusse where he was lying in State in a Tarpaulin. They held a very sad Funeral Service for this brave Gen.

On Jan. 1. 1916, did he give through the daily Core Order New Year's Wishes to the Troops. They hoped that the New Year would move them from the Trench War to an Offensive move into France.

At the Hill 542, north of Les Collins, were at start of the New Year a Mine blasted which did big Damage to the Enemy Mine Work. The brave German Pioneers and Mine Workers from the Saar Area RIR. 70 were at these under Ground Works, which mostly was they're civil Job, enthusiastic, even so the Mine Work in Enemy Area was very dangerous. When he had to go through these dark Passages he was always astonished of the creative ability of the Men to work in this rocky Environment.

The Bulgarian Oberstlt. Rakoff became Permission to look at the German Trench building so he could get Experience as an Engineer Officer in Mazedonien and Saloniki. He arrived on Jan.14 with a few other Men at the KHQu. My Grandfather drove with them to Beulay. Then they walked for to La Frapelle. Oberstlt. Rakoff spoke acknowledgement about the Work in the Face of the Enemy. On the next Morning they rode from Moussey up to the Hill Ridge. It was a Pleasure for him to show the Bulgarian Ally they're Work in the Forest between the Cliffs. The brave Man worked, in Places only 12m. From the Enemy, and stood Guard. They had good oversight from the Observation Post.

On Jan. 16 did the Core loose the 13cm. Canons on order of the AOK. These Canons were already before the War taken out of use, but did in this Trench War splendid work. The Battr. Leaders and Men knew how to bring this Weapon to good use. Many times had the Enemy found out, at St. Leonard and Area, what the heavy Grenades could do, that the

Battr. Between Lannequin Ferme south of Chatas and Belfay les Braques did send.

On Febr.1 fired the French with 5 Field Battr. And a few heavy Battr. At they're Position at Frapelle. Sometimes became the Fire so violent that an attack might be imminent. At 4.30 in the Afternoon became the 30st. RD. an order, one light and one half heavy Field Howitzer Battr. To hold for insertion at the 39st. RD. The Core kept 2 Comp.of the Bav. Ers. Battl. 1 in Saales for Reserve at this Division. Since the Fire continued were shortly thereafter from the Army Reserve south, 2 Battl. And 6 MGs. and a Truck Column made ready. At beginning of dark calmed the enemy Fire. The French had not attacked.

At the east Edge of the Bois de la Garde was a Patrol Operation prepared with the Code Name "Nachtigall".(Nightingale) The 39st. RD. was ordered with the Preparation. The Division became for reinforcement the Bav. Ers. Battl. 1 and 2 and the Jaeg. Battl. 8 came to the Core from the Army as Reserve to Weiler.

On Febr. 12 did, in spite of heavy Fog who later left, begin the "Nachtigall" Operation.

He was with his Staff at Noon at the Observation Post at Hill 690, 2km. northeast of La Parriee. At 1 in the Afternoon were a Mine blasted and the German Artillery started, which the French replied. The German Artillerist's thought that they're Fire had effect and reported that the French Battr .was destroyed. At 3 in the Afternoon moved a German Patrol at the Hill, called "Fernsterberg" (furthest Mountain), for but were with heavy Curtain Fire stopped in Front of the French Trenches. Further south succeeded the Bav. Ers. Battl. 9 with a heavy attack to break into the French Fortress and brought 30 French Prisoners from the Jaeg. Battl. 120.

The Fortress became occupied but had to be evacuated at Night because the French Artillery took it under Fire. This Operation had cost 22 dead and 65 wounded. The Enemy first Position which was destroyed by the Mine blasting came in their defense Line and was build up.

At the 30st. RD. was on Feb. 16 a Patrol Operation prepared at which with a sudden attack at a Field Guard southeast of Celles Prisoners were to be caught.

The Kdr. of the R. Hus. R. 9, Maj. Bleibtreu Ul. R. 15, who was commanding in this Section of the Plaine Valley, was ordered to lead this.

The pre works which he had planned because of the arrangements between the 30st. RD. and the 84st. Ldw. Br. gave the Operation the impression of a big attack. It was a big number of Battr. Made ready. The success of the attack was based on the result of the Artillery and a surprise move forward after demolition of the Obstacles. The Artillery had fired on previous Days and the French became wise because of that and had send Patrols in the Area for 3 Bav. Comp. under Maj. Rietzschel (22nd. Bav. IR.) Had positioned themselves in the Forest and the Enemy Patrols were to harass them in Flank and Back.

The assault Columns were at dark already at the Area and waited for the demolition Fire of the Artillery, who because of Fog and rain did not start. They did not want to be a Danger to their own Troops.

In the Morning he went with Maj. Baron de la Motte Fouque and the Staff Officer, 2nd. Lt. Luehmann from the RHR. 9 to Maj. Bleibtreu. He was sad about the bad Weather which hindered the Operation. Several Messengers confirmed French Patrols in the Area. With his Companions a few Hussars and Artillerists did they went through the wire impediment down in the Area to the attack Troops. On the Path there they met a Master Sergeant who reported that Maj. Rietzschel had ordered to move back and he was ordered to prepare Provisions for the 3 Comp. A few Min. Later he was taken Prisoner by the French, without him been able to call them for help In a wide Front did they go for and he met 2 Soldiers who took down the Telephone wire. Directly after that came the retreating Detachment towards them. The Maj. reported that he had to give up the Operation because the French Obstacles where not destroyed and they had time to bring reinforcement.

The Path back was hard especially for the MGs. and Ambulance Core.

On Top of the Master Sergeant did the French take 2 more Men from They're Troops. That he went personally so far for was probably careless but it made a big Impression on Officers and Men since the Mood was down because of the missed attack.

Since a few Days they could hear the Canons at Verdun. They envied the Comrades who could attack forward while they were tight to the Trenches.

On March 14 did the French Fire with Artillery and Mines at the Hill positions at the left Wing of the 39st. RD. and the German Positions at the Border Ridge. Maybe it was a Demonstration for the Operation at La Frapelle, and at 4.30 in the Afternoon they attacked in that Section. The German Artillery and MG. Wall Fire did keep the Enemy from moving for in a wide Front. They could only break into a forward Trench and take a few Men there Prisoners.

On March 31 did a 10cm. Canon of the Core shoot down a French Captive Balloon. The delight of the Battr. Was big and they gave him a painted Caricature. After a few days later came a Letter of a French Officer in their Hands that said that the Observer had lost both Legs.

In the next Days were several Patrol Operations taken. At the Border Rim of Hill 786, the Bernhartstein, and at the Hill 950, the Tete du Violu, were 7 Alpine Jaeger from the French Jaeg. Battl. 13 taken Prisoners.

The Corporal Seybold from the 3rd. / Bav. Ers. Battl. 1 took in the Fave Valley 2 Prisoners from the Territorial Reg. 115. He gave this Man the Iron Cross 1st. Class.

On April 10 came the Chief of the Bulgarian Gen. Staff, Genlt. Jostow, to Heilig Blasien to look at the Core Positions. My Grandfather chose the Hill 670 north of Senones. They walked over the Road Cross to the first Line and back to the Observation Point 670 from where you could overlook the Ban de Sapt, the Ormont and the Hortomont. The Bulgarian Gen. was interested how the Trenches where fortified and he was thankful for the instructive Tips. They parted as good Friends. Unfortunately did the Gen. Not live much longer

Gen.Oberst Baron von Falkenhausen became on April 25 the Pour le me rite and was promoted to upper Kdr. of the Shore Defense. His successor was the Gen. of the Infantry d'Elsa who was soon promoted to Gen. Colonel. The Army Detachment became the Name "Army Detachment A".

On April 25 was, to better the Positions of the 84st. Ldw. Br. North of les Collins, the Operation "Schnepfenstrich" to be executed who's Leadership he kept for himself. Gen. Neuber led the Infantry, Colonel Fehr the Artillery.

These were to be used: under Maj. von Goerne the Jaeg. Battl. 8 with the Pi. Comp. 249 at the right Wing at the French Positions on the Slope of Hill 542 south and west from Allencombe.

Under Maj. von Broesigke the Br.Ers. Battl.82 with the R. Pi. Comp 88 at the French Positions west of the Forest Office.

At the left Wing under Maj. Schubert the Bav. Ers. Battl. 4 from the Hill North of Les Collins at the Hill 585.

With his Chief and a few Officers of his Staff did he go in the Morning to Allarmont. They drove with the Cable Car to the Command Post, the Adlerfelsen, (the Eagle Rock) were the Telephone wires where laid. The Artillery Fire surprised the Enemy who after a long time answered. At the appointed time broke the attack Column for and got to the first French Trenches. At the Jaeg. Batt. 8 stayed the second waves at they're starting point and did not have the Courage to follow. Since the first French Positions at the Slope at Hill 542 were overrun with the first brave attack and the attackers, west of the Sawmill resistance became, did they from the overrun French, who came out of their Bunkers, got shot to pieces in the back. Since they were forsaken from their Comrades, they were, after brave Resistance, taken Prisoners. The personal influence of the Battl. Kdr. who's Command Post was far behind the Front, was missed.

The Br. Ers. Battl. 82 came from the Hill through the Forest down and stood in Front of the not destroyed Barriers and became involved in Combat.

The Bav. Ers. Battl. 4 that moved for against the Hill 585 could win Area but Flank Fire stopped them, it came back with 84 Prisoners from the French RR. 363 and Territoral R. 43 among them 1 Officer, 3 MGs. and 1 MW.

The German losses where substantial: 70 dead, 180 wounded and 34 missed.

The first Reports of the Battl. Were good. He personally checked if they were exaggerated and could find on the next Day that the Positions were not better.

At they're right Wing had the Saxonian Troops of the 19st. Ers. D. with they're Fire intervened and had accomplished that the French could not use their success to hit the 8st. Jaeger any more. Again he had to mention how important it was to give correct Reports.

The next Day brought Patrol Operations in several Places mixed success. At the" Schlangenburg" (Snake Cassel) at Senones were 9 Prisoners from the French RR. 299 brought in. However at the Position

"Felsengrund" (Rock Ground) they lost because of French MG. Fire 1 Officer and missed 4 Man, also at La Faite south of Launois they missed 3 Men.

On May 25. 1916 became finally the Badische Ers. R. 29 the right Name of the Battl: Br. Ers. Batt. 58 (1 to 4 Comp.) I. Battl. Br. Ers. Battl. 84 (5 to 8 Comp.) IInd. Battl. Br. Ers. Battl. 82 (9 to 12 Comp.) IIIrd. Battl.

On May 17 was Lt. Ziegler from IR. 87, who later as second Lt. and Leader of the Fighter Squadron 41 and on Sept. 3. 1917 was deadly shot down at Ensisheim, and Lt. Baron von der Tann from Badischen Leib Gren. R. 109, who on Feb. 2.1918 at the Fighter Squadron 24 at Bellemengliese in Aerial Combat died, from the Fl. Abt. 65, Kdr. Captain Pretzell, who was put with the XVst. RK. Involved in an Aerial Combat with a French Fighter Plane over the Area from Ban de Sapt. They had to land with a shot up Propeller at Salzern and the Airplane tumbled over. Both Officers where not hurt.

On Aug. 18 he inspected at the Airport in Schlettstadt at the Fl. Abt. 65 an Airplane that in the Area of St. Leonhard was hit with a direct hit. The Airplane Bottom was ripped off and the Fuel Tank was hit. The whole Airplane Body was riddled with Holes. Both Men were lifted up from they're Seats. The Pilot did not lose Control of the Airplane and flew through French Fire over the Vogesen Ridge to Schlettstadt and landed. He gave the Pilot for his brave deed the Iron Cross. The Observer, Lt. Baron von der Tann was congratulated that he was again saved from Death.

The continued Operations of the French at the Border Ridge were to get a counter Reaction. The 61st. Ldw. Br. became the order the Operation "Laubheu" (Leaf Hey) at the Hill 950, Tete du Violu, and the Hill 786, the Bernhartstein to prepare. It was supposed to demolish the French Trenches and Obstacles.

On June 10 did he observe from the Hill opposite of the Hill Violu, Hill 950 that the Artillery and MWs. In spite of Rain and bad sight had good results.

The dashing lead Patrols from the Ist. and IIIrd. / IR. 80 and from IInd. / Ers. R. 29 broke in 3 Places in the French Trenches and demolished them. They came back into their Positions with 1 Officer, 16 wounded and 1 wounded French from Jaeg. Batt. 22. They're own losses where: 3 Men dead, 1 Officer and 12 Men wounded.

The Artillery and Mine Thrower Observers went with the Patrols to see the result of they're Fire. With Core order did he tell everybody his appreciation?

On June 17 was at 12 Noon at Hill 542 north of Les Collins a Mine explosion done in which the first French Trench was buried and according to Enemy reports, which were overheard, 2 French Post Places with 41 Men demolished.

On June 24 brought an Operation southwest of Lusse at the Bav. Ldw. IR. 15 after the Enemy Fortifications were destroyed 16 Prisoners from witch 12 where from the French IR. 227 and 4 from the French Pi. Battl. 11. They only had a few wounded.

From the Bav. War Ministry was now the already done new Distribution and designation of the Bav. Br. Ers. Battl. From June 22. 1916 ordered.

To the first Bav.Ers. Br. belongs: Bav. Ers. R. 1 (I.II.III.) (Up to this time Ers. Battl. 1,3,4) and Bav. Ers. R. 3 (I. II. III.) (Up to this time Ers. Battl. 10. 11. 12.) To the 5. Bav. Ers. Br. belongs: Bav. Ers. R. 2 (I. II.) (Up to this time Ers. Battl. 7. 8.) and Bav. Ers. R. 4 (I. II.) (Up to this time Ers. Battl. 5. 6.) To the 9. Bav. Ers. Br. belongs: Bav. Ers. R. 5 (I.II.) (Up to this time Ers. Battl. 2. 9.)

On June 30 were at Senones 7 Prisoners from the French Trenches brought in. Against that did they have no luck in the Night to July 4 in the Position Fuchsengrund.(Fox Ground) 3 Patrols from Infantry and Pioneers under the Leadership of vice Sergeant Bohrer from the IInd. / Bav. Ers. R. 2 came, after overcome the wire Obstacles, which they had destroyed with long Sticks with Dynamite, up on the watchful Enemy, who hindered the Bav. With they're Gun fire from moving for. They had no losses.

On July 10 were on the Violu 8 Prisoners brought in and a Deserter. At Senones was 1 French caught. It stayed with such small results.

On July 20 at 6 in the Morning did he drive with the upper Kdr. to Senones. They inspected the Positions all the way down to Allarmont. G.O. d'Elsa was satisfied with what he observed. The Troops had worked hard and he did acknowledge it.

On July 24 did he go to Schlettstadt to the Funeral of Lt. Pretzsch from the Field Fl. Abt 65, who a few Days before at the Train Station Wenzel in the Leber Valley had crashed and burned.

The Army Leader was with him on Aug. 10 in the Positions of the Bav. Ers. R. 5 on the east Edge of the Bois de la Garde. It was a nice and hot Day and the Path up from the Bottom of the Blanc Ruisseau, a side River of the Fave in the Wiesembach Valley from Le Mont. The walking through the narrow Trenches in the Area south of Merlusse was hard after they had walked from the Col de St. Marie through the Forest north from there. You had to go bend down through the deep Dugouts or you would hit your Head. Excellence d'Elsa was still good at walking and gave high Praise about the Trench work. Also the Divisions Kdr. Gen.Grueber, was fresh and untiring, but the peculiar Gen. Mark, who lead the 10st. Bav. Ers. Br. was in spite of his slim Figure panting and complained about the Path. When they reached the Rim, they ate a little Breakfast, which they had brought, and then they went down to La Parriee, were he gave Iron Crosses to some Men.

There waited they're Horses and they rode over the Hills to Lubine.

On Sept. 5 was his Chief, Oberstlt. Hassenstein, transferred as Chief of the Gen. Staff to the Gen. Kdo. Also were the Captains of the Gen. Staff von Tippelskirch and von Wangenheim transferred.

Chief of the Gen. Staff at the Core became the Bav.Maj. Knight von Reinhardt. As Gen. Staff Officer came Captain von Hoesslin.

The XVst. RK. Became on Sept.7.1916 the XVst. Bav. RK. In the following Days were also other Officers of the Staff and many Corporals and Men transferred to the Gen. Kdo.

Because of the changes in the Staff did he have more work and was often with the Troops to keep the connection between the Gen.Kdo. And the Troops smooth until the new People were established.

A few dashing Patrol Operations brought several Prisoners.

Again did an Airplane from the Field FL.Abt. 65 crash after a hit from Enemy Artillery Fire. It fell on the German wire Obstructions. The Pilot Lt. Hangy and the Observer Lt. Baron von der Tann, where not hurt.

He was many times Guest at the Officers of the Flight Detachment, they're Leader, Captain Pretzell, was a good Friend of his.

The Chief of the Gendarme in the German Areas, GenMaj. Baron von der Borch was with him for a Conference. His Gendarmes did have before the War, because of the political conduct of the Government opposite of the People, not an easy time. Therefore they often did not know what to do with the People. In his Core Section they always had support.

In the Afternoon he drove to Schirmeck was an Ldst.Battl. Was loaded up and he wanted to say good bye. While there he visited a Field Hospital. There he had a moving Experience. The devoted Nurse Else, the Daughter of Gen. Grueber, had asked him, in accord with the Chief Dr. to give Iron Crosses to heavy wounded. A Jung Pioneer was from a Mine heavy wounded on Head, Shoulder and Breast. He was unconscious. As my Grandfather bends over him and told him that he would get the Iron Cross in the Name of the Kaiser, did he take a deep Breath and tried to come up a little and said "Thanks, Thanks a thousand times."

On Oct. 14 did he get his first Leave in the War and he drove to Baden Baden. There he was greeted by his Wife and younger Daughter. On Oct. 16 did he celebrate the Birthday of his Wife, when a Telegram arrived:

"Big Headquarters, Oct. 15. 12.50 Afternoon.
To Gen. of the Infantry von Eberhardt,
Leader of the XVst. RK.
I appoint you for the duration of the War Leader of the
Xst. RK.

Wilhelm R."

He was very happy, even so he was sad to say good bye to the brave Leaders and Soldiers of the XVst. Bav. RK. Because he hoped to get out of the narrowness of the Trench War and get to be moving forward.

As Leader of the XVst. Bav. RK. Was the Gen. of the Artl. Knight von Hoehn promoted.

On Oct. 25 did he say good bye in Heilig Blasien.

It was a peculiar Emotion as he drove from Strasburg over the Rheine and seeing the Tower of the Cathedral for the last time. Would he see one more time this Landmark of German building Art? The Vogesen disappeared on the Horizon, what all had he experienced there. How much Blood had flown! On French Soil did he succeed the German Border from the Hills south of the Donon to the Violu east of the Bluttenberg to defend and hold against all Attacks. His Whish was that this Beautiful German Elsa's may further stand against all French Attacks. He was Shure that his successors would see to that.

He drove with a happy Mood in a new Future.

In Galician

In Berlin he had with his Wife and younger Daughter a comfortable Evening in his Apartment.

In the Evening of Oct. 26.1916 did he drove with Ordinance Officer, from the XVst. Bav. RK. Lt. Lang von Langen from the R. Hus. R. 9. In the Night towards East. The drive through Galician was interesting. Krakau, with their high Fortresses and the many Graves, were brave Austrian and Russian and some German Soldiers rested.

Tarnow and the blood soaked Area who's destroyed Villages witnessed of heavy Battles. On Oct. 27 in the Evening they came to Przemysl and arrived in the Night in Lemberg.

At the next Morning they viewed the Town. It was full of Jews and Adventurers looking People, Galician, and Ruthenia and in between Austrian and German Soldiers. The Churches were full of devout People, and at the Markets and Streets where all possible Things sold.

At Noon came the Ordinance Officer, Lt. Schuster from Drag. R. 16 with the Car from the Xst. RK.

We drove over totally neglected Streets, they often were covered with Knee deep Mud, to Rohatyn were he reported to the upper Kdr. of the south Army, the Bav. Gen. of the Infantry Count von Bothmer. He was received with a pleasing manner. The Chief of the Gen. Staff of the south Army, Colonel Knight von Hemmer, was at that time on leave, his substitute, GenMaj. Baron von Nagel to Aichberg, which he had met in Berlin and later in the Vogesen, informed him about the Situation and the Task of the Xst. RK.

The South Army belonged to Army Group of Gen.Colonel Boehm Ermolli. At 8.30 in the Evening was he in his Core HQu in Martynow Nowy introduced to the Chief of the Gen. Staff of the Xst. RK. Maj.von Westhofen, who introduced him to the Officers of the Staff.

The Commanding Gen. of the Xst. RK. So far, Genlt. Fuchs was transferred as Leader of the XIVst. RK. Witch stood in the Somme.

The long shaped Village at the left Shore of the Dnjestr was scenically very pretty. The not so big Manor had plenty Room for Quarter for the intimate Staff and Office Rooms. Especially nice were the Stables for his Horses, who came after 7 Days Train ride, in good Hands from they're Hostler.

The Food was different than in the Elsa's but very good done. Meat was from many different Animals, because an Austrian loves his roast Beef, the Turk roast Mutton and the many Bav. Soldiers from the Xst. RK. Wanted something from a fat Pig.

The Russians did on Oct. 16 at Herbutow and Kunaszow, after they did they're Artillery Fire raise to Drumfire, attack. On Oct. 17 were the German Positions again under Drumfire but they did not again attack. The German attack Troops brought southwest of Herbutow 2 Officers, 350 Man, and 4 MWs. and 12 MGs. after hard Battle from the Russian Positions.

On the next Morning did he ride with the Ordinance Officer from the Vogesen for the last time, because he had to go back to the XVst. Bav. RK. They rode to observe the Area and he visited the Kdr. of the 119st. RD. witch was under my Grandfather, GenMaj. Gruenert in his DSTQu. In Ruzdwiany. It seemed hard for him, because of the Mud in the Streets to get to the forlorn Village and the deplorable Quarter of the Gen. And jet he was to learn even more of the deplorable Roads in Galician.

He was out every Day. The Horses, with a few Men from the Staff Guard, were send for. As much as possible he drove for and then rode to the Positions and then on Foot. The Horses walked on the Streets up to the Belly in Mud. They used so called Column Path who became wider every Day because the Tracks were unusable after heavy use. At the Village Bouszow was a loaded Pack Wagon with the Horses sank, the Driver was with effort saved.

They rode from this Place on the Gnila Lipa to Boslzowce for and came to an Austrian heavy Battr. That belonged to the Xst. RK. He greeted them in they're Positions.

In the first Positions before Boslzowce, were the from north coming Narajowka in the Gnila Lipa flows, the defense Line. There stood, to his Joy, the RIR. 46 who had the Number of the Regiment who's Kdr. was his Dad from 1870/71 till 1874. Also was at this Division the IR. 58 who's first

Battl. His Dad Commanded 1866 at Nachod, Skalitz and Koeniggraetz. That gave several times cause Officers and Men to tell his Relation to those Regiments and to mention the reputation of those Troops. The active Regiment 46 that also belonged to the 119th. RD. was sadly transferred, instead came the Bav. Ldst. R. 2 to the Division. The Bav. Regiment had in this Place done very well.

Since the Narajowka and further down to the Dnjestr the Gnila Lipa a good Front Barrier were, so were the Fortifications in a few Places not enough build up and wired, especially at the left River Shore where Posts moved for.

Reinforcements had to be built since Russian Patrols had taken Prisoners.

The Russian Troops opposite of the Germans, Siberian Cores, were heavily mixed and could not be called good. Almost every day where Telephone calls from the German listening Commando overheard mostly from Officers who gossiped about Leaders. They also brought in many Renegades often 10 to 20 Men, who reported at their Posts and were given from they're good People Coffee and Cigarettes. At his first Observation of the first Trenches were a few Renegades brought before him. He greeted the Troop in Russian and they answered in a Chore the Russian Soldier Greeting. As he asked in German, he only spoke a little Russian, if one of them spoke German, there answered a blond blue eyed Man whose Grandfather had moved from East Prussia in the Area of Kiev. His Name was Christian Froehlich and was then commanded by him as Horse Handler to the Horses.

The Renegades complained about the imperfect Food and the bad Treatment from the Superiors at the Siberian Core.

The Kdr. of the 75th. RD. witch also belonged to the Xth. RK. Was Genlt. Von Hoeppner. He knew him from his Lt. Time. Sadly could they only work a few Days together since he became Commanding Gen. of the Air Force. His Successor was Genlt. Von Eisenhart Rothe whom he also knew from Berlin. The DStQu. Was in Bursztyn, the RIR. 249, 250, 251 and the Bav. Ldst. R. 3 was under the Division.

Only in his Staff did he have Hanoveraner, even so the originally in the Province of Hannover mobilized RR. Were assigned to the Xst.RK.

He rode in the first Days with Gen. Gruenert to the Positions were they could see from the distance on the right Wing of the Gnila Lipa to Halicz. Because of that they had to get down early and walk, while his upper Torso sweat under the heavy Overcoat were his Feet cold because of the 1/2m. Deep Water in some parts of the Trenches. The Mood of the Men was good. At the time it was a quiet Front. Russian Artillery fired a few times but they had no big losses.

When it at times not rained and the Wind blew over the Area, did the Roads dry fast, but they became not better because the Ruts were deep and hard and a nasty Dust bothered Men and Horse.

On Sunday Nov. 5 broke for the first time the Sun through the Clouds and a blue Sky beamed as the King from Bav. With his Brother Prince Leopold and his Son, the Prince Georg got of a special Train at the Train Station Bortniki and witnessed the Parade of the Bav. Ldst. And other Formations. Next to the upper Kdr. was his Neighbor, the Wuert. Gen. of the Infantry von Gerock, Commanding Gen. of the XXVIIst. RK. There. My Grandfather was happy that his Majesty the King and his accompaniment and especially the Bav. War Minister were kindly to him and remembered his work in the Vogesen. The King gave a Speech to his Countryman and bestowed the "Big Cross of the Max Joseph Medal" to Count von Bothmer.

As dirty and deteriorate the Houses of the People from the outside were, because of the pyramid like hang Tobacco Leaves, like Hottentotten Kraals, the more pleasant you were surprised of the exact cleanliness in site of the scarcely furnished Houses. The Orthodox had always sacred Pictures and Pictures of the Czar and his Wife.

Old Man, Woman and Kids were the only People, because all Men who were able to fight were on the Front.

It was nice at the Shores of the Dnjestr who's left Shore was steep and the Garden of their House was nicely inserted. Beautiful was the Look at high Water, far over the Water Area at the low laying right River Shore you could see in the background the harsh Hills of the Karpaten. At Sunshine or Evening light was the magnificent look at the old Castle Halicz who was at a Hill near the formerly Crowning Town of the Kings of Galician and overlooked the whole Area.

You had a good overlook from there at the Russian Positions at the east Shore of the Gnila Lipa. This River flowed at this Town in to the Dnjestr. The Russians had the Street Bridge blown up in 1915. The middle Pillars with the Iron Structure lay in the River, who had in spite of the enormous weight, moved everything with the Ice Flow down River. The Pioneers had a hanging Gangway constructed over 60m. Long. It was for him, who was not swindling free, a risky Tour to get to the other side. He always looked to the other End, where the holy Nipomo stood and who shielded him from the back on the return Trip.

On the left Wing of the Xst. RK. Stood the 75th. RD. he viewed they're Positions at the Narajowka with the Genlt. Fink von Finkenstein, Kdr. of the Infantry, who was later Kdr. in Strasburg. Also in this Section did he order Improvement in the defense Installations.

He became a Report that in the previous Night 2 Sergeants, who were transferred from Home to him, both trustworthy from Elsa's and 1 with the Iron Cross, where deserted to the Russians.

About transferring Elsa's Men to the East Front was Questionable. They stopped at they're Relatives before the Trip east. There they were instigated and hoped that by going to Russia they would get better Positions in France.

He took a long ride with Lt. Schuster to visit his left Neighbor, Genlt. Von Lindequist, Kdr. of the 3rd. GD. Who had in 1911/12 in Hannover the I.R. 74 commanded that was in my Grandfathers Division. He greeted him in his DStQu. And shuck Hands with his Gen. Staff Officer, his Nephew Maj. Schroeder, who was heavy wounded but in spite of not been totally healed had come back to the Front.and Second Lt. von Koenig from the Garde Fusilier Reg. twice heavy wounded was also in this Staff.

He accompanied him on Nov.13 to the Regiments Staff of the "Maikaefer". They had sent the Horses for to Bursztyn, from there it was a hard ride to Sarnki Dolne. The Horses were already 2 hours on the Road, when they at 8 in the Morning mounted and at the soft, sticky Ground trotted along. In the RStQu. He was greeted first from the upper Music Master with the Music Regiments March."Fridericus Rex". Colonel Count von der Schulenburg, his Adjutant second Lt.Baron von und zu Gilsa and Captain von Dewitz Krebs escorted him in to the nice Casino. In the Garden played the Music his favored Marches. Then came all the

Officers that still knew him as they're Regiments Kdr. and later when he was Chief of the Gen. Staff of the Garde Core. The Maj. von Amman, Baron von Werthern, Captain von Kroecher, second Lt. Hinkelday and Lt. von Schulz. That was the rest from all the Officers that were still with the Regiment. 20 Officers were slain.

Soon he had to leave and while the Music played there Parade March, did they mount the Horses and with the Sound of the "Maikaefer Song" and a long Halali did they Gallop over Galician's Meadows, accompanied from the Jung Officers, like they had done at the Tegeler Place in Berlin. They rode with them to Ludmikowka. This was fantastic and this Day was one of the nicest of his Memories of the War.

He could spend a lot more time at the Front in Galician and not so much at a Desk, like in the Vogesen, were he had to look at the Fortress Strasburg and Land and Forest. At the time was heavy Snowfall and an icy Wind blew over the Area. In spite of that he rode much and observed the Installations behind the Front.

A ride over the Dnjestr Meadows was in spite of Snow and Ice fantastic. At one of such rides did he inspect the Austrian Air Force Comp.11, which was under his Command. He liked to talk to the brave Pilot Officers. They had at that time not many occasions to fly.

On Nov. 10 was Captain Zeitz transferred as Gen. Staff Officer to the 205th ID. Maj. von Wolff came as first Gen. Staff Officer to the Xst. RK.

From End of Nov. was the Army Leader for a few weeks on Leave in the Home Land. My Grandfather was ordered, as Service oldest, to be substitute, but stayed Leader of the Xst. RK.

On Nov.27 did he drive with Captain Wagner from his Staff to Chodorow, were the AHQu. Was moved to. After the upper Kdr. instructed him about the Situation and asked him to inspect some Troop parts and Installations in the Trenches and behind of the Front. He spends 3 Days in the AHQu. And 3 Days in the KHQu. Captain Wagner was ordered to be on his side.

The Chief of the Gen. Staff of the south Army introduced him to the Officers of the Army Staff. He came in close contact with some of them. The k.u.k. Austrian Quarter Master Oberstlt. Ferjientsik, the Bav. Maj. in the Gen. Staff Knight von Ruith and Maj. in the Gen. Staff Feeser, the first Adjutant Maj. Knight von Braun, the Information Officer Maj. Prince

George of Bav. The Osmanische connections Officer Maj. Rifaat Bey and the Kdr. of the AHQu. Maj. Knight von Porschinger.

He drove with his Adjutant, the Cavalry Captain von Pavel Rammingen, on Nov.28 again to Chodorow and on the 29st. with him and Maj. Feeser to Stryj to look at the communications Area. They passed on this long Trip the Battle Fields from May 1915 at the River Stryj. Many Crosses pointed to Graves where brave Soldiers, also some "Maikaefer" found they're resting Place.

In Chodorow reported to him the Kaiserlich Osmanische Gen. Djevad Pascha, who had the Command of the 15th. Turkish AK. Under the south Army. He spoke fluent German and was often with his Majesty the German Kaiser. He also accompanied the Kaiser Couple on their Journey to Jerusalem. He had in the World War at Gallipoli Commanded and was a splendid Soldier.

Kaiser Franz Joseph of Austria died on Nov.21. What political consequence his death, that from Destiny hard imprinted Monarch, would have for Germany, could nobody foresee at that time.

While he was in Chodorow they drove from there to a Bath, which was beautiful situated in a Spur of the Karpaten, where a School was opened under the Leadership of Maj. von Roeder from the 1st. G. R. on Foot. There were Officers, Sergeants and Men from the German, Austrian and Turkish Army instructed. It was interesting to observe the different Attitude of the Man. The most diligent and handy were the Officers of the Turks. They were not afraid to work and show they're ability.

From Chodorow he inspected the Positions of the XVst. Kaisers. Osmanische A.K. witch stood at the left Wing of the south Army. He was accompanied from his Staff by Cavalry Captain von Mach and from the upper Kdr. of the Turkish Maj. Rifaat Bey and Maj. Knight von Poschinger. They drove over Rohatyn to the KHQu. Czesniki, were Gen. Djevad Pascha greeted him in his, with Turkish Rugs pronounced Room.

It was an especially cold Day. The Path iced and in Places slick. They had to drive from there to the Place where the Horses where. He was horrified about the Saddle and Bridle of the brown Horse witch a Turkish Soldier brought. It could not be any worse, String held everything together. The Pascha rode a beautiful white Arab Horse. The Path leads through hilly Area, much Forest and many Villages, who were occupied with Turkish Reserves. In Places was the riding hard because the Horses slipped. Finally they reached the Place in a Forest opening were the to be decorated Officers and Men and a big Detachment of Troops from the first Line stood ready for a Parade. First they went on Foot in a big Shed were the to be decorated waited. He gave a short Speech, which Rifaat Bey translated, where he mentioned how much his Majesty the German Kaiser appreciated the bravery and stamina of the Turkish Troops. He then decorated the Officers with the Iron Cross IInd. Class the Men became the War Merit Medallion on black white Ribbon on the Breast. All crossed they're Arms and bowed and said thanks. The whole Ceremony made a big Impression on all. They then mounted the Horses and rode on the Slope of the Forested Hill to the right Wing of the Parade.

At the Moment that he called the Greeting "Machala! Machala!" to the Troops, broke the String which was the Saddle Strap and the Saddle slipped down and he fell in front of the Wing Men. Everybody was horrified! Choke white, knowing of his doing, called the Ordonnance who had saddled the Horse " O Pascha, Pascha! " As unpleasant as it was for him, he took it with Humor and asked the Pascha and his Companions to get down and walk along the Parade.

Then came the Parade March, who was hard on this uneven Ground. The Men gave a lot of effort but the impression was not good because of the horrible Dress especially the Foot ware which was mostly badly tied Rags. The Officers had the most adventures Weapons, from old pretty Turk Swards up to the "Hammelschwaenzen" (Sheep Tails) which the old Militia used and they saluted with them.

Cleanliness and order in the Camps and Barracks was not like in Prussia. Horrible were the Sentry Boxes, who were used for other uses.

The Kaisers. Osmanische XVst. AK. Did very good in the Defense. It was later pulled out of the Front of the south Army and send back in their Homeland were they fought in Palestine.

Before he gave up his substitute Position in the upper Command did he have many interesting talks with the Chief of the Gen. Staff of the south Army about aspiring Operations. He knew that the south Army had a big Task and that they had, following the Dnjestr towards south, to attack. He found at Colonel von Hemmer Agreement.

The hopes from this talks became true, only he could not take part in it, since he was from the begin of 1917 again on the western Front.

On Dec.12. 1916 at 12 noon were the Peace offer of his Majesty Kaiser Wilhelm IInd. With the agreement of all German Princes, given to the Alleys and at 4.30 in the Afternoon was the Peace offer of his Majesty the Kaiser Karl to the Austrian Hungarian Troops, announced.

The Divisions reported that the Troops were very happy about the Peace offer, but they all thought it would not be accepted and they would have to further fight.

Begin of Jan. was his Chief of the Gen. Staff on leave. Shortly thereafter on Jan. 13. 1917 did he became a report from the upper Command that said on order of the OHL. One Gen.Command of the south Army had to be given up. The upper Kdr. decided for that the Gen. Command of the Xst. RK.

On Jan. 14 were they supposed to be ready for Transport. He said good bye to the Troops in a Core Day order, in it he said to all Officers, Sergeants and Men of the Detachment under him live well and best wishes. He thanked them for their Performance of Duty and the completion of the Positions.

The AOK. Of the south Army ordered on Jan. 14. 1917 an Army Command:

"With heavy regret I see that the Gen. Kdo. Of the Xst. RK. After 4 month long work from the Kaisers German south Army has to leave. The Battles from Herbotow and Kuneszow connect the Name of the Gen. Kdo. Always with the History of the south Army. But also in the Trench Battles at the Narajowka did the Gen. Kdo. Carry out exemplary Duty. The fresh and military spirit, which is in the Person of the Commanding Gen., was visible in his Staff and his Troops, so he is granted to leave the Place of his work in Peace. May the Gen. Kdo. Always have rich success!"

On the Evening of Jan. 14. 1917 did they turn the lights out and left the nice Martinow Nowy in order to get to the Freight Station Bukaczowce. The Commanders of the Artillery and Pioneers stayed in the Area of the 119st. RD.

In Chodorow stood the upper Kdr. with his Staff and said personally good bye to him and his Officers. He was very sorry that he had to leave the Detachments of the south Army.

With a Foot Sack and a warm Blanket and a small Cushion under his Head could he sleep very nicely on the long Train Trip. At Daylight he read or looked at the nice Area and they exchanged Thoughts. This lasted Day and Night through north Galician over Lemberg, Przemysl, Tarnow, Krakau, Oderberg and Oppeln. Then further over Breslau, were his Chief came on the Train, Goerlitz, Chemnitz, Hof, Ansbach, Heilbronn, Karlsruhe, Germersheim, Zweibrucken, Saarbrucken, Diedenhofen, Luxemburg and then into France to Montmedy Sedan where they arrived at 1 at Night.

His oldest Son, who took leave from the big Main Quarter, came to him and could tell them that they came to the 7st. Army at Laon. He accompanied them to Moyon near Charleville.

They're unloading was done after a Trip of 5 Days and 6 Nights on Jan. 20.1917 in the middle of a Field. There was a small Station with a normal Field Train Track at Roberchamps Ferme west of the Street Laon Neufchatel north of Reims at 7 in the Morning.

In the Champagne and at Bremond

An ice cold Wind blew.—

With his Chief and a few Officers of the Staff did he drive to the KHQu. Villars Devante le Tour, from there to Laon to the upper Kdr. of the 7st. Army, Gen.Colonel von Schubert, whom he reported the Arrival of the Staff.

It was a funny chance that the Quarter for him belonged to the French Gen. Weis, and for a time had the German Gen. Lequis lived there.

On Afternoon did he drive to both Divisions Kdrs. Who were under the Xst. RK.

Genlt. Mueller (Friedrich), Kdr. of the Saxonian 47st. Ldw. D. in St. Germainmont and GenMaj. Kuester, Kdr. of the 222nd ID. In Berrieux. On Jan. 24 did he take Command of the Group Eberhardt.

With an Ordinance Officer did he went on Jan. 25 to Pont Givart, were the Horses were send to. There he spoke with 2 brave Patrols, who on the Evening of Jan. 24 brought 1 Officer and 18 Man, 1 MG. and other Booty. He acknolished and gave them Praise. He did not have Iron Crosses at that time.

From there they rode as far as possible for. At Bremond, the old Fortress from Reims, build at the end of 1870 like the Strasburg Fortress, was 1914 not defended because it could not have resisted the heavy Battr. There they left the Horses and walked to the Positions in the first Line. In the heavy Lime they had to use Pickaxes like in the rocky Ground in the Vogesen.

They were Shure that in the Spring French attacks would come on they're Front. Because of that was a lot of work to be done in order to be ready. There was a lot of work for the Officers of the Gen. Kdo.

In the many Villages and Towns in this Section, and in the first Positions, were Installations and Troops to be inspected. The Inhabitants were still there. They were later transferred to more northern Villages. The Area at the Aisne and Snippes were pretty. From the right Wing of the Front Section were the Hills from Craonne to be seen. On the left

Wing they could see from Bremond the coveted City of Reims with her Cathedral, at which they could not shoot. The Ground of the Champagne was fertile, a deep humus layer under that Lime, penetrable and crumbly. On several Places had the Troops Grief with Ground Water.

The 222nd ID. Was relieved and in their Place came the 9st. Bav. RD. GenMaj. Knight von Clauss, included were Bav. RIR. 11 and 14 and the Bav. Ers. R.3. Officers and Men greeted my Grandfather happily who had fought under his Command in the Vogesen.

Lt.Colonel von Westhoven was transferred, to the regret of my Grandfather, as Chief of the Gen. Staff of the Vth.RK. At his place came Lt. Colonel Hasse (Otto) who had been Chief of the Vth. RK. On Feb. 8 did the new Chief report to him, his clear and charming Personality spoke for him?

By going often through the Trenches he became a good knowledge of his Core Section. The Ground was tough because of the rain and walking in the Trenches was hard. It formed quickly a hard white mess on the Boots witch could only be removed by knocking and scraping with Hammer and Knife. How much did the Troops endure in the Trenches? The only consolation was that the French had the same Problem.

The 47st. Ldw. D. was end of Feb. pulled out of the Front and replaced with the 43rd. RD. Kdr. Genlt. Von Runkel. The DStQu. St. Germainmont had, since the Place had a Hospital, for the Core Staff better Room and Board as Villars deviant le Tour. Because of that was the KHQu. Moved there.

The newly build 235th ID. Kdr. Genlt. Zietlow, collected themselves as Army Reserve in the Area of Sissonne. The inspection of their training became my Grandfathers Task, more work, but with the performance of the Troops it became Joy.

On March 10 did he visit his Neighbor at right, the Gen. of the Infantry von Liebert, who 1866 in the Battl. Of his Grandfathers Father at the 58th. Took part in the Campaign against Austria and later as Governor in East Africa and Kdr. of the Protection Troops earned many Merits and was then Leader of the Gen. Kdo. 54. Also he could greet there his Chief of the Gen. Staff, Oberstlt. Hassenstein and Officers and Men who were under him at the XVst. RK.

On this Day was his Car several times stuck in snow The Population said, they had not seen so much snow in a 100 Years.

Gen.Ob. von Schubert was decorated with the black Eagle Medal and relieved of the upper Kdo. Of the 7st. Army. Gen. of the Infantry von Boehn became the Army Command. The departing Army Leader was for him a benevolence and good Companion.

In the last Days of March was the Front of the Group Eberhardt (from April 10. 1917 on Group Bremond) because of insertion of the Group Hoehn (from April 10. 1917 on Group Aisne) at they're right Wing made smaller. Fresh, fight robust Divisions where put in.

The following Flight Formations, with whom the Gen. Kdo. And the Troops in close accord worked, whose brave Pilots, with no regards of their own Safety, achieved big successes for the Xst. RK. Belonged to the Group Bremond: Grufl. 10, Capt. Geyer; Fl. Abt. 226, Capt. Spranger later Cav. Capt. Hohl; Fl. Abt. 248, Capt. Neumann later Capt. Kranz; Fl. Abt. 286, Capt. Seudel; Fighter Squadron 17, Cav. Capt. von Brederlow (Anton); Guard Squadron 1, Oblt. Seldner; Guard Squadron 5, Oblt. von Schikowski; Fl. Abt. 254, Cav. Capt. Baron von Loewenstern; Fl. Abt. 278, Capt. Schueller; Guard Squadron 19, Oblt. Hahn; Bav. Guard Squadron 29, Oblt. Vogeley.

Originally extended the right Wing west of the Aisne over La Ville aux Bois to southeast Craonne to left over the Street Neuschatel Reims to north of there. From then until summer was the Aisne from Guignicourt to Berry au BAC the west Border, while the east stayed the same with little movements. Because of that was the 9st. Bav. RD. no longer under his Command.

The Group Eberhardt had under them beginning of March: The 10st. RD. Kdr. Genlt. Dallmer, the 21st. ID. Kdr. GenMaj. Von Suter and the 43st. RD. Kdr. Genlt. Von Runkel.

If you crossed the Core Section from north to south so came the 4, for the defense favorable Positions behind the Aisne, the Retourne, the Suippes and the Aisne Marne Canal. Insight.

The right Wing leaned on the from Guignicourt to Berry au BAC to southwest flowing Aisne who had on left Shore a connection Canal. Between River and Canal, were much Forest and partly swampy Ground. In the Corner, whom this Canal at Berry au BAC with the Aisne Marne

Canal formed, was the Hill 108 with a Stone Quarry, who abruptly fell to the Enemy side. This Hill was build up as a good Bulwark. From there protracted the defense Line to Hill 91 northeast to Sapigneul and from there on the Slope of Hill 100, utilizing the Forest parcels north of the Canal to Loivre. This Place and the Hills south of the Canal, also the Hill 101, closely west of Courcy, the Hill 92 east from there and the Canal in connection, were used as defense. East from there went the defense Line over the Champ de course to south of the Modelin Ferme at the Street Fresnes Betheny.

A solid strong point was the Bremond with his old Fortress and the Battery's de Loivre and Cran de Bremond. He wanted that the forwards Positions were hard fortified so they could stop Enemy attacks. On the Place at Loivre did he point out that the French were Masters using the terrain and in using hollows and ravines. Therefore it was necessary to block these hollows and ravines, because tightly each other following Columns, could break through, in spite of Flank Fire.

The second Line, who from Conde sur Suippes over Aguilcourt Merlet Orainville Point Givart Aumenancourt Boult lead, was for the active Reserves and heavy Flat Fire Battr. Favorable. At the Hills at Prouvais were a Battle Observation Post and a Signal Station established.

On March 17 did he drive to Pont Givart and from there with Genlt. Von Runkel to several Battr. Positions to the Fortress Bremond, from there they had a good overview over the Divisions Sector and the Positions of the French.

On March 18 was the upper Kdr. Gen. von Boehn, in the Core Sector and informed himself. They exchanged and recollect about Berlin events and they're Gen. Staff Trip under Gen. Baron von Falkenhausen in the Year 1887.

On March 20 did they observe the Section at Loivre were the Fuselier Reg. 80 stood under Maj. Von Nickisch. Sadly it was Snow Storm and Rain so the crawling through the Trenches and Bunkers, who were at this Train incision east of Loivre build in, was very hard. There stood in Feb. when he took the Command, the Militia of the Ldst. Battl. Weimar, from Enemy not much bothered. Now it became unpleasant. South of the Bremond were a few Russians taken Prisoners, who belonged to a Russian Br. who was inserted opposite from them.

At the time was changing Weather, presently was Snow and very cold and then magnificent Spring Weather with warm Sun. It brought Anemones and Snowdrops out. On March 26 was the 19st. ID. Left of the Group Eberhardt put in. The Div. Kdr. Genlt. Von Huelsen (Walther) reported to him the arrival of his old Peace Div. who under his strong Leadership until Wars End was very prominent. (The French Marshall Foch wrote after the War in his Book: "The Reasons of the German Capitulation from Nov.11. 1918", that the 19st. ID. until the End should have been called Storm Div.)

On that Day did the French Canoers put they're Grenades right and left of the Road on which they walked, for so they were not hit. He wanted to find out, why after several hours of Artillery Fire at a forward Dugout, at witch 2 Guards got wounded, a French Patrol was able to break in and take the Crew Prisoners.

The Comp. Leader reported to him, that he had during the Enemy Firing from the second Line, standing next to his Dugout, observed but could not see because of the Powder Cloud. Neither he nor somebody else had at the German Artillery curtain Fire ordered. The Officer had only been there shortly and did have no connection with the forward Guard.

On March 29 had the Upper Kdr. of the Army Group, the Kaisers. Highness the Crown Prince, announced his arrival for observation in the sector of the Group Eberhardt. With Maj. von Wolf and sec. Lt. von Heyden (Ul.R. 9) did he drive to Tuilerie east of Prouvais. Genlt. Dallmer with his Gen. Staff Officer Capt. Franke came also. Soon came the Crown Prince with his Companion Gen. Staff Officer Maj. Baron von Esebeck and his Adjutant Maj. Mueldner von Muelnheim. They went up on the Hill were a Signal Station had been installed. From there they had a wonderful Oversight over the Aisne Suippes Valley to the Bremond and west at the from Enemy occupied Hills south of the Canal from Cormicy to Villers Franqueux.

At Hill 108 in the Area of the 10st. RD. was it conspicuous that the French enlarged they're moved for Position at the Hill 108 and 91. Daily reported the Regiments of the 10st. RD. the advancement of those works and had overheard that they would bring heavy MWs. And MGs. With a proposal of the 10st. RD. to attack first did he agree and came to the Resolution with a strong attack the attack Lust of the French to stop.

With his Chief, the Divisions Kdr. and his efficient Gen. Staff Officer Capt. Franke, did they plan right there the attack and decided that the move forward of the 10ˢᵗ. RD. towards Sapigneul, had not to go over the Canal. After the Enemy was pushed back and they're attack works destroyed, had the troops to go back in to they're start Positions. The Reason for this was the low Position of the Canal and it was in the Area of the superior Artillery Fire. Details of this Plan where reported to Genlt. Dallmer.

Group Eberhardt   KHQu. 21. March 1917

    Gen.Kdo. X. RK.
    Ia Nr. 43 op. secret
             Group Command

1. The Group Eberhardt will occupy the east Shore of the Aisne Marne Canal about from the blue Point 105 (southeast of the Hill 108, Map 1: 12500) to the Section of the Canal with the first Position Line of the IR. 81.

    They will so the Canal and the Lowland of the Fontaine Creek make into an important Front Barrier for they're right Wing.
2. It is not intended to move the main Battle Line. The Ground that is won to hold and the Lowland of the Fontaine Creek to block for the Enemy is the task of the advance Guards.
3. The leadership of the attack will be the 10ˢᵗ. RD. For that they become under them the right Wing of the 21ˢᵗ. ID. (Ist. / IR. 81)

    For Artillery to assist is the Group Hoehn of the 21ˢᵗ. ID. and 43ʳᵈ. RD. to bring here.
4. 10ˢᵗ. RD. gives as soon as possible to the Gen.Kdo. An attack Plan with calculation of Artillery and MWs. Ammunition and Statement of time.
5. At the other parts of the Group Front are further Patrols to prepare. The decision is to be reported.

                              The Commanding General.

Group Eberhardt   KHQu. 31. March 1917

Gen.Kdo. X. RK.
Ia Nr. 685 secret
To Ia Nr. 43 op. secret

Group Command
For the attack at the French Bridge Head
East of the Aisne Marne Canal

1. The Enemy has they're attack preparations increased. To really disturb them on the right Wing of the Group is the aim of this attack.
2. The reinforced 10st. RD. is now executing the attack according to they're Plans.
3. The won Enemy Position is north and east at Sapigneul to be building up and to incorporate in to our Trench System. Main defense Line remains the present German Line
4. The other Positions of the French Bridge Head are to be cleaned, important Installations to be destroyed, the Bridges over the Fontaine Creek to be destroyed. All these parts of the Bridge Head are before Daybreak from the attack Troops to clear. It is important to leave the Enemy in the dark over our move back and to take Measures that the Enemy Infantry can be taken under Fire if they try to reoccupy. It is at the discretion of the 10st. RD. to leave Patrols for this.
5. The Artillery of the 9st. Bav. RD. 5th. Bav. RD. 21st. ID. and 43rd. RD. will take part in the destroy and Wall Fire, also in the combat of the French Artillery and observation Stations. The 10th. RD. gets in touch with these Divisions.
6. The group Hoehn and the VIIst. RK. Are ordered in the Area north of Pontavert and north of Reims to do pretense Operations.

The Commanding General.

On April 4 at 4 in the Afternoon begun the German Artillery and MWs. Fire. At 4.40 in the Afternoon begun the French Artillery with slowly increasing Fire to answer. The German Artillery caused 2 big Detonations and Flames in Cormicy and the Fire at a Munitions Depot. At 6.30 in the Afternoon broke the German Storm Detachments for and immediately started the French Wall Fire. In the Section Steinmetz came the dashing Fusiliers of the IR. 37 in spite of heavy MG. and Gun Fire in the Enemy Trenches. The Storm Detachments of the IR. 155 succeeded, in spite of Enemy Artillery and MG. Wall Fire, the first Enemy Line to overrun. Lt. Christiansen earned himself a lot of Praise.

The Suippes Lowland was covered with Shrapnel. The German Battr. Was hit with heavy Calibers. Enemy attacks were repulsed.

The operation was successful. 12 Officers and 909 Men where taken Prisoners. 12 MGs. 18 Hand MGs. 13 light MWs. were also taken. Several Observation Posts and MW. Battr. Each with 4000 shots was destroyed.

The preparations of the French MW. Big style attack at Hill 108 was shattered. The German losses where: 3 Officers and 101 Men dead, 2 Officers at 305 Men wounded, 30 Men missed.

The French Prisoners belonged to the AR. 1, 22, 25 and 45 and the IR. 150, 261, 267 and 269 and to the 3rd. Suave Regiment. These Troops where not all Battle troops but work Troops who stayed at they're work in spite of the Fire and were caught by the German Troops.

After Dark brought the French strong Reserves over the Canal who's Bridges were in the Fire Line of the Artillery. Prisoners told later that they had heavy losses.

The stormed Positions were slowly, like ordered, left. An extreme important Booty was brought in. From the Storm Detachment C4 under Lt. Pfeifer of the RIR. 37 were from Pi. Sergeant Lambrecht of the 2nd. / R. Pi. Battl. 5 in a French Officers Dugout important Papers found which were immediately from the Kdr. of the IIIrd. / RIR. 37, Capt. Witting, at the 10st. RD. to the Xst. RK. Send.

Under these Papers was a Command of the 5th. Battl. Of the Suave Regiment for the coming attack, whose Content was of extreme consequence for the Germans. In it were next to Instructions for the Conduct of the Movements of the various Battle Phases and Statements over Force, Structure and attack Direction of big parts of the 5th. French Army.

Translation of the French attack Command captured
On April 4 from the 10st. RD. southeast of Berry au BAC
3rd. Suave Regiment. 5th. Battl.
Attack Plan

I. Order of the VIIst. Army Core.

The VIIst. A. K. operates at the right Wing of the 5th. Army between the XXXIInd. Core in Northwest and the XXXIIIrd. Core in the South.

The VIIst. Core has the order Bremond from north to encircle and to take.

The Divisions of the VIIst. Core attack in good contact with each other like so:

41st. ID. And Russian Brigade right

14st. ID. In the middle

37st. ID. Left

The movement is from the left Wing started; The Russian Br. builds the middle.

Left: The XXXIInd. Core at both sides of the Aisne has to reach on Day J: Prouvais Proviseux Evergnicourt Brienne east Edge of Forest of Grand's Usages Aumenancourt le Grand.

Right from the 37st. ID.: The 14st. Div. has on Day J to reach the Line inclusive Bremond Crane de Bremond Fermi Landau.

II. Order for the 37st. ID.

After breaking through of both first Enemy Positions they should reach first the Suippes at Merlet in connection with the XXXIInd. AK. Then is the Operation of the VIIst. Core at Bremond with an encircle attack to lighten and to cover by successively the crossings over the Suippes (Opening to North) to make accessible and finally to lay the hand at Aumenancourt and the Hill south of there (Opening to Northeast) after

167

the connection to Pont Givart with the XXXIInd. Core is established.

III. Order for the 74st. Br.

Capture of the first German Positions at Hill Spin, then the second (at the Train) and then to win the Suippes between Merlet and Orainville.

IV. Battle Section and attack Goal of the 3rd. Suave Reg.

a) Attack Section. The 3rd Suave have left from the XXXIInd. AK. And right the 3rd. Turks. North Border towards the XXXIInd. Core: Point 45/46 (first German Line at XXXIInd. AK.) Bois de la Chenille. Hill 751 (at the 37st. ID.) Battr. 63.54 (at the 37st. ID.) Battr. 71.59 (at the XXXIInd. AK.) Underpass of the Train. Hill 576. Course of the Suippes upwards Hill 576 Orainville. South Border towards the 3rd. Turks. See Sketch 41. 39, 55. 45, 71. 45, 76. 46, Bridge over the Vesle River, 94.45.

b) Attack Goals. See Sketch.

1. Goal: Line Battr. 67. 54, 82. 2.

2. Goal: Merlet and Bridges over the Suippes north and east of Merlet. Entrance into Trench at 56. 6

3. Goal:

c) Begin Distribution of the Battl.

The Battl. A and B put in next to each other east of the Canal. Battl. A right, Battl. B left, each with only 1 Comp. in first Line; The other both in deep Echelon behind. 18st. Comp. first. Behind the 19st. Comp. with 2 Platoons MG. behind the 19st. the 17st. With 2 Platoons MG. (The 17st. Comp. gives before the attack 2 Groups of Voltages to The 18st. Comp. to clean the Vampire Trenches. Those 2 Groups go back to they're Comp. when they reach the Trench.) Connection between Battl. A and B. Projection of the Vampire Trench at Point K (middle of the Bois en Deutelle at point M (southeast Corner of the Bois d'Alger). (The Bois d'Alger all to Battl. B.) Northwest Corner of the Bois Abbique (Bois Abbique all to Battl. A). West projection of the Fabric Douaumont (the Fabric All to Battl.

A). Crossing of the Trench of the 15. Dec. and the Trench Douaumont East Edge of Merlet (Merlet and Bridge of Merlet to Battl. B). Battl. C behind of the Canal.

V. Course of the Movement.

The Movement is in 3 Phases. Each Phase embraces the accomplishment of the 3 attack Goals.

1. Phase: At the hour "H" starts everything to move fore.

Battl. A and B take the first German Positions

The Point Comp. of each Battl. Arrange themselves again in the Heely Ditch, is going to be past from the other 2 and the attack Movement to the first attack Goal.

About 150m. Before the first attack wave is to be put a Wall fire Line, witch at the hour "H" starts at the first German Trench and with a speed of 100m. In 3 Min. moves fore. In the course of this Phase is the Wall fire twice adjusted:

1. from hour H + 37 to H + 40 especially at Line 56.49, 66. 32.

2. from hour H + 55 to H + 1, 05 especially at Line 61. 53. 66. 32.

This fixed Artillery Wall fire, after taking of the second and 3rd. Line of the first Enemy Position, has as purpose to allow the Infantry to get back in order, in case they got mixed up in the course of the Battle. On the other side of the first attack Goal is the Wall fire at a Line about 300m. West of the Train and parallel of there to be fixed, while the heavy Artillery continued to pound the second Enemy Position Storm ripe.

All Detachments arrange themselves as fast as possible after reaching the first attack Goal and make needy repair at the captured Line and stand by to continue the move forward at hour H + 2.

VI. Attack disposition of the Battl. During the first Phase.

18st. Comp. at point in attack wave.

2 Groups of the 17st. Comp. is added for cleaning of the Vampire Ditch. The 18st. Comp.Stops in the Ditch. The 2 Groups join again they're Comp.as soon as the 17st. Comp. has

reached the Vampire Ditch. The 18st.Comp. stops in the Heely
Ditch, is going to be past There from the 19st. And 17st. Comp.
and follows then as Reserve about 150m. Behind the Middle of
the first Line. 19st. Comp. with 1 Platoon MGs. 70m. Behind
the middle of the 19st. Comp. is as soon as the Heely Ditch is
occupied to give 1 Platoon MG. up. The whole move forward
of the Battl. Is to secure the Connection to the XXXIInd. AK.

She is to pass the 18st. Comp. in the Heely Ditch and
builds then at a further move forward in the same height
with the 17st. The left Wing of the first Line of the Battl. 17st.
Comp. follows from beginning at 100m.behind of the middle
of the 19st. Comp. passes the 18st. Comp. in the Heely Ditch
and builds the right Wing of the first Line of the Battl. At
their move forward at the other Positions. She detaches in a
half move with the order to Keep continues connection with
the first Battl. MG. 5 detaches 1 Platoon to the 19st. Comp.
1 Platoon to the 17st. Comp. 2 Platoons Following the 18st.
Comp. as Reserve from Heely Ditch.

End Goal: Occupation of a Position which dominates
the Roads to the Suippes and to Merlet. Guarantee and Fire
protection for the Place of connection to the XXXIInd. Core.

VII. Cleaning of the Ditches.

Vampire Ditch: 2 Groups of Voltages of the 18st. Comp.
from the 17st.given for disposal.
Ditch du Talus and Heely Ditch from the 18st. Comp.

VIII. Magnet Needle (Compass).

From the start Ditches to the Heely Ditch: 83 Grade to
north south Line.
From Heely Ditch to A—attack Goal: 83 Grade to north
south Line.
From the first to the second attack Goal: 92 Grade to
north south Line.
2. Phase: At hour H + 2 take the Battl. To move forward
to the second attack Goal again up.

Task of the Battl. B: The second German Position between Fabric Douaumont and Point 74 53 57 6, also Merlet and Bridges of Merlet to take. Connection with the XXXIInd AK. To secure. In the course of this Phase is the Artillery Wall Fire, Which until hour H + 2 was firm about 300m. West of the Train Line, starting new with Tempo of 100m. In 3 Min.

Because of the same Reason like earlier said breakup of the move forward of the Wall Fire from hour H + 2 H 12 to H + 2 H 20 at a Line about 150m. East of the Train Line.

After reaching the second attack Goal is the Wall Fire to move forward about 150m. All Detachments arrange themselves as fast as possible make needy repair at the captured Line and stand by to move again for at the hour H + 4.

IX. Insertion of the Battl. In the second Phase.

First Line: 17st. Comp. right (south), 19st. Comp. left (north).

18st. Comp. as Reserve 150m. Behind of the Middle of the first Line. MG. 5: 1 Platoon

To the 17st. Comp. 1 Platoon to the 19st. Comp. 2 Platoons to the 18st. Comp.

X. Borders between both first Comp.

North Corner of the Alger Forest (Alger Forest to the 17st. Comp.) Battr. 7455 (of the 17st. Comp.) North Edge of Merlet (Merlet to the 17st. Comp.)

Move forward to the 17st. Comp. and order of the Comp. to secure connection with the I. Battl. Take the second German Position, take the Battr. East and west of Train, Enemy resistance which could come against the Ist. Battl. Encircle (Ditch de Gouvelle Ditch of Dec. 15). To take Merlet and occupy the Bridges.

Move forward and task of the 19st. Comp. Secure connection with the XXXIInd. AK.

Take the second German Position and occupy crossings over the Suippes down River from Merlet.

Move forward and task of the 18st. Comp. Following 100m.behind of the middle of the first Line. To establish themselves in the Area of the Battr. 7755 7855 to

Assist the Comp. of the first Line with help of 2 Platoons MGs.

Move forward of the MG. 5. One Platoon with the 19st. Comp. (secure connection

To the XXXIInd. AK.) 1 Platoon with the 17st. Comp. 2 Platoons with the 18st. Comp. One of them stops at the Train Line until arrival from a Platoon MG. from a Territorial Regiment.

XI. Cleaning of the second Position is in every Section guaranteed from a Comp. of the first Line.

XII. Command Post of the Battl. Commander.

      Begin: At the Point of the 19st. Comp.

      After capture of the Heely Ditch: East Edge of the Bois en Deutelles (Point B)

      During the occupation of the first Position: Movement Ditch on Hill Spina, 500m. West of this Position.

      After capture of the second Position: At the Battr. 7775.

      3. Phase: More Commands will be established for the further movement.

      Post Sector 132, March 23. 1917

      The Chief of the Battl. De Metz, Battl. Kdr. of the 5th. Battl.

      Signed: De Metz.

News Officer 7   AHQu. April 7. 1917

Br. Nr. 678

For the Correctness

von Wiedebach Nostitz

Cav. Capt. and N.O.

Distribution:

III.6. West 1 NO. 2 and NO. 3 each 2

News. Abt. Gr. HQu. 2 Groups and Div. 26

N. 5 German Kr. 2 NO. 1, 4, 5, 6 each 1 4
NO. Kr. v. B. 2 NO. 7 9
Total 50

Extremely valuable was for the Germans the knowledge that came from this Command that the beforehand attack of the French would not reach over the Bremond towards east. They now knew where his rights Wing were and could plan counter Measures.

It is not said too much, if you maintain, that the knowledge of this Command did help the big Nivelles Offensive did break down almost on the first Day.

In this captured Command were Day and hour of the attack not stated but in a French MW. Command was talk of a 10 Day Fire preparation. For the 10st. RD. was also a captured MW. Shooting Plan extremely valuable who made it possible the Enemy MW. To attack.

From end of March on did they have the Towns who were on the Suippes, the La Retourne Creek and the Aisne from Neuchatel to Guignicourt from the People evacuated. This hard Measure was in the Interest of the People necessary since they needed these Places for Quarter of their Troops and who's security against sudden attacks and Treachery Intrigues were important. It was a sad look as the People with their belongings had to leave their Houses under Tears. War is hard and jet they tried not to hurt the civil Population any more than necessary. A few days' later were this nice Villages totally demolished by heavy French Artillery Fire. The French tried to hit the Aisne Bridge at Neuchatel which they could not do. The Destruction of Evergnicourt, were important economical Installations in the big Fabric Buildings were, was very bad.

On April 6 did he speak with his Chief, Oberstlt. Hasse, because of the found attack Command, about what counter Measures they have to take, in case of an attack in the Area of St. Etienne, Bourgogne, Bermericourt and Orainville, with the Gen. Staff Officers of the Front and Intervention Divisions.

On this Day started the French Drumfire at the German first Positions, the systematic Destruction Fire at they're Battr. And Villages too far in to the back Ground. German Artillery answered lively.

On April 7 did he inspect one more time the Position on the Canal south of the Bremond. This Position was hard to defend since the Canal there was deep cut in between Forested Shore Walls. Towards La Neuvillette was this deep Gorge, in which the Canal de l'Aisne was installed, with a big Sandbag Barricade towards the Enemy closed. If this could take Artillery Fire was doubtful.

There he spoke with a Soldier and 3 Men who were in a MG. Position of the RIR. 201. The Soldier, a Jung Volunteer, had taken the Observation Post. "One does this so the Comrades have Rest", he said to him. "Where are you from? "I was born in Brazil were my Father is a Merchant, but since 2 Years are my Brother and me in Germany; because my Father wanted that we were taught in Germany. Then came the War, we joined immediately. My Brother was taken later; I am already Private first Class in this nice Regiment 201".

He will never forget the Inspiration of this Boy who had a Spanish first Name. 2 weeks later did he learn that he and his 3 Comrades had died at they're Post.

He inspected on April 8 with a few Officers the Battr. Cram de Bremond. The French fired at the German Battr. Which stood at both sides of the Street Reims Pont Givart and the backward Lines on the Suippes and Aisne with heavy Calibers. They observed and steered they're Fire from Balloons. The Fortifications, which had been done since 1914 and the Cram de Bremond became many hits. They thought they could not be so soon being destroyed, but a few Days later it came to that. The Mood of the Soldiers on the Front was confident. They had to think of the move back, which would have lead through heavy Enemy Grenade Fire.

On April 9 became from the Group Bremond, because of the found French attack Command, the Infantry and Artillery Commands in writing

Because of the continued connection of the Officers in his Staff, especially of his untiring Chief, with the Troops under the Group, even in the first Lines, and because of the knowledge of the Area and Positions, there build up and reinforcement, was a close and understanding work together inside of the Group Bremond guaranteed. Only because of that was it possible for the Troops to get Success. On that Day took the GenMaj. Count von Moltke the Command of the 21st. ID.

A Core Command of the Commanding Gen. of the XXIInd. French Core, Passage, was found. In it where ordinary and vulgar words to whip up the French:

> "Heroes of the Marne, from Ypern, from the Argonnen, from the Somme
> And from Verdun!
> Officers, Sergeants, Privates second Class, Jaeger and Soldiers of the XXIInd. Core!
> With support from a frightful Artillery, Divisions joined who are proud to fight on your side and determined to show Courage in rivalry with you, so You will once more show the Force of your Courage to the unworthy Enemy, Who plundered and destroyed your Stove, violated your Woman, mutilates Your Kids and old Folks and tortured our Prisoners.
> When you leave your Trenches to attack the Enemy, then will the dead come Far from they're Graves and you will be surrounded by an illuminated shine Of Glory. It will bless you to see the attack of the living from the famous XXIInd. Core.
> Be worthy of your Heroes! May they be proud of you, Comrades, strike hard, Revenged them.
> Passage".

On April 9 visited the Commander of the G.Ers.D. Genlt. Von Larisch, in St. Germainmont. They were together 1865/66 in Glogau at the Gymnasium, then in the Kadett Core in Walstatt and Berlin as Lt. in the IR. 93. They stood both later in Berlin and were at the same time Regiments Commanders in the 2nd. G.I.Br. Now he came with his G. Ers. D. under his Command.

They both inspected the Area northeast of St. Etienne, which was viewed for the G. Ers. D. as Intervention Division at the start of the French attack. On April 10. They were at the Hill south of Aumenancourt Le Petit were a Battle Post was installed. There in the Terrain did they talk about the task of his Div., which in case of an Enemy break through east or west of the Bremond, they should push the Enemy back.

It was clear for both that the French planed a heavy attack towards northeast on both sides of the Berry au Bac, who's right Wing should pass west of the Bremond and then after they broke through, the Fortress

Group from north to attack. They were sure that the Crew of the Bremond could hold this important Point, but that the Enemy could overrun the German Positions west of the Canal, since this Terrain lay partly deep and these Positions where not good to fortify. His Chief and he had decided to position the G.Ers. D. South of Aumenancourt for counter attack as soon as the Enemy attack started. Before were 2 Battl. Of this Division north of the Suippes positioned as support for the tired 21ᵗʰ. ID. The Command of these Battl. Did not come under the 21ˢᵗ. ID.

At 3.15 in the Afternoon came from the Group Bremond, which was the Name of the Group Eberhardt since April 10.1917, a Command:

"1.to 3.not mentioned

4. The Battl. IIIrd. / G.I.R. 6 and Ist. / G.I.R. 7 come under the 21ˢᵗ. ID. But Must not, without order from the Group, towards south of the Suippes put into Battle. Both Battl. Arrive on April 10 in the Evening in Poilcourt, Houdilcourt. They are from there from the 21ˢᵗ. ID. To lead, that they arrive on April 11 at 5 in the Morning in The Suippes Section.

5. to 6. The G. Ers. D. lead on April 11 until 10 in the Morning Ist. and IInd. / GIR. 6 to Poilcourt, IInd. and IIIrd. / GIR. 7 and 1 Pi. Comp. to Houdicourt. There Quarter."

On April 11 Commanded the Group both Reserve Divisions of the G. Ers. D. and 4ˢᵗ. ID. Kdr. Genlt. Freyer to move closer to the Battle Front, so all Forces of the Div. at the Bremond would be free for the Battle at the first Positions. Part of the Artillery of the G. Ers. D. came under the 21ˢᵗ. ID.

They were still changes and new distribution done at the 7ˢᵗ. And 1ˢᵗ. Army. The Group Bremond was so far at the left Wing of the 7ˢᵗ. Army, was from April 16 in the Morning on, the right Wing of the 1ˢᵗ. Army, under the upper Command of the Gen. of the Inf. Fritz von Below. Chief of the Gen. Staff of the 1ˢᵗ. Army was Maj. von Klueber, who was I b in the Staff of the Garde Core, When my Grandfather was Chief of the Gen. Staff.

Gen. von Dommes, who was in the Operations Department of the OHL. Came to inform himself to St.Germainmont. The Artillery Kdr.

of the Army, GenMaj. von Berendt was also in the KHQu. This excellent Artillerist had the Gen.Kdo of the Xst. RK. With his Advice in all things assisted.

On April 15 at 12 Noon came from the AOK. 1 a Report that the French Military Attaché

In the Hag in a Wine Mood said that on April 16 with Sun ascent the decisive Battle of the War would start.

Since April 6 were the Positions at the Hills 108 and 91 under heavy Drumfire. This heavy Fire and the Nerve shattering work digging out buried Soldiers was hard on the Forces of the 10st. RD. The Group Bremond became, because of that the 54st. ID. Kdr. GenMaj. Baron von Watter, as Support. On April 14 did my Grandfather Command:

> "4st. ID. Relieves as Front Div. the 10st. RD. 54st. ID. Moves for the 4st. ID. As interlock Div. in the Sector of the 4st. ID. The 10st. RD. moves as rest Div. to be available to the OHL. In the Previous Sector of the 54st. ID. The 10st. RD. leads until April 17 at 11 in the Morning the Upper Command in they're Sector."

In the Evening of April 14 became the G. Ers. D. from the Group Bremond an Order to give 1 Battl. As Reserve to the 21st. ID. The relieved Ist / IR. 81 take over the Task of the Garde Battl.

Ice-cold Wind and Sunshine dominated since a few Days and brought a fine Dust from the dry Champagne Stones who went in Eyes and Noses and caused Pain.

On April 15 became the G. Ers. D. from the Group Bremond at 9 in the Morning an Command:

> "Enemy attack is imminent. G. Ers. D. is to move for. They assembled The Forces at Poilcourt, Houdilcourt in the Forest Area northeast of St. Etienne, the at Blanch stationed parts in the Area Sault—"

This Command was right away given to the 21st. ID. And 43rd.RD.

The Observations of the Pilots contradicted the Observations of the Battle Div. they reported:

"No movement in the Trenches."

At 5 in the Afternoon commanded the Group Bremond the G. Ers. D. to move back in to they're Quarters and on April 16 from 5 in the Morning to be ready to March.

In the Night from 15 to 16 April was at the 10st. RD. each one Battl. In the first Line relieved with each one Battl. Of the IR. 140, 49 and 14 of the 4st. ID. In the first Position was therefore 3 Battl. Of the 10st. RD. and 3 Battl. Of the 4st. ID. for Aisne defense was 1 Battl. Of the 54st. ID. with a light Howitzer Battr. At Conde sur Suippes positioned.

At 3.40 in the Morning started a raging Fire. The Officers of the 10st. RD. stayed because of the relief in the Positions and also had stopped the moving back Battl. At 6 in the Morning begun the Enemy Infantry to Storm for. The Germans started immediately Wall Fire and Prisoners said it had a big effect.

In the KHQu. In Germainmont came the first reports of the Enemy Infantry attack at 7 in the Morning from Air and Ground observation Fresnes.

The French had at the whole Front, the way that they expected, because of the found Command and from the Troops and Air reports, attacked. West of the Aisne where at the Group Aisne Battles fought, east of the Aisne was a heavy Battle to and inclusive of the Bremond. Further northeast of Reims was only Artillery Battle.

At the right Wing of the Group Bremond did the brave Regiments of the 10st. RD. and the 4st. ID. Repel the attacks. At Hill 91 did the Enemy advance to the east Slope.

Because of a counter attack from the IIIrd / IR. 49 were they pushed back. A French counter attack failed in the Fire of the MG. Comp. / IR. 49.

Extremely hard was the Battle at the Hill 108. There did the Enemy several times advance over the first Positions but always came in the middle Area in the MG. Fire and had heavy losses.

In this Battle Section proved the mesh position of the MGs. True. The mobility of the MGs. on April 16 and the following Battle Days hindered they're discovery, so they had not many losses.

The Group ordered to the 54st. ID.:

"IInd. / IR. 27 come under the 10st. RD. I. / IR 27 is through the 54st. ID. from Avaux to Prouvaiser Forest to put in March and comes also under the 10st. RD. Details arrange both Div.

And to the 10st. ID. At 10 in the Morning:

"2nd Battl. IR. 27 of the 54st. ID. Is immediately to put in March from Villars deviant le Tour to St. Hubert. 1st Battl. Moves immediately further to Guignicourt it comes to the seam Command Aisne (Command becomes oldest Battl. Kdr.) The other Battl. Stays for disposal of the Group in St. Hubert. Ensure Telephone connection. 4st. ID. Became at 9.55 in the Morning a Command to alarm both Battl."

At the 21st. ID. intensified the Enemy Artillery and MG. Fire to a heaviest Drumfire. At 6 in the Morning did it become the heaviest and also there broke the Enemy Infantry for.

The Wall fire for the 21st. ID. could not start in time because of heavy Ground Fog. Impenetrable Smoke and Dust of the Drumfire, which made Observation in the deep laying Area of the Aisne Marne Canal, impossible.

In the Sections of the IR. 81 and 87 did the Enemy overrun the Trenches, the valiant resisting Soldiers in the first Trenches where caught from Flank and Back and were put out of Combat. That in the back Section of the IR. 81 Battle ready IIIrd. / G. I. R. 6 pushed in quick and vigorous counter attacked the Enemy back and maintained the intermediate Positions.

Brilliant fought that at the left Wing of the 10st. RD. R.I.R. 37 that because of the forward move of the French was threatened in Flank and back and in spite of that held they're Positions.

The French pushed then, while in and around of the Trenches Men on Men fought, with heavy Forces north of the Canal to the Train Guignicourt Reims, for. The Trench Soldiers of the IR. 80 fought hard for every Foot of Ground, until the Ammunition for MGs. and Infantry and all Hand Grenades where used up. The Villages Loivre and Bermericourt were lost. The Enemy pushed to the Train Station Loivre for. There did the 6st. / IR. 80, MG. Comp. and the Regiments Staff of the IR. 80 give heavy Resistance. At 9 in the Morning was the Enemy forced to move back to the Train Notch at the Village Bermericourt. From the 21st. ID. was the Ist. / G. I. R. 7 in the second position and the Ist. / IR. 81 that had been moved back moved fore to Bertricourt, 2km. northwest of Pont Givart.

On order of the Group was the Ldst. Battl. Hannover put under the 22nd. I.Br. south of Pignicourt, 2km. east of Men Neville, south of the Canal.

At 10.25 in the Morning reported the Group to the 21st. ID. That 2 Battl. Of the IR. 90 of the 54st. ID. in Avaux were alerted to march in the Position of Pignicourt. There they were put under the 21st. ID.

At the 43rd. RD. held the R. I. R. 202 at the south Slope of the Bremond in the Battr. De Loivre. Courcy was until Evening tenaciously defended but was lost and the Trench Position at the Canal were with Artillery Fire destroyed and became a big Grave. The French could not take Area north of the Canal towards the Bremond. There held the R. I. R. 203 and 201 in valiant resistance and caused the Russian Ist. Br. who were in this Place, heavy losses. Also the 19st. ID. Who connected with the 43rd. RD. took part with the IR. 91 in this defense Battle.

At 7.15 in the Morning became the G. Ers. D. from the Group an order to start immediately to march for to the on April 15 taken assembly Places.

At 10 in the Morning became the G. Ers. D. a further Command:

> "Enemy broke in the Position of the 21st. ID. And in moving forward to the Train Line Guignicourt Reims. G. Ers. D. is ready south of the Suippes in the Area from Aumenancourt to counter attack between the Suippes and Bremond under security of the left Flank. At 11.15 in the Morning came to the G. Ers. D. a Command from the Group:
>
> "1. Enemy moved for at the 21st. ID. In Orainviller Forest at 43rd. RD. to the Canal. Heavy Enemy Fire at the Bremond Mountain.
>
> 2. G. Ers. D. leads the attack for assistance of the 21st. ID. Has to secure Left Flank."

Meanwhile were the French broken through at the right Aisne Shore at the 5th. Bav. RD. in the first attack to the vicinity of Guignicourt. The leader of the Observation Post there "Max", a Corporal, had reported to the 10st RD. that the French were direct in Front of him. After an hour he appeared again and signaled that the Enemy had been pushed back, but there came fresh Infantry Columns and Tanks on the Street Pontavert Guignicourt. The Kdr. of the Fusilier Regiment Steinmetz reported to the 10st. RD. that his Battle Post became Fire in the back. Genlt. Dallmer gave immediately order for the Battr. Field AR. 108, who stood in the Forest south of Prouvais, to open Fire. He also Commanded 1 Battl. From there as Seam Commando to Guignicourt, and a second to closure at the Aisne Canal, were the French with MG. Squads fired in the back of the German Positions. There at the Canal stood a Platoon Field Artillery, to protect the Flanks of the Aisne Marne Canal, in Concrete Bunkers. They turned around and fired at the Tanks on the other side of the Aisne. Likewise fought the Battr. Of the Seam Commando (Field AR.108) the Tanks until the loss of the last Canon. From about 50 Tanks were 28 destroyed. The Fusilier Regiment Steinmetz was able to contain the Front at the Canal. The German MGs. flanked the moving back Enemy and helped because of that the counter attacks of the 50st. ID. Who were during the day at Juvincourt successful.

At 2 in the Afternoon came Gen. von Below with his Chief in the KHQu. To learn about the course of the Battle.

At 3 in the Afternoon did the 21st. ID. The Ist. / G. I. R. 7, which was under her Command, Commanded to attack. The Battl. Broke from the south Slope of the Orainviller Forest for towards Bermericourt. The attack moved with ardor for. In all Forest Parcels south and southwest of the Orainviller Forest resisted the Enemy with all Force, who was finally broken with Men against Men. The Enemy moved half right over the Tracks back and had heavy losses because of the pursue Fire of the G. Ers. D. The first Battl. Reached at 3.30 in the Afternoon the Hills east of the Street Pont Givart Reims. The Street was crossed from both attacking 6st. And 7st. G. I. R. Only now became the Infantry Fire, at first Shrapnel, then Wall Fire. The move forward of the Infantry continued heroic. The breaking through of the French was because of that caught and repelled.

Even the enemy, Officers and Man, who became later Prisoners, gave Praise about the attack of the G. Ers. D.

The Enemy had lost in this attack 700 to 800 dead, 600 Prisoners, 36 MGs. 83 Mitrailleusen (a French Gun with several Barrels) and 1 Trench Canon.

At 6 in the Evening Commanded the Group to the G. Ers. D. 21st. And 43rd. RD. the Rest of the lost German Positions again to take. The IR. 80, that in the between Position at Bermericourt was, came under the

G. Ers. D. the Village Bermericourt was in the Night from parts of the G. Ers. D. and the IR. 80 occupied.

In the second Position of the 21ˢᵗ. ID. Were on Command of the Group the Ldst. Battl. Hannover moved for. At Guignicourt was the Force of the Troops so far consumed, that at the 10ˢᵗ RD. a breakthrough was feared. The forward Move of the Battl. Was very hard and time consuming. At Midnight came just then at the 10ˢᵗ. RD. the report that still a Battl. Of the 54ˢᵗ. ID. south at Guignicourt and 1 Battl. At Menneville steep Slope hat arrived and 1 Battl. Were in March to the Hill 108, with an extra safe Leader.

So raged the Battle through the Night and in the Morning of April 17 got more violent. The losses were also at my Grandfathers Div. heavy. One heavy Grenade hit a Dugout, that was supposed to be bomb secure, and killed 10 Officers and 80 Man.

The Artillery Munitions consumption at the Group Bremond was on April 16: 104248 Grenades. On April 17 at 12.15 in the Afternoon became the G. Ers. D. from the Group a Command to take as soon as possible the Area south of the Village Bermericourt until the connection at the right Wing of the 43ʳᵈ. RD. at the Canal to relief the right Wing of the brave Regiments of the 43ʳᵈ. RD. who had kept their Positions without reinforcement of other Troops south of the Battr. De Loivre. The 21ˢᵗ. ID. and the 43ʳᵈ. RD. had on order of the G. Ers. D. the attack to Advance with heavy Artillery help. The Troops of the G. Ers. D. stormed the French Positions to 300m.south of Bermericourt, so the connection with the Troops of the 43ʳᵈ. RD. was made. Until Evening were more 12 Officers and 700 Men taken as Prisoners and 3 MGs.

To the 10ˢᵗ. RD., 4ˢᵗ. ID., 21ˢᵗ. ID., 54ˢᵗ. ID., 43ʳᵈ. RD. and the G. Ers. D. was a Core Command given:

"The heavy attack of the French yesterday hit the whole Front of the Troops under my Command. In tenacious Battle did the valiant Regiments, reinforced with Artillery, MWs and Pioneers, stopped the Enemy, who broke in to several Places, and in brave Counter attacks pushed them back. I speak to the Leaders and Men of all Grades, also those that with the rescue of the wounded Ambulance Soldiers, those that under the hardest circumstances working Telephone and Signal Core and the never tiring Columns that work to bring Munition and Material, my heartfelt Gratitude. Those Detachments that leave the Group. I thank for their Bravery in the Battles of the last weeks."

In order to speak with the Kdrs. Personally, did he drive with his Chief to the Battle Field witch looked dreadful. Some of the dead were buried or gathered up the wounded were taken care of. Many dead Horses, destroyed Wagons and piles of Munitions were big Obstacles. The nice Villages on the Suippes and the Aisne lay in Ruins.

On this Day where all attacks of the French repelled, counter attacks brought no results in winning Area.

On April 18 came from the upper Kdr. of the 7st. Army, Gen. of the Inf. von Boehn, a Letter:

"The Group Bremond is changed from the Formation of the 7st. Army to the 1st. Army. She has during the time that she belonged to the 7st. Army stood out with her energetic attacks, but also on April 16 the attack from superior Forces valiantly repelled and a planned brake through prevented.

Your Excellency and the Troops under you, I tell my Heartfelt Gratitude and Thanks with the best wishes for the coming serious Days."

The Russians and French attacked on April 19 several times. They were repelled with losses. 200 Prisoners and much Material fell in German Hands.

It seemed the French planed a new heavy attack. The Troops in the first Lines had because of that to be relieved. On April 20 in the Morning came the 4st. ID. To the Group Aisne. The Div. had in the days that they belonged to the Group Bremond fought valiantly and took from the Enemy 8 Officers, 415 Man, 11 MGs. and 16 Muskets.

The Border of the Position at the right Wing of the Group Bremond was not deemed appropriate since the Aisne as Flank obstacle gave valuable services. At 5 in the Afternoon came the upper Kdr. with his Chief for a discussion over the Position in his Group Section to the KHQu. It was discussed about the insertion of the Divisions at the Front of the Group and to make the Div. Sections smaller since the Group Section was too wide for 2 Front Div. On April 21 was the 21st. ID. Relieved with the 54st. ID. The 21st. ID. Had by themselves the attack of the French in the first Positions to bear and she took from the Enemy 9 Officers, 532 Man, 12 MGs. 19 fast loading Guns and 3 Muskets. Also were from 10st. to the

20st. April at the Ambulance Core of the Div. 421 French and 2 Russians treated.

In Place of the 43rd. RD. with they're valiant Regiments 201, 202 and 203 entered the 34st. ID. Kdr. GenMaj. Teetzmann. The 43rd. RD. had also in the defense Battle on the Bremond brought hundreds of Prisoners and Enemy Material.

In the Evening of April 28 attacked the French and Russians the Train and Canal Position on the Bremond. All attacks where completely repelled. From Prisoner Statements was this Position the outlet Position for the attack at the Bremond, which was intended soon, and had to be taken. It followed again heavy Battle Days, where the Front Div. in heavy Artillery and MW. Fire had to hold out. Enemy attack attempts where stopped from begin. They had the Impression as if the Elan of the French attacks from the previous Days had eased off. They succeeded no more to break into they're Positions. You became particularly heavy and horrible Impressions with a look at the first from German occupied Train Line south of Bermericourt. There had the Enemy Artillery at begin of April caused much Destruction, and at the Storm at April 16 did the French with Flame Throwers all Men, who were in that Dugout, suffocate and burn. Even so in this No man's land were also many dead French, did the Enemy not allow anybody to bury the dead. The German first Line stretched there in connection on their Position at the Hill 101 south of Bermericourt at the Slope of the Battr. De Loivre and the Bremond until the Sluices at Courcy.

Despite the grueling service in the Trenches, took the Soldiers every free moment to create little Souvenirs from the Champagne Lime that testified from the artistic knowhow of the Men. Also there where quite peculiar Stone Formations in this Lime, smooth like a Ball and in the Form of a Billiard Ball, when broken in half they had crystal Vanes. One such Ball did he, after the War, give to a well—known Professor von Zahn in Jena for his Collection in the University. He had such Form never seen and could not find anything in his Books about their Formation.

Beginning of May did Enemy Airplanes bomb the Supplies and Munitions Magazine at Neuvizy and burned it. Slowly Sub side the Battle so on May 4 was a Core Day Command:

"The Divisions under him had many Days withstood the heavy Artillery Fire. They had the Enemy Masses, who followed the Fire Storm, in hard Battle victoriously repelled. For their tenacious bravery he spoke to all Troops his Recognition. Our Victory in this War deciding struggle has to be followed by more Victory's."

The 39st. ID. Kdr. GenMaj. Muenter, relieved as Front Div. on May 7 the G. Ers. D. and shortly thereafter was the 54st. ID. Relieved with the 187st. ID. Kdr. Genlt. Sunkel. In order to greed the new Troops in their positions he had with his Officers to walk several hours, because in the prevailing clear Weather at that time and the observation possibility from 26 French Balloons, they could not drive very far for. The French even went so far as to use Artillery Fire on single Persons in the Area.

His Majesty the Kaiser had announced his arrival on May 24. In the KHQu. In Rethel, to hear a Lecture from the Upper Kdr. about the Battles of the 1st. Army. The Statement of the Army Leader gave an overlook over the gigantic defense Battle. After the Lecture awarded his Majesty the Kaiser with appreciating Words to Gen. of the Inf. von Below (Fritz) the Cross and the Star of the House Medal of the Hohenzollern with Swords, to the Saxonian Gen. of the Inf. von der Planitz, Commanding Gen. of the XIIth. Saxonian AK. And to my Grandfather the Pour le me rite. It was an unforgettable Moment, when he became from his Kaisers Hand the Medal, which he from his Youth on made it his Target and his Grandfather carried for 61 Years.

After he came back did he give a Speech in St. Germainmont in Front of his Staff and stressed the particular merits of his Chief and the other Officers of his Staff, who in the heavy Battle Days, each on his Place, had helped to gain the Victory. With the distribution of a Series of Iron Crosses could he give his thanks even more. It was touching how much Devotion, Loyalty and Gratitude was in the many congratulation Letters that were send to him. Many made him proud. Only a part of the Letters from former Soldiers of all Grades to they're higher Superiors were published to show the population how warm and trusting the ratio was between Officers, Corporals and Men.

On May 26 at Noon came the 187st. ID. To the Group Aisne, the 19st. ID. To the Group Bremond. With that came his old Peace Div. under his Command. In the next Days did he visit the Kdrs. And Regiments in their Positions and could greed many old known Soldiers from the Years 1911to 1913.

The big Offensive of the French and English in April and May, who was done with powerful Forces, had failed. While the Englander with 34 Div. and a Front width of 34km. had attacked and only at Arras and Wytschaete small successes attained, who was not of Influence at the whole Situation, was the attack of the French at the Aisne and in the Champagne in which they used 72 Div. almost all repelled. Only in a few Places could they move they're first Line a few 100m. Fore. The loss of Men, Material and Mood of the Troops was heavy at the Enemy.

The 7st. RD. Kdr. Gen. of the Inf. Count von Schwerin, were in a Section of the Group employed. In mid—June came the 239st. ID. Kdr. Genlt. Schmiedecke, as Front Div. to the Group Bremond, in Place of the 19st. ID. Slowly became the Front of the Group Bremond again wider. They became the Div. Sector at the right Aisne Shore west of Guignicourt to the Forest north of Juvincourt—Damery and south to Berry au Bac. The 231st. ID. Kdr. GenMaj. von Huelsen (Bernhard) came under the Command of the Group Bremond.

From July 21 until Aug. 7 was he on Vacation in the Homeland and used this time for Treatment in the Spa Ems, were he was with his Wife and youngest Daughter. On Aug. 8 did he come to Kreuznach where his oldest Son went with him to report to Gen. Field Marshal von Hindenburg, who invited them for Dinner. He sat next to him and later could hear a Lecture from Gen. Ludendorff.

From Aug. 1 on was the Army Command in the Section from the Group Aisne for a short time given to the Group Bremond. Since the 227st. ID. Kdr. Genlt. Von Leyser, was pulled out, had this big Section to be held with 3 Div. 243. Kdr. Genlt. Von Schippert, 231 and 239. On Aug.1 was Capt. Guderian, so far Quarter Master at the Group Aisne as indigenous Ic, transferred to the Group Bremond. They soon learned this qualified and lovable Comrade to appreciate.

Excellence von Below and his Chief came often to the KHQu. And drove then from St.Germainmont with my Grandfather and his Chief to the Front Div. On Aug.26 at 4.45 in the Afternoon came suddenly Enemy Fire at the left Wing of the 231st. ID. Two heavy Enemy Patrols penetrated but where repelled from the shock Troop of the IR. 443. 4 dead French and 2 wounded Prisoners from the French IR. 252. Of the 15st. French Div. were brought in, 1 German double Post was missed. Shortly thereafter brought Thuringische and Hessische shock Troops from the IR. 441. of the 227st. ID. which was again in this Core Section whose Gen. Staff Officer was the intelligent Capt. von Zobeltitz, a former "Maikaefer", and north of the Aisne Canal at Sapigneul 12 Prisoners and 2 fast loading Rifles from the French IR.217 of the 71st. Div. from the French Trenches.

On the Mauchamp-Ferme brought a shock Troop from the IR. 417, of the tenaciously defending Enemy, 8 Prisoners from the Turku Reg. and 1 light African Jaeger of the 45st. French Div. The 6st. Bav. RD. Kdr. GenMaj. Knight von Koeberle came under the Xst. RK.

On Aug.26 did he drive at dark with 1 Orderly Officer to Merlet at the Suippes for; from there did they walk with they're Driver cross Country towards Hill 108 to the first Line. For the Artillery did he on the previous Day order for the Night heightened State of alert. The in the Area behind the Positions build in MG. Nests where observed and the attentive MG. Posts where praised. Suddenly started a French Fire surprise at the Hill 108. The getting red morning Sky glowed in the Sea of Flames and they thought a big Battle Day started. What now? As responsible Leader of the Group was he with the 2 Officers 1km. behind the first Trench Position without a possibility of connection to his Staff. Soon came the Signal "Gas". For the first time did he have to put on a Gas Mask. The French shot they're Grenades luckily over the Artillery Positions and the Wind went to north, so they could not smell much of the Gas.

He went to the next Inf. Battle Post. There reported the Adjutant the Kdr. went fore to the Troops. It involved a Patrol Operation against the Position at the south Slope of the Hill 108. At the first Aid Station of the Regiment were a few wounded. He walked in their Position for and were told from the Trench Soldiers about the break in of the French Patrol. They did with a short Fire attack penetrate the Trenches and had killed the double Post with Hand Grenades. The in the Dugout resting relief was immediately there, several wounded, one heavy. The French left Torches which they wanted to use to burn the Dugout but the brave Soldiers prevented this. The Leader of the French was dead; He laid on the

Embankment, in the cold Hand an Amulet. One of the Posts was taken away; A Blood Trail was visible in the Obstacle.

First Aid Station People alerted him that in the Dugout where a heavy wounded Soldier. He went to him and gave him the Iron Cross; if he noticed, he did not know; he breathed heavily and had earned this Medal.

The lively Patrol Activity of the French and the observed firing of their Artillery and MWs. Let the AOK. Determine that the Enemy wanted to attack. Because of that was on Sept. 9 a Meeting with the Div. Kdrs. Under him and they discussed the extension of the Positions, the building of Obstacles and the caring of the Men.

A Decree from the Chief of the Gen. Staff of the Field Army, concerning measures against incitement of Hate Speech in the Army, was announced. At Command of the OHL. Was an Organization created, who was supposed to keep and strengthen Victory and fighting Spirit in the Army and in the Homeland, in spite of Peace yearning. The Men at the Front and in behind of the Positions had to learn through skillful evidence from they're Officers, why they had to endure until acceptable Peace Negotiations could be obtained. The harmful influences from the Homeland and the Propaganda of the Enemy's, with the Phrase "Democratization" did the moral conscience and the Authority in Army, Navy and Nation destroy, this had to be countered. From the Div. had to be suitable Officers found, who could give the Troops and Officers advice. With this were good results obtained, even so in some Places were the wrong Officers chosen. Generally can one say that at the Front the Input of good Leaders was good to the End and the Troops kept they're moral Attitude. Older and younger Men had the solid Will to do their Duty, which he can attest to through personal Experience by constant connection with the Troops.

On Oct. 4 came at the 239st. ID. a French Corporal from IR. 214 and gave important statements about an imminent attack. The Instruction about the Enemy Artillery Positions was after verification correct.

On Oct. 6 drove he and his Chief with the Ia and Id to the 239st. 231st. And 242st. ID. Kdr. GenMaj. Von Erpf, to talk about the necessary measures in case of an Enemy Attack at the Bremond. Pretty was the Valley of the Aisne with they're green Trees and the juicy Meadows, which they nursed and cultivated. Sadly was at the begin of the War not enough care given to the Fisheries, because some People preferred instead of the Fishing Rod Hand Grenades, without thinking that with that everything is destroyed. Interesting was a Trial, who was done behind the Front, with Romanian Buffalos. They were supposed to be used as Draft Animals. In the Conde-les-Harpy was such a Herd. To observe these big Animals in the Aisne, were only the Heads were visible and it looked like Monsters. They're Horses did not want to go in the Water only slowly did they got used to.

About 100 French attacked on Oct.18, after a heavy Fire surprise, at the 242st. ID. They captured in the section of the 475st. IR. A light MG. and took supposedly the whole Crew as Prisoners. On the next Day were 2 Men, who were reported as Prisoners live, dug out. One of the French from the IR. 222., who was on the 18st. With the attack, was brought in.

On Oct. 20 did he become the following News:

On Command of the OHL. separates the Gen.Kdo. Of the Xst. RK. From my Army Group. The Commanding Gen. and his highly regarded Helpers for their faithful performance of Duty and they're outstanding Service, to thank, is my utmost necessity. With the fullest appreciation do I remember the energetic leadership of the Group Bremond during the Aisne Battle. Purposeful and cheerful to attack did the Gen.Kdo. Of the Xst. RK. in those heavy Battles lead his Troops to full Victory. My Whishes accompany the Gen.Kdo. Of the Xst. RK. On his further Roads to Glory and Success.

The upper Commander:
Wilhelm,
Crown Prince of the German Empire and of Prussia.

The Gen.Kdo. Of the XVst.AK. Took over the Group Bremond. With the Kdr. Gen. Genlt. Ilse and a few Officers of their Staffs did he drive out to show them the main Points of the Positions.

On Oct. 21 did the upper Commander order him for a few days as substitute and he had to greed at this time a Delegation of the Empire who took an Information Trip to the Front of the first Army. In Rethel were the Gentleman received. At the Table Speech did he emphasize the Devotion of the brave Men who's Mood to hold out until Victory was evident. He contested the complaint about not enough Food. He explained that in heavy Battles Troops have to go hungry, when the Artillery and MG. Fire makes it impossible to bring Food forward, but so far did no German Soldier ever starve to death. We all were from the oldest to the youngest Soldier ready to give our best for the Welfare of our beloved Fatherland. In this Mindset did he welcome the Representatives of the People on the Front of the first Army.

On Oct. 22 gave the Chief of the Gen. Staff of the 1st. Army him, as substitute Army Leader, a report. The Army intended an attack in bigger proportion to create a field before the Front for the defense of the Bremond. The Group Bremond gave a proposal to stretch this attack to the Aisne towards north in order to create better Battle conditions between the Aisne and the Bremond.

On Oct. 26 at 9 in the Morning stormed Storm Troops of the IR. 442. under Lt. Schellkopf into the second Enemy Line for and came back with 3 Prisoners from the 252st. French IR. With that was the insertion of the French 157st. Div. opposite confirmed.

At the nicest Fall Weather was the KHQu. In St. Germainmont handed over. He dismissed himself from the Troops with the following Core Day Command:

> "Tomorrow goes the Command of the Group Bremond over to the Commanding Gen. of the XVst. AK. I leave with the Gen. Kdo. Of the Xst. RK. This Sector, to be used in another Position. Nine Months did I experience here on the Aisne heavy and diligent times and glorious Battle Days in April and May of this year. A big Number of Div. of all German Ancestral was under my Command at this time. With Pride and Joy do I look back to my official Activities, which brought me and my trusty Companions together with brave soldiers and they're outstanding Leaders. To all Troops of all Weapons, who right now belong to the Group and all working Governmental Authorities and Men, who in faithful fulfillment of their Duty, working behind of the Front, I call a hearty good bye and thank them for their dedication with which they in this Place work for our beloved Fatherland to get the final Victory and a glorious Peace. Wherever it is to be, will we all do our Duty,

this may be our mutual Pledge. Forward with God for Kaiser and Fatherland!"

On Afternoon of Oct.31 drove the Gen. Kdo. in 3 Carriages from the Train Station Asfeld over Rethel, Charleville, along the nice Maas Valley to Namur and from there on the next Day without break over Brussel, Gent to Bruegge where they arrived at 9 in the Evening.

In Flanders

Group Ijmuiden

The Impression of the old Sea and Commerce Town is great, one think to be back in the middle Age. In the Harbor were parts of the German Torpedo Boot Flotilla, many Workshops and Magazines were build. To their defense were a Number of Aviator defense Gun Battr. Put in while they were there they witnessed a few Bombing Raids, which were supposed to destroy the Harbor but did not much Damage.

Before Noon on Nov.1.1917 did he drive with his Chief and the first Gen. Staff Officer, Maj. Von Wolff, to report to the upper Commander of the 4st. Army to Kortrijk, were a big Monument reminds of the Liberation struggle of the Flames from the French under Philippe. On June 11. 1302 were in the Spores Battle more than 8000 French killed, among them over 1000 Knights of the noblest Families of France.

The Army Leader, Gen. of the Inf. Sixt von Armin greeted them heartily. The Chief of the Gen. Staff of the 4st. Army, GenMaj. Von Lossberg explained the Situation. From Spy reports seamed an English attack at the Coast Front of the Marine Core or in Dutch Flanders, possible. In this case had the Gen. Kdo. Of the Xst. RK. To take over the Command over 3 to 5 Div., who were for defense of such an attack, made available, and with that came under the Group North.

The Leader of the Group North was Admiral von Schroeder, whom he knew from the Year 1894, as they were in the War Ministry in a Commission to build Island Guards on the North see Coast. His Chief of Staff was Colonel Berlet, who he knew from Gen.Staff.

As soon as a Coast attack was not likely any more was the Gen. Kdo. Of the Xst. RK. To take over a Group to be built from 2 to 3 Div. called

Group Ijmuiden. Also informed Gen. von Lossberg that the Enemy at this time was doing big Troop movements from the Ypern Bend towards north and an Enemy big attack on both sides of the Ijmuiden to the Houthoulster Forest was expected soon.

As KHQu. Was Lop hem proposed, 6km. south of Bruegel, in the Castle of the Belgian Baron de Calhoun, which proved to be suitable for the Staff. His Quarter was in the Parsonage of the Catholic Priest. The Village Lop hem was immediately furnished with all Telephone Connections, which took a few Days, who were used to explore the Section Blank Enberg—Knocked.

On Nov. 10 was the Command of the AOK. 4, with which the Gen. Kdo. Of the Xst. RK. Came under the Group North in case of an Enemy attack, lifted. The Gen. Kdo. Moved on that Day in to they're Quarter in Lop hem. With the Chief and the first Gen. Staff Officer did he drive in the Afternoon to talks with the Div. Kdrs. And Gen. Staff Officers of the 4st Div. that belonged to the Group Ijmuiden.

The 26st. Wuertemberg RD. Kdr. Genlt. Von Fritsch, the 54st. Wuert. RD. Kdr. Genlt. Von Wencher, the 187st. ID. Kdr. Genlt. Sunkel were as Front Div. in Position, behind stood the 24st. Saxonian RD. Kdr. GenMaj. Baron von Oldershausen, as Army Reserve.

On the Morning of Nov.16 broke under Leadership of Petersdorff the 9st. / IR. 187. At the left Wing of the Group Ijmuiden in the Enemy Position and took 1 Officer and 63 Man from the Belgian IR. 108. As Prisoners, captured several light MGs. and pushed the first Line in 500m. Width 200 to 300m. For.

With the rides in the Area of Lop hem, were Village was on Village, in which all were Troops of the Group Ijmuiden, also work Detachments, Aviation Detachments, big Wood Saw Mills, and the Core Butcher Place. He got to know the fertile, highly cultivated Land. The Food in Flanders was good; there was excellent Meat and plenty Poultry. In the bigger Places were Stores put in were the Troops in the Positions could send their Vehicles to buy. Venison was scarce. At the Gen. Kdo. Was a Forest Supervisory Officer, Capt. Hedicke, who had lost one Arm, but still was an excellent Marksman. He was a good Hunter and tried to conserve the Stock of Game.

The Front on the Yser Canal, once lush and scenic, was very much destroyed from the War ravages. After going across of the Line Eernegem—Koekelare—Houthoulst was only seldom a Village not destroyed or a Tree with his Crown intact. That gave the Area a special Character and underlined the fall and sad Flanders Mood. Most terrible it looked in Ijmuiden, the surrounding of the Place and in the Houthoulster Forest who was almost Daily Target of Enemy Fire attacks. The German first Positions lay outside of the Forest Edge, but the Regiments and Battl. Dugouts were inside of the former Forest. There he met the Kdr. of the IR. 61. Oberstlt. Von Kaiser, and had a talk with this brave, with the Pour le me rite decorated Officer about the Situation, the Position and the task in this Section. He thought that his Dugout was adequately covered against view and Air Observation; 2 Days later as he walked for to his Troops did a Grenade hit his Dugout and killed his Adjutant, the Scribe and his Orderly.

At a visit at the pretty positioned Position at the Blanchard Lake did he talk with his Guide, a Vice Sergeant of the Militia, about Politics, he spoke open about many Questions, but did not want to see a shabby Peace. This Man was not War tired and his Comrades thought like he did.

Several times could they drive in a Motorboat on the Handzomevaart Canal to Ijmuiden, there they stopped at the old, dating back to the 15th. Century Bridge, which was heavy shot to pieces, and then walked to Town. The north part of this Front Position was not so much interesting.

On Nov.17 was the Army Leader with his Chief for talks in Lop hem about the buildup of the Winter Positions and on Nov.20 was the Chief of the Army Group Crown Prince Rupprecht, Gen. of the Inf. Von Kuhl with Gen. von Lossberg for talks about the structure of the Troops for the Winter Month in Lop hem. With Army Command became the Group Ijmuiden (at the time 3 Div. strong) also the Group Houthoulst with 2 Div. It came new under the Group Command the 8st. Bav. RD. Kdr. GenMaj. Jehlin, the 58st. Saxonian ID. Kdr. GenMaj. Count von Vitzthum von Eckstaedt, also 2 engaging Div., the 185st. ID. Kdr. Genlt. Von Uthmann and the 35st. ID. Kdr. Genlt. Von Hahn.

On Nov. 24 was a Meeting at the AOK. Where all commanding Gens. With they're Chiefs were there. In connection was the following order given from the Group Ijmuiden to its subordinate Div. Kdrs. witch was also talked about:

"Starting thereof, that at this time a new big Battle Area at the 2nd. 6th. and 7th. Army also east of the Maas with attacks and threat of the Enemy started, had on other Places substantial departure of Battle hard Troops taken place. Also the 4th. Army was for that used; even so here were further big attacks, especially in the middle of the Army Front, expected.

It is not excluded that Enemy attacks come against the Group Ijmuiden, that the preparations made by the Enemy against the Houthoulster Forest and at Ijmuiden will be used. In spite of that had this Group to give up 1 Div. and several Detachments, heavy Artillery, Aviation Detachments, Riveting Balloons, Marksman and MWs. Detachments. There will be high demands on the Leaders of the Div. and efficiency of the Troops made. It is desirable that we in the next spring with Battle and attack Force Div. and good Artillery can start. For this Task it is necessary that the Front is sparsely occupied so half of the Troops can be pulled back outside of the Enemy Fire for training.

A continuing observation and watching of the Enemy Positions is required, so Troops are timely at hand, when an Enemy attack is imminent. Thorough preparation for such an Operation is necessary. It is not recommended with Inconspicuous Fire of the Artillery the Operation to prepare. He found this Phase absurd, because the Enemy will notice such firing and the" inconspicuous" will be obvious! Summarize of MWs. And a sudden Fire attack with those is preferable in many cases, then Artillery participation. The Div. has to plan a few Patrol Operations, so that they are ready to order one, when observation make it necessary.

He recognized that already much happened and He expressed his Appreciation to the Patrols of the 187st. ID. And the 8st. Bav. RD. to they're successes. The seriousness of the Situation, which comes with the weakening of the first Front, causes an increased load of the Officers and Men. It is the Duty of the Leaders, as often as possible, to observe the first Lines and to tell the Troops the reason of their increased Job performance. Our Men should be told quite frankly what the immediate Situation is and how the General War Situation asks for various demands and tasks for the Army Fronts."

The 24st. Saxonian RD. and the 185st. ID. left the Area of the Group Ijmuiden. On Nov.29 was the 58st. Saxonian ID. As engaging Div. moved back and the 35st. ID. Moved in their Position. At the 8st. Bav. RD. brought a Patrol 1 Officer, 46 Belgian, 2 MGs. and 1 Grenade Launcher, in. The Chief and the Ia explored the main Position at the Yser in the Regiments Sectors of the IR. 121. And 180. And 119. While my Grandfather on Dec.3 inspected the Positions in the Houthoulster Forest. The Chief and Ia informed themselves mainly in the first Positions and daily did my Grandfather observe the training of the Troops.

It was reported At a Question from the upper Command, which Experience at the Div. Were lately observed at the Troops in view of losses on Prisoners and Deserters, because of the weakening of the Battle readiness and the will to resist,

"To AOK. 4. from Dec. 4. 1917 Ia Nr. 66/ Dec.

The Div. under the Group at this time found no such experience. But the Div. Kdrs. and they're substitute's report that the Troops in their moral and training no longer correspond to the previous state. The young Comp. Leaders do not have partly the Influence, which the Peace Officers had.

While the Troops in the first Battle Lines in the bigger Dugouts get wear down with Enemy Drumfire and then the Officers and Corporals cannot get the Men attack ready. So failed at the Moment, at an Enemy break in, the Resistance. This experience is already made with good Troops 1915 at Ban de Sapt under capable Leaders. At that time there was a lack of depth Structure and the first Lines were to heavy manned. The experiences, which have been made with the relative thin manned first Lines, showed that the Enemy could not take so many Prisoners.

He was of the Opinion, also all the Kdrs. and older Leaders of the Div. under him, that the not so good trained Troops will be equally as good as the well trained from the first War Years, when they because of the imposed War defense Situation can go forward to attack. Then there is no need for cover or fear from Enemy destruction Fire.

That the Enemy is not losing so many Prisoners is because they are easily given up their first trenches as soon as the German Artillery Fire starts. Especially at Patrol Operations, because they know that the Germans, after a victorious end of the Battle in most cases the won Trenches leave, since they do not try to further they're Positions."

His Chief, Oberstlt. Hasse, became on Dec. 23. 1917. for his outstanding Performance from his Majesty the Kaiser the Medal Pour le me rite. On Jan.18. 1918 was in the KHQu. In Lop hem at 8.15 in the Morning a Meeting on which his Excellency Ludendorff with a few Officers of the OHL. The Leaders and Chiefs of the Groups North (Navy Core), Ijmuiden (Xst. RK.), Staden (GRK.), Ieperen (G.K.), the IXst. RK. The Chief of the Army Group, Genlt. Von Kuhl, the Chief of the 4st. Army, GenMaj. Von Lossberg, the Chief of the 14st. Army, Genlt. Krafft von Dellmensingen, participated. Oberstlt. Hasse explained the attack design of the Group Ijmuiden against the north Flank of the Ieper Bend.

Gen. of the Inf. Ludendorff informed himself especially about the various Proposals for the average Front widths and depth of a Div. and stipulated widths of about 2km. The high Interest which Excellency Ludendorff gave the Troop Leaders and the Army and Core Chiefs was evident at all these Meetings. In the lively exchange of Ideas were military, tactic and operative questions mentioned. My Grandfather could again admire, like so often, the calm and clarity in the views and descriptions of the first Gen. Quarter Master, at the end gave Gen. Ludendorff a summary of the political Situation, which he thought was good, since in Brest-Litowsk another sound had taken effect. The Negotiations with the Ukraine where good and Romania had on the previous Day asked in Berlin about a Peace Offer.

Certainly were, like the first Gen. Quarter Master further explained, because of the not clear Situation, the evacuation of Troops from the east limited; A few Div. would come to the West Front, but it should stay a heavy Border defense in the East. In the near Future would come 4 Div. from Romania and all Troops, who were in the fall send to Italy, to the West Front.

These Meetings should only give the OHL. A Global View, in order to enable them to make up their Minds and to ask his Majesty the Kaiser for a Decision. Gen. Ludendorff pointed at the End again, like at the Start, to absolute Secrecy about everything discussed. If it was necessary to send Troops to the Homeland should only reliably Battl. Used, like Storm Battl. but at present would be no reasons for any Concerns.

This Day should not pass without a big Shock for my Grandfather. In the Afternoon he learned that his Wife got very sick. He asked for leave for

Berlin and in connection on that for the Command to a Gas Course, for which he was already chosen. Shortly before he left on Jan.21 he became the news of her Death. A true German Soldiers Wife separated from them; they had lost very much.

After he came back there was much to do, a Presentation of a Pioneer Trainings Course about learning to build Train Bridges in a Funnel Area. Meetings about Plans at the 38st. Ldw. D. and the 54st. RD. Battle exercises and so on.

Maj. Von Wolff was on Feb.28. 1918 promoted to Chief of the Gen. Staff of the Detect Inspection 4. He was for him a very efficient first Gen. Staff Officer but also in his Prussian thinking a true Comrade.

In his Place came the wise energetic Maj. Reuter who even in the hardest Situations was fresh and cheerful On March 6st. At 6 in the Morning took a Shock Troop of the IR. 50, 358 and 363 of the 214st. ID. Kdr. GenMaj. Maerker, 3 Officers and 114 Men of the Belgian KD. As Prisoners and Captured 2 MGs. Shock Troops of the 35st. ID. Took in the Afternoon of that Day 2 Officers and 30 Man of the 3rd.Belgian ID. As Prisoners and captured 2 MGs.

On March 8. 1918 was at 6 in the Afternoon in the KHQu. Of the Group Wytschaete a Meeting at which Gen. Ludendorff with several Officers of the OHL. Excellence Sixt von Armin with his Chief and the first Gen. Staff Officer, also Gen. Von Kuhl, the Commanding Generals. Of the Groups Ijmuiden, Ieper, Wytschaete with they're Chiefs and the Chiefs of the Groups North and Staden, were present.

It was about the implementation of Operation in the Area of the 4st. Army, especially the storming of the Kemmel Mountain. Gen. Ludendorff let himself accurately report how the execution was planned. This Meeting had for the Officers of the OHL. Only Information Character.

On March 21 started the big Battle in France who was soon followed by a further attack at the Lys. A wounded English Man of the 32nd. English Div. was brought in on March 22 and a Patrol Operation at the 36st. RD. Kdr. GenMaj. von Rantzau, brought 1 Officer and 3 Men of the 3rd. Belgian Div. as Prisoners in. 4 Days later took again a German Patrol 20 Men of the Belgian Jaeg. R. As Prisoners.

Abruptly started on March 28. 1918 at 9 in the Evening heavy Enemy Fire at Aschkop and with this Fire moved heavy Enemy Patrols for and took the Crew of a Dugout, 2 first Lt. and 27 Men as Prisoners.

Group Flanders

On April 3 was commanded that the Gen.Kdo. Of the Xst. RK. Give up The Section Ijmuiden to the Group North and the Group Ieper; it will be pulled out for extra Utilization. On April 5 became the Gen.Kdo. Of the Xst. RK. For Disposal of the AOK. 4 and was as Army reserve stationed in Tourcoing.

The Army Command of the AOK. 4 from April 5. 1918 Nr. 122 had the following orders:

"Gen.Kdo. of the Xst. RK. Take over the Command over the sector of the Group Wytschaete south of the Lys as Group Flanders. Timing of the Command takeover arranges the Xst. RK. With the Group Wytschaete. The in the Group Wytschaete stationed 31st. ID. And parts of the 36st. RD. remain under the Gen. Kdo. Of the Xst. RK. The 49st. RD. takes over on April 6 the Village Frelinghien from the Group Lille. On Artillery becomes the Xst. RK. All of the so far to the 49st. RD. belonging Artillery. In all:

10 Field Canon Batteries	4 Mortars
5 light Field Howitzer Battr.	5 10cm. Canon Battr.
10 heavy Field Howitzer Battr.	3 13 and 15cm. Canon Battr.

In addition becomes the Xst. RK. From the 6st. Army:

7 Field Canon Battr. Motionless
7 light Field Howitzer Battr. Motionless
2 heavy Field Howitzer Battr.
1 Mortar Battr.

Storm Battl. 4 without 1 Comp. who stays further under the Group Wytschaete come under the Xst. RK. Drawing arranges the Xst. RK. Themselves with the Group Ieper, Storm Battl. 4 and Bba 4."

On this Day were his Chief and the first Gen. Staff Officer for Instruction in the duties of the Xst. RK. At the AOK. 4 at the Group Wytschaete and the 49st. RD. Kdr. GenMaj. Von Ueschtritz und Steinkirch.

Gen. Von Lossberg came on April 6 to the KHQu. Of the Xst. RK. To talk about the details of the preparation for the attack, especially the Procurement of Ammunition, the Control of replenishment necessary to overcome the Lys Crossing and the Funnel Areas, this was complicated in this short time. Following was at the Gen.Kdo. In presence of the Divs. Kdrs. and they're Gen. Staff Officers an in depth Instruction and discussion of the Tasks, who the Front Divs. would encounter.

The Group Flanders had the order to join the attack of the 6st. Army. (Upper Kdr. Gen. of the Inf. Von Quast, Chief of the Gen. Staff Oberstlt. Knight von Lenz), who stood left from them, and with the 31st. ID. Kdr. GenMaj. Von Wissel, over Waasten between Dove-Creek and Ploegsteert, with the 214st. ID. The over Deulemont and Frelinghien should have moved for, between Ploegsteerter Forest and Lys to attack. The 36st. RD. and the 49st. RD. stood as Army Reserve behind these attacks Divs. First attack Day was for the 6st. Army April 9 for the 4st. Army April 10. Code Name for this Operation was" Oster Fest". (Easter Celebration)

On April 7 did he drive to Lille for a Conference with the Commanding Gen. of the IInd. Bav. AK. Gen. of the Cav. Baron von Stetten (Chief of the Gen. Staff Maj. Count von Tattenbach). At beautiful Weather was heavy Aviator Activity, which gave a special Impression, since in the Town Lille, the Life and Carry on of the elegant dressed Woman, the happy and worry free playing Kids in the Streets, stood in stark Contrast to the heavy visible from afar Air Battles and the lively Artillery Activity.

The 6st. Army was to move for with they're right Wing from Fromelles to Baillieu. The Group Flanders with they're 4st Div. under them, also the on the right connecting Group Wytschaete with the 17st. RD. had to attack the north of Armentieres facing Enemy as soon as the 6st. Army had moved for over the Lys. The cleanup of the Area south of the Lys from Hiplines to Erquinghem took the 6st. Army with they're attack over.

At the Xst. RK. Had as Div. of the first Wave the 31st. ID. Right, and left next to it the 214st. ID. To attack, as Army reserve had first of all in the middle the 36st. RD. to follow. The 49st. RD. had by advanced attack, first behind of the middle to pull Forces quickly in the Area from

Waste together and to get ready to march for as Army reserve in westerly direction.

It was important, as soon as possible, to get the connection to the right Wing of the 6st. Army. First attack target was the taking of the Enemy Battr. Between Douve Brook and the Lys. The Ploegsteerter Forest was with encirclement from the inner Wings to be taken by the 31st. And 214st. ID. A further attack Target was the Kemmel and the red Mountain south of Westoeter, in connection on the 6st. Army, respectively XVIIIst. RK. (Kdr. Genlt. Sieger, Chief of the Gen. Staff Oberstlt. Buerkner). As soon as possible to take over.

On April 8 was at the Group Flanders a Prisoner of the 25st. English Div. brought in, witch confirmed Enemy Force Distribution. His Chief drove on this Day to the 31st. And 214st. ID. And 49st. RD. and to the Group Lille (IInd. Bav. AK.).

The Attack on April 9 south of Armentieres of the 6st. Army was in this Group Section not noticeable. At 10 in the Morning stood the 31st. ID. In the Area Komen, Wervik, La Montagne, Le Vieil Dieu and the 36st. RD. in the Area of Bousbecque, Roncq, Linselles. At 1 in the Morning came the first relay of the Gen.Kdo. To the Group Battle Post Linselles. The Rest of the Staff remained KHQu. In Tourcoing.

The 6st. Army had the attack between Fromelles and Givenchy until 9 in the Evening in the Line Bois Grenier (inclusive) L'Armee south of Armentieres—Fleurbaix—Estaires—La Gorgue and La Casan (This was taken) Richburg L'Avoue – East Edge of Festered—Givenchy (was not taken) moved for.

In the night of April 9 to 10 moved the 31st. ID. Not bothered from the Enemy, in the Storm starting Position. The 214st. ID. Pushed at Pont Rouged and Frelinghien Bridge Heads over the Lys and led the Bridge building on those 2 Places until 1.15 in the Morning. The brave Pioneers did not interfere in their hard work by the losses witch the Enemy Artillery Fire caused.

From 2.45 in the Morning on was the Enemy Artillery gassed. The attack started from the position east of the Lys River from south Komen over Waste, Delamont, Frelinghien, and Hiplines. At the 31st. ID. started from 5.09 in the Morning until 5.15 in the Morning abruptly own destruction Fire on to the first Enemy Line with MWs. And at the second

Line with Artillery Fire, At 5.15 in the Morning followed the Storm of the Infantry.

At the 214ˢᵗ. ID. Lasted the own destruction Fire from 4.45 in the Morning until 5.15 in the Morning and then came the Infantry attack. At 5.45 in the Morning had both Divs. reported to the Group that they're starting Positions had been reached without interference and the Inf. attack had started on time and they had taken Area. At 8 in the Morning came for Directions in the Gen.Kdo. The Staffs of the 11ˢᵗ. Bav. ID. and 22ⁿᵈ. RD. He gave both Div. Kdrs. Genlt. Knight von Kneussel and Gen. of the Art. Schubert, the Battle Situation and they're Tasks.

The Divs. were to follow as Army Reserves in the Section of the Xst. RK. The 11ˢᵗ. Bav. ID. stood at 8.30 in the Morning for the Gen.Kdo. At Verlinghem for Disposal. There upon he ordered that the Div. at Quesnay should hold themselves in readiness the Lys at Pont Rouged or Freilinghien to cross. The 22ⁿᵈ. RD. at Wambrechies was at 10 in the Morning from the AOK. To the XVIIIst. RK. Put in March.

The right Wing of the 31ˢᵗ. ID. following a Fire Roller was quick stormed over both first Lines of the Enemy Position. It then became from the Trenches from Dove Farm, Damiere Farm and from the northeast Corner of the Ploegsteerter Forest heavy MG. Fire. In the thereby incurred stay was the connection to the Fire Roll lost and the attack was stuck in the heavy wired marshy Area.

Heavy Fog in the Morning and Haze during the Day prevented any Flyer activity. An energetic Infantry Flyer could have, by ascertain the German first Line and by bringing up the Reserves, on this Day provide valuable Services.

This Day was for the IR. 174. And 70. Very hard. The Kdr. of the 174ˢᵗ. Maj. Mueller—Loebnitz, was able, even so he was wounded, after loss of all Battl. Leaders, under ruthless use of his own Person, the Detachments to organize and his Regiment again put to Storm.

At the left Wing of the 31ˢᵗ. ID. Came the attack of the Inf.Reg. 70, Kdr. Oberstlt. Siehr, at the buildup of heavy Strongpoint Sugar Fabric, at heavy Resistance. Only at 8 in the morning was the Fabric, after fight with losses in German Hand. In further moving forward came the left Wing of the Div. to the southeast Corner of the Ploegsteerter Forest. The 214ˢᵗ. ID. To whom the IR. 363. Kdr. Maj. Roeschke, IR. 358. Kdr. Maj. Hahn and

IR. 50. Kdr. Colonel von Paczynski—Tenezin, belonged, had at 5.15 in the Morning under the Umbrella of the Fire Roll, the Enemy position overrun and could already at 7.25 in the Morning report the taking of the Rabeque Farm, at 10.15 in the Morning the Village Ploegsteert and the taking of several Canons also over 200 Prisoners. There on moved the Gen.Kdo. The R.I.R. 61, from the 36st. RD. to the southeast Corner of the Ploegsteerter Forest, as Core Reserve for. The rest of the 36st. RD. stayed east of the Lys, south of the Deuel. Enemy heavy Artillery shelled from 8 in the Morning the Lys Bridge at Pont Roget and destroyed it temporally with a hit.

The Viscous Resistance giving Enemy (19st. And 23rd.English Div.) Were, after what Prisoners said, by the attack completely surprised. In the Noon hours were an Enemy counter attack against Ploegsteert from the Area of the big Munque Farm repelled. Calva ire Farm was with heavy Enemy counter attack lost, but was retaken by the IR. 358. The moving forward at the left Wing by the 214st. ID. Was with MG. Flank Fire from the South Shore of the Lys, from the Area of Hiplines, made Difficult.

The Kdr. of the Pi. Battl. 93. Capt. Luedecke, which was allocated to the 31st. ID. Led the Repair work of the totally blown Road through Wasting. The Div. Push Battr. Could already in the Night, at this Road through Wasting over their own formerly Positions, follow the Inf.

At 2 in the Afternoon was the first Line of the Group Flanders: 31st. ID. East of Dove Farm, South east Corner of the Ploegsteerter Forest. West of this Line prevent Enemy MG. Nests a move forward. At the 214st. ID. was the Line west Edge of the Ploegsteerter Forest- Calva ire—Big Rabeque Farm—Westhoeck.

From the Gen. Kdo. Of the Xst. RK. Was Capt. Baron von und zu Gilsa from G.Fus.Reg. As Connection Officer to the 32nd. Saxonian ID. Kdr. GenMaj. Von der Decken, to the Group Lille commanded. Capt. Baron von und zu Gilsa did continually report to the Gen. Kdo. About they're left Neighbor. The 32nd. Saxonian ID. At the right Wing of the 6st. Army came at Erquinghem not over the Lys; because of that ordered the AOK. 4 at 2.30 in the Afternoon, that the Xst. RK. Not to swing to northwest, but for relief of the crossing of the 32nd. Saxonian ID. Further to west advance to the Steen Works.

The Gen. Kdo. Ordered at 3 in the Afternoon to the 31st ID. To occupy the Rossignol Hill north of Ploegsteert, to the 214st. ID. Regardless of the

31st. ID. To attack towards West until connection to the 6st. Army. For security of the right Flank followed the Div. the R. I. R. 61. Kdr. Oberstlt. Von Jacobi, as Core Reserve. The 36st. RD. became order, a second Inf. Reg. with push Battr. To move forward for Advance towards West.

The attack of the 31st. ID. Came Opposite of the numerous, in the Area hidden MG. Nests, until Evening not further for. The 214st ID. Became, On their Application, at 5.50 in the Afternoon the Ist. / RIR.61. Under Capt. of the Reserve Risch, to they're disposal. It did, under rejection of several Enemy counter attacks, move the attack for until the Line Big Munque Farm-East Don Farm—Osthove Castle—Pont de Nieppe and came in this Line opposite tenacious resistance to a halt. In the Evening moved the IInd. And IIIrd.RIR.61 into the south part of the Ploegsteerter Forest.

At 6 in the Evening ordered the AOK. That the Xst. RK. Again Attack towards Kemmel and Nieuwekerke, since the 32nd. ID. had taken Erquinghem.

My Grandfather gave the following Core Command:

"The Enemy is moved back in Front of the 31st. ID. In the Afternoon in the Ploegstetter Forest and North from there. Against the 214st. ID. Were strong counter attacks until the Evening hours.

The English apparently to move they're Battr. During the Night back to escape the Threat of encirclement west of Armentieres. Both have to be prevented. It is therefore necessary the Enemy, who at this time apparently has no heavy reserves, immediately to attack,:

> 31st. ID. In their attack Section,
> 214st. ID. With they're right Wing towards Nieppe,
> To make Connection with the Right Wing of the IInd.
> Bav. AK.

The in the Group Command from April 7 Ia Nr. 309 ordered attack Sections will be in effect again, also inside Wing towards Nieuwekerke, west Slope Kemmel.

From the 36st. RD. remains RIR. 61 under the 214st. ID. It is up to the one for Deployment open Battl. To pull back after the Right Wing.

The 36st. RD. follows inclusive the Comp. of the Storm Battl. 4 at the right Wing of the 214st. ID. South of the Ploegsteerter Forest. The kept back Reg. crosses at 5 in the Morning the Lys.

The 11st. Bav. ID. crosses at 5 in the morning at Frelinghien the Lys and follows behind the left Wing of the 214st. ID."

After, on before Noon of April 11 the 31st. ID. Did not come forward against the Rossignol Hill, gave the Gen. Kdo. At 12 Noon for support the 36st. RD. It was intended, that this Div. after taking of the Rossignol Position would come for the 31st. ID. And later take over this Section.

The attack was from the Kdr. of the 31st.ID. GenMaj. Von Wissel, planed as follows:

31st. ID. With IR.174 from East against the Strong Point at Dove Farm, Dammar Farm; IR. 70 against St. Yves from South and IR. 166 against the Rossignol Hill from South. 36st. RD. in the Gab between the left Wing of the IR. 166 and the right Wing of the 214st. ID. at Pouxcelle.

Artillery Preparation from 6.15 until 6.30 in the Evening, then Storm.

At 3 in the Afternoon came his Majesty the Kaiser to him in the Battle Post and became on hand of Maps Lecture on the Situation. He asked him to express the brave Troops his Recognition for their Achievements in the Battle. From there drove his Majesty along the Front and greeted everywhere the Troops who marched for, who cheered him enthusiastically, very happy to see they're Supreme Commander.

In the meantime took the 214st. ID. In continuing Attack Le Romarin north of Nieppe. Until Evening had the Div. taken 28 Canons, many MGs. and MWs. and big Stocks of Munition.

At 6.30 in the Evening stormed IR. 174 the opposite Enemy Position and took in one MG. Nest 16 MGs. The IR. 70 took at the same time St. Yves. The attack of the IR.166 was delayed, when the approach of the Reg. got stopped by the attacks of low flying Enemy Airplanes,. At 7.45 in the Evening Stormed the Reg., after preparation with MGs. and MWs. The Rossignoll Hill. The dashing Kdr. of the IR.166. Oberstlt.Polmann was for his determent conduct mentioned in the Army News.

To west joining filled the 36st. RD. the Gab between the 31st. ID. and the 214st. ID. At 8.30 in the Evening attacked the RIR. 5. Kdr. Oberstlt. Brehme. Of the 36. RD. again and came to the Line La Hutte—Le Petit

Pont. At 12 Midnight (On April 12. 1918) was the following Command given:

"Troops of the Core did today, tenacious resistance breaking, achieved beautiful successes. The 31st. ID. Has taken the Rossignol Hill and is with the Reg. of the 36st. RD. moved for south of the Hill towards west.

The 214st. ID. has stormed the Enemy Positions on both sides of Le Romarin. At they're left Wing did they connect with the 32nd. Saxonian ID. Who stays at Les trois Tilleuls.

North of the Douve Brook did the 49st. RD. make no progress. The XVIIIst. RK. Has first of all the taken Area to hold and should no more moving forward. It is reliant, with heavy Artillery, the further attacks of the Xst. RK. To support. The 31st. ID. with the 36st. RD. under them attacks tomorrow the whole Line Wulvergem—Nieuwekerke and should take the Hill there.

The 214st. ID. Goes at Daybreak from Le Romarin towards west for in order to connect with the 117st. ID. Who is moving forward to Le Papol.

Nieppe is at 6 in the Morning attacked from south from the 32nd. Saxonian ID. The 11st. Bav. ID. has, at moving for, the 214st. ID. Over Le Bizet to Le Romarin to follow."

At before Noon of April 12 did he drive with Capt. Von Goeckel to Waste and on Foot from there to the Ploegsteerter Forest to talk with the Kdr. of the 31st. ID. And other Leaders. The Weather was beautiful, Sunshine and long sight so they had a good overlook over the Battle Area. The output of the Pioneers at the building of Bridges and Roads over the Lys and the Funnel Area, earned high Praise. Continually had the Bridges, because of Enemy Fire, to be repaired, or totally new build.

Endless Trains of Columns moved for to the fighting Troops, picturesque Bivouacs right and left at the shot to pieces Homes and in a wide Flat in which the English could look from the Kemmel. It was no wonder that suddenly Heavy Grenades exploded in the midst of these Columns and resting Troops. The English had fortunately only a few Canons and no good Ammunition.

The XVIIIst. RK. Had at 9.15 in the Morning reported that the left Wing of the 49st. RD. towards Wulvergem, without finding real resistance, had moved for 800m. Because of that became the 36st. RD the Command, if the Enemy moved back, to push sharply behind, if possible over the Line Wulvergem—Nieuwekerke.

Through Core Command 82 of April 12. 1918 before Noon were ordered that it was necessary for the Preparation of the Attack against the Kemmel and the red Mountain that the Hill Area of Wulvergem, Nieuwekerke and Bailleul on April 13 came early in German Hand.

The at 4 in the Afternoon following attack of the 31st. ID. and 36st. RD. thrust at tenacious resistance of the Enemy, in the heavy build up Position west of Lerche, and came only to the Line Big Douve Farm— Leeuwerk Farm—Lerche, 300m. West of Petit Pont.

Indeed had the Artillery resistance of the Enemy, against April 11, significantly strengthened. The 214st. ID. led in the Morning hours the attack further for. The Enemy stayed in the Line Romarin—Le Papol. At 5 in the Afternoon reported the 214st. ID. That the tenacious resistance of the Enemy at Le Papol was broken and the Village towards north were passed; The Enemy went back to the height of Nieuwekerke. The Gen. Kdo .ordered to strongly follow and to take the Hills of Nieuwekerke. The Div.reached at 7 in the Evening the Line south of Fache Farm—Grove 600m. East of de Seule but came there to stop because of Enemy resistance.

The 11st. Bav. ID. had at 4 in the Afternoon the Area from Le Bizet, Osthove Castle attained. At 9 in the Evening took the 36st. RD. Over the Command in the Battle Section of the 31st. ID. She kept until further the IR. 166. and all the Artillery. The rest of the 31st. ID. Collects itself in the west part and south of the Ploegsteerter Forest. The Div. had with heavy losses on dead and wounded taken many 100 English Prisoners, among them an American Officer and much Booty of Weapons and Munition.

At 11 in the Evening commanded the AOK. That the Xst. RK. On April 13 occupies the Hills at Nieuwekerke. At 12 Midnight ordered my Grandfather that the 36st. RD. and the 214st. ID. On April 13 had to occupy the Hills of Nieuwekerke and if possible the Hill at Zwartemolenhoek. The attack was to start at 7 in the Morning and the heavy point should be at the left Wing of the Div. The 11st. Bav. ID. became order to follow behind the left Wing of the 214st. ID.

The dashing sweeping advance of the 214st. ID on this Day had succeeded Armentieres to take; witch was from the troops of the IInd.

Bav. AK. And the Xst. RK. From north and south encircled. The English Crew, 50 Officers and more than 3000 Men gave the Weapons up after brave resistance. 45 Canons and many MGs. came in the Hand of the storming Troops.

On April 13 at 7 in the Morning started, at heavy Fog, the attack against Nieuwekerke. The 36st. RD. came, because of heavy Enemy resistance, not forward. The 214st. ID. was able in heavy Battle to win Area. IR. 363 came within 300m. At the Village Nieuwekerke. IR. 50 came until the Hill west of that Village. But since the IInd. Bav. AK. In this attack, as provided, not took part, but without reporting to the Xst. RK. Had moved it to 12 Noon, were the IR. 50, in the because of that open Flank, from a heavy Enemy counter attack seized and had to go back to Drie Koningen. The Reg. became an order of the Group a Battl. (IInd. / 22. Bav. IR.) of the 11st. Bav. ID.

That at the left Wing of the 214st.ID. Moving forward IR. 358 could not storm forward since it was involved in a Battle at the left Flank against De Soule. This Village was, against the report of the IInd. Bav. AK. Still heavy from the Enemy occupied. Since the Frontal Attack of the 36st. RD. at the heavy Enemy Position brought no success, became the Div. at 11 in the Morning an order, the Enemy with only weak forces to hold on the Front, while the left Wing with heavy forces had to strike out toward south to in this way to take the Position and to ease the moving forward of the 214st. ID. Towards Nieuwekerke. The 214st. ID. became the order at 5 in the Afternoon to frontal attack against the Hills of Nieuwekerke and from left staggered over Westhof.

From the 11st. Bav. ID. was 2nd Inf. Reg. moved for. The 22nd. And 3rd. Bav. IR. Came under the 214st.ID. The 22nd. (Colonel Carl) had Nieuwekerke to storm, the 3rd. (Colonel Baron von Stengel) Zwartemolenhoek. The attack was conducted in accordance with the recommend, Nieuwekerke and the Hills west of the Village came in German Hand, because of the dashing advance of Capt. Langbein from the IIIrd. / 22nd. Bav. IR. The, at the same time started Attack at the left Neighbor Div., the 117st. ID. Kdr. Genlt. Von Drabich-Waechter, from 16. April with Kdr. GenMaj. Hoefer, did not yield any significant benefits.

On Afternoon at April 13 came the 22nd. RD. under the Xst. RK. And from Gen.Kdo. In the Area southeast of Ploegsteert moved for, Div.

Combat Post Le Bizet. In addition became the Xst. RK. In the Evening the 117st. ID. And on April 14 before Noon also the 32nd. Saxonian ID. After Implementation from April 13 from the IInd. Bav. AK. Ordered Attack, tactically subordinate. Economically remained the Div. Under the Command of the IInd. Bav. AK.

The AOK. Ordered the Xst. RK. To occupy on April 14 the Hill Ritch which runs from Nieuwekerke to west towards Bailleul. On Afternoon came his Majesty the Kaiser again to his Battle Post and was very happy that everything moved forward. It was detected that the Enemy Artillery with their main Forces had moved into new Positions northeast and southwest of Groote Vierstraat. On April 13 in the Evening came from the AOK.an order:

"Xst. RK. Did with the 36st. RD. brake through the Enemy Position south of Nieuwekerke and penetrated Nieuwe Eglise. The 214st. ID. Has produced the connection with the 36st. RD. and has with the 11st. Bav. ID. towards the Hills west of Nieuwekerke won Area. The 117st. ID. Who was put under the Gen. Kdo. Has taken De Seule. The Xst. RK. Has to proceed as follows: The 36st. RD. is with the middle to be set at the Kemmel. They're follows the 31st. ID. As Flank Defense against Wulvergem. The 214st. ID. reinforced with the 11st. Bav. ID., has, after taken the Hills from Nieuwekerke, the Ravets Mountain to take from east. The 11st. Bav. ID. reliefs the 214st. ID., who is to be pulled back for use at the Army, and goes between the 36st. RD. and the 117st. ID. With the Middle against Dranoeter and Red Mountain for. They're follows the 22nd. RD."

For April 14 was from the Gen. Kdo. Ordered the continuing of the Attack with Group Command (Xst. RK.) Ia Nr. 97:

"After the so far known News is the Situation as follows:

Left Wing XVIIIst. RK. As until now east of Wulvergem. 36st. RD. with right Wing close south of the Road Wulvergem-Nieuwekerke, left Wing penetrated to Nieuwekerke east. 214st. ID.had with right Wing Nieuwekerke and Hill west from there taken. Left Wing is moved for to Zwartemolenhoek, Bonte Katte. Success not now known.

117st. ID. Has taken De Seule and Le Seau and is with right Wing moved for over De Brooken and to Berthof. The Alpine Core shall from the Chaussee Bailleul—Metern (1.5km.west) towards St. Jans (1km. north of Bailleul) on April 14 attack.

Further Tasks for the Core is, as soon as possible, to move for against Kemmel, Red Mountain and Mont Noir, so that the Kemmel, on who's Foot is much resistance expected, can be taken as soon as possible also from the west. To this have the Divs. to forge ahead in their Battle Sections.

36st. RD. pulls in the Night as much as possible Artillery for under whose protection she works for against the Kemmel. Security at the right Flank and heavy echelon Formation is necessary at coming down to the Dove Brook. 11st. Bav. ID. takes over Command at 3 in the Morning in the previous Section of the 214st. ID. Who comes under they're Command."

On the Morning of April 14 attacked the Enemy with heavy Forces the middle of the 36st. RD. but where repelled, in which 2 Officers and 50 Men stayed in they're Hand.

The 36st. RD. intended the ordered attack at 11.30 in the Morning to perform. Artillery helps from the 49st. RD. was asked. The Attack of the 11st. Bav. ID. was fixed for 4.30 in the Afternoon. The Relief of the 214st. ID. From the 11st. Bav. ID. was done according to order. The 214st. ID. Gathered itself in the course of late Morning in the Area Drie Koningen, Kortepyp and were later pulled back to the Area Quesnoy, Wambrechies, Linselles.

The 214st. ID. had fought magnificently. They're energetic Kdr. Gen. Maerker, supported with his efficient Gen. Staff Officer Capt. Langemeyer, were in continuing connection with the Gen. Kdo.

12 Officers, 1 Doctor, 708 not wounded and 281 wounded Prisoners, 38 Field Canons, 2 heavy Canons, 150 MGs. and other Booty, took the Div. from the Enemy. The losses of the Div. were heavy, but the Troops and they're proven Leaders made an excellent Impression, when my Grandfather greeted them in their Rest Quarters. He praised the services of his brave Troops and his successful Leadership

He did find Gen. Maerker worthy to award him the Oak Leaves to the Pour le me rite, and presented him the Decoration with the following Words:

"GenMaj. Maerker is an outstanding Leader of the from himself exemplary trained Div. He has with his Troops on April 9/10 surprisingly crossed the Lys, on April 10 Armentieres towards north isolated and taken the Village Ploegsteert. On the 10th. And in the following Days conquered Gen. Maerker, everywhere on his own and brave in the first Line, the Village Nieuwekerke and the Hills west of there. He deserves the fullest appreciation for the success of those Battle Days."

> The German Army News from April 14.1918 reported:
> AT the Battle Field on the Lys were in hard Battle Area won. South of Dove Brook pierced the Troops of Gen.Von Eberhardt the Enemy Positions southwest Of Wulvergem and stormed after bitter struggle with Englishmen who tried to counter attack, Nieuwekerke. A carried out attack in the Evening hours under Leadership of Gen. Maerker brought us into Possession of the Hill west from that Village. At Bailleul was fought. The Villages Merris and Vieux Berquin were taken. To the Battle Field marching Columns became through our Ground and Air Observation led Fire, heavy losses."

On late Morning on April 14 came the 11st. Bav. ID. into Possession of several big resistance Nests east of Nieuwekerke. Thereby came 2 Officers and 100 Men into German Hand. At 6 in the Afternoon were from IIIrd. / 22nd. Bav. IR. 5 Canons, 4 MGs. and 150 English brought in. During the Day became the Enemy Artillery Fire much stronger, several Enemy Battr. Were seen at the Kemmel, also Enemy Trench work was reported at that Mountain.

The for 11.30 in the Morning from the 36st. RD. and the at 4.30 in the Afternoon from the 11st. Bav. ID. ordered attacks, brought no considerable Progress. The reason for that was at the 36st RD. Flank MG. Fire from the direction of Wulvergem, at the 11st. Bav. ID. heavy Enemy MG. Fire from the Front and Flank Artillery Fire. The Attack of the 117st. ID. Brought them into Possession of Le Seau, the Railroad Claw at La Creche also the Broken Berthof and Le Lethe.

For April 15 was a renewal of the attack at the 36st. RD., 11st. Bav. ID., 117st. ID. Ordered, in such a Way, that the right Wing of the Core (36st. RD. and right Wing of the 11st. Bav. ID.) held back, while the left Wing of the 11st. Bav. ID. and the 117st. ID. at 4 in the Afternoon, after 1 hour of Artillery preparation, starts to occupy the Hills of Zwartemolenhoek, Sebasto, Le Ravets Mountain and Liller Mountain. As further Day Target was the Line Red Lager, 1km. southwest of the Train Baillieu—Wulvergem 1km. north of Zwartemolenhoek, Salon Farm—Hagedorn fixed.

The ordered attack Command for April 15 was expanded by subordination of the 32nd. Saxonian ID. Under the Command of the 117st. ID. And 1 Infantry Reg. (R. I. R. 71) of the 22nd. RD. under the Command of the 11st. Bav. ID. before Noon of April 15 ordered the Army, that the Xst. RK. Kept the Command over the 117st. And 32nd. Saxonian ID. Until after the Implementation of the attack.

At 9.15 in the Morning could his Chief tell the Divs. That a Battle Squadron of 6 Airplanes of the Battle Squadrons 23. And 30. Under Command of first Lt. Ertl would participate in the Battle. This was warmly welcomed by the Battle Troops.

The Attack of April 15 from the XVIIIst. RK. Had result. After taken Wulvergem they subsequently moved for to the Street to Wytschaete. With this advance of the 49st. RD. did the Reg. of the 36st. RD. from own Initiative, join and were moved for to the Street Wulvergem-Nieuwekerke—Stemcor Mill. In the Morning moved the Div. further for and stood in the Noon hours with the right Wing from Dove Brook to the Train Facilities there in the Plan Quadrat 7650. From there bent the Front to southwest, about in the direction q in the Plan Quadrat7651. 98 Prisoners where brought in. At this advancing became the Div. almost no Artillery Fire.

The 11st. Bav.ID. Had at 8 in the Morning north of Nieuwekerke the Attack of an English Battl. Repelled. The Attack of the 11st. Bav. ID. the 117st. And 32nd. Saxonian ID. Against the Hills west of Zwartemolenhoek, the Rivets and Lille Mountain went according to Plan after the Artillery preparation and they occupied the Hills west of Zwartemolenhoek after overcoming tenacious Enemy resistance. A very forceful lead Enemy attack against the Hills of Zwartemolenhoek were repelled.

The at Evening reached Line was about 500 to 800m. South of the Train Wulvergem—Baillieul. After Report of the 117st. ID. Had towards Evening the 32nd. Saxonian ID. North of the Liller Mountain the Street Zwartemolenhoek—Bailleul towards north crossed and was with parts to the Lunatic Asylum St. Antonius advanced. The first weak Enemy Artillery Fire became more forceful towards Evening. The Fire was particularly on Nieuwekerke and at the Hills west of Zwartemolenhoek.

From the 22nd. RD. was the R. I. R. 71. Kdr. Maj. Volkmann, as Reserve of the 11st. Bav. ID. moved for to Westhof, R. I. R. 82. Kdr. Oberstlt. Du Vignau, moved into Bivouac at Kortepyp, De Seule, R. I. R. 94. Kdr. Oberstlt. von Goerschen, at Lampermisse, le Romarin.

The Core Command for April 16 ordered that the 11st. Bav. ID. the Hill Ridge at Salon Farm and further east the Dove Bottom had to contain and the attack of the left connecting G. R. K. Kdr. Gen. of the Cav. Baron Marschall, Chief of the Gen. Staff Maj. Humser, in his right Flank by also move for, to secure. Otherwise was the Day to be exploited to organize the Detachments and move the Artillery for.

In the same Night was the Command about the 117st. And 32nd. Saxonian ID. Given to the G. R. K. witch was put in at the right Wing of the 6st. Army. After storming of the Enemy Positions at Wulvergem by the 49st. RD. started the Enemy also before the Front of the 36st. RD. his first Line to the Dove Brook and between the Dove Brook and the Kemmel Mountain to clear. Until Noon was the Line I—o in the Plan Quadrat 7550 reached. The 11st. Bav. ID. cleaned in connection of the results of April 15 the Area before they're right Wing to the Dove Brook.

Before they're Front was the 29st. English Div. found, who was supposed to be used at Ypern and were with Trucks brought to the Battle Front. Also were Men from a training course at Ypern taken Prisoner.

The appointed attack of the 11st. Bav. ID. for April 16 at the Hills of Salon Farm had little result. The Infantry came closer to the Enemy Position to about 400m. And took Keerseboom but it was not possible for them to take the Hills. The reason for that was heavy Enemy MG. Fire, which hit the for moving Infantry, also was no connection to the left.

Since the occupation of the Hills at the Salon Farm was very important for the Preparation of the 11st. Bav. ID. for the intended big attack on April 17 was the Div. ordered to attack at the Salon Hill Positions early on April 17. In the Evening of April 16 repelled the Div. an Enemy counters attack. In the Evening of April 16 was the following Group Command given out:

"XVIIIst. RK. Took today the Hills at Wytschaete and South from there. At they're left Wing is Battr. K North of Wulvergem and the Area about 500m. West of this Battr. In they're Possession. G. R. K. stays with they're right Wing at the Railway Installations about 600m. Northeast of the Lunatic Asylum. Direct connection in the Area of the Prisoner Camp Keerseboom is at this time not known.

Left Wing of the 4st. Army and right Wing of the 6st. Army attack on April 17. Start of the Inf. attack at 11 in the Morning.

36. RD. occupies the Kemmel and the north from there positioned Enemy Artillery. The attack is with the main Forces at the left Wing with most probable encirclement from southwest to perform.

The XVIIIst. RK. That largely stays defensive, has been asked to follow the 36st. RD. at the attack with they're left Wing. One Inf. Reg. of the 31st. ID. Shall come under the 36st. RD.

11st. Bav. ID. has at 8 in the Morning, together with the right Wing of the 117st. ID. to win an appropriate assembly possibility, to occupied the Salon Hills. Target of the main attack is the enemy Artillery at Loker and Red Mountain. The attack is to perform with heavy left Wing. The R. I. R. 71 of the 22nd. RD. stays under the 11st. Bav. ID. The 117st. ID. Moves for towards Mont Noir.

31st. ID., without one Inf. Reg., follows by advancing attack, the left Wing of the 36st. RD. 22nd. RD. without one Inf. Reg. follows the 11st. Bav. ID. 36st. RD. has the At the Kemmel Mountain found Battr.From 8 until 10 in the Morning to Gas with Bunt Gas and during the attack to hold down. XVIIIst. RK. Keeps the Battrs. In the Castle Park Kemmel down. 11st. Bav. ID. has with Blue Cross, before the main attack, to gas and during the attack, the At Locker found Battrs.to keep down.

36st. RD. and 11st. Bav. ID. prepare to storm from 10 in the Morning on."

The At April 17 at 8 in the morning ordered attack of the R. I. R. 71. At the Salon Farm and Hill 70 could not reach the established Target because of heavy Enemy MG. and Artillery Fire. Already at the Preparation had the Reg. heavy losses, it only came for to the south Edge of the Salon Farm. The Farm itself and the Hill 70 stayed in Enemy Hand. For support became the R. I. R. 71. The R. I. R. 82. Of the 22nd. RD. It became the order to move for in the Area of Westhof, in their place was the R. I. R. 94. Moved for.

The attack of the Xst. RK. At 11 in the Morning at the Kemmel and Dranoeter Hills west from there encountered tenacious resistance and came only in a few places for. The 36st. RD. advanced with R. I. R. 5. And 54. To the At the south Edge running Field Train and took with the R. I. R. 61. The Enemy Position 500m. Southeast of Den Molen. In connection to the 36st. RD. worked the right Wing of the 11st.Bav. ID. against Dranoeter from southeast and south, while the R. I. R. 71. Could not come far Over the Storm Starting Position. The Enemy defense was, because of cleverly in the Area hidden MG. Nests, very heavy, also the Enemy Artillery Fire became stronger. In the Evening became the R. I. R. 71. From The Div. The Order to take the Salon Farm Hill. But before this attack, hit an Enemy counter attack the Reg., so the ordered attack was not executed.

The Situation on April 17 was so, that at the whole Army Front only small results were made, with the exception at the left Wing of the 36st. RD. who towards Den Molen could put a Whole in the Enemy Position. The Gen.Kdo. Intended this Result on April 18 to exploit and early in the morning, through this Whole, to get to the Kemmel and there for to take the Hill. For this purpose were ordered that the 31st. ID. Takes over the Command in the right Div. Section of the Group and at 5.30 in the morning the Kemmel under security of the left Flank from the 11st. Bav. ID. to attack.

At 6 in the Afternoon were his Chief and the first Gen. Staff Officer at the Kdr. of the 31st. ID. To talk about the Possibility of an Attack at the Kemmel. Since the Enemy Artillery at that time was low and a heavy defense of the Kemmel from the English was not deemed organized, agreed the 31st. ID. To do the Attack.

The for April 18 planed attack at the Kemmel could not be carried out because the Inf. came at the march to the positioning under heavy explosive force and Gas Fire from the Enemy Artillery. The taking of the Storm starting Position at the ordered time was not possible.

At 11 in the Morning was he at the Div. Battle Post of the 31st. ID. At the northeast Corner of the Ploegsteerter Forest and could hear from the Leaders and the Troops they're impressions. At the Afternoon was heavy Artillery Fire at the German first Lines especially the Area at Nieuwekerke and the Dove Bottom came under heavy Fire. From the right Wing of the 31st. ID. Were 2 Turncoats of the 28st. French Div. brought in.

Storming of the Kemmel

At Evening came the order from the AOK. 4 that the Uniform Attack on both Sides of the Bailleul Was temporally stopped. The 4ˢᵗ. Army wanted to bring the main pressure of their further attack at the Front of the XVIIIst. And Xst. RK. To Occupy the Kemmel and Force the Enemy to Clear the Ypern Bend in which the Xst. RK. Had to put they're main point to attack the Kemmel. Precondition of the attack was the taking of the Hill Area at Dranoeter and at the Hill Ridge witch ran towards north of the Bleugelhoek from west to east. In Addition to the Troops already under the Xst. RK. Became the Core for the Attack the 4ˢᵗ. Bav. ID. Kdr. GenMaj. Prince Franz of Bav., Gen. Staff Officer Maj. Leyh, the German Alpine Core, Kdr. GenMaj. Knight von Tutschek, Gen. Staff Officer Capt. Von Kluge, this had the force of an Inf. Div., for disposal, and if possible a further fresh Div. in prospect. The attack of the Core was supposed to take place after thorough preparation.

Because of this Army Command gave the Gen. Kdo. Already in the Evening of April 18 the first Preparation Orders. In the Night from 18 to 19 was brisk Artillery Fire at the German Positions. The German Battr. Attacked the Enemy Artillery and gave destructive Fire at Positions and MG. Nests. According to Troop reports was a strengthening of the Enemy Artillery not found.

Before Noon came the Chief of the 4ˢᵗ. Army, GenMaj. Von Lossberg for a Meeting about pertinent Measures to my Grandfathers Command Post, also came the Gen. Staff Officers of the German Alpine Core and the 4ˢᵗ. Bav. ID.

Airplane reports and Pictures revealed that the Kemmel Mountain seemed not to be heavily built up for defense. The deep Tunnels, who were dug into the Mountain, had entrances partly towards the German Positions, which came after the occupation to be very handy.

After this Meeting where the preparations for the earliest attack at the Kemmel for April 24 ordered, which first requires the storming of the Enemy Positions southeast of Vyver and the small Kemmel Brook with the XVIIIst. RK. The Villages Dranoeter and Haegedoorne with the X.st RK. The Alpine Core had to take Quarter in the Area of Verlinghem, the 4st. Bav. ID. in Armentieres and east, both Divs. had to do the necessary Exploration. The Commands for the Artillery were given in agreement with the Art. Kdr. from the Alpine Core, Oberstlt. Herold, the Art. Kdr. of the 4st. Bav. ID. GenMaj. Kollmann, the Art. Kdr. of the 22nd. RD. Colonel von Oertzen, and the Command and Instructions for the Alpine Formations with the Kdr. of the Air Detachment at the Xst. RK. Capt. Zuehlke. (Group Flyer 7, Kdr. Capt. Zuehlke, Group Pictures Department Flight Detachment 13; Flight Detachment (A) 256, Leader Capt. Felmy; Flight Detachment (A) 258, Leader Capt. Petri; Flight Detachment (A) 266, Leader Capt. Gaede; Battle Squadron B, Leader first Lt. Ertl; to him belonged: Bav. Battle Squadron 23 26 and 30 Leader first Lt. Ertl, Battle Squadron 10, Leader first Lt. Lerche; Battle Squadron D, Leader first Lt. Missfelder, to him belonged: Battle Squadron 9, Leader Lt. Janson, Battle Squadron 12, Leader first Lt. Missfelder, Battle Squadron 16, Leader first Lt. Ramdohr, Bav. Battle Squadron 24, Leader Lt. Alberthausen.)

In the Afternoon was he at the Div. Battle Post of the 11st. Bav. ID. And could tell the Commander Genlt. Knight von Kneussel his appreciation for the performance of the brave Troops.

With Core Command from April 20.1918—Ia Nr. 173—were the detailed arrangements for the attack of the 22nd. RD. to the Salon Farm and Hill and the Hills north and south of Vleugelhoek, given. The attack was to happen on the second Day in the Evening.

About Relief of the 11st. Bav. ID. in the Night from April 21 to 22 with the 22nd. RD. and the 4st. Bav. ID. came a Command who pointed out that the attack of the 22nd. RD. coexistent with the attack in the section of the G. R. K. had to take place. Together with the Capt. Baron von and zu Gilsa did he drive to both of his Div. Kdrs. at the left Wing, GenMaj. Prince Franz of Bav., Kdr. of the 4st. Bav. ID. and Gen. of the Art. Schubert, Kdr. of the 22nd. RD. over Lille to Armentieres. From there they walked further for to the Observation Posts.

The losses in the time from April 10 to 20 where at the Xst. RK.:

Dead—	64	Officers,	1159	Corporals	and	Men
Wounded—	219	"	4910	"	"	"
Missed—	8	"	586	"	"	"
Prisoners—	0	"	15	"	"	"
Total loss	291	"	6670	"	"	"

The 36st. RD. Was on April 20 at 6 in the Evening put in March. They had fought magnificently and took from the Enemy hundreds of Prisoners, 8 Canons, and 2 Trench Canons and over 30 MGs.

On April 21 in the Morning was in his KHQu. A Meeting at which Gen. Ludendorff attended. They talked about the attack Plan for the storming of the Kemmel. The Kemmel had, after the storming, to be held with all means, since the big Attack "Hagen" (Code Name for the, end of July planed, large attack in Flanders.) His Chief stressed at this Meeting that, to hold the Kemmel, the attack should go further over the Kemmel and at Opinion of the Xst. RK. Should the Sharpen Mountain be included in the Attack.

The German Alpine Core was at the right Wing of the Xst. RK. And they're left Wing had to move for to the Street Marie rug—Den Molin, next to that the 4st. Bav. ID. and left from there until the Core Border had the 22nd. RD. to move for. As second Wave followed the 214st. ID. The 233rd. ID. Came to the XVIIIst. RK.

On this Day ebbed the Enemy Artillery Fire substantially, the German Battrs. Continued to fight the Enemy Artillery and took occasional Targets under Fire. In the Evening was the Farm Salon from Patrols of the 11st. Bav. ID. occupied. From the Command of the Xst. RK.—Ia Nr. 186—from April 21. 1918:

"1. 4st. Army attacks probably April 25. With the XVIIIst. RK. And Xst. RK. The Line Hill Ridge between Kemmel and little Kemmel Brook—Burggravehof— Hill Ridge to the north Vieugelhoek—Haegedoorne.

2. At success of the assault is a further moving for planed of the XVIIIst. RK. With Heavy Point at the Left Wing Towards North Against the Street Vlamertingen—Poperingen to Strangulate the Ypern Bend. The Xst. RK. Has the Task to

take over the security of the left Flank of the XVIIIst. RK. In fact by moving for at the right Wing and turning left to about Scherpenberg.

After reaching the first attack Target, is, regardless of a further move forward, to see to it, that this Line will be held by building Field Fortifications, Position echeloned in depth, especially MGs. arrangement of the Artillery defense against an expected heavy counter attack.

3. The Xst. RK. Has for the attack available: As Divs. in first Line: Alpine Core, 4st. Bav. ID. and 22nd. RD.; As Divs. in second Line: 214st. ID. And 31st. ID.

4. And 5. —

6. Attack Strips.

7. Time Table for the attack of the Xst. RK.: 3.30 until 5.30 in the morning: Gas Fire, 6.00 Until 7.00 in the Morning: Destruction Fire against Enemy Positions, 7.00 In the Morning: Storm.

8. from the 233rd. ID. Who is under the XVIIIst. RK. Is one Inf. Reg. (IR. 450. Kdr. Maj. Kaulbach to follow the right wing of the Alpine Core. That Reg.is to take the Village Kemmel

For his successful and prudent Leadership on April 25, whereby the tenacious defended Village

Kemmel were stormed, became Maj.Kaulbach from his Majesty the Kaiser the Pour le me rite.)

9. —

10. Preparation of the Divs. in second Line in the Night from April 23 to 24. 31st. ID. without Artillery and MWs. Bivouac in the Area of Le Romarin, Le Bizet, Pont de Nieppe. 214st. ID. Ploegsteert, South part of the Ploegsteerter Forest, Le Gheer. Both Divs. are at attack Day at 7 in the Morning March ready in their assembly Area—".

In the Night was lively Enemy Artillery Fire at the German Inf. and Art. Positions and the approach Routes, it became less in the Morning but got again stronger from 12 Noon on. German Artillery Fired at Enemy Battrs. At 9.30 in the Evening started Enemy Artillery and MG. Fire at the whole Front and lasted a half hour, an attack did not come.

The 11st. Bav. ID. left according to order on April 22 from 10 in the Morning they're Section. The 4st. Bav. ID. moved during the Night in there, and left from there took the 22nd. RD. the Section over. The 11st. Bav. ID. was pulled back in the Area Le Romarin, Rossignol, Lampernisse and stayed with one Inf. Reg. under the 22nd. RD. and with 2 Inf. Reg. under the 4st. Bav. ID.

At 9.40 in the Evening started suddenly Enemy Curtain Fire at the Front of the 31st. ID. Observations revealed that 2 specially selected Sergeants from the Alpine Core, who were supposed to find preparation Areas in the Div. Section, in darkness went over the first Lines and came against the English Position. The English had both brave Men recognized, thought an attack was imminent, and gave the Curtain Fire Signal. This Signal was from the German security Posts falsely passed. From the 2 Sergeants came 1 wounded back and the other fell dead or wounded in Enemy Hand. The 31st. ID. reported to the Gen.Kdo. By Funk of this Event. April 23 was generally quiet.

At 8.55 in the Evening attacked the 22nd. RD. the Hills at Vleugelhoek with good result. In spite of heavy counter defense were the ordered Line everywhere reached, only at the left Wing pushed an immediately taken Enemy counter attack the Div. a little back. 4 Officers and over 200 Men of the 34st. French Div. were captured and 5 MGs. taken.

In the Night from April 23 to 24 moved the 11st. Bav. ID. into the Quarters at Wambrechies, Londures, Linselles and were on April 25 at Noon as Div. Lokeren to Base Inspection 4 promoted. The brave and good lead Troops had heavy losses in these Battle Days, but they took from the Enemy hundreds of Prisoners and much Material also gave them heavy losses.

The 214st. ID. marched in this Night into the staging Area in the Ploegsteerter Forest, the Alpine Core into the first Position to relief the 31st. ID. Who moved into the staging Area of Le Romarin, Le Bizet, Pont de Nieppe. The 31st. ID. was sad that they were not allowed to do the Storm at the Kemmel, supported with heavy Artillery, but the Alpine Core in force of a Div. seamed with they're Men Power (Battl. 800 to 900 Men) better suited for this order.

On April 24 in the Morning came an Enemy counter Attack who was against the newly won Positions at Vleugelhoek but was repelled with MG.

and Artillery Fire. In the course of the Day ebbed the Enemy Artillery Fire at the Front of the Xst. RK. German Battrs. Gave disruption Fire at Traffic Points and battled Enemy Artillery.

At 10 in the Morning reported the Alpine Core the takeover of the Section of the 31st. ID. at 9 in the Evening started, because of a red Signal given by the Enemy German Curtain Fire that lasted until 10 in the Evening. At 9.15 in the Evening tried the Enemy in Front of the left Wing of the 4st. Bav. ID. to leave they're Trenches but was prevented with MG. and Artillery Fire.

In the Night were lively Enemy disruption Fire, also with Gas Munition, at the German Inf. and Battr. Positions. The Weather was cloudy.

The preparation for the attack of the Inf, Pioneers and Shock Battr. Continued amidst heavy Enemy Artillery Fire. From 3.30 to 5.30 in the Morning was the Enemy Artillery gassed. From 6 until 7 in the Morning was German disruption Fire against the Enemy Position.

At 7 in the Morning stormed the German Troops for. The Enemy Artillery was at first weak. The Kemmel itself was in dense Fog and Smoke; the Hollows were hard to see through the Fog. The 56st. ID. stormed at the left Wing of the XVIIIst. RK. From Vroilandhoek at the Village Kemmel to witch 2 Battl. Of the IR. 450 from west stormed, subsequently moved the Alpine Core for with the Prussian Jaeg. Reg. 2. Kdr. Maj. Bronsart von Schellendorf, the Bav. Ist. Leib Reg. Kdr. Colonel Knight von Epp, the first Bav. Jaeg. Reg. Kdr. Oberstlt. Paulus, left from them the 4st. Bav. ID. left beside that the 22nd. RD. with the R. I. R. 94 and 82.

The Attack of the 10st. RK. Had full success. After overcoming tenacious resistance, especially at Den Molen and Louis Mill, were the Kemmel Hills at both Wings of the Alpine Core at 8.45 in the Morning in German Hand. The Alpine Core reported by Telephone at 8.45 in the Morning to the Xst. RK.:

"After own observation and Prisoner Statements was the Kemmel already past."

Thereupon gave his Chief by Telephone the following Statement to the Alpine Core:

"Change of the Battle Section so, that the Scherpenberg will be in the middle of the Battle Section of the Alpine Core."

The Enemy held out in a few Nests with tough resistance, especially at the Farms east of the Louis Mill. The brave Bav. From Inf. Leib Reg. went around these Positions and at 12.30 in the Afternoon was the last rest of the Kemmel Position in German Hand. There had 400 French, with they're Reg. Kdr. gave up, many MGs. where taken.

The 4st. Bav. ID. had in connection to the Alpine Core taken Dranoeter and was stormed over Den Molen towards west for. At the left Wing had the 22nd. RD. taken the Hill north of Vleugelhoek. Prisoners were brought in from the 28st. 34st. and 159st. French and the 49st. English Div.

The first attack Target of the Day was already reached at Noon on April 25. Parts of the Jaeg. Reg. 2 had penetrated De Kleit, Patrols of the Goslaer Jaeger climbed the east Slope of the Scherpenberg. Thereon did he give the following Core Command (Ia Nr. 232 from April 25. 1918, 11.26 in the Morning):

> "1. Left Wing of the XVIIIst. RK. Had reached Vyver and the small Kemmel Brook, also Xst. RK. Comes close or has reached the first attack Target.
>
> 2. XVIIIst RK. Continues attack with left Wing at Street Kemmel—De Kleit—Reningshelst.
>
> 3. Xst. RK. Attacks likewise further to win the General Line Scherpenberg—Loker—Dranoeter.
>
> 4. Alpine Core takes, with heavy right echelon turning to left with the middle the Scherpenberg. Left Wing over Lager at Street Brulozze—Loker to Krabbenhof.
>
> 5. 4st. Bav. ID. wins turning to left the Line Krabbenhof— Dranoeter possibly by taking the Village Loker.
>
> 6. For the moving forward of both Divs. is it crucial to have Artillery close with plenty Munition.
>
> 7.—
>
> 8. 214st. ID. follows behind of the right Wing of the Alpine Core. They're deployment, to fill an about emerging Whole at a further forward attack, between the XVIIIst. RK. And the Alpine Core."

So the fixed Event from Core Command 186 from April 21 had occurred. The Measures for the necessary execution of this Command were repeatedly discussed between the Kdrs. of the Front and intervene Divs. and they're Gen. Staff Officers with him and his Chief.

In the Morning was the 214st. ID. moved further for. The energetic Gen. Maerker was during the Day in Constance connection with the Gen. Kdo. In Linselles and from him became the Gen. Kdo. The best Battle Reports, who Gen. Maerker obtained, partly with personal Observation and partly with Exploration of the Battle Troops.

The attack happy 214st. ID. placed IR. 358 in the Area south of Lindenhoek, IR. 50 in the Area northwest of Leeuwerk Farm, IR. 363 in the Area east of Lerche, to use.

At 1.57 in the Afternoon reported his Chief to the Chief of the Army about the Situation, what the Div.sofar had reported:

"A quarter hour ago per Letter Pigeon: Bav. Inf. Leib Reg. penetrated in Brulozze, had at 8.15 in the Morning reached Kemmel. The Field Artillery of the Alpine Core is in Position change to Kemmel, the 4st. Bav. ID. to Den Molen. Alpine Core moves with the middle to Scherpenberg, right Wing to Dem Lager 1km. northwest of De Kleit, left Wing to Krabben Farm. IR.358 follows right Wing of the Alpine Core. Remains of the 214st. ID. marched.

4st. Bav. ID. with right Wing to Krabben Farm with the middle to the Hill Ridge between Dranoeter and Loker. Left Wing stays. 22nd. RD. stays in they're Position."

The Army Chief answered thereupon with:"31st. ID. becomes Army Reserve. 10st. Ers. D. moves in the Area of Ploegsteert. 2 new Divs. coming (probably 29st. And 121st.). One of them can be accommodated in Linselles, the other in the Area of Wambrechies and west from there."

In the Afternoon came the Staff of the 10st. RD. Kdr. GenMaj. Rumschoettel, Gen. Staff Officer Capt. Dinglinger; The Div. was until Evening gathered in the Area of the Village Ploegsteert. The Div. was to follow later in the Night to the XVIIIst. RK.

At 4.15 in the Afternoon came a Report that the 4st. Bav. ID. had taken Loker Farm at 1.15 in the Afternoon. In Loker were still French. The Div. had in dashing attack taken 850 Prisoners with them a Battl. Staff.

The Alpine Core had they're attack at the Scherpenberg scheduled for 6 in the Afternoon. When the News of the success of the 4st. Bav. ID. came to the Gen. Kdo. Came his Majesty the Kaiser in to his Battle Post.

He hurried to meet him and reported the conquest of the Kemmel by the Alpine Core and informed him about the Situation and further attack intensions. His Majesty was full of satisfaction about the success and dictated the following Telegram to Gen. Ludendorff:

"Situation at Xst. RK. Is at 4 in the Afternoon: Alpine Core first Target at right Wing reached at small Kemmel Brook left Wing moved for at De Brulooze 4st. Bav. ID. reached north Dranoeter, now taken Loker Farm, also 22nd. RD. has reached Target Alpine Core moves with middle to Scherpenberg. 4st. Bav. ID. moves with middle to Loker for. At Neighbor has left Wing of the XVIIIst. RK. Reached Kemmel Brook, moves further for to De Kleit. Middle supposed to have reached Groote Vierstraat and Eckwald. Kemmel Mountain this Morning at 8.15 from Bav. Inf. Leib Reg. taken, Louis Mill a little later. Heavy Battle till Noon for Farm in between, in which 400 French also Reg. Kdr. and MGs. were taken. From Prisoner Statements was Gen. Foch shortly before in Poperingen. Mood of the French over use between the English very bad, tell of heavy losses from our Artillery Fire, made harrowing War tired Impression. Have Gen. Von Eberhardt the Pour le me rite awarded.

With Gods help a nice Victory, for which I congratulate your Excellency.

Wilhelm."

That was a beautiful Moment, when he, from the Hands of the Kaiser, at the Battle Post in the midst of the Battle, this high Decoration became.

The Core Day Command said:

"His Majesty the Kaiser lingered today again in the Battle Post of the Core and charged me, the Troops his full recognition for their bravery and courage at the storming of the Kemmel and the Hills at Dranoeter and Vleugelhoek to convey. I gave his Majesty the reassurance that the Troops under my Command also further will do they're obligation and Duty."

At 5.15 in the Afternoon informed the Army Chief by Telephone:

"Wireless Telegraph of the 22nd. English Gen. Kdo. To the 6st. 9st. 21st. 30st and 49st. Divs. said: French reports Kemmel from Enemy taken. Resistance Line Scherpenberg—De Kleit—Loker is to hold. Train Line

Scherpenberg—De Kleit—Train Claw Groote Vierstraat until counter attack at 10 in the Morning (11 in the Morning German time)."

At 5.30 in the Afternoon reported the Alpine Core that a part of the Field Artillery is already in Position and fires at the Scherpenberg. Enemy Artillery Fire at the approach Streets delayed the march of the Artillery. Enemy Fire at the southeast Slope of the Kemmel.

His Chief gave per Telephone to the 4st. Bav. ID. and 22nd. RD. the Situation and discussed Measures to be taken for the planed, at 6 in the Afternoon, attack of the Alpine Core. In spite of repeated telephoned Questions at the Alpine Core, became the Gen. Kdo. Only in the Evening at 9 News from the 214st. ID. That the Alpine Core on April 25 did not want to attack but changed the attack to the 26th. The reasons were as follows: The Artillery of the Alpine Core, because of the blockage of the Douve crossing, could not in time have taken the Position change at the Kemmel. The Inf. Reg. of the Alpine Core was, because of the first attack, totally mixed up. That in the middle located Bav. Inf. Leib Reg. was at this unstoppable storm forward, strayed towards left and had the 1st. Bav. Jaeg. Reg. that so far at the left Wing of the Alpine Core was located pushed out. The 1st. Bav. Jaeg. Reg. had now to be collected behind the Front of the Alpine Core. The 4st. Bav. ID. could not carry out the attack at Loker and Krabbenhof, since the connection to the Alpine Core was lost.

At 9.15 in the Evening came from the Alpine Core this Report:

"Inf. Leib Reg. (middle Reg. of the Alpine Core) had in the attack at Scherpenberg missed the direction and moved for at Brulozze, because of that heavy mix up of the Detachments. Left Reg. of the Alpine Core 1st. Bav. Jaeg. Reg. was pushed out of they're Section. Continuing of the attack stopped at Alpine Core because of the big mix up of the Detachments at the 4st. Bav. ID. since Alpine Core is not enough for and the 4st. Bav. ID. would be too far for to have connection to the Alpine Core were the Situation was not known and would have been in Jeopardy."

This Report of the Alpine Core was for him and his Chief a big disappointment, because of the so far incoming Reports and Information by Telephone was from a postponement of the attack to 7 in the Evening spoken. The pre—approved assurance of the Gen. Staff Officers of the Alpine Core at the Telephone, that the attack of course would take place, had all consideration pushed back. Had the Alpine Core the Gen. Kdo.

Of this Report earlier notified, so were the attack happy and resolute lead 214st. ID. to the attack at the Scherpenberg from him used. At that time it was too late.

The 214st. ID. was with one Inf. Reg. to Kaite Kerkhof, one Inf. Reg. to Lindenhoek and one Inf. Reg. to Leeuwerk Farm moved for. The Div. Battle Post was at the Rossignol Hill. The Staff of the Alpine Core was during the Battle Days in the Forest of Haubourdin, 600m.northwest of the Street Fork south of the Number 7846; the Observation Post was at Nachtigall north of Haubourdin.

Already in his first Commands on April 10 did he noted that it was important that the higher Leaders (Div. and Brigade Leaders) move they're Battle Posts timely for, to personally lead the Battle, especially in critical Situations. He had this as his Opinion in many Meetings expressed.

In Core Command of April 25—Ia Nr.240—did he Command:

"The Xst. RK. Had today after victorious Battle reached the Line: Alpine Core: Gleisdreieck Plan quadrat 7252 over De Brulooze to a few 100m. South from there. 4st. Bav. ID. in connection towards east Hospiz Loker, towards west Loker Farm to Plan quadrat 7554.

22nd. RD. in connection towards north to the Inn at Vleugelhoek. XVIIIst. RK. Attached with they're left Wing at Gleisdreieck towards north at Groote Vierstraat. The attack is to be continued on April 26.

22nd. RD. has to hold the taken Line. She stretches in the Night, the 4st. Bav. ID. relieving, they're right Wing to q south of Loker Farm. 4st. Bav. ID. occupies Loker and Krabbenhof. Alpine Core takes the Line De Nieuwe Lenie Chapel—Scherpenberg—q in the Plan quadrat 7053. It has in the Night to stretch they're right Wing to the Core Border.

XVIIIst. RK. Is to move for with they're left Wing to the Street De Kleit—Reningheist. The attack of the 56st. ID. The Alpine Core and the 4st. Bav. ID. is to start together, after the Artillery preparations at 9 in the Morning. G. R. K. is from 5 in the Morning on, the enemy Artillery towards west of the Line q in the Plan quadrat 7455, west Exit Loker, middle Scherpenberg, t in the Plan quadrat 7052 to gasify and then to hold down, also the Area and the Streets west of this Line to spread from the Flank.

The Divs. battle from 5 in the Morning on, as much as possible, with Gas the Enemy Artillery in their Battle Sections. The Artillery of the 22nd.

RD. has as main Task to hold down the Enemy Artillery at Lokerstraat, Vidaigne Hill, Westoeter all during the Day. The Enemy Artillery north of the Street De Kleit-Lokerstraat is with disturbance Fire during the Night to be prevented from Positions change.

Cover of the Street also at Night: Alpine Core Poperingen—Reningheist—De Kleit. 4st .Bav.ID. Poperingen—Westoeter. 22nd. RD. Poperingen (southwest Exit)—Westoeter. 214st. ID. Stays ready to follow the right Wing of the Alpine Core.

10st. Ers. D. is from 7 in the Morning on at they're Bivouac places ready to march that they can start a half hour after the order. The Road Kemmel towards Kemmel Village is to explore. 31st. ID. Stays in their rest Places."

The own Munitions use on April 25 was 102411 shots.

The Weather was alternating, at times Thunder Storms witch made it difficult for the Aviators. Early in the morning of April 26 came a heavy Enemy attack against the Prussian Jaeg. Reg. 2 at the right Wing of the Alpine Core and against the 56st. ID. of the XVIIIst. RK. The Jaeg. Reg. 2 under the Leadership of Maj. Bronsart von Schellendorf, repelled the attack. But the Enemy succeeded to push back the 56st. ID. 800m. Because of this counter attack came the attack of the Alpine Core at 9 in the Morning not to execution.

The attack of the 4. Bav. ID. could not be executed because of heavy Enemy Artillery Fire. The Div. ordered, because of that on their own, to move the attack to the Afternoon. Brought in Prisoners of the 39st. French Div. had told that they were supposed again on this Day take the Kemmel. The French attack on the Morning started with a violently Artillery preparation mixed with heavy Calibers.

Since from Aviation Reports with Pictures, heavy occupation of the Enemy Positions were visible, they had to be reckoning with Enemy attacks. Because of that decided the Army the further attack to continue after planed preparation. Corresponding Commands were given immediately to the Divs., however this Command did not reach the Inf. Reg. of the 4st. Bav. ID. Both Reg. of the first Line moved in the Afternoon to Loker. After turbulent Battles took the 9st. Bav. IR. Kdr. Colonel Jaud, the Loker Farm. At the same time pushed first Lt. Von Westernhagen with his IInd. / R. I. R. 94 of the 22nd. RD. on his own Initiative the Enemy from Hill

Ridge southwest of Loker. 34 Prisoners and a Number of MGs. came in they're Hand.

With his first Gen. Staff Officer, Maj. Reuter, did he drove late in the Morning to Waasten and from there they walked over the Rossignol Hill towards the Kemmel. He talked among others with Gen. Maerker who told him about his observations about the Storm at the Kemmel and his Impression from the Battle Situation. The Div. Battle Post was at that time at Leeuwerk Farm. The 214st. ID. had on this Day the Impression that the attack at the Scherpenberg, with success in connection with the taking of the Kemmel Mountain, should have been done, when on April 25, after you had the Impression that the Alpine Core with his own Force could not come anymore for, immediately a new Div.Had been used for the attack. The Attrition of the Enemy was so heavy that seriously resistance at the Scherpenberg against fresh Storm Troops would not have been. Gen. Maerker gave his View in writing.

At the Battle Post of the Alpine Core did he meet with GenMaj. Knight von Tutscheck, who also told him of his Impressions, about the performance of his Troops. His Gen. Staff Officer rode for to the Jaeg. Br. 1, Kdr. GenMaj. Knight von Kleinhenz. GenMaj. Knight von Tutschek made efforts to produce the extremely difficult connection to his Inf. who was in direct contact with the Enemy. There he met also the leader of the Bav. Inf. Leib Reg. Colonel Knight von Epp, whom he could personally tell his Praise for the Performance of his glorious Reg. The Colonel reported to him of the very high losses of his Reg. and was extremely deeply moved of the heroic death of the Leader of the Ist. / Bav. Inf. Leib Reg. Capt. Count von Holstein from Bav, who since 1914 took part in all the Battles of the Reg. The Bav. Ist. Leib Reg. had at the Storm at the Kemmel lost 5 Officers and 350 Sergeants and Men. The GenMaj. Knight von Kleinhenz told him at his Battle Post from the overwhelming Storm of his Inf. and Jaeg. But also of the big Trouble, for the under heavy losses fighting Artillery, to keep connection with the Storm Troops. The successes of these brave Troops of the German Alpine Core were indeed significantly. Besides of the taking of the important Kemmel Mountain and the Area before, had the Alpine Core taken 152 Officers and 4184 Men Prisoners and 119 MGs. 80 Muskets, 7 MWs. One heavy 18cm. Canon, six 10.5cm. Canons and

15 Field Canons captured. The Troops that they met, made a fresh and attack ready Impression.

In the Core Day Command for April 27 was the preparation of a further attack ordered. The Day of the attack should be announced.

Before Noon of April 27 was lively disruption Fire at the German preparations Positions and at the behind Terrain at Streets and Villages. In the Afternoon became the activity of the Enemy Artillery considerable more. In the Evening started own Wallfire, caused from a red Flare from the Enemy. At 11 in the Evening slacked the Enemy Artillery Fire.

During the Night to April 28 was mutual heavy destruction Fire. On the Afternoon of April 27 was the IR. 371. Kdr. Maj. Reich of the 10st. Ers. D. moved for and came under the 4st. Bav. ID. with Army Command was the 52nd. RD. Kdr. Genlt.Waldorf, Gen. Staff Officer Capt. von Heydebreck put under the Xst. RK. The 29st. ID. Kdr. Genlt. Von der Heyde, Gen. Staff Officer Capt. Schmidt, came and was housed in the Area of Linselles and Roncq.

In the Core Command of April 27—Nr. 261—were the following ordered:

"On April 29 will the XVIIIst. And Xst. RK. Resume the attack. Penetrate wide as possible in towards north and northwest in the Enemy to reach the Street Ypern—Poperingen and the threat of the still in the Ypern Bend staying Enemy Forces, is the next Target of the Operation.

XVIIIst. RK. Goes with left Wing along the Street Village Kemmel—Reninghelst over De Kleit—Reninghelst for. Alpine Core attacks over Church Reninghelst—crossing of the Train with the Street Westoeter—Poperingen at m in the Plan quadrat 6857, left Wing over De Nieuwe Lenie Chapel to Farm Heksken 500m. Towards north of Westoeter.

4st. Bav. ID. connecting with left Wing at Red Mountain—Street De Brulooze—Road crossing 1km. north of Loker—Reninghelst belong to the Alpine Core, Street Loker—Road crossing 1km. north of Loker—Westoeter belongs to the 4st. Bav. ID.

To create a free left Flank for the further to north moving XVIIIst. RK. Is it important to reach the Line Poperingen—Westoeter—Red Mountain as soon as possible. 22nd. RD. is at favorable continuing Battle of the 4st. Bav. ID. in the position, by slowly moving forward of their right

Wing, the until then necessary becoming long left Flank of the 4st. Bav. ID. to shorten.

214st. ID. Follows the right Wing of the Alpine Core towards Reninghelst. It is intended to put the Div. in a possible resulting Gab between the XVIIIst. RK. And the Xst. RK. At Poperingen.

From the 10st. Ers. D. stays 1 Inf. Reg. behind the 22nd. RD. Otherwise comes the Div. under the 4st. Bav. ID. the Kdr. of the 10st. RD. must be in a position, by possibly later pulling out of the Troops of the 4st. Bav. ID. to take the Command at any time in this Section.

Time Table for the attack of both Cores:
From 4 until 6 in the morning Gasification of the Enemy Artillery.
From 6 to 6.40 in the Morning preparation Fire.
At 6.40 in the Morning start of the Inf. attack."

On April 28 was a Meeting of Oberstlt. Hasse with the Gen. Staff Officers of the Alpine Core, the 214st. ID, the 22nd. RD. the 10st. Ers. D. and the 4st. Bav. ID. at the Battle Post of the 214st. ID. about the coming attack at April 29.

My Grandfather was in these Days and in the following, as often as the Situation aloud, in accompaniment of one or another Officer of his Staff for at the leaders and the fighting Troops. The Mood of the Divs. under him was excellent and confident. The day was in all quiet. The 29st. ID. Came under the XVIIIst .RK. The 121st. ID. Kdr. GenMaj. Bressler, Gen. Staff Officer Capt. von Wiedner, so far at the G. R. K. Came under the Xst. RK. The Div. was in the Evening moved for in the Area Ploegsteert, Le Gheer, Ploegsteerter Forest.

Like ordered started on April 29 at the appointed time the gasification of the Enemy Artillery, the preparation Fire and the Inf. Storm. The Enemy Artillery counter effect was at first weak, but begun then to get conciderable stronger. The attack of the Core came, because of heavy Enemy Artillery Fire and the cleverly hidden MG. Nests, not really forward. Also the attack of the XVIIIst .RK. Won little Area.

At 9.30 in the Morning was the enemy counter attack against the right Wing of the 4st. Bav. ID. repelled. The following Reports came in:

From Alpine Core at 7.15 in the Morning, that the right Reg. like planed had started, that Enemy Artillery, during the Storm of the Inf., had only light scattering Fire done. 8.30 In the Morning, that the right Wing encountered resistance of many MG. Nester and became Flank Artillery Fire from northeast. The connecting Troops at the XVIIIst. RK. Seemed to lag and the Storm of the Bav. Inf. Leib Reg. to be stopped. German Aviaters reported that at 8 in the morning German Inf. was at the Foot of the Scherpenberg.

At 10.20 in the Morning from the Alpine Core, that the Bav. Inf. Leib Reg. had reported the Enemy moves back to the Scherpenberg Mill. On the Street Scherpenberg—Dickebusch were heavy MG. Nester. Since 9.15 in the Morning were the Artillery Fire condensed at this Street.

At 8.30 in the morning had the Alpine Core become an Airplane report that the German Inf. were stormed for over the Scherpenberg. At 8.10 in the Morning was the Street northeast of the Scherpenberg crossed. The Art. Kdr. of the Alpine Core, Oberstlt. Herold had thereupon reported that the Scherpenberg seemingly was only half taken and he has captured the left Fire roll.

At 11 in the Morning was the Situation at the Xst. RK. Following:

The Alpine Core had with they're right Wing reached about the Intersection of the Train Line with the Street Kemmel—De Kleit—k in the Plan quadrat 7252—k in the Plan quadrat 7253—q in the Plan quadrat 7254. There connection with the 4st. Bav. ID.

The 4st. Bav. ID. stood from q in the Plan quadrat 7254 until 100m. east of Krabbenhof past until west Edge of Loker after the first 4 in the Number 7454. There connection with the 22nd. RD. The 22nd. RD. stood connecting 50m.east of Burggrave Farm at east Edge of the little, on the Burggrave Farm past flowing Brook, along to m in the Plan quadrat 7554. From there in the old Line.

At this time was a new heavy Enemy counter attack against the right Wing of the 4st. Bav. ID. the Enemy succeeded to push the Div. Back, to the between De Brulooze and Loker situated Supply Store and the Hospize Loker.

The 4st. Bav. ID. intended because of that, the IR. 370 of the 10st. Ers. D. to use in order to take back what was lost and the south of De Nieuwe Lenie Chapel opening up Gap to close.

The Alpine Core reported at 12.02 in the Afternoon, that the Bav. Inf. Leib Reg. had reported that the German Artillery at the Scherpenberg had not achieved the Fire Wave effect. It would now be a new Artillery Firewall at the Scherpenberg ordered and at a time still to be determined, would the Inf. Storm ordered.

His Chief repeatedly admonished the Gen. Staff officer of the Alpine Core that with a Firewall it cannot succeed such a Mountain to Storm, only through concentric combined Artillery Fire.

Towards Noon was a new attack for taking of the Scherpenberg, after heavy Artillery preparation combined with an attack of the XVIIIst. RK. Against the Hills of De Kleit, ordered.

The time of the attack was for both Cores at 6 in the Afternoon decided. The 214st. ID. became order, at this attack, to follow the Alpine Core at the right Wing. The Kdr. of the Aviation of the 4st. Army, Capt. Wilberg, had the important Task for the Xst. RK. For the whole Operation of the 4st. Army, recognizing, 2 Battle Sqadrons of 48 Airplanes each, for support at the Storm at the Scherpenberg, allocated to the Xst. RK. Already in the morning hours where 17 Airplanes, because of earth defense, Battle incapable. 4 of them had to land right behind the German Positions. In spite of that attacked the brave Aviators of all Squadrons until late Evening in tight Formation the enemy Positions, Barack Camps at Dickebusch and the Traffic in the Area Dickebusch—De Kleit and the Quarters at the Street Reninghelst—Westoeter. There were 66000 shots fired with MGs. 8000 throwing Mines, 1088kg. Bombs and 38 Hand Grenades thrown at the Enemy Troops, in the behind Area.

The Alpine Core reported that at 2.56 in the Afternoon at the Scherpenberg white luminous Balls were fired, also at De Nieuwe Lenie Chapel. The Bav. Inf. Leib Reg. had there 2 Comp. put in March. The Kemmel stand under very heavy Artillery Fire with heavy Calibers. The Chief gave immediately orders to the Alpine Core, to get into connection with the 4st. Bav. ID. and to find out if the Wings of both Divs. were at De Nieuwe Lenie Chapel. If tis were the case, it were intended from here to move for against the Scherpenberg.

German Aviators had several times reported that at the Scherpenberg, also at De Nieuwe Lenie Chapel were white Light Balls fired, several Troops of German Soldiers were seen there and when the Airplane came

close they had spread white Towels. The Gen. Kdo reported to the Alpine
Core at 3.19 in the Afternoon about the attack of the XVIIIst. RK. That at
6 in the afternoon wanted to Storm and about the mentioned Air Reports
the from the Kdr. of the Flyers at the Gen. Kdo. Capt. Zuehlke, and
because of inquiry at the Squadron Leaders, were confirmed.

The Gen. Staff Officer of the Alpine Core reported at 3.15 in the
Afternoon again that the Alpine Core would try to Storm at the same time
then the XVIIIst. RK. But already at 4.30 in the Afternoon came a report
that the Alpine Core could only Storm at 7 in the Evening. The Storm
would be done with 2 Battls. One Battl. 1st. Bav. Jaeg. Reg. would move for
against the Scherpenberg. One Battl. Of this Reg. was supposed to hook
up with the right Wing of the attack of the 233rd. ID. Therefore became
the Alpine Core communicated, that the Gen. Kdo. Had ordered the 214st.
ID. with one Inf. Reg. at the Gap of the attack between the Alpine Core
and the 233rd. ID. to follow.

The XVIIIst. RK. Insisted therefore to do they're attack at 6 in the
Afternoon. The Alpine Core became immediately the News and also
notification that the Xst. RK. From 5.15 in the Afternoon until 6 in the
Afternoon would support the attack with Artillery at they're right Wing.
At 8.15 in the Evening reported the Alpine Core that the preparation
Position of the 1st. Bav. Jaeg. Reg. witch were supposed to do the attack at
the Scherpenberg, could not be finished by 7 in the Evening. The Reason
was the heavy Enemy Fire at the Kemmel. Since the preparation Position
only at 8.30 in the Evening could have been done, ordered the Alpine
Core from their own Initiative, that the attack at the Scherpenberg should
be omitted. My Grandfather was against this unauthorized Decision and
ordered that the Alpine Core still in the Evening had to attack and until
Daybreak had to occupied the Scherpenberg. The Alpine Core decided
because of that to do the attack at Daybreak on April 30.

From the 4st. Bav. ID. came in the Evening a Pigeon Letter Report,
that the Gap between the 4st. Bav. ID. and the Alpine Core, also between
De Nieuwe Lenie Chapel—Hospice Loker, were closed. Since the Reg. of
the 4st. Bav. ID. were very exhausted, intended the Div. the IR. 369 and
370 from they're subordinate 10st. Ers. D. as long as it was not already
done, to employ in the Night from 29 to 30. April and the 5th. Bav. IR.
and Bav. R. I. R. 5 to relieve and pull back.

The 22nd. RD. had in the Afternoon Koukot occupied but had to give it up because of a heavy Enemy attack. The 22nd. RD. intended to attack Koukot again but the Gen. Kdo. Did not allow it, since the possession of this Village was not necessary for the continuing of the Operation and it would have caused unnecessary Blood. The R. I. R. 94 of the 22nd. RD. had heavy losses and had to be pulled back from the first Line. The Div. became as replacement 2 Battls. Of the IR. 371 of the 10st. RD. while one Battl. Of this Reg. should stay as Reserve at Zwaartemolenhoek. To get a favorable Line was the right Wing of the 22nd. RD. pulled back to they're starting Positions; the conquered Area stayed as for field occupied with Posts.

At 9.15 in the Evening became the Alpine Core from the first Gen. Staff Officer of the Gen. Kdo. Communicated, that the Chief again had asked the Leader of the Battle Squadron, who had reported that German Troops were at the Scherpenberg, that this was so.

The 1. Bav. Jaeg. Reg. had reported to the Alpine Core that they're attack could not have happen before 9 in the Evening since they're preparation Position would not be done until that time.

The Jaeg. Br. 1. Had reported to the Alpine Core that the approach to the Position where not possible. The Alpine Core gave on April 29 at 10.30 in the Evening the following Command:

> "1. Should the Scherpenberg really not be in German Hand, which was immediately to determine with especially Officer Patrols, so had the Jaeg. Br. 1 to take the Scherpenberg at April 30 at 5.15 in the Morning by surprise.
>
> 2. The attack is to start with a short, abruptly Fire assault with all the Artillery for disposal. Fire time 5 min. 5.15 in the Morning start to Storm behind the Fire roll.
>
> 3. Fire roll—
>
> 4. The Inf. attack is lead from the Commander of the Jaeg. Br.1. For the implementation of this Attack are available the 3 Battls. Of the 1st. Bav. Jaeg. Reg. and as many parts of the Bav. Inf.Leib Reg. as are necessary for the protection of the left Flank of the 1st. Bav. Jaeg. Reg. (advance at the Street Loker—De Kleit.)
>
> 5. 214st. ID. has one Battl. To move for behind the Gap of the Jaeg. Reg. 2

6. Special Measures are to take from the Br. that the report of the starting of the Reg. come Immediately to the Core Command.

Signed von Tutscheck.

At 10.20 in the Evening were Gen. von Lossberg again from the Chief of my Grandfather informed, about the Situation at the Alpine Core, that they stopped the attack on their own accord, further about, that from Aviation reports the Scherpenberg were in German Hands and therefore became the Alpine Core the Command in the Night or early in the Morning to move for to the Scherpenberg. The continuation of the attack past April 30 is in the Opinion of the Xst. RK. Not possible because of heavy counter attack of the Enemy.

The Army Chief agreed with the directive to the Alpine Core. After the moving for, of the Alpine Core to the Scherpenberg, was everything to be set for defense. Gen. Maerker should have, regardless of the Task for the Alpine Core and the 4st. Bav. ID. Take over the defense of the Kemmel. The 121st. ID. stayed in their Quarters in the Area of Ploegsteert.

Late in the Evening reported the Alpine Core, that the one Bav. Jaeg. Reg. who probably did not get the order from the Alpine Core in time, had started to attack. This attack was not done, because the Alpine Core on April 30 in the Morning reported that the 1st. Bav. Jaeg. Reg. had gotten the Command on time.

The at 1 in the Morning incoming Army Command ordered that on April 30 the reached Line was to be held and made ready for defense in depth. During the Night were 2 heavy Enemy counter attacks at the 4st. Bav. ID. repelled. A 3rd. attack brought the Enemy to take the Hospize east of Loker. An immediate counter attack from 2 Battls. Of the IR. 371 and 5th. Bav. IR. Kdr. Oberstlt. Fels, pushed the Enemy back; The Hospize was taken again. That during the Night heavy Enemy Artillery Fire calmed towards 8 in the Morning down.

The Alpine Core reported at 9 in the Morning, that the Bav. Inf. Leib Reg. on their own accord during the Night had retreated to they're starting Position at De Brulooze since a holding of the first Line was not possible, because of Flank Artillery Fire from all sides.

At 10 in the Morning gave the Alpine Core the following Command to the Jaeg. Br. 1:

> "1. To share with the Inf. Leib Reg.-
> 2. Core Command: The Brigade has they're disposal Battl.
> And one Batt. Of the Core Reserve to Move so close to the Bav.
> Inf. Leib Reg. that both Battls., in case that the Scherpenberg
> is Taken from Bav. Inf. Leib Reg. can be used to the following
> Storm further over the Scherpenberg.
> Signed von Tutscheck."

At 1.25 in the Afternoon reported the Gen. Staff Officer of the Alpine Core, that the Jaeg. Br. 1 has no knowledge about the taking back of the 4st. Bav. ID. The Commander of the Bav. Inf. Leib Reg. were determined to take the Scherpenberg today. It had been found towards Noon that the taking back on their own accord of the Bav. Inf. Leib Reg. at the left Wing had not been done. So it came to be that the left Wing still, from q in the Plan quadrat 7254—k in the Plan quadrat 7253 far jutted, while the right Wing moved back. Both Inner Wings, Alpine Core and the 4st. Bav. ID. Build, because of that, a far, before the whole Position jumping, acute angle. My Grandfather therefore had ordered the inner Wings of the 4st. Bav. ID. and the Alpine Core in the Night from April 30 to May first to pull back in a better backwards preferred Position north of De Brolooze.

At 6.25 in the Afternoon did he Command the Alpine Core on order of the Army:

"It is immediately to uncover who gave the Command to clear the foremost Positions at De Nieuwe Lenie Chapel at April 19 in the Evening and why was it of no concern that this Command was made knowing to all Troops there."

Towards 5 in the afternoon was a heavy, against the inner Wing of the 4st. Bav. ID. and the 22nd. RD. pointed, Enemy attack repelled. A further, with heavy Forces taken attack between 9 and 10 in the Evening, against the left Wing of the Alpine Core broke down before the German Line with heavy Enemy losses. The 214st. ID became Instruction to move 1 Inf. Reg. further back, the 121st. ID. stayed in they're Quarters.

The losses of the Xst. RK. From April 21 to April 30 were:

Dead	59	Officers,	1008	Corporals	and	Men
Wounded	182	"	4435	"	"	"
Missed	7	"	294	"	"	"
Prisoners	21	"	"	"		
Total loss	248	"	5758	"	"	"

Trench Battles in Flanders

Core Command Ia Nr. 300 on May 1.1918:

"1. The Army is temporarily at defense positioned. The preparations for the soon to be taken up Attack, especially Artillery, is therefore vigorously to advance. The Troops are not to be told from the temporary breakup of the attack.

2. The Section of the Xst. RK. Is towards right made wider by a Div. Section. In them is in the Night from May 1 to May 2 and 2 to 3 the 233rd. ID. with the 29st. ID. relieved. A part of the left Div. Section (22nd. RD.) Is to give up to the G. R. K. Time of the takeover of the section to the G.R.K. May 4 at Noon.

3. In the new Core Section will be 3 Divs. put in Line. Right 29st. ID. Middle Alpine Core left 121st. ID. About exact Section Borders follows Map. As Div. second Line has the Core the 214st. ID. and 31st. ID. At disposal. 4st. Bav. ID. Become Army Reserve.

4. The Inf. of the 4st. Bav. ID. and 10st. Ers. D. is in the Night from April 1 to April 2 and April 2 to 3 with The 121st. ID. under Leadership of the 4st. Bav. ID. to relief. About relief of the Artillery follows order. The other Formations are until 4 in the Morning to relief. Takeover of the Command with the Staff of the 121st. ID. on May 3 at Noon. 4st. Bav. ID. leaves 1 Gen. Staff Officer and 1 Officer of the Staff of the Art.Kdr. Until the total familiarizing of the Staff of the 121st. ID. 10st. Ers. D. comes to the G.R.K. The relieved parts of this Div. are in Armentieres to bring to Quarter. Further Directions to get from the Gen. Kdo. The relieved parts of the 4st. Bav. ID. is first to bring together in the Area of Lampernisse— Ploegsteert (exclusive)—Le Bizet—Rossignol. About Quarters in the backwards Core Area follows order.

5. The Task of the defense of the Kemmel stays with the 214st. ID. She has to make Shure, that by Tense Battle Situation immediately the necessary Measures are taken. The

preparations are set down in writing. One Inf. Reg. stays in the Area Lindenhoeck, the rest of the Div. is to bring to Quarter in the Area Ploegsteert—south part of the Ploegsteerter Forest Le Gheer.

6. 31st. ID. remains provisionally in they're Quarters.

7. About new formation of the Artillery follows orders.

8. The Staffs of the Divs. in the first Line stay for the time being at they're Battle Posts. About later Staff Quarters will be passed an order.

9. The Divs. in the first Line report as soon as possible, at the latest on May 3 at 10 in the Morning, The forces outline of the Inf. in they're Sections. Over the course of the relief is in the Day Report To report. "Assessment of the Situation on May 2.1918 (Ia Nr.318):

Enemy Forces outline: On May 1st. at Noon stood before the Front of the Xst. RK. The 39st. 31st. And 34st. French Divs. and moved for parts of the 2nd. And 3rd. French K.D. The 28st. and 154st. French Div. Are from the Front moved back. The 31st. French Div. is identified on May 2nd. From Deserters in Front of the 4st.Bav.ID.

Enemy Artillery: While the Artillery counter Fire of the Enemy at the German attack at the Kemmel on April 25 was relatively weak, increased the strength of the Enemy Fire in the Following Days substantially. For the attack on April 29 was the Gasification of the in the Meantime reinforced Enemy Artillery not enough. They were deep structured and widely disbursed. The German first Line and the backwards Area were at Day and especially at Night under heavy and lively distraction Fire, and at times got heavy. About the Force of the Enemy Artillery is at this time not really known. It seems that they are about equal to the German Artillery.

Enemy Inf: After the Enemy attack on April 26, with the fresh put in 39st. French Div. did the Enemy on April 28 in the Night from April 29 to 30 and on May 1 again attacks, especially in the middle Divs. Section, but all where repelled.

Intention of the Enemy: Since the shortly after the storming of the Kemmel, in large scale but not uniformly taken, Enemy counter attacks failed, it can be assumed that the Enemy would not repeat this in this art.

However it has to be assumed that he with a planned prepared attack with heavy Forces would try to reoccupy the Kemmel.

Battle worth of the Divs: The Alpine Core, the 4st. Bav. ID. the 22nd. RD. the 214st. ID. and the 10st. Ers. D. needs 3 to 4 weeks training after recruitment replacement. The 31st. ID. needs 2 weeks of training the 29st. ID and the 121st. ID. is full Battle ready."

From May 3 on were Enemy Planes, contrary to the previous Days, very active. Especially was a heavy Air Lock, with many Battle Squadrons, to observe at the Kemmel.

On this Day dropped the 4st. Bav. ID. out of my Grandfathers Command. The Div. had done excellent during their Mission at the Xst. RK. They're Inf. had rousingly stormed, the Artillery always kept connection with the Sister weaponry, the News connection from the Troop to the Staff and to the Gen. Kdo. Were in good order. They're young Leader was personally always involved and earned Love and Honor from his Subordinates.

My Grandfather entered him for the award of the Pour le me rite, because of his determent Leadership in the Kemmel Offensive, were the GenMaj. Prince Franz von Bav. For the Task of his Div. on April 25, taking of the west Slope of the Kemmel and the Village Dranoeter, did take all necessary observations personally, witch lead to the total success. On April 26 did he attack with his Div. Even so to the right of him was the Alpine Core for the attack at the Scherpenberg with the preparation not finished, on his own accord the Village Loker and the Hills on both sides, knowing that you have to stay on the beaten Enemy.

In the Evening of May 3 came at an Enemy attack Prisoners of the French IR. 122 (31st. Div.) in German Hand. Since the Leader of the Alpine Core asked my Grandfather to relief his battered Troops, was the relief of the Alpine Core with the 31st. ID. In the Night from May 6 to 7 and from May 7 to 8 ordered. It was supposed to go to Quarters in the Area of the 31st. ID. The takeover of the Command from the Staff of the 31st. ID. Was on May 8 at 10 in the Morning done. Already on May 4 came the Command from the Gen.Kdo. Of the Xst. RK. That the relief of the Alpine Core from the 31st. ID. Were to be 24 hours earlier.

The Troops of the German Alpine Core were great in Battle. The proposals of Gen. Knight von Tutscheck, for the award of decorations to the Troop Kdrs. could he in every aspect agree. He was especially happy to enter the Kdr. of the Bav. Inf. Leib Reg. for the award of the Pour le me rite, which he did with the following words:

"This personal outstanding brave Reg. Kdr. did on the 25th. And in the following Days employed his whole Personality to further hold the gained advantages. I support the exceptional decoration of Colonel von Epp all humbly."

For preparation of an attack on May 8 at the 52nd. RD. of the XVIIIst. RK. Did the Artillery of the Xst. RK. Take part. About 5 in the Morning started heavy Enemy Artillery Fire, whom an attack on both sides of the Street Kemmel—De Kleit against the inner Wings of the 31st. and 39st. ID. Followed. On schedule at 5 in the Morning started destruction Fire and cost heavy losses at the Enemy Positions. The forward storming French waves came in Flank MG. Fire and were for the most part killed. Parts reached the German Line and were in close combat repelled or taken Prisoners. From testifying of Prisoners was the first Enemy Target the Depot on the Street Kemmel—De Kleit. After winning this Target was the attack to continue with fresh Forces. Many Prisoners from 4 different Reg. of the 129st. and 32st. French Div. were brought in.

Since of this Battle Action of the Enemy could both Comps. Of the 52st. RD. (XVIIIst. RK.) Who from the Section of the 29st. ID. Were to attack, because of Flank Enemy Artillery Fire not reach they're preparation Position. In their place attacked a few Comps. Of the IR. 112. (29st. ID.) on their own Initiative and had big success. Over 200 Prisoners of the 32nd. French Div. and a few English were brought in.

A Patrol of the 121st. ID Found Burggrave Farm free from Enemy and brought a heavy and 2 light MGs. as Booty back. In the Evening started a very heavy Enemy counters Attack against the 29st. ID. And 52nd. RD. who in places, in bitter close Combat, were completely repelled.

On May 9st. at Noon moved the Battle Squadron of the Xst. RK. Again to Tourcoing, that they 1 Month ago had left hopefully. On May 10 came the 8st. Inf. Div. Kdr. Genlt. Hamann, under the Xst. RK. The Army ordered on May 15, to make the preparations more sustainable and uniform for the later planed attack of the 4st. Army, the new Formation of the Army Area according with the attack Plan for "Hagen". (A Code Name for an Attack).

The thereto adopted Core Command from May 15 (Ia Nr. 331) gave the necessary Instructions. The Group Sector was therefore, by giving up the east Reg. Section to the XVIIIst. RK. And the west Reg. Sector to the G. R. K. made smaller and in 2 Divs. Sections split up. In the right Div. Sector ("G"right) was the 58st. ID. Supposed to put in. While the left Div. Sector ("H"left) was taken over from the 121st. ID. This new structure was supposed to be done until May 24.

In the next Days where larger and smaller attacks of the Enemy at the Positions at the Kemmel taken, but where all repelled.

His Majesty the King of Bav. Had announced his visit to see the Bav. Troops who took part in the storming of the Kemmel. It was held in a beautiful Park in Tourcoing. His Majesty spoke nicely about his brave Troops. Also my Grandfather became honorable mention especially from the Bav. War Minister and a few old Acquaintances from the Vogesen.

In the Night from May 19 to 20 came heavy Fire and it increased towards 6.15 in the Morning to heavy drum Fire at the whole Group Front. In connection thereto did the Enemy attack on the whole front. The main push was against the middle and the left Wing of the 31st. ID. and against both right Reg. of the 121st. ID. here succeeded the Enemy to push the German Line quite a bit back. The Attack against the 8st. ID. And middle of the 121st. ID. We're repelled. The left Wing of the 121st.ID. We're not attacked. An immediately started counter Push at the R. I. R. 7 of the 121st. ID. pushed the Enemy some back. Otherwise came quick counter attacks, because of the difficult Command transmission and the heavy Enemy Fire, not to implementation.

In the Night to May 21 started the relief of the 31st. ID. with the 58st. ID. undisturbed from the Enemy. During the Day was the Kemmel lively with heavy Calibers shelled. In the Noon hours came an attack at the German captive Balloons, at which one was shot down. The attack at the other Balloons where repelled with Flak Fire.

Between 12 Noon and 1 Afternoon discovered an Inf. Aviator of the 121st. ID. in Brulooze a few People who waved at him. Because of this Report and to find out the unclear course of the Enemy Positions, ordered the Gen. Kdo. Again verbally and in writing, in the course of the Night with Inf., eventual using Reserve Detachments, to push for to chase away

Enemy Posts and to determine the Enemy Line and establish connection with the parts that are in Brulooze.

All retaking of the old Line, without the projecting corner at De Brulooze was planned for May 26, and after consultation with the Group Wytschaete (XVIIIst. RK.) At the same time with the intended undertaking of this Group"Johanniswuermchen"(Code name). In the Section of the 121st. ID. Were the IR. 60. To be used, because it was the least burned out.

Towards 10 in the evening increased the Enemy Fire again at the whole Front of the Xst. RK. To greater Violence. At 10.30 in the Evening attacked the Enemy at the left Wing of the 8st. ID. but were repelled. Also were the Attack against the R. I. R. 7. Of the 121st. ID. with timely starting German destruction Fire with MG. and Inf. Fire repelled.

That from the Gen. Kdo. For May 22 ordered push forward of the first Line did not happen, because of the lively activity of the Enemy. At 9.30 in the Morning reported the Inf. Aviator Lt. Haellnink again German Inf. in Brulooze and at V in the Plan quadrat 7353. The Gen. Kdo. Ordered again the Div. to forceful move forward and to create Connection with the Posts, before it will be too late. At 5.30 in the Afternoon reported Lt. Haellnink that he, in the before Noon from German occupied Trenches at Brulooze, has seen French. The Gen. Kdo. Ordered destruction Fire at Brulooze. The 31st. ID. reported, that the IR. 166. Were too exhausted, that they could not move for at De Brulooze.

The new Formation of the Core Section in 2 Div. Sections was done on May 24. At 10 in the Morning was in Linselles a Meeting between the Army Chief and Oberstlt. Hasse, the Gen. Staff Officers of the 121st. ID. and the 16th. Bav. ID. witch on May 21 came under the Xst. RK. Because of bad Weather was the Operation"Johanniswuermchen" and the push forward of the Xst. RK. From May 26 moved to May 27. Since the 121st. ID. could not be left in the Position that long, where the 16st. Bav. ID. determined to participate.

The Attack of the 58st. And 16st. Bav. ID. Kdr. GenMaj. Knight von Moehl, was under his Leadership on May 27 according to Plan carried out. At the same time was at the XVIIIst. RK. the Operation "Johanniswuermchen" carried out. Reason of the attack was the improvement of the Line positioning and deflection of the Enemy from the big attack at the 7ˢᵗ. Army at Chemin des Dames. The Attack of the XVIIIst. RK. Was pointed at Seewald also Hill 47 and 44. The Xst. RK. Had both sides of the Street Kemmelberg—De Brulooze to attack, in order to reach the Line: 150m.southerly N (7252)—P (7252)—N (7353)—Q (7353)—point 12km. on the Street Dranoeter—Loker. The Attack was to move so far over the Line that a deep Fore field would be established.

After the Gasification of the Enemy Artillery and the German destruction Fire at the Enemy Facilities started the Inf. at 4. 50 in the Morning to attack and reached the ordered Targets. The Enemy Artillery was in spite of the Gasification quite lively. Enemy counter attacks pushed the German Troops back to close to their starting Positions. 180 Prisoners and several MGs. were brought in.

On May 29 shot Lt. Roeth, the Leader of the Bav. Fighter Squadron 16, at 4 in the Afternoon in 1 Flight between Ijmuiden and Haze brook, 5 Enemy Balloons down. On May 30 was the Enemy Air block especially lively.

On June 2 became the Xst. RK. From Army Command the order, the Enemy Forces before the Front to tie up to make it hard for the Enemy to move his Reserves to the Aisne Front. For that were 2 Operations prepared: At the 58ᵗʰ. ID. on June 4 in the Morning and at the 16ˢᵗ. Bav. ID. on June 5 in the Evening. Both Operations went according to Plan: 5 Prisoners of the IR. 103 of the 7ˢᵗ. French Div. were at the 58ˢᵗ. Saxonian ID. Brought in. The 16ˢᵗ. Bav. ID. took with they're push for in the Enemy Trenches 2 Officers and 50 Men Prisoners.

From their own accord entered on June 13 at 5.40 in the Morning, it was already Daylight, a Patrol of the 2ⁿᵈ. / IR. 103 of the 58ˢᵗ. Saxonian ID. In the Enemy Positions, surprising a sleeping Guard and brought, in spite of heavy MG. block Fire, 10 Prisoners from the French IR. 104 of the 7ˢᵗ. Div. back, whereby the Insertion of this Div. were confirmed.

On June 16 discussed his Chief, with the Gen. Staff Officers of the Positions Div. 1 from the Army incoming Telephone call who said, according to Spy News and Prisoners Statements, it were with Enemy attacks in Flanders to consider. At strongest Observation of the Enemy and checking of the defense Measures were especially pointed.

On June 27 was his old Driver from the Vogesen, Sergeant Hermann Dippon killed in Air Combat over La Bassee. The Aviation Detachment were he belonged to was not far from Tourcoing and only a few Days earlier did he visit my Grandfather and his Brother, who was his Orderly. He drove with his Brother to the Funeral of this valiant and magnificent Man. An Oak Wreath was the outer sign of his loyalty and Gratitude for the 2 Years of faithful service as Driver to begin of the War.

On July 1. 1918 was the Kemmel shelled with 38cm. Caliber, while so far only 28cm. Grenades at the Kemmel shelling were used from the Enemy.

The Inf. Soldier Stemmler of the IR. 107 from the 58st. Saxonian ID. Took early in the Morning on this Day 3 English Prisoners and provided with that, that the 7st. French Div. were relieved with the 41st. English Div. Like always, when his time it aloud, did he asked this brave Man at his Post Position to tell him the course of his Patrol walk. The brave Saxonian had observed, that the French opposite from him did sleep at they're Guard Duty, which was because of lack of sleep in the previous Night. With the firm resolution, to take those French Men, did he go for alone and was very happy when he found in the Position English, who also slept, who he then took. My Grandfather praised him for his resolute conduct and gave him, in the Name of his Majesty the Kaiser, the Iron Cross 1st. Class.

From July 6 on started the incoming transport for the big Flanders Attack "Hagen". At the daily shelling of the Kemmel, shelled the Enemy the German Observation Posts with 10 shots of 38cm. Caliber. Otherwise past the Month of July in normal Trench War without particular Combat Action.

The Shadows of the Events at the Marne, which started since July 15. 1918, gave also with them rise to the presumption, that the big Attack "Hagen" at the Kemmel Area and north from there would not happen. They had to give up many Troops, especially Artillery Detachments, MW. Columns and Munition.

Oberstlt. Hasse, his reliable Chief, was on Aug.4. 1918 promoted to Chief of the Gen. Staff of the 9st. Army. This big Honor he had earned with his services. On May 12 did he get from his Majesty the Oak Leaves to the Pour le me rite.

"When on April 7 the Gen. Kdo. Of the Xst. RK. Was to set in to take over the Command at the left Wing of the 4st. Army, succeeded the Chief with his prudence and skill in a short time to master all Obstacles, which were tied with the solution of the new Tasks. The building of the

Bridge over the Lys, between Waasten and Armentieres and the following of the Munition to the victorious for moving Troops, took next to the Leadership of the Operation, the highest requirements of his capacity for work. Oberstlt. Hasse did also in this War Section so great that my Grandfather deemed him worthy for the Oak Leaves to the Pour le me rite."

This is what my Grandfather gave in. It was hard for him and all Officers of the Staff of the Xst. RK. To part from this lovable and smart Comrade and War tested Man. His successor was Maj. Reuter, who was for him and all the Staff, with his Freshness and Energy a valued Co Worker.

On Aug. 6 became my Grandfather the following Telegram:

"General of the Inf. von Eberhardt, Leader of the Xst. RK.
I appoint you in trust of your insightful and Energy to the upper Commander of the 7st. Army.
GrHQu. Aug. 6. 1918.
Wilhelm I. R."

Had his lovely Wife this experienced! She would have been so happy with this Honor. He was very thankful to the Kaiser and confirmed that he had received the Telegram and promised to use all of his know how to justify his Trust!

On Aug. 7 came before Noon the Army Group Leader, his Royal Highness the Crown Prince Rupprecht von Bav. With his Chief, Genlt. Von Kuhl and the Army Leader Gen. of the Inf. Sixt von Armin to him, to congratulate him and say good bye. The farewell from his Core was for him very difficult. As they're Leader he had lived a hard but successful Life.

As his successor was the Gen. of the Inf. von Gabeln to Leader of the Xst. RK. Appointed.

Leader of the 7st Army

In the Morning of Aug. 8. 1918 came News, that the Enemy had achieved a break through at the German 2nd. Army, since a few Divs. were run over by a big Tank attack. At his departure from Tourcoing to Avesness, were the OHL, at the time operated, was the seriousness of the Enemy success not yet known. In Avesness did he encounter Field Marshall von Hindenburg on the Street, who told him, after his report that he was on the way to see Gen. Ludendorff, to talk with him about the events at the 2nd. Army. Soon came the Gen.Field Marshall back and my Grandfather could report at Gen. Ludendorff. In detail did he inquire of his Impressions from the Front and the spirit of the Troops. Both found the failure from a few Divs. at the 2nd. Army unexplainable. How brave and unafraid had the Divs. of the 7st. Army, in the heavy July Days, the sudden Tank attacks from the Forest at Villers Cotterets withstood, even so the Enemy had at first success. My Grandfather could only assure, that the Spirit of the Div. who he had under his Command at the Kemmel, were absolutely reliably. He suggested the excellent 58st. Saxonian ID. To put in at the threatened Place at the 2nd. Army. Gen. Ludendorff had the full confidence to the from him fresh put in Divs. that they would master the Situation. His calm and objectivity in this difficult Situation convinced my Grandfather, that the English would have no further success.

In Marchais, his new KHQu. Met him on the same Day (Aug. 8. 1918) in the Evening his predecessor, GenOb. Von Boehn, with the Officers of his Staff. The Chief of the Gen. Staff of the 7st. Army was the Wuertemberg Colonel Reinhardt, Quarter Master the Wuert. Colonel Woellwarth, oldest Gen. Staff Officer Maj. von Blomberg, who he knew from Hannover, were he stood at the IR. 73. When he took the 7st. Army over it had the following Cores:

> Genlt. Von Etzel, XVIIst. AK.
> Genlt. Of the Inf. von Schoeler, VIIIst. AK.
> Gen. of the Inf. Wichura, VIIIst. RK.
> Genlt. Count Eberhardt von Schmettow, Gen.Kdo.65.

Behind the Front the Gen. Kdo. IXst. RK. Kdr. Gen. of the Inf. Dieffenbach.

22 Inf. Divs. were in this Army Section employed. Over 30km. Front width was the Vesle Position, in which the Army had the attacks of the Enemy to repel. The Battle Force of the Battls. Was in the Position about no more than 150 Men.

The Army stood with they're right Wing south of Laon von Conde sur Aisne over Courcelles at the Vesle, 10km. west from Fismes, over Breuil sur Vesle to Jonchery. The left Wing of the first Line in the Area west of the Bremond.

The brilliant Leadership of GenOb. Von Boehn and the extremely efficient Officers of his Staff had reached, that the Troops of the 7st. Army escaped the threat of constriction from the Enemy successes at Soissons in the July Days and could be pulled back fighting to the Position at the Vesle. The Spirit of the Troops was because of this move back unbroken, the brave Divs. had in counter attacks and in defense Combat caused the enemy heavy bloody losses and took from them the ambition further to push against the 7st. Army. GenOb. Von Boehn was promoted to Leader of the newly build Army Group who stood connecting right on the Army Group German Crown Prince.

It was of Interest for my Grandfather to see again the Places of his activity from the Year 1917. At an inquiry drive he drove past his old KHQu. In St. Germainmont and through the totally shot up Town of Neuschatel to the former Positions between Bremond and west from there.

On both sides of the Street St. Thibaut—Bazoches and 1km. west of Fismes attacked, after very violent Fire, on Aug. 27 American Battls. The 17st. And the right Wing of the 29st. ID. Both attacks where repelled. The 17st. ID. brought 100 Prisoners in.

An attack Operation from the 29st. ID. at the same day, which was in the most careful way prepared from Maj. Grohe of the IR. 113. Snatched after a short Fire attack from the Americans the Town of Fismette and pushed for to the Vesle. The Bridges there were busted and 106 American Prisoners brought in. The neighboring IR. 112 of the 29st. ID. had at the defense of the Enemy attack 2 Officers, 1 was a Capt. and 12 Americans taken Prisoners.

At suggestion of the 29st. ID. was at the Army Group Crown Prince from the 7st. Army requested, that each Army became a few Tanks for disposal, so that the Troops in rest behind the Front get used to this Weaponry. They thought that they could obtain better results than with only theoretical instruction. A Man who sees a Tank, after a Nerve shattering Artillery Fire, for the first time in his Life react different than one who knows this Weaponry and his weakness and has seen it before.

On Aug. 31 was the first big training with Tanks at the 1st. Army under the Leadership of the upper Kdr. Gen. of the Inf. von Mudra. They used captured French and English Tanks. Over wide and deep Ditches, through dense Forests and various huge Obstacles could the Soldiers See which big Progress had been done compared to the first ones. Also live shots were fired at these Tanks, unoccupied, to show the effect of the German Artillery.

At the West Front they came in to an ever serious Situation. They had to compensate with the Material Superiority of the Enemy. In addition came that the fresh American Troops in ever increasing Measure, purely numerically, the ranks of the Enemy Army's reinforcing, who because of that came in the lucky Position they're exhausted Div. to relief, to strengthen and to give them the necessary Rest.

At the End of Aug. won the 7st. Army through News and Prisoner Statements the impression that the Enemy before the Army Front became thinner and also because of leaving of 2 Gen.Kdos. (French IIIrd. and XXXth. AK.) They're Section got wider.

The Situation nevertheless remained tense. The Force of the Enemy Artillery, the increase of their Funk Telegraph Stations and they're brisk Traffic with Airplanes, the lately often before attacks observed intentional restrained of the Artillery and the Combat Planes, the visible low activity at Trench building also the dense occupancy of the Villages and Depots, pointed to attack intentions. The time of this expected attack was obviously not known and probably dependent from the outcome of the Operation against the, at the right of the 7st. Army, positioned 9st. Army. The 7st. Army had nevertheless with surprising part and whole attacks to figure.

Often did he look at the Positions at the Vesle and his thought of the defense expressed to the Troop Kdrs. The German Positions were favorable, since they almost everywhere stood at the higher north Shore in buildup Trenches and dominated the Fore field.

At the 5ᵗʰ. ID. who stood at the right Wing of the 7ˢᵗ. Army, could he greet his old IInd. / Gren. R. 12: The Posts of the 6ˢᵗ. Gren. R. 12 oriented him about the Enemy. The Comp. Leader expected an Enemy attack and was relieved when he left the Position. In the Evening he was at Gen. von Etzel, who had his KHQu. In the Area of Bruyeres, as a powerful Enemy Fire attack at the German right and left Wing of the Group Stabs started. The Prussian Leib Gren. Reg. 8 from the 5ᵗʰ. ID. supported, with a few Comps. The left Wing of the 9ˢᵗ. Army, so the Enemy could not perform the attack successfully.

The Enemy was successful, with large Forces of Artillery and fresh Troops, the 9ˢᵗ. Army and the left of the 7ˢᵗ. Army positioned 1ˢᵗ. Army, to push back, therefore had also his Divs. to be pulled back (view Map). The Cores were unseen from the Enemy moved back from the Vesle. Not until Afternoon moved they're Points, from the German Combat Patrols shot and hinder, against the Mesas north of the Vesle.

On Sept. 4 won the Combat Squadron 5 of the 7ˢᵗ. Army with the downing of the 14. Airplane by Lt. Rolfs, the 500ᵗʰ. Air Victory.

At the 216ˢᵗ. ID. (Core Wichura) did the Corporal Kastran with 2 Men of the 10ˢᵗ. / IR. 59. East of Merval take 31 Americans of the 77ˢᵗ. American Div. as Prisoners and took 1 MG. On the whole Army Front were continuously dashing Patrol attacks done and Prisoners brought in, whereby the opposite Enemy could be ascertained.

It was not a nice Task to give only withdrawal orders. He was daily fore at the Troops to find out the Situation and to learn of the needs of the Divs. Splendid was help for him his smart and energetic Chief. Also the Quarter Master and the first Gen. Staff Officer of the Army had always good knowledge and kept him up to Date. And indeed all Officers of the Army Staff supported him superbly, in this difficult End Month of the War.

From Sept 14 on were under the 7ˢᵗ. Army the Core Luettwitz I. Wichura and Schmettow, behind the front Gen. Kdo. XXXIXst. 34. RK.; The Cores Etzel and Schoeler had left the Army Detachment.

On Sept.14 at 12 Noon attacked the Enemy the Romain-Riegel, 6km. northeast of Fismes and was with heavy losses from the 4ˢᵗ. G. I. D. (Core Wichura) repelled. In a counter attack pushed the Ist. 5 GR. Under

Command of Capt. von Stietenkron the Enemy through Glennes back. An Enemy counters attack pushed them again from the Village. 80 Prisoners and 10 MGs. of the 62nd. French Div. were brought in. On the next Day attacked, after short Artillery preparation, at 6.25 in the Morning 1 Battl. Of the 216st. And 1. Of the 4st. G. I. D. from the Core Wichura, the in Glennes penetrated Enemy and pushed them over the old defense Line back. The G. Gren. Reg. 5 had joined in the move for the 5th. GR. On Foot and took 1 Officer and 46 Men of the 62nd. French Div. as Prisoners. From Prisoners Testimony was learned, that at the attack on the previous Day at the Romain-Riegel the 9st. 45th. And 62nd. French Div. had taken part. The Enemy had suffered heavy losses. At the Core Wichura were 6 Officers and 184 Men, 9 heavy and 15 lights MGs. brought in.

At the Core Luettwitz II swam the Grenadier Schmit of the 1st. IR. 119 through the Canal and brought 2 Prisoners and 1 dead from the 52nd. French Div. back

The very busy German Army Flyers started in the Night from Sept.15 to 16 with 20 big Airplanes for the attack at the Fortress Paris. From 2000 to 4000m. High were a total of 1069kg. Bombs at the Town dropped.

An especially brave Patrol of 8 Men from the 4st. IR. 42 of the 216st. ID. (Core Wichura) under Leadership of Corporal Wiese brought south of Revillon 1 Officer and 33 Men of the 8st. Italian Div. in.

On Sept. 18 took my Grandfather the Command over the previous Section and the Cores Luettwitz II. (XXXVIIIst. RK.) Schoeler (VIIIst. AK.) And Petersdorf (XVIIst. AK.) Of the right from the 7st. Army positioned 9st. Army, who's right Wing was 5km. northeast of Coucy-le-Chateau-Crepy. The AOK. of the 9st. Army were pulled from the Front, so the 7st. Army connected on the left Wing of the 18st. Army, who's upper Kdr. was the Gen. of the Inf. von Hutier.

The 19st. ID. pushed on Sept.19 they're Fore Field 150m. For in spite of heavy Enemy counter Combat. 46 Prisoners were at the Core Petersdorf brought in, who confirmed the Deployment of the 41st. French Div. Under the Leadership of the Officers Locum Schoenfelder, Vice Corporal Luedecke and Privat first Class Helmer broke 8 Men of the R. I. R. 230 of the 50st. RD. south of Chalons sur Vesle in the Enemy Position fore and brought 1 Officer and 80 Men as Prisoners back.

On Sept. 24 attained the 19st. ID. 84 Prisoners of the 45th. And 62nd. French Div. to bring in. At the 29st. ID. Were 1 Officer and 29 Men at an Operation against Vailly brought in.

On Sept. 20 did he give Notice in an Army Command, that the Enemy the Front Line Ailette—Aisne with new Troops reinforced had, that because of the Troop movements the occurred Battle Pause was happening and with their ending must now be figured.

Opposite of the German Line north of Ailette stood still Battle ready, but already for weeks used Divs. Between Ailette and Aisne were the already long in Position standing, with the previous Battles weekend French Divs. 29., 5., 128. And 25. They by only a short time or all fresh put in Divs. 59. 36. 127. 41. And 162. Were reinforced. While south of the Aisne until the Area from Reims the old Enemy Divs. in middle Battle Force stood.

The Enemy Artillery was in the Area Laffaux—Vregny—Neuville sur Margival with the main Direction Pinon—Vaudesson—Malmaison—Jouy remarkable heaped, they were medium strong, also opposite of the Romain—Riegel, less strong opposite of both Army Wings north of the Ailette and at the Mesas of the Vesle.

The Enemy use of Force, the many single Observations and Prisoner Statements indicated a continuing of the Enemy attack intentions. Part and large attacks were further to be expected. As next Main Target of the Enemy was considered: Pinon, Vaudesson and Jouy with the Intention to push through to Chavignon. They thought that the Enemy simultaneously would attack the Romain—Riegel and against the Aisne and Vesle Front exploration advances would try, since he could figure there with a German withdrawal.

The Army wanted the expected new Battle take on in their current Position and the attacker beat in a defense Battle. The Structure was from Sept. 29 on the Cores Luettwitz II (XXXVIIIst. RK.) Schoeler (VIIIst. AK.) Luettwitz I (IIIrd. AK.) Wichura (VIIIst. RK.) Schmettow (Gen. Kdo. 65)

To the Cores were send exact Commands and orders about the Development of action, positioning of the Artillery and the continuing connection with the Neighbors.

Decree of the Chief of the Gen. Staff From Sept. 4. 1918

The Decree of the Chief of the Gen. Staff of the Field Army from Sept. 4. 1918 –II Number 10162 says under Nr. 3:"The Fore Field Crew behaves like fore Posts. And under Nr. 2: The decisive fight is to be about the main defense Line, not the Fore Field. And in Nr. 4: In and behind the main defense Line has to be held.

From this follows: In each Section has the main defense Line to be accurately determined and all Officers and Men have to know. Since they, in the present Battles, had no prepared Trench Positions, but an incoherent Terrain exploiting and with a few support Points, marked Line. So it has to be at the Start of the Battle occupied from those Troops who have the order to they're defense.

The connection to the Neighbor Section is very important; for this are Stitch Commandos to select, who at Enemy break in, can immediately intervene. The For Field Crew has to be ordered how they should behave also the For Posts. Is the For Field narrow so you leave only week Posts, who's Task it is the Enemy to stop at an Obstacle, to give the fighting Troops in the main defense Line time to occupy the defense Line.

They're move back in the main defense Line must correspond to the circumstances. Each Detachment has to know were they have to move back to create a Front or if they should stay in the For Field to the last Bullet even so if the Enemy has broken in. Is the For Field wide, one is forced to give the Enemy heavy resistance. Also this has to be ordered to the For Field Crew. In this case have local Crews and especially MG. Nests, in spite of Enemy break in, to stay in the For Field.

While the from the OHL. From Aug. 24. 1918—Ia / Nr. 9963 secret reported experiences from the Battles at the southwest Front under Nr. 2 say: The deep For Field did, after the Judgement of the Reg. (of the 78st. RD.) Proven to be effective, asks GenMaj. Daenner (1st. Bav. ID.) on Aug. 31. 1918—4109—after his experiences the Question: The development of the Enemy attacks, they're daily progress and achievements, had him in cohesion with the News from the other Battle Fields a Question imposed, whether the Div. of the Battle Area in the For Field, the main resistance Line and main Battle Zone and the at the time valid principles for the elastic Battle Leadership in the defense, still at the time in Section attack process of the Enemy, correspond. He had the impression, as if the Enemy had they're attack method adopted to the German defense method and daily tried to win an Area Parcel with certain depth. The Attack of the Enemy started with the break in and taking of the For Field on the 17. And 18. Aug. The in the for field used Troops of the Position Div. moved back to the main defense Line or came in Enemy Hand.

After the loss of the For Field was the main defense Line the first Line. The Crew of the first Line had therefore the Obligation the first Line decisive to defend. Alone after the real operations has this Thought not come into awareness of many Troops. The Troops looked rather habitually to get again new For Field; since it was not possible forward so they looked backwards and left the Enemy without fighting more Area. This Act was made easier for the Troops since the main defense Line was often not visible with Trenches.

Also the practical experiences confirm the previous written. The defense has to use all they're Forces for the Battle at the main Resistance Line. The Leaders become, because of the almost never coherent defense Position and the in certain circumstances in the For Field moved for, points, many changing Tasks. They have to bring the Battle from the depth and the Flanks and they have to bring the success with counter attacks.

From Reports of the Front Officers did my Grandfather became the conviction, that the consumption of the Battle Force of the Div. has its reason, not so much from bloody losses but from lack of Sleep, inadequate Rations in the first Line and too many Lice.

He asks the commanding Gens. And Divs. Commanders to look especially at those points. He told them to avoid mixing of Detachments and make Shure of proper structure in depth. The Objection, that in the first Line at the weak Forces no Men could be missed, them is to encounter, that if all Comps. Stay in the Fire Area, that the Forces condition inevitably starts to sink and after a few Days will be conciderable weaker then at fresh Forces. The Duty to prepare everything for a threatening Battle does not absolve from the other Duty the Forces possibly to conserve. Between both demands is quiet Blood and sharp Enemy Observation also sober assessment asked from the Leaders. For that there is no Recipe.

He told his lower Leaders that a relief of the Div. after short use was not possible at the General Situation. It had to be the Duty of the higher Leaders the fighting ability of the Troops with appropriate application to keep high.

There were sure signs that the Enemy wanted to attack at the Romain—Riegel. In expectation of this did he give on Sept.29 the necessary Commands. A special Impediment for the Leaders was that without prejudice of the defense readiness, on Sept. 30 the preparations had to be started for a further move back during the next 3 Nights.

In his operations Command did he emphasize that if on Sept. 30, when the Enemy attacks, without a look backwards is to be implemented. A defense success is the best cover of a move back."

After a half hour of heavy Artillery preparation attacked the Enemy on Sept. 30 with help of Tanks at 6 in the Morning, the 19st. ID. (Left Wing Core Wichura) and the right half of the Core Schmettow (2nd. Bav. And 5th. ID.). the 19st. ID. repelled all attacks. The Enemy broke in at the Core connection at the 2nd. Bav. ID. until Vantelay and forced at Jonchery the crossing over the Vesle towards Pevy. Between 9 and 10 in the Morning attacked the Enemy also the right Section of the Core Wichura, the 216st. ID. the Battle was in full course. At the broke in Position moved the Enemy for with Tanks from the side against the 19st. ID. At the 2nd. Bav. And 5th. ID. were at the Hills west of Vantelay fought and at Montigny and southwest of Pevy.

In the Afternoon was the impact of the attack broken, especially because of the brilliant attitude of the 216st. ID. The Enemy success was because of the break in at the 2nd. Bav. ID. and of the menace of the Flanks of the connecting Troops. Towards Noon were the 19st. And 5th. ID. and through parts of the 4st. G. J. D. successful, to catch the attack and then to hold the Line Glennes—Vantelay—Pevy—Prouilly. The only, in the course of the Morning starting Enemy attacks against the 216st. ID., were from the often proven Troops repelled. The Enemy managed, in spite of 5 attacks; at no place to break in the Main defense Line. Many Prisoners were brought in.

The 7st. Army was in the course of Sept. in the Battles for and in the Siegfried Position according to they're Tasks successful. It followed then until Oct.9 the Trench Battles north of the Ailette.

At the begin of Oct. left the Core Luettwitz II the Army Association. In their Place came the Core Petersdorff (XVIIst. AK.)

In the Frame of the total Situation became the 7st. Army the Task from the OHL. To hold out to fight and important Battles to dodge gradually until the Hunding Position. The Task for the Army was more difficult than a straight defense or an attack and made it necessary for solid Leadership which must be imbued with the thought not to avoid the Battle but to do it in another form which postpones the decision since at that time was the Balance of Power not favorable. He ordered that there, were Battles started, these always with emphasis and when possible be performed attack wise. Nobody had, without order, a delegated defense to break up. Every Leader had his Position to hold and maybe lost Area to gain back, if not a counter attack was strictly not ordered.

The new Situation had the higher Leaders and Troop Commanders with deduction of immovable Combat Equipment, limitation of the Supply Train, Deportation of everything dispensable to the Recruit Depot, to think of. Long-term Buildings and Facilities should not anymore be done, only make shift. Streets and Trains in the Area of the current Battle Zone had to be destroyed and changed into Tank impediments.

At the election of the rear Guard and evasive Positions had the 7st. Army with good success continuous straightness avoided. By on purpose building of corners and Bastions, especially also from re-entrant angels, were the Enemy the recognizing of the new Position made difficult and flanking use of close Combat Weapons made the defense easier, so that the rear Guard Battles were for the Enemy very bloody and the rule of Action was on the German side.

The German Artillery had there many Tasks witch cost them highest requirement. At their current state it would have been wrong to expect too much from the Individual units. It had to be thought to distribute the Tasks so that each Battr. Had certain Tasks to do. The necessary wave art use and deep structuring, because it mattered in this retreat fight that the Inf., in no Battle phase, was without help.

The Enemy did not follow the 7st. Army directly, for them evidence of their heavy losses.

On Oct. 12. 1918 did he give the following Army Day Command to all the Troops under him to make it clear to everybody why the 7st. Army had to move back unchallenged from the Enemy.

7st. Army   AHQu. Oct.12.1918

Upper Command
Ia Nr. 112 / Oct. 1918

Army Day Command!
Why did the 7st. Army move back?

The answer views every Officer and Men of the Army. Twice did the Enemy attempted with the biggest Force to overpower the 7st. Army. In the Spring 1917 should have the Chemin des Dames been taken and a brake over Laon-Sissonne been forced. But we stayed victorious, solid stood the 7st. Army at the Hills of Laffaux, Malmaison, Cherny and Craonne! Instead of brake through was collapse the result of the big Offensive of the French.

Then came for us a big Mishap in the autumn of 1917. The Enemy took from us, under the cover of Day long Gasification; against we had no Air movement or Raindrops for help, the Laffaux Corner. We were because of that, put at the Chemin des Dames in an unfavorable Situation; Vacated this 8 Days later voluntarily and not disturbed from the Enemy and positioned us behind the Ailette for the winter.

In the spring of 1918 we moved again forward, not only at the Chemin des Dames, no, everybody has not forgotten, deep into the Enemy until over the Marne. Never have the French something like that done. That was our Target and everybody gave they're best. Honor and thanks to the Heroes who gave they're Life for that!

But the Enemy became too numerous, since they pulled everything together to counter the 7st. Army. For a second time had the Army to beat a great defense Battle. This time we were not like in 1917 on our solid place in the big German West Front but in the Front of a big Bulge much more forward without Positions. The first start was against our Neighbors right and left at Soissons and Reims, whereby our Flanks where constricted. Then attacked the Enemy comprehensive the 7st. Army. We had to repel him and then take our place slowly moving back over Marne, Qurcq and Vesle. It was a good Plan, according to the Situation of the 7st. Army, then still under the Command of the GenOb. Von Boehn who completed it, thanks to the bravery of Leaders and Troops, like ordered, successful on every defense Day, in good order on every back march Day.

When we again stood at Malmaison, Cerny and Craonne, came the Enemy in full force at the Chemin des Dames, but solid stood the 7st.Army and bloody were French and Italians repelled.

In the meantime is our Enemy successful with mass use of People, Munition and Machines the German Positions to overwhelm between Cambrai and St. Quentin also in the Chmpagne. There had the German Army's to move back after hard Battles and take new Positions in the Area of Le Chateau—Bohain and from Rethel—Vouziers.

Since then had the Enemy the 7st. Army no harder attacked. Only Patrols tested the Front; At times was it very quiet. The intention of the Enemy is clear; we should now no more be attacked, the progress right and left was to box us in, in order to finish us from all sides, the so far solid staying middle part of the West Front .The German is so sluggish, he is not going to give up Laon and they're nice Forest Mountains, he will stay in his good Positions, he is Battle tired, too passive to relearn to move fighting in the free Field. Then comes a new Sedan for the Germans, but reversed."

We anticipated these cunning Plans. The Situation is similar like at the Marne, similar is also our Task: Move in a whole Front Line.

We do it bitter unwillingly, but we understand that it is a good Plan who is adapted to the big Situation. Solid stood the 7st. Army for 4 Years at the Damen Road. Twice did they storm the big Hills from Craonne, twice evacuated but never lost in an Enemy Storm. Solid has to be the 7st. Army also further, wherever she has to fight, to hold or to march.

I expect, that also in the new Situation, every Officer and Men of the Army as until now, fights and works and holds out, that each Troop as until now do their Duty, so that the 7st. Army stays in Honor until Peace, which they were for 4 Years; The solid middle part of the West Front!

This Command is to be read to all Officers, Corporals and Men and to explain with the Map.

Signed
The upper Commander
Von Eberhardt

The AHQu. Was first moved to Rozoy and Montcornet, later to St. Michel east of Hirson. Until Oct.13 fought the Army before the Hunding and Brunhild Position later in these Positions.

Enemy Artillery shelled; with they're lack of restraint, on Oct. 15 the Liebfrauen Church in Liesse, after the Germans had this Pilgrimage site for 4 Years protected. A Lyoner Radio Signal reported in these Days, Laon where in Flames. This Lie lined up with others. What was in and around Laon destroyed was the work of the French Artillery. The Germans had left this Town at they're retreat totally unshelled, since the People of this Town and the Area, with German caring, were gathered there. Also in the Eifel tower reports were more false reports. To the French Radio Reports from Oct.15 and 16. 1918 is to say, that no French Bombs fell on Montcornet, also that La Selve was taken by the French and that at Marchais 400 Prisoners fell in their Hand, 3 French Reports, 3 Lies!

On Oct. 17 could he say the following Recognition:

"Almost all Divs. of the Army had success in their new Positions in the defense, in counter attacks and Patrols to bring Prisoners in. Therefore was in short time clarified the structure of the Enemy before the Army. I speak for this my appreciation, especially to the Patrol Officers and Men, which is to be announced to all."

The good lead and brave 24st. Saxonian RD. under GenMaj. Baron von Oldershausen brought on Oct. 19 at a successful defense of Enemy attacks over 100 Prisoners of the 31st. French Div. in. These heavy attacks, which were probably the initiation to near big attacks, were also at the left Wing of the Core Petersdorf (XVIIst. AK.) Repelled from the brave IR. 133. The Reg. brought in counter attack 2 Officers and 133 Men of the 31st. French Div. as Prisoners in.

At the 86st. ID. became the main defense Line lost; a counter attack was planned for the next Day. At the Core Luettwitz I (IIIrd. AK.) Were through Prisoners the 72nd. French Div. found out. At the Core Wichura (VIIIst. RK.) Took the 19st. ID. in counter attacks the Macquigny Ferme and the Troops of the 2nd. Bav. ID. the Village La Selve again, after both Places where lost before Noon. Lt. Umbach and Private first Class Twickler from the Eastfriesischen IR. 78 of the 19st. ID. walked alone to the Enemy and came back with 22 Prisoners. From Testimony of Prisoners, was the Target of this Enemy attack the enforcement of the Serre—and Souche Section. Then should the whole Front of the 7st. Army be attacked. The German losses were high, but the attack Spirit of the Troops was unbroken.

The 86st. ID. whetted the Stain from Oct. 19 on the next Day completely and took they're old Positions again. Prisoners and Material came in German Hand.

The Leader of their Army Group, His Imperial Highness the Crown Prince were on Oct. 25 in the Area of the 7st. Army. He informed himself intensely at the Div. happily greeted from Officers and Men, and gave much Praise about Attitude and successes of the Troops.

On Oct. 26 were heavy Enemy Tank attacks repelled and on the next Day between 5 in the Afternoon and 8 in the Evening attacked the Enemy 3 times in several waves with the help of Battle Airplanes against the Fronts of the 10st. RD. and 26st. Wuert. ID. The attacks where started with heavy Fire but were bloody repelled from the proven Regiments, in part with Men to Men Combat, R. I. R. 37, Gren. R. 119 and IR. 121.

The Army expected a continuation of the Battles, especially at the left Wing at the Core Schmettow (Gen. Kdo. 65) were large attacks with heavy tenacious Men to Men Combat had ensued. Several times tried the Enemy, the Inf. with support of heavy Artillery and participation of Airplanes and Tanks and obscuring, to penetrate. All his attacks failed with heavy Enemy losses at the tough defense and counter attacks of the brave Troops.

It was for the Battle Troops a hard time. While the Troops of the second Line moved in to they're backwards Positions, had these brave tenacious Combatant they're Positions to defend, make shift expand and to secure. As much as possible was he in constant touch with the Staffs and Reg., had especially brave Men come to him, talked with them and tried in personal talks to make clear to them the current Battle Situation, especially for the in the fight standing Troops. The Troops did not understand the move back according to Plan, because they thought they were stronger then the Enemy.

On the same Day (Oct.26) was Gen. Ludendorff been removed from his Position. Which seemed to them, since they still had Hope of change of the Situation, depressing.

On Oct. 28 at 7.15 in the Morning did he come back from a drive to the Front. His Chief told him that something important existed. He would come in Person to him and go with him to the Casino to eat.

At the End of his talk about the events at the Fronts and the various official entries, told Colonel Reinhardt that he has something more to tell, which were for him, the Staff and the whole 7st. Army very hurting and gave him a Telegram, which had come in the Afternoon from the Chief of the Military Cabinet in Berlin:

"His Majesty the Kaiser and King want to, because of dissolution of the Army Group Boehn, the GenOb. Von Boehn at Nov. 1 again make the upper Commander of the 7st. Army, accordingly your Excellence will be transferred at the 31. Of the Month to the Officers of the Army. Your Excellency should for reuse, as soon as an opportunity arises, be taken into consideration."

This him deep touching News could not be mitigated, that not only his Chief of the Gen. Staff and the Officers of the upper Commands, but also the under him Commanding Gen. and many Troop Kdrs. let him know, how reluctantly they seen him go.

On Oct. 30 came the following report:

"His Majesty the Kaiser and King have your Excellency at Oct.31 transferred to the Officers of the Army. His Majesty the Kaiser and King have your Excellency in grateful appreciation of your performance on the top of the 7st. Army the Red Eagle Decoration I. Class with Oak Leaves and Swards awarded."

Already on Oct. 29 had his Imperial Highness the Crown Prince told him, how much he was surprised at this recall, especially as Gen. Ludendorff had told him that he would stay in his Position; GenOb. Von Boehn would get a different use. He sends him on Oct. 31 the following Telegram:

"The surprisingly recall of your Excellency was known to me from a communication of the Military Cabinet on Oct. 28. I can only painfully regret your Excellency Departure from my Command Area and have to thank you for everything you did as upper Commander of the 7st. Army. Next to the bravery of the Troops are the outstanding deeds of the 7st. Army in the present Battle your clear, unerringly Leadership to thank. I wish that your Excellency soon becomes opportunity your proven force to use in the service of the King and Fatherland.

Wilhelm, Crown Prince."

On Oct.31 did he drive to the Gen. Kdos. Who were under him, to say good bye. In the Evening did he say to the Officers and upper Officials of the AOK. Good bye and were then with the closer Staff for a few hours in the Casino. In his good bye Speech did he tell the Chief, Colonel Reinhardt, that he thought him suitable to be once War Minister.

Colonel Reinhardt had, to honor his Old Prussian feeling, for this farewell Party instead of the Pour le me rite the Commanders Cross of the local decoration of the Hohenzollern put on.

Very hard was the good bye from his Horses!

To the Officers of the Army transferred.

As he came to Charleville he met his, from many Years earlier, old Chief Oberstlt. Hasse, who was employed as Chief of the Gen. Staff of the 1st. Army. He oriented him about many Questions. Both did not know that in a few Days they would come together in the old Relationship. After a boring Train Trip did he arrive with great delay on Nov.2. 1918 in the main HQu. In Spa. He went first to the Operations Section, were Colonel Heye told him that he would only shortly be without a Position. The first Gen. Quarter Master, Genlt. Groener, was in those Days not in Spa. The Chief of the central Section, Colonel Tieschowitz von Tischowa, told him also that ha soon would become a Command. The Chief of the Military Cabinet, GenMaj. Baron Marshall named Greiff, was more reserved. On the Street did he meet Gen. of the Inf. von Guendell, who, was scheduled for the Armistice Negotiations, was ordered to Spa for Information. An excellent choice was taken with this appointment; Excellence von Gruendell mastered several Languages and hid dexterity, which already came at his utilization as a Delegator at the Conference in the Haag and in the Gen. Staff of the east Asien Expedition Core, to recognition. He might have been a guarantee for a relatively favorable course of the Armistice Negotiations. The sudden appearing of the Center Delegate Erzberger forced Gen. von Gruendell to leave the Commission. He told me that the Rumor, that he also heard several times from Oct. 7 to 10, that he should have been his successor as upper Commander in Elsa's. He was thankful that this had not come to be, so he was spared the Pain to give the German Elsa's to the French.

He asked the Gen. Adjutant of the Kaiser, GenOb. Von Plessen, to give him an audience with his Majesty the Kaiser. He refused to do that.

At 11 in the Morning he reported to Gen. Field Marshall von Hindenburg, who, like always was kind and sympathetic. He regretted his Fate and promised him to get him the next open Position. The Gen. Field Marshall told him literally:

"Now I have the Kaiser here in Spa transported from the influences of the Berliners. Now there can be no more talk from Abdication or other restrictions from the Imperial Power. I will make Shure of that."

They from the Front, even he as Army Leader, did not know that it already was seriously for the loss of the Crown!

On Nov 3 at 8 in the Morning did he reach Berlin. On Nov. 8 in the Morning was he surprised by a Telephone call, that a Telegram from the Chief of the Military Cabinet had come in, which said, he was right away to go to Spa, were he was again to be used as upper Commander of an Army. Immediately afterwards he was told by Telephone from the Hospital of the Surgeon Professor Unger, that his oldest Son, who was on Business in Berlin, in the Evening of Nov. 7 at the Anhalter Train Station at boarding the Train to Spa had broken the Knee Cap of his wounded leg. In spite of the preparation for his Trip to the Front did he visit his Son, who was for some time tied to the Bed. Then he went to the Command Post and became the necessary Information and Papers. He noticed the great excitement of the Employees but he did not think of any Dangers. At the Street were many Officers in Battle Uniform who had followed the public calls to report at the Command Post. They were without any further orders send home. The Soldiers who he seen in the Street did not look like Revolutionary's. Towards Evening he became the following Telegram:

"I appoint you to Upper Commander of the 1st. Army.
Big Headquarter, Nov. 8.1918.

Wilhelm I. R."

Upper Commander of the 1st. Army.

2 strong Grenadiers from the 2nd. G. R. on Foot were given him and helped to bring the Baggage to the Train Station. There it was not sure if the Train could go to Spa. He went to Town to eat. He encountered a few Processions. He did not notice any harassment of Officers. Between 9 and 10 in the Evening was he again at the Anhalter Train Station were the Train stood ready to leave. An Officer Deputy with 12 Grenadiers of the Kaiser Franz G. Gren. Reg. 2 in Uniform, with sharp Munition, were given the Train as security. In the sleep Car, in which his Compartment was, were also his Excellence von Delbrueck, Chief of the Civil Cabinet of the Kaiser, a few Officers and a number of Civil Persons. From them did he meet a nice Train Official from Colon with whom he came in political discussion. The majority of the Civil People were Industrial Bosses who wanted as fast as possible to get over the Rhein and in to they're Homeland. They seeing the Situation as very dangerous and were afraid that at the Rhein were already bloody Revolution.

On the Morning of the disastrous Nov. 9. 1918 was he in the Train on the Route Nordhausen—Kassel. The friendly Conductor made him a Cup of Coffee; his orderly brought him a piece of dry Bread. The News, which the Train Personal got at various Train Stations, was very serious. From Kiel had the seditious Movement of the Sailors spread to the Province Capitals, the Troops, was said, had mutinied, Deputy Gen. Commandos were stopped, Magazines stormed and plundered. The Danger, that the Train Stations were occupied from Rebels, the Train Line blown up, and that also his Train could be hindered from the Trip to Spa, was very real. During the Morning came more News of the establishment of Worker and Soldier Councils and from they're terrorist doing against Officers and Men. Before they reached Kassel did he order the Officer Deputy to him and ordered him before the Entrance into the Station to post Guards on the doors. The Train Personal said, that from all points incoming News, the Train Stations of the Garrison Towns were in the Hands of the reds. He told the People in his Railcar that he would in all circumstances use

265

his Revolver if somebody would try to take his Sabre. As his Express
Train in the Kassel Station arrived, were many Soldiers, who were from
Leave Trains pulled out from young people with red Armbands. On his
Train did the Man from the Soldier Counsel not dare to approach. After a
short stop did the Express Train continue. As soon as they had left Kassel
came 2 young Gen. Staff Officers and asked for his order for the further
conduct of the Train Guards. Since he said it were obvious not to allow
unauthorized People to come in and that he would hinder anybody with
the Weapon who would dare to take Weapons, Decorations and the likes,
said the Officers it were possible that in Giessen, how it was in Kassel surely
planed, red Battl. At the Station was and the entrance deny. To this he
said, that they could not force the entrance and the transit with they're 12
Man Guards, in case this were already planned. He said that they had to
defend themselves to the last drop of Blood. He gave everybody his Word
of Honor the he would fight, if a Bloke from the Soldier Counsel would
ask for his Sabre. Both Gen. Staff Officers left the Car. Then came the
People in Civil to him that had overheard the talk in the side walkway of
the Car and said;

"But Excellence! You are not going to shoot? You're going to get killed,
think of us, since we are uninvolved! You are not going to use the Revolver
just for your Sabre? The Sabre you would have to give also in the Field
when you are encircled by the Enemy. Think of your Family." He answered
this People that he had given to the Officers his Word of Honor that he
would shoot when red Rebels came to him. His Sabre, which he got from
Prince Friedrich Karl from Prussia 45 Years ago, when he became Officer,
he would not have given to the Enemy, unless he were unfit to fight. His
Family and Kids thought like him and would be proud if he had saved
his Honor.

Then he sat alone in his Compartment. Both young Lt. who he had
taken from Berlin as orderly Officers, did not come anymore in sight. His
faithful Orderly, Karl Dippon came to him. He had during the past 4 War
Years got to know him and knew how he thought and felt!

At a Station, he thought it was Treysa, brought the Conductor deeply
moved the Limburger Special Edition with the from Prince Max von
Baden signed Decree of the Empire Government after witch the Kaiser
had resigned. He took it to Excellence von Delbrueck, who gave it back to

him with the words:" That is totally against the agreement that is a Coup d'etat!"

In the Afternoon they came close to Giessen. He laid his Revolver handy; The Train suddenly stopped before the outer Station. From the Train you could see nothing. After a long time begun the Train again to move. They drove into the Station Giessen. At the Station were the Dispatcher and the People that checked the Wheels with Hammers, everything else were empty. They continued after 10 Min. over Wetzlar into the Lahn Valley. In the site walk way of the Car did he meet Excellence von Delbrueck, who told him smiling, that after he had said he would shoot in case Rebels would come near the Train, the People in civil and the 2 Staff Officers had a meeting and from then on did not come back into the Car. The Train Driver had to stop before Giessen and a delegation was send to the Station who met with the Soldier Counsel and told them the Train is Military occupied and the Commander had ordered to shoot. One shut not spill Blood over that. So the Soldier Counsel thought it wise not to use force. So had Diplomatic Negotiation, started with his will to shoot, and worked!

The Train could not at Koblenz cross the Rheine, because the Bridge there was closed from red Troops who did not want to let any more Trains from the Homeland over the Rheine. He thought it was thanks to the Train Command Center in Cologne and the Train Conductor that the Train from Ehrenbreitstein over the Bridge at Engers did move.

In the meantime it had gotten dark. They had on the left Rheine Shore at a big Station a long wait, because for the Trip through the Eifel they needed a different Locomotive. Slowly moved the Train on. He was quite hungry because other than the slice of Bread earlier he had nothing to eat.

The Morning dawned as they passed the Belgian Border. After a 37 hour Trip did the Train at 7.30 in the Morning arrive in Spa. One look to the Place were the Royal Train normally stood, it was gone! His Kaiser had gone at 5 in the Morning to Holland into Exile.

After he had changed Close in the Hotel de Rosette he went to the Military Cabinet to report. The Chief, GenMaj. Baron Marshall called Greif, was very pessimistic and had a terrible View if the Situation, so he could only assume that a very bloody Revolution had started. Berlin, it was said, swam in Blood. All Troops had deserted and went to the Rebels — 3rd.G. Reg. Alexander, G. Fues. Only the 2nd. G. Reg. had fought. All Officers were dead, the Kdr. Count Castell at the point of the Reserve Battl. Fallen. Red Troops were in march to Spa, the Rheine line in the Hands of the Reds. Those were News who came to the big HQu. And were meant for his Majesty. They were wrong! Why were they not checked out?!

Whatever did happen on Nov. 9. 1918 in Spa and who had told the Kaiser to go to Holland?

All these Questions and many more and nobody could give him a clear answer. It always was said it were inevitable, the Army were falling, it had now be necessary to lead the Army properly back.

Treason and Lies and Inaction, as had occurred with the Prussian People and Prussian Officers in 1806, had brought about the Disaster in the Homeland during the Nov. Days 1918.

Back to his personal Experience in Spa. At Colonel von Rauch of the Detachment "Foreign Army's", at witch his oldest Son stood, did he find, next to full Sympathy for the Mishap of his Son, a totally different Perception of the Situation. The Colonel thought that the Departure of the Kaiser had not been necessary. The Storm Battl. Rohr and the many Battle ready Officers in Spa had the safety of the Emperor guaranteed. He spoke to Gen. Field Marshal von Hindenburg at his report in the Garden of the Hotel were the meeting Rooms were. He reminded him of his Words from Nov. 2 and asked him why his Majesty had abdicated. He answered that at the time and Situations it would have not been possible otherwise. At the Chief of the Operations Detachment, Colonel Heye, did he achieve to order by Telephone a Car from his Upper Commando of the 1st. Army to Spa. He then talked to the Chief of the Central Detachment, Colonel Tieschowitz von Tischowa, and then to the first Gen. Quarter Master Genlt. Groener, whose assessment of the Situation did not correlate with his.

At 1 in the Afternoon did he drive with Excellence von Delbrueck to the Villa of the Gen. Field Marshal. There were about 20 Persons at the Table. The Menu was the same as on Nov.2 – Herring Potato's. He sat between the Gen. Field Marshal and the Bav. Colonel Knight Mertz von Quirnheim. The Conversation was naturally about his Trip experience and the happenings of Nov. 9. You could not have a Picture of the real

Situation. You were in Spa much under the impression of the News from Berlin, witch were considered literally.

In the Afternoon came his Car. In a rapid pace on good Streets through nice Area did he drove to Rochefort, his AHQu. They had to cross the Danger Zone, in which at the opinion of the OHL. Red Troops were to be. The Deputy Officer who picked him up in Spa did not see anything like that on his Trip to Spa. Also at the Trip back did they not see anything. Only in 1 Village where 2 drunk Militia Men who would not move from the Street. They were at they're Driver, who himself at the Soldiers Counsel of the Car Column of the AOK. Of the first Army involved was, badly seen. He almost would have run over them.

At 9 in the Evening was he greeted from his Staff, on who's Point Oberstlt. Hasse was Chief. There he also found other Acquaintances, the Quarter Master Oberstlt. Von Caprivi, the Adjutant Capt. Baron von Boenigk, who in 1914 had lost 1 Eye and he also knew him from Kaiser Franz Reg. also the Gen. Surgeon Dr. Paalzow, with whom he had worked in the War Ministry. An especially outstanding Personality was Maj. Klewitz, first Gen. Staff Officer in the Gen. Staff of the Army, who as a born Prussian came from the Wuert. Army. His clear and sharp Mind and his Energy were in the following hard Days, priceless.

Gen. of the Inf. Otto von Below, who had lead the 1st. Army, was on Nov. 9 with a special order send to Germany.

The Business Rooms of the Upper Commando were in the School Building in the middle of the Village. There he became on the next Day Orientation from the Chief about the Situation of the 1st. Army. The 3 Cores, Lindequist (VIIst.RK.) Borne (VIst.RK.) and Langer (XXIVst. RK.) were under him. They had reached the Area between the Maas and the Luxemburg Border north of Givet.

The next Days brought them the whole Tragedy from that in the Forest of Compiegne signed Armistice to awareness. That the German OHL. Took this disgrace on them belongs to the Incomprehensibilities; of witch this War was so rich. The Illusion that the Troops would not fight anymore, that it were impossible, they one more time to a last resistance at the Maas to inflame, was there in all the Heads. The biggest part of the Front Officers and Men thought it as shameful, the occupied Land hastily and with abandoning of valuable Material, to leave. The Rogues, who had sharpened the Knife in the Homeland, pressed it in the Neck of the Army, and were already happy with the Thought soon to be in Power.

The Task, the German Army in short time, followed from the Supply Troops, from the conquered Area, to lead back over the Rheine was for the OHL. And the lower Command Structure a huge Task. Especially the from Flanders and North France returning Army's had trouble with March Streets. It was important to move Daily through certain Sections whose west Border was reached on the same Day also from the Enemy. When you think of the inhibitions and delays, the already in Peace time with the best preparations at such mass movements would occur, so remains the Masterpiece of this Retreat an astonishing performance of the German Gen. Staff and Pioneers, who, hurrying ahead of the Army's, had to build a big Number of Bridges from War Bridge Columns and big Construction Companies, also the Water Engineering Department for the completion of the few existing crossings, to make the crossing of the Rheine fluent. The 3 Cores of the 1st. Army had become 2 March Streets from Belgian through north Luxemburg assigned, from which the southerly had to be used in places from parts of the 3rd. Army. At Elerf (Evreux) had the Core of the 1st. Army, at the move through the Pass, only use of 1 Street and could only after, use again 2 Streets. Before the Army marched the Supply Depot Troops with their Vehicles of any kind.

In all were the Supply Depot Columns in order and in the Hand of they're Leaders. All Vehicles were decorated with the Flags of their relevant German States. There had been formed, at order of the OHL. Worker and ·
Soldier Counsels. The Chief had immediately given appropriate provisions in which each Formation should have voted Confidence Councils, whose wishes the Chief would accept then the from the relevant Superiors. On the 2nd. Day that my Grandfather was there, did the Chief suggest, that he give several Men, who were members of the Staff, who every Day not directly with a Weapon in the Hand, but nevertheless in any event with appreciation to devotion of Duty, they're often hard work at the AOK. Had done, the Iron Cross second Class. He did this very much so, since he knew how hard these Men had worked in seemingly minor places, for the interlocking of the many wheels of such an important Task, which the AOK. were. The Chief suggested the awarding not to do in the Name of

the Kaiser. He could not follow the recommending and did the awarding in the Name of the Upper War Lord. He thereby experienced the following:

He greeted the Soldiers of the Staff to be decorated, about 50, with" Good Evening, Comrades!" witch all happily answered, and continued:" As it is known to you, did his Majesty the Kaiser on Nov. 8 appointed me to the Upper Commander of the 1st. Army on who's point I came with Pride and Joy, because I know that your performance through the hard Years of the War earned on all Battlefields highest recognition. Not only the fighting Troops who stood directly in front of the Enemy, but also those Corporals and Men, who in many Positions at the AOK. Did they're Duty and Obligation. They did often at responsibly Posts at Day and Night they're hard work and could therefore help for a happy ending of our Operation. Many of you have for Years stood on French and Belgian Ground and earned full recognition of your Superiors so that they had given a Number of proposals to bestow the Iron Cross. I am very happy that I can give this Decoration, which you earned under the Upper Command of his Majesty the Kaiser, to you. In the Name of his Majesty the Kaiser, whom you served faithful during the War, I bestow on you the Iron Cross second Class!" During the last Words went a happy movement through the Rows of the Men. He could hear the whispered words:" Also still from the Kaiser!" and when he then on each personally the Cross on the Breast pinned, shook each Hand and asked were he came from and other relationships, was nobody who was not proud the nice Decoration to become in the Name of the Kaiser.

On Nov. 11 in the Evening came from the Army Group a Telephone Message, that his Imperial Highness the Crown Prince had resigned the Upper Command. He would go to Holland at neutral Ground and he would on the next Day at 8 in the Morning at the AOK. Of the 1st. Army arrive to say good bye to my Grandfather.

On Nov.12 at 7 in the Morning came in Rochefort the Chief of the Gen. Staff of the Army Group German Crown Prince, GenMaj. Count von der Schulenburg. He asked him if it were possible to make the Crown Prince to stay, for his Security he would guarantee, because the in the Army present Divs. were very trust worthy. Count von der Schulenburg denied this, since the consequence of the presently politic Situation and with regard of the threatening attitude of the Enemy, who would want the extradition of the Crown Prince, would make it to dangerous. At 8 in the Morning arrived the Crown Prince there. He signed the Army Group Command to the Army, in which he said good bye to the Troops. Then came the farewell from the Crown Prince of the German State and of Prussia. Once had my Grandfather got to know him at his fresh and merry Rider Nature, his Talent as Leader of tactical Tasks and his Interest in performance of many Sports at a Gen. Staff Trip of the Garde Core, who my Grandfather in 1907 lead and which lead over the Battle Fields of Jena and Auerstaedt also to the Kyffhaeuser. In the War was he in 1917 and 1918 under his Command and accompanied him several times to the Front, when he personally wanted to see the Troops or wanted to know about the Position of Friend and Foe. Always the same, with the utmost Kindness, clear political Judgement and complete understanding for Military Questions and Needs. In War was he as Army Leader at the right place. He only had Trouble with him when he had to contain his personal Courage and had to stop him from going to very dangerous Points. The Adjutant brought an Inf. Cap." No, I want to wear on this last Trip my Hussar Cap. Nobody will hurt me!" A last Handshake:" Your Imperial Highness can rely on my being Faithful until Death!" Loyal German Soldiers of all grades came together at the Garden at Rochefort, to give the leaving Crown Prince a last Salute.

The Director of the 1st. Army, the real secret Council of War Lange, informed my Grandfather of the critical Situation in which the 1st. Army would come in the next few Days. The Workers and the Soldier Counsels at the Rheine were stopping the Food allowance Trains. A pass of a single Gen. Staff Officer or an Official were impossible, because mutinous Soldiers and Deserters do the worst insubordinations in the rear Area. Of a proposal from his Chief flew an Office Supplies Officer, whose Name he did not remember any more, to Bonn. On the 3rd. Day did this brave Man come back, who had lead 1 of the Supply Trains personally and had the other Trains properly instructed. He had at the landing in Cologne trouble with Rebels and also at Negotiations with the Soldier Counsels did he have to use all of his Agility and Energy to get what he wanted. My Grandfather awarded him the Iron Cross 1st. Class.

On this Day came a Radiogram from the OHL. To the Army Group in the West:

"It is understandable, that at the momentary Situation in the Homeland, which is made worth by difficulty with the Post delivery to the Front, Rumors spread about conditions in the Homeland. In contrast it is emphasized that these Rumors are far exaggerated. In the Empire is everywhere quiet and order, only at a few places is on Nov. 9 and 10, with regrettable excesses of a few, Blood spilled. The Food requirement is with Notification from the War Ministry ensured. So there is no reason to worry about the Family in the Homeland. This Notification is immediately to announce to all Soldiers of the Field Army.

Signed: Groener."

They had first the excellent G. Kav. Schuetzen Div. under Genlt. Von Hofmann, who's Gen. Staff Officer was Capt. Papst, to march ahead, to have a reliable Troop at Hand, if the moving back rear Troops and Mutineers should commit somewhere improprieties. The AOK. Had for this reason the not so nice Task, to get as fast as possible in the backwards Area, to bring order and get the necessary preparations for the Rheine crossing, particularly to build a Bridge between Weissenthurm and Neuwied.

On Nov. 18 was the AOK. Moved to Gerolstein in the Rheine Province. It was a cold Nov. Day when they started. With him were the Gen.Surgeon Dr. Paalzow and Capt. Baron von Boenik. Soon they had reached the North March Street on which the long Wagon and Automotive Columns moved towards they're Target. The Chief had driven in the Night with Maj. Klewitz and a few Officers of the Staff ahead, to try before Daybreak and the March movements, to prepare the Business Center in Gerolstein. Many times had they to insert themselves into the Columns and wait before they could use the side, that was supposed to be kept free, but many times was not. At Clerf, were the deep cut Valley of the Rivulet, with the same name, forces the Street into big Serpentines, arose a long stop. The many Vehicles accumulated more and more. The supposedly undisciplined accompaniment Men kept an admirable quiet and followed the orders of a few Officers without trouble. So after 2 hours stop was the Road again free. During this time did he walk next to the Vehicles fore to the Clerf Bridge. During this time did he never hear an unpleasant remark, the Soldiers made readily they're salute. They were thankful for every friendly Word.

273

So also here by the generally in bad reputation standing Supply Train was nowhere a sign of beginning Mutiny. Only on the subsequent path did they overtake a few Troop Detachments from the rear Area, among them a Field Draft Depot, were the March order was bad. Inappropriate orders of the Battl. And Comp. Leaders were to blame. The Trench War on the West Front excluded mostly long Marches. Many of the Young War Officers, who lead Battls. And Comp. did not have the Piece Experience for the care of the Troops on long Marches. On a few places did he see overturned Artillery Vehicles and even a left behind Canon of heavy Caliber already on German Soil in the Ditch. At Dasburg did they cross the Border of the Rheine Province; they were again in the German Homeland!

When he on Sept. 1. 1914 at Markirch the French Border crossed, was the thought never occurred to him, that he would not victoriously come back into the Homeland, unless that he had found his last Rest Place in foreign Soil. It blew in the Villages and Towns which they drove through, the old German Flags and green Garlands greeted them with" Welcome in the Homeland!" But his Heart was heavy with hurt and suffering, and so was it probably with all German Front Soldiers!

In Gerolstein in a Hotel was a conjoint Lunch for the Staff of the 1ˢᵗ. Army. There were about 50 Officers and Officials. He raised his Glass and said:

"For the first time again on German Soil, since us 4 Years ago crossed the Border. Different we thought of the Homecoming. We want first to greed our precious Fatherland. May God shield it! We want secondly think of our Comrades, with whom we once marched out, who fought with us, who heroically gave they're Life for the Fatherland and now rest in foreign Soil. Thirdly we want to commemorate our Upper War Lord, under whose Leadership we went to Glory, Honor and Victory in the Field and over 4 Years did fight: His Majesty the Kaiser—Hurrah!"

He did not know if the roaring Hurrah of the Guests, from all Participants was sincere and honest applied. This much is sure, that there were People in the Hotel, maybe under the Orderly's or other Hotel Guests, who had nothing more urgent to do, as his words to report to Berlin!

At the Train Station in Gerolstein was a wild Chaos, because a large quantity of Men required immediate back Transit to the Homeland. A Reserve Officer in Garde Uniform had established himself as Chairman of the Worker and Soldier Counsel and Station Commander. He was sure of the best Intention, but not able of the Position, since he had no knowledge of the requirements of the Army at the necessary Railway Operation. He was ordered to the AOK. Since he had told a Gen. Staff Officer, that the Soldier Counsel would use Force over the measures for the Troops. The Chief told him in his fine manner how much he was wrong, since it is only a matter of the AOK. Orders from so far reaching importance to give. He was told, he should stay there with his knowledge of the Station Facilities in Gerolstein, who he had learned in these Days, as Commander of the Station Guard without Soldier Counsel, which he did.

In these Days visited him the GenMaj. Edler von der Planitz, a former "Maykaefer", who with 74 Years old, also went into the War. He was in various Positions, at last 1918 in North France and Belgian as Commander of the Armament Battl. 189. And he had lead this Battl. Under the hardest conditions, at the March back of the 1st. Army, after the Armistice, in total order and Discipline, in spite of his 78 Years mostly on Foot, in order to give his Men a good Example. He was able to celebrate Christmas with his Family. On Dec.31. 1918 did this exemplary Man, this splendid Type of an Old Prussian Officer, die.

On Nov. 23 was the AHQu. Moved to Neuwied. He was happy to get to know a part of the Eifel and decided to drive over Maria-Laach, to see the Monastery there. It was already quite winter and in the Mountains in places quite slippery, since they had Frost. They drove though several Villages in whom the G.Kav.Sch.D. Where in Quarter, the Men where staunch and made a good Impression. His following Decree from Nov.20 had the People welcomed with Enthusiasm, which was told him from several Officers.

Army Main Quarter, Nov.20. 1918.
Proclamation:

Since the 1ˢᵗ. Army reached the Rheine Province, is the Area from the German-Luxemburg Border to the Rheine, Operations Area. I took on Nov. 18 power of Command in the Area Asselborn— Arzfeld— Walsdorf—Heckenbach—Brohl—Neuwied—Mayen—Daun— Birresborn—Carlshausen and Niederwampach. All Military and Civil Offices are requested to support me in upholding quiet and order. Should in the forenamed Operations Area Soldier and Worker Counsels have formed, so they have of course subordinated themselves to the Military Force. The carrying of red Emblems is prohibited on the strictest.

The smooth March through of an Army in Force of 150000 Man and 60000 Horses requires that my orders and arrangements from everybody are accurately followed. The orderly accommodation of so many Troops, in such a small Area, takes large requirements of the Residents. I would be thankful, if the Inhabitants our brave Troops, after the heavy hardships of the War, would give any possible relief. On the other Hand is the Army ordered, to be most considerate towards the Homeland.

The Upper Commander."

Inclined to the Revolution was the small Town Mayen. At the Houses decoration were many red Flags used. In the Afternoon did they reach the Monastery Maria-Laach, which was beautiful situated on the Laacher Lake, in the middle of a nice Forest. It made a peaceful Impression. Also the Monastery had they're billets, the Commanding Gen. of the XXIVst. RK. Genlt. Langer with his Staff. The Abbot showed them the Treasures of the Monastery, under which were also Gifts from the Kaiser. It was dark when they reached, at the continuing Trip, the Rheine at Weissenthurm. Without any ado did they cross the Rheine with the Ferry, deeply saddened and shaken to the Heart.

In Neuwied was he quartered at the Prince Friedrich zu Wied, who he knew from his Berlin and Potsdamm service time, and was greeted with great Kindness from him and his Wife. Also in the following Days, with so much Agitation and Hardship for him, did he enjoy the Hospitality at the Princely House with Gratitude. Since from reports of several Officers, the saluting of the Men had largely failed, were they asked and they said, it were told to them, the greeting Duty were abolished. Therefore did he give the following Army Command:

"AHQ. Nov. 23. 1918.

It has spread an Opinion that the military greeting were abolished. This Opinion is false. Everybody has to his military Superior, like always, to render the salute.

The Upper Commander."

On Nov. 24 did he get a Telegram from Colon-Klettenberg:
"To the Upper Commander of the 1ˢᵗ. Army, Excellence von Eberhardt, AHQu.—Gen. Kdo. Inquire Koblenz through rear Area Inspection 1 Neuwied.

For the manly Words in the Proclamation from Nov 20 witch your Excellence at entry in the Rheine Province had announced, our Thanks, hoping that more brave German Men will follow your Example. Colon Citizens greet your Excellence, Klettenberg—Park."

The following Letter did he gets on Nov. 24. 1918 from Colon-Lindental in Typescript:

Distinguished Excellence!

In dire Distress of our Fatherland and for the Abyss, before we all stand, have all Nationalist People read your Proclamation on the Rheine Area and that you rightly forbid all red Emblems, because we are Germans and want to stay that. You will have read from the last reports of the Berlin Gatherings, how the decent Social Democracy under Scheidemann, more and more with Force gets pushed to the left, how even the most radical Independent under Haase, give more and more Space to the Liebknecht's

George von Wurmb

People, because they have the Terror of the armed lowest Mob Masses, because of the shameful own disarming of the Home Army's, which I could see here in Colon, based more on Surprise, Stupidity and lack of Energy, are the Bourgeois and also the Government Socialists completely defenseless against the handful Bawler and ultra-Socialists, better called Anarchists. Those have, because of the more and more left leaning Executive Counsel on Nov. 22 a one in 5 points culminated Agreement issued, that the Power continuously will be in the Hand, of the not from the People elected Workers and Soldiers Councils stays; also that, if a National Assembly would be elected, they should become only an advisory Voice. The Berlin Clique beliefs, with they're democratic Decree to terrorize the whole Empire. In Bavaria and here in the Rheine land are already strong Voices calling for Separation. After already the North Republic had established itself, shall the German Empire very quick disintegrate into 100 States and Towns. Without End will the inside Battles continue, and the Century-long aspired welded together German Empire, which gave us Power and Esteem, will sink in disgrace and weakness and would give room for a scare regiment of Bolshevism. Only a strong Man, a Dictator like you, Mister General, could all of us free from this terrible Incoherence. You still have your Troops in the Hand, nor has the Government Counsel a red Gard put together, the already Armed Proletariat, which stood behind Liebknecht, is today against an organized Military Force almost powerless. With 50000 Men and maybe less, could, with a light Coup, the old Government friendly Social Democracy under Scheidemann, again be helped to govern alone with the Bourgeois Party, which would then have to oblige itself to immediately convene the National Assembly and then to follow the Majority of this Assembly. After only 14 Days of Power, do the People have had enough of the Worker and Soldier Counsels and my personal observation, from the moving through Troops and at the local Workers Circles, gave me the Conviction, that an energetic occurring General from our incomparable Front Army, alone is more in the Situation to force down and ward off the Chaos and the Bolshevism from our Fatherland, with whom Foreign Countries can make no Piece and it will also grant no Bread. But highest rush is necessary, before the far left have organized they're Forces and before your last Troops, Mister General, are demobilized. You take the Leadership, Mister General, and 99 % of the whole People would cheer you as Savior of the Fatherland in highest Distress and would follow you. Let follow your wonderful Proclamation a glorious Act."

How well—meaning these Demonstrations where, and as much as he in their meaning would have acted, so unfeasible were all suggestions contained in them. The Upper Command of the Field Army had GFM. Von Hindenburg. A single Action would have promoted the Chaos. GFM. Von Hindenburg alone—this was at that time they're Opinion from Order and Discipline— could have done an independent Deed. The Army would have gladly followed this call and would have under his Leadership marched against the Rebels. That he did not do this, is because firstly to follow the Will of the Kaiser, who in order to avoid a Revolution, did abdicate and went to Holland into Exile. Then it was also the dreadful Situation, in which the German Army came, because of the nonsensical Armistice, which forced them to a hasty retreat over the Rheine, leave big amounts of important War Material and brought the Enemy close to follow. The Freedom of Determination was so completely taken from the OHL.

His orders for the 1st. Army and the Proclamation for the People of the Rheine Province caused in Berlin great Consternation. It started there Propaganda against him. The" Vorwaerts" (a Newspaper) headlined a lead Article" Der Saebelrasselnde General." (The Saber rattling General). They're Demand was:" Dieser alte Haudegen muss weg!" (This old Broad sward has to go). Other Papers agreed with this rubble-rousing. The OHL. Demanded a report about his Conduct. He gives about the Process and report the following extracts from the Files:

"Transcript from Army Group German Crown Prince
Army Group secret IV.Part.

To HGR.B					November 23.

The Imperial Chancellery requests the OHL. To determine, if the following Facts are correct and to give tomorrow morning here answer:
1. Telegram to Ebert from Colon:

AOK.1. Eberhardt dissolves the very sensible occupied Worker and Soldier Counsel Neuwied. Salute forced, Kaiser greeting, strict Ban of red Emblems, Intervenes and prevents further disquiet.

Worker and Soldier Counsel Colon.

2. to Ebert from Koblenz:
AOK.1 commands with Decree 4466 to all rear Inspections the dissolving of the Workers and Soldiers Councils. Request urgent telegraphic directive to AOK. That this order will be cancelled, also Notification here. Soldier Counsel Donath.

3. Worker and Soldier Counsel Koblenz say in long Telegram inter alia: So far good work together, at the 3rd. Army so far not the case.

AOK.1 has supposedly the following order issued:
Command Power in Operations Area taken. All Military and Civil Authority's I call on, to help me in maintaining quiet and order. Should in the pre named Operations Area Soldier and Worker Councils have been established, so must they of course come under Military Force. The bearing of red Emblems is strictly prohibited. For eccelerated message about the facts in the present matters is asked.

I S November 23. 11.55 At Night	OHL.
AOK. 1	November 24. 1918

To HGR. B.
Pertain Inquiry about taken Arrangements.
To 1. Worker and Soldier Council Neuwied were dissolved in the sense of the designated of the HGR. Ia 7311. I and II Matter under Ia 7383, were its specifically ordered, that Worker and Soldier Councils, who are not confirmed from the Government, OHL. Or HGR. Or who cause Trouble, must be eliminated. Worker and Soldier Council Neuwied is not installed from either of those Authorities, but has formed itself; Twice summoned, to come to a Meeting with the delegated Rear Area Inspection, were not complied with. Many Men have told, that the Soldier Council have spread (not only in Neuwied) that the forced Salute is stopped. There is here no doubt that the forced Salute is not stopped. He is to be maintained. The

usual Correspondence between the OHL. And the HGR. Confirmed this Conception.

According to HGR. Ia 7291 was the use of red Emblems banned. The prohibition does not exceed the necessary Military Framework.

I have on the first Evening at Home Ground in remembrance of the Upper War Lord, who lead us into the Field, in the circle of my Staff a "Hurrah" to S.M. the Kaiser proclaimed. Trouble had never occurred, on the contrary, local Authority's felt grateful for the creation of Order and elimination of Bodies, who under the Name of Soldier Council, committed Mischief and Pillage. That behind the Front, especially in Gerolstein, Mayen and all the Way to the Rheine spreading Marauder System, whom the so-called Soldier Councils steered and encouragement gave, is now shrinking.

To 2. Order to dissolving the Worker and Soldier Councils was only in the Army Section and only at rear Area Inspection 1 given, since according to Decree of the HGR. Ia 7383, Soldier Councils build outside of the Field Army have to be pushed aside. Since also the AOK. Has only to deal with Military and Civil Authority's, is they're establishment not necessary. They're participation in keeping quiet and Order was expressly permitted, but the Name "Soldier Council" was not allowed to avoid misunderstanding.

With the affairs in Koblenz, which does not belong to the Army Section, has the Army nothing to do.

To 3. The specified Command is in close imitation on that from the HGR. Recommended to spread and by Telephone dictated design.

All Orders are for the Purpose of the Government and Army Groups Decrees to maintain discipline and Order in the Army.

The Upper Commander:
Signed: von Eberhardt, Gen. of the Inf.
Ia 4468

Army Group B.   Nov. 24. 1918, before Noon.

12.35 Afternoon to Capt. von Bodecker, OHL.
To OHL. Operations Department.

To I S from Nov.23, 11.15 in the Evening.

W. and S. Council Neuwied is neither from the Government nor a Military Authority set-in, it had built itself. Twice ordered, to come to a Meeting at the rear Area Inspection, was not followed. The Soldier Council damaged the Discipline and got involved in the inner Affairs of the Field Army, since he spread the repeal of the forced Salute (not only in Neuwied). Disturbance witch W. and S. Council in Colon claims, did at Authority's and Population not happen, on the contrary, Population and local Authority's did felt grateful for elimination of organizations, who under the Name of Soldier Council, get up to mischief. Example: To the Upper Commander of the 1st. Army, Excellence von Eberhardt. For the manly Words in the Proclamation from Nov. 21 which you're Excellence at entering the Rheine Province announced, our thanks. Hoping that more brave German Men could be found which would follow this Example, greeting your Excellence, Colon Population.

Wearing of red Emblems is from the OHL. For the Field Army forbidden. The Ban is also in Force with Home Troop Detachments which, because of the move back of the Army, come under they're Command.

Command of the 1st. Army refers to, not on all rear Area Inspections, to the present wild Councils in the Operations Area of the 1st. Army, which was formed with uncontrollable Personality's.

Soldier Council Koblenz is not resolved.

Army Group B.
Ia Nr. 7440."

So much of his Report and the Operations taken from the Files.

For the time being was next to the further measures for Accommodation, Provisions and Munition replenishment of the Army in the various Sections, the completion of the Pontoon Bridge between Weissenthurm and Neuwied, they're Chief Task. It was a pleasure to watch, how under the Leadership of the Gen. of the Pioneers, Colonel Nigmann, who as Kdr. of the Garde Pioneer Battl. Had moved into the Field and got great Merits at the Battle against the Rebellion in German East Africa in 1905, the Work was completed, for the most part from older Pioneers under young Officers and Corporals, with the biggest calm and order and in spite of Interruptions, because of the strong Current, in a few Days without

Accidents. On Nov. 27 was a part of the Pontoon Bridge taken from a String of Barges. The Rheine crossing occurred in spite of that, according to Plan, first alone over the Crown Prince Bridge at Engers. The efficient Pioneers had in short time the Pontoon Bridge at Neuwied fixed, so it could be further used.

On Nov. 30 crossed the 8ˢᵗ. Bav. RD. which belonged to the VIst.RK. The Bridge at Engers, the Rheine. Under the Sounds of old Army Marches, moved the Bav. R. I. R. 19 under his Commander, Oberstlt. Von Weech, in correct order, with all Vehicles, past of my Grandfather; Many Officers and Men knew him from the time in Flanders and returned his Salute with obviously heartfelt Joy. Next to him stood his old Cadets Comrade Kurt von der Borne, with whom he had in Walstatt the War Year 1870/71 in the Tertia (3ʳᵈ. Class) experienced, as Commanding Gen. What a long eventful and fateful time between then and now – at least something became of them. After the March past did he gathers the Officers of the Reg. and gave them a brief Farewell Speech. In the process did he mention, that he at the start of the War, as Prussia, did not have it often easy, to have won the Hearts of the many Bav. Under him. But he then managed, and in Loyalty would he always think of his brave Bav. With whom he fought in the Vogesen, at the Narajowka, on the Bremond, in Flanders, at the Kemmel and at the Vesle. Amongst other things did he mention, that he would never forgive them, if they not right away would call it quits with the horror Regiment in Munich, because it would be incomprehensible for him that the Bav. Of all from Berlin a Polish Jew, Mr. Eisner, did fetch, and then in Munich dance after his Pipe! Now, the Listeners seem all to be of his View, the sequence has indeed shown, that the Bav. Can manage without such Leadership.

On Dec. 2 at 1.30 in the Afternoon did he get the following Telegram:

"General of the Inf. von Eberhardt, Upper Commander of the 1ˢᵗ. Army.

Your Excellence is under Dec.1ˢᵗ. With the statutory Pension for Disposition posed.

Berlin Dec. 1. 1918. On behalf of the War Minister. Military Cabinet.

Baron Marschall."

This Farewell Decreed has the following interesting past history. On Nov. 28. 1918 came a Resolution with the following content:

"The National Government has decided, the Gen. of the Inf. von Eberhardt to relief of his Duty's. The War Ministry shall be commissioned to cause the further.

Signed: Ebert Signed: Haase."

"To the Mr. War Minister:

I testify that this decision today is unanimously approved from the Cabinet.

Berlin, Nov. 28. 1918. Signed: Baake."

The allegation that the Decision was unanimously made is false, which from the Memo listed below shows:

"Memo (Hand writing from Mr. War Minister).

To the Imperial Government is on Nov. 29 a Letter to send, in which I ask, that I in the Future, when brought out such Resolutions, will participate.

Signed: Scheuch. Nov. 28."

When my Grandfather in Dec. 1920 to Genlt. Scheuch, without knowing the above Memo, made the reproach, he had the Resolution of his Discharge on Nov. 28 consented, did he find out from this Memo with the addition from Genlt. Scheuch, that he in a Letter to the Imperial Government on Nov. 28. 1918, said correction, then also in Person to Mr. Ebert repeated had, and that the Government, as long as he was Minister, no more got mixed up with Personnel questions for Officers and they're positions occupation.

This was also the End of an almost 45 Year Service Career, to which one can add 5 War Years." This old Broad sword has to go!" So had the Berlin Soldier Council it required and they're claim to Power pushed through against the OHL. His Report was not liked there.

On Dec. 4. 1918 did he walk with Capt. Baron von Boenigk onto the Rheine Bridge at Engers. There he on hooked his Sabre, whom he had carried with Pride all through his entire Service time, said good bye to him and threw him in the River. The Waves engulfed him, now could no Villains threaten to take it from him or break it. At the Rheine Bottom should he rest with the "Nibelungenhort", until his Grandson will raise him to Germanys Liberation!

They drove deeply moved towards east, in order to reach the new AHQu. In Giessen. It came now the Question, what he as discharged and retired Upper Commander could do. He was reluctant, with the Situation of the Fatherland, not to do anything. His Chief advised him to stay at the Upper Command, there were still many Signatures and Service Matters for him to do and he were not dispensable at that time. A Successor was not named. So he stayed. Officers of his Staff had assured him, that his staying at the ripping aimlessness of the Upper Leadership must be a big Sacrifice, which he would bring. He did not see it as such, instead as self-evidence.

The drive to Giessen through the Rheine Province and through Hesse was very nice. The clean Villages, the nice Towns shined with Decorations of Flags and Garlands to greed the Home coming Warriors. An especially friendly Impression made the picturesque small Town Benndorf. Any sign of Revolution was nowhere to be seen.

On Dec. 16. 1918 was the work at the AOK. 1 in Giessen finished. He started his last Service Trip; a special Train brought them to Potsdamm. Once there he said good Bye to the Officers of his Staff and from his long time high esteemed Chief.

His 45 Year work in the service of the Kaiser had reached the End.

End Word

No Army has until now in the History done more sublime that the German in the Years 1914/18. Certainly had, like General Ludendorff said, the World not seen a better Army, than the German from 1914. Was the defeat necessary? Marshall Foch, who already doubted in Victory, said in the Year 1928 to a Reporter of the" Neuen Freien Presse" (Newspaper new free Press) in Vienna the following:

"Even in the spring of 1918 could Germany have won the War but even in the July Offensive 1918 was Germanys Situation not hopeless. I go even further and maintain that Germany in Nov. 1918 behind the Rheine could have withstood.

If the German People had a Gambetta (a French Politician) the War would have been extended—and who knows—? I believe that a Nation, who refuses to be defeated, also must not be defeated. In Nov. 1918 had Germany of course no more Victory prospects. Had however his Army behind the Rheine withstood, so had many things taken another turn."

He gave Marshall Foch, who next to Clemenceau— certainly from a Fear Psychosis before the indeed Enemy Predominance but notably trough Treachery forced down, but still feared Enemy— our Inexorable Enemy became, right. Only he who abandons himself is lost. Because Government, Parliament and after the leaving of General Ludendorff, also the Army Leadership, gave themselves lost, in which the motives of this 3 Factors should not be identified, did the Enemy won the War.

Acta, non Verba (Latin for Deeds not Words) was the Motto of his Family. Not the Deeds of their Enemy were for the Germans dangerous, but they're Words, the unfortunately with so big success lead Lie Propaganda. Therefore you're Germans, do not believe the Word, if it comes from the Enemy's Mouth, and believe only the Deed! A Poet came to the conclusion, that in the Beginning not the Word, but the Deed stood. In reality is at every Beginning the Resolution. Is this to be a successful Deed, so he has to come without Fear from Will, Experience and the ability to bring the existing Resources, with the reachable Target for Unison. Of that was the German Leadership and also the German People missing at the end of the

War. You could also there still require Greatness from Army and People. The bitterest experience of his Life, the Nov. 1918, did not make him into a Pessimist. He believes in Germany and the German People. May the Knowledge of his Experiences contribute in the rising Generation, above all in the Hearts of the leading Men in future War times, to promote the proper valuation of the Word, the Joy of the Deed and the necessity of powerful Decision Situations to revive and strengthen.

One should after the Victory tighten the Helmet, so one should also after the defeat in Trust at the from God to the People given forces and self—criticism, in believing in yourself and his People, to step up to the Future in purposeful upward movement!

Appendix

The Governors of the Fortress Strasburg in the Elsa's during the War of 1870 General Uhrig until Sept. 28.1870.

1. 1871/75 Genlt. Von Hartmann, Sept. 1873 promoted Gen. of the Kav. 1875 retired.
2. 1875/78 Genlt. Von Schachtmeyer, March 1876 Gen. of the Inf. 1878 Commanding Gen. of the XIIIst. AK.
3. 1878/81 Genlt. Von Schkopp, 1881 as Gen. of the Inf. retired.
4. 1881 Genlt. Von Gottberg, 1881 Commanding Gen. of the Inf. AK.
5. 1881/84 Genlt. Von Massow, 1884 as Gen. of the Inf. retired
6. 1884/87 Genlt. Von der Burg, 1887 Commanding Gen. of the IInd.AK.
7. 1887/89 Genlt. Von Verdy du Vernois, April 1887 Gen. of the Inf. April 1889 Minister of State and War Minister.
8. 1889/90 Genlt. Von Lewinski II. Jan. 1890 Gen. of the Inf. Nov. 1890 Commanding Gen. of the XVst.AK.
9. 1890/92 Genlt. Von Sobbe, Jan. 1892 retired. Sept. 1892 promoted Gen. of the Inf.
10. 1892/96 Genlt. Von Bergmann, Jan.1893 promoted Gen. of the Inf. Jan. 1896 retired.
11. 1896/99 Genlt. Von Jena, Sept. 1896 promoted Gen. of the Inf. May 1899 transferred to the Officers of the Army, then retired.
12. 1899/1903 Genlt. Von Sick, Sept. 1901 promoted Gen. of the Kav. April 1903 dismissed from This Position.
13. 1903/10 Genlt. Von Mossner, Sept. 15.1904 promoted Gen. of the Kav. Oct. 16.1906 Gen. of the Kav. Of the Leib G. Hus. Reg. Jan. 1910 retired, in the World War substitute Commanding Gen. of the XXIst. AK.
14. 1910/13 Genlt. Baron von und zu Egloffstein, April 1910 Gen. of the Inf. March 1913 retired From IR.26, in the World War Commanding Gen. of the VIIIst. RK.

15. 1913/14 Genlt. Von Eberhardt, Aug.1914 Gen. of the Inf. Sept. 1914 Commanding Gen. of Core Eberhardt Dec.1914 Commanding Gen. of the XVst.RK. Sept. 1916 Commanding Gen. of the XVst. Bav. RK. Oct. 1916 Commanding Gen. of the Xst. RK. Aug. 1918 Kdr. of the 7st. Army, Nov. 1.1918 transferred to the Officers of the Army, Nov. 1918 Kdr. of the 1st. Army, Dec. 1918 retired.
16. 1914/16 as substitute promoted Genlt. Von Vietinghoff called Scheel, 1916 Kdr. of Strasburg, Juni 13.1916 Kdr.of the 92nd ID May 13 1917 deceased
17. 1916 Genlt. Von Redern, June 1916 transferred to the Officers of the Army, commissioned With the Business of Governor of Strasburg, Aug. 1916 Genlt. Dec. 1916 Kdr. of the 82st. RD. Nov. 2.1917 Leader of the Gen.Kdo. Nr. 59, Dec. 1918 transferred to the Officers Of the Army, Dec. 1918 retired.
18. 1916/17 Genlt. Zu der Mootz, Dec. 1916 substitute Governor of Strasburg,
19. 1917/18 Genlt. Herhuth von Rohden, Dec. 1917, Governor of Strasburg, Jan. 1919 retired.

Scheduled War Garrison of Strasburg in the Elsass 1914.

Governor with Staff	2nd. / Ldst. Pi. K. XIVst. AK.
Gen. of the Foot Artillery with Staff	Fest. Teleph. Abt. Strasburg
Gen. of the Pioneers with Staff	Fest. Teleph. Abt. Fest. Kaiser Wilhelm II
Traffic Officer local	Fest. Funk Abt. Strasburg
Staff of the 30st. RD.	Fest. Funk Abt. Fest. Kaiser Wilhelm II
Staff of the 60. R. I. Br.	Fest. Airship Squad 14
R. I. R. 60	Fest. Airship Squad 15
R. I. R. 70	Fest. Fl. Abt. 2
R. I. R. 99	Fest. Telegraph Comp.2
Staff of the 3rd. Bav. R. I. R. Br.	Fest. Searchlight Detachm. 7, 8, 23, 29, 37
Bav. R. I. R. 4 (4 Battl.)	Fest. Railway Constr. Comp. 7 and 8
Bav. R. I. R. 15 (3 Battl.)	Fest. Survey Abt. Nr. 2
Staff of the 10st. Bav. R. I. Br.	Immobile Ldw. Railway Constr. Comp. 4
Bav. R. I. R. 11. (2 Battl.)	Fest. MG. Abt. 1 with 6 Guns
Bav. R. I. R. 14 (3 Battl.)	Fest. MG. Abt. 2 with 8 Guns
Staff of the 44st. Ldw. Br.	Fest. MG. Abt. 3 with 6 Guns
Ldw. I. R. 71 (3 Battl.)	Fest. MG. Abt. 4 with 6 Guns

Ldw. I. R. 82 (2 Battl.)

Staff of the 52nd. Ldw. I. Br.

Ldw. I. R. 120 (3 Battl.)

Staff of the 42nd. Ldw. I. Br.

Ldw. I. R. 80 (3 Battl.)

Ldw. I. R. 81 (3 Battl.)

Substitution Kdo. 59st. I. Br.

Substitution Kdo. 84st. I. Br.

Ers. / Ldw. I. R. 60

Ers. / Ldw. I. R. 99

Res. MG. Abt. 3

Res. Hus. R. 9 (3 Squadrons)

Inspection of the Ers. Abt. Of the Field Art.

Ers. / Field Art. R. 15

Ers. / Field Art. R. 51

Ers. / Field Art. R. 80

Ers. / Field Art. R. 84

II. / Pi. Battl. 15 (4 Comp.)

1st. / R. Pi. K. 15

2nd. / R. Pi. K. 15

1st. / Ldw. Pi. K. XIII. AK.

2nd. / Ldw. Pi. K. XIII. AK.

1st. / Ldw. Pi. K. XV. AK.

2nd. / Ldw. Pi. K. XV. AK.

E. / Pi. Battl. 15

E. / Pi. Battl. 14

E. / Pi. Battl. 19

1st. / Ldst. Pi. K. XIV.AK.

Ldw. Foot A. Kdo. 10

Ldw. Foot A. Kdo. 14

Fest. MG. Detachm. Nr. 1 with 4 Guns

Fest. MG. Detachm. Nr.2 to 4 with 3 Guns

Fest. MG. Detachm. Nr. 5 to 13 with each 2 Guns

3 Fest. Signal Detachm.

San. Comp. 1 and 2

4. Bicycle Comp.

7. / Foot A.R. 13

8. / Foot A. R. 13

I. / Foot A. R. 14 (Staff, 4 Battr. 1 Park Comp.

R. Foot A. R. 10 (Staff)

I. / R. Foot A. R. 10 (1 Mun. Col. and 1 Park Comp

II. / R. Foot A. R. 10 (1 Mun. Col. and 1 Park Com

III. / R. Foot A. R. 10 (1 Mun.Col. and 1 Park Com

R. Foot A. R. 13 (Staff)

I. and II. / R. Foot A. R. 13 (with each 1 Mun. Col

and 1 Park Col.)

R. Foot A. R. 14 (Staff)

E. / Foot A. R. 13 (Staff and 6 Battr.) 2 Recruit

Depots, Horse-Team Detachm.

E. / Foot A. R. 14 (Staff and 6 Battr.) 1 Recruit

Depot

Ldw. Foot A. Battl. 1 XIV. A. K.(Staff and 4 Battr.)

Foot A. Br. Kdo. 4

Park Kdo. 4

Park Battr. Staff 5 and 8

Ldw. Foot A. Battl. 10 (Staff, 4 Battr.
1 Park Comp.)
Ldw. Foot A. Battl.14 (Staff, 4 Battr.
1 Park Comp.)
Ldw. Foot A. Battl. 18 (Staff, 4 Battr.
1 Park Comp.)
7 overplaned Foot A. Battr.
E. / Foot A. R. 10 (Staff and 6 Battr.)
2 Recruit Depots, Horse-Team
Detachm.

Persons Register

Abel (Oberstlt. Colonel)

Adam (Teacher in Heilig—Blasien in Vogesen

Armin Sixt von (Gen. of Inf.)

Alberthausen (Lt.)

Altrock von (GenMaj.)

Amann von(Maj.)

Auwaerter von (Genmaj.)

Baake (Office Secretary)

Backhaus (Assessor)

Bahls (Kav.Capt.)

Bartenwerffer von (Maj.)

Bauer (Bav. Maj.)

Beck Baron von (Quarter Master)

Beck von (GenMaj.)

Below von Fritz (Gen.of the Inf.)

Below von Otto (Gen.of Inf.)

Beneckendorf von (Gen. Field Marshall)

Borch Baron von dem (GenMaj.)

Borne von dem (Gen. of Inf.)

Bowien (Capt.)

Brederlow von Anton (Kav. Capt.)

Bressler (GenMaj.)

Buerkner (Lt. Colonel)

Caloun Baron de (Belgian Castle Owner)

Carl (Colonel)

Christian Viktor (Bav. Militia Man)

Clauss Knight von (Bav. GenMaj.)

Cossel von (Capt.)

Berchem Baron von (Maj.)

Berendt von (GenMaj. Genlt.

Berlet (Oberstlt.

Beseler (Colonel)

Bismarck Prince (Chancellor)

Bleibtreu (Maj.)

Bleichert (Constr.Comp in Leipzig)

Blomberg von (Maj.)

Boeckmann von (Oberstlt. Colonel GenMaj.)

Bodecker von (Capt.)

Bodungen von (Genlt.)

Boehm-Ermolli (Gen. Colonel)

Boehn von (Gen.of Inf. Gen.Colonel)

Boenigk Baron von (Capt.)

Bohrer (Vice Sergant II. Bav. Ers. R. 2.)

Benzino Knight von (Bav. Gen. of Inf.)

Bothmer Count von (Bav. Gen. of Inf.)

Braun Knight von (Bav. Maj.)

Brehme (Lt. Colonel)

Breyer (Lt. Colonel)

Busse Eberhard (Commiss.Council)

Caprivi von (Lt. Colonel)

Castell-Ruedenhausen Paul (Colonel)

Christiansen (Lt.)

Clemenceau (French Prime Minister)

Dallmer (Genlt.)

Dallwitz von (Governor of Germ. Area)

Dame (Genlt.)

Daenner (Bav. GenMaj.)

Dayler (French Lt.Colonel)

Decken von der (Saxonian GenMaj.)

Deimling von (Gen. of Inf.)

Delbrueck von (Chief Civil Cabinet)

Deppert (Bav. GenMaj.)

Dewitz-Krebs von (Capt.)

Dieffenbach (Gen. of Inf.)

Dinkelacker von (GenMaj.)

Dinglinger (Capt.)

Dippel (Director of Musik)

Dippon Hermann (Sergeant/ Pilot)

Dippon Karl (Corporal)

Dirichsweiler (Forest Master)

Dittler (Capt.)

Dommes von (GenMaj.)

Donop von (GenMaj.)

Drabich-Waechter von (Genlt.)

Dubail (French Gen.)

Eben von (Genlt.)

Dellmensingen Kraft von (Bav. Genlt.)

Eberhardt Gaspard von (Genlt.)

Eberhardt von Friedrich-Wilhelm-Magnus (Maj.)

Eberhardt Heinrich von (GenMaj.)

Eberhardt von Hans-Joachim (Capt.)

Eberhardt Klara von born von Kalitsch

Eberhardt von Klara born von Reuss

Wife of the Gen. of the Inf.

Mother of the Gen. of Inf.

Eberhardt Wilhelm von (Genlt.)

Eberhardt von Walter (Genlt.)

Ebert (State Chancellor)

Eberhardt von Wilhelm-Magnus(Maj.)

Egli (Colonel, Chief of Swiss Gen. Staff)

Eichhorn (Bav. Genlt.)

Eiermann (Lt. of Reserv.)

Eisenhart—Rothe von (Genlt.)

Eisner (Bav. Prime Minister)

Eitel Friedrich (Prince of Prussia)

Elner (Infan. 3. / Bav. Ers. Battl.)

d'Elsa (Saxonian GenOb.)

Emmich von (Gen. of Inf.)

Epp Knight von (Bav. Colonel)

Erpf von (GenMaj.)

Ertl (Bav. Colonel)

Ertl (Bav. sec. Lt.)

Erzberger (Centrum Deputy)

Esebeck Baron von (Maj.)

Etzel (Bav. Maj.)

Etzel von (Genlt.)

Falk von (Gen.of Inf.)

Eckstaedt Bitzthum Count von (GenMaj.)

Falkenhausen Baron von (Gen. of Inf.)

Falkenhayn von (Capt.)

Falkenhayn von (Gen. of Inf. Prussian War Minist. Chief of Gen. Staff)

Feeser (Bav. Maj.)

Fehr (Government Assessor)

Fehr (Oberstlt.)

Feilitzsch Baron von (Bav. Colonel)

Felmy (Capt.)

Fels (Bav. Oberstlt.)

Ferjientsik (Oberstlt.)

Ferling von (Genlt.)

Fink von Finkenstein Count (Gen. of Inf.)

Fischeneuer (Corp. 3. / Bav. Ers. R. 1.)

Foch (French Marshall)

Foerster (Oberstlt.)

Francois von (Gen. of Inf.)

Franke (Capt.)

Franz (GenMaj. Prince of Bav.)

Franz Ferdinand (Duke of Austr. and Ungarn)

Franz Josef (Kaiser of Austria and Ungarn)

Freyer (GenMaj.)

Frick (Gunner Fortr. MG. Comp. 7.)

Friedrich Prince zu Wied (GenMaj.)

Friedrich II. (King of Prussia)

Friedrich II. (Gen. Field Marshall, Duke of Baden)

Friedrich III. (Germ. Kaiser / King of Prussia)

Friedrich August (King of Saxonian)

Friedrich Karl (Gen. Field Marshall, Prince of Prussia)

Friedrich Karls Wife, Princess of Prus. born Prnc. Maria-Anna von Anhalt

Friedrich Wilhelm IV. (King of Prussia)

Fritsch (Colonel)

Fritsch von (Genlt.)

Froehlich Christian (Russian Soldier)

Frommel Knight von (Bav. Gen. of the Kavalry)

Fuchs (Genlt.)

Gabain von (Gen. of Inf.)

Gaede (Gen. of Inf.)

Gaede (Capt.)

Galland (Mayor of Heilig-Blasien Vogesen)

Galland (Merchant in Heilig-Blasien/ Vogesen

Ganser (Corporal 3. / Bav. Ers. R. 1.)

Georg (Maj. Prince of Bav.)

Gerock von (Gen. of Inf.)

Geyer (Capt.)

Gilsa Baron von und zu (Capt.)

Glasenapp von (Genlt.)

Glasenapp von (Capt.)

Gorad (Sergeant (3. / Bav. Ers. R. 1.)

Goerschen von (Oberstlt.)

Grassman (Bav. Oberstlt.)

Gratier (French Gen.)

Grolmann von (Gen. of Inf.)

Grueber (Bav. GenMaj. Genlt.)

Gruenert (GenMaj.)

Guendell von (Gen. of Inf.)

Guth (Lt.)

Haase (Member of Socialdemocracy)

Hahn (Maj.)

Hahn von (Genlt.)

Hamann (Genlt.)

Hindenburg von (Gen. Field Marshall)

Hammerstein-Equord Baron von (GenMaj.)

Hansi (Painter)

Hasse Otto (Gen. of Inf.)

Hausmann (Capt.)

Heeringen von (Colonel, GenOb.)

Hegel (Philosopher)

Hemmer Knight von (Bav. Oberstlt.)

Heyde von der (Genlt.)

Heydebreck von (Genlt.)

Heyden-Linden von (sec.Lt.)

Hinkelday von (sec.Lt.)

Hoefer (GenMaj.)

Hoetzendorf Conrad von (Quarter Master, Chief Austian Gen. Staff)

Hohl (Kav. Capt.)

Hoiningen Baron called von Huehne (Gen. of Inf.)

Goeckel von (Capt.)

Goerne von (Maj.)

Gossler von (Gen. of Inf. Pruss. War Minister)

Grohe (Maj.)

Groener (Genlt.)

Grueber Else (Red Cross Nurse)

Guderian (Capt.)

Guenther (Maj.)

Guenz-Rekowski von (GenMaj.)

Hellningk (Lt.)

Hahn (sec.Lt.)

Hahnke von (Gen.Colonel)

Hangy (Lt.)

Haenisch von (Gen. of Kav.)

Haenisch von (Genlt.)

Hartmann (Capt.)

Hassenstein (Maj.Oberstlt.)

Hedicke (Capt.)

Hegel (Bav. Oberstlt.)

Helmer (Core R. I. R. 230)

Herold (Colonel)

Heydebreck von (Maj.)

Heydebreck von (Capt.)

Heye (Colonel)

Hinzler (Bav. GenMaj.)

Hoffmann (Oberstlt.)

Hofmann von (Genlt.)

Hohenlohe Duke (Gen. of Inf.)

Hoelderlein (Bav.Maj.)

Hoehn Knight von (Bav. Gen. of Art.)

Hoeppner von (Genlt.)

Holnstein Count von (Bav. Oberstlt.)

Hosse (Capt.)

Hopfgarten von called Heidler (Genlt.)

Hoesslin von (Bav. Capt.)

Huf (Riflem. Fortr. MG. Comp. 7.) Huelsen Bernhard von (GenMaj.)

Huelsen Walther von (Genlt.)

Humser (Maj.)

Hutier von (Gen. of Inf.)

Ihssen (sec.Lt.)

Ilse (Genlt.)

Ipfelkofer (Bav. Genlt.)

Isenburg (sec.Lt.)

Jacobi von (Oberstlt.)

Jahn (sec. Lt. Resv.)

Janson (Lt.)

Jaud (Colonel)

Jehlin (GenMaj.)

Johannsen (Forest Master)

Jost (Riflem. Fortr. MG. Comp. 7.)

Jostow (Bulgarian Genlt. Chief of Bulg. Gen. Staff)

Karbe (Oberstlt.)

Karl (Kaiser of Austria, King of Ungarn)

Kastran (Sergeant 10. / I. R. 59)

Kaulbach (Maj.)

Keiser von (Oberstlt.)

Kessel von (Gen. Colonel)

Klewitz (Maj.)

Kleinhenz Knight von (Bav. GenMaj.)

Klueber von (Maj.)

Kneussl Knight von (Bav. Genlt.)

Kluge von (Capt.)

Knoerzer von (Genlt. Gen.of Kav.)

Koenig von (sec. Lt.)

Koeberle Knight von (Bav. GenMaj.)

Kollmann (Bav. GenMaj.)

Koepke (Genlt.)

Kortgien (Maj.)

Kranz (Capt.)

Krause (Genlt.)

Krenker (Capt.of Reserv.)

Krieger (Bav. GenMaj.)

Kressenstein Kress von (Bav. Gen. of Kav. Bav. War Minister)

Kroecher von (Capt.)

Kuhl von (Gen. of Inf.)

Kuehn von (Maj.)

Kumme (Oberstlt.)

Kuester (GenMaj.)

Lachemair von (Bav. Genlt.)

Lambsdorf Count von (Capt.)

Lambrecht (Sergeant 2. / R. Pi. Battl. 5.)

Lange (Vice Sergeant II. RIR. 70.)

Langen Lang von (Lt. War Volunteer R. Hus. R. 9.)

Lange (Privy Councillor)

Langenmeyer (Capt.)
Langenhaeuser (Bav. GenMaj.)
Lentze von (Gen. of Inf.)
Leopold (Prince of Bav. Gen.Field Marshall)
Lerche (sec.Lt.)
Leyser von (Genlt.)
Lignitz von (Gen. of Inf.)
Loewenstern Baron von (Kav. Capt.)
Lossberg von (GenMaj. Gen.)
Loewenfeld von (Capt.)
Ludendorff (Gen. of Inf. first Gen. Quarter Master
Luedecke (Vice Sergeant 1. / RIR. 236.)
Luettwitz Baron von (Gen. of Inf.)
Mach von (Kav. Capt.)
Mandel (Secretary of State)
Markschiess (Riflem. Fortr. MG. Comp. 7.)
Marshall called Greif Baron (GenMaj.)
Max Prince from Baden, Chancellor
Metz de (French Battl. Kdr.)
Meyer von (Capt.)
Michahelles (Bav. GenMaj.)
Missfelder (sec. Lt.)
Moeller von (Genlt.)
Moltke Count von (Gen. Field Marshall, Chief of Gen. Staff)
Muehlnheim Mueldner von (Maj.)
Mueller (Bav. Genlt.)
Mueller (Kav. Capt.)
Mueller-Loebnitz (Maj.)
Nagel Baron von zu Aichberg (Bav. GenMaj.)

Langer (Genlt.)
Larisch von (Gen. of Inf.)
Lenz Knight von (Bav. Oberstlt.)
Lequis (GenMaj.)

Leyh (Bav. Maj.)
Liebert von (Gen. of Inf.)
Lindequist von (Genlt.)
Lindow (Maj.)

Loewenfeld von (Gen. of Inf.)
Luedecke (Capt.)
Ludwig III. (King of Bav.)

Luehmann (sec. Lt.)

Lussy (Riflem. G.Fues. Reg.)
Maerker (GenMaj.)
Mark (Bav. GenMaj.)
Marshall Baron (Gen. of Kav.)

Mathy (Genlt.)

Mertens von (GenMaj.)

Mewes (Capt.)
Meyer (Bav. Genlt.)
Michelmann von (sec. Lt.)
Mittler & Sons Publishing House
Moehl Knight von (Bav. GenMaj.)
Mohs (Maj.)

Mudra von (Gen of Inf.)
Mueller (Saxonian Genlt.)
Mueller Friedrich (Genlt.)
Muenter (Bav. GenMaj.)
Neuber (Genlt.)

Neumann Walther (Kav. Capt. of   Neumann (Capt.)
Reserve. Publisher)
Nigmann (Colonel)   Nikolai (GenMaj.)
Nikolaus II. (Kaiser of Russia)   Nivelles (French Gen.)
Oldershausen Baron von (Saxonian   Oertzen von (Oberstlt.)
GenMaj.)
Ostini Baron von (Bav. Maj.)   Paalzow (Chief Phys. Dr.)
Pacczynski-Tenczin von (Colonel)   Pascha Djevad (Osman. Gen.)
Papst (Capt.)   Passage (French Gen.)
Pau (French Gen.)   Pauli (Privy Councillor)
Paulus (Oberstlt.)   Pavel von (Genlt.)
Pawel-Rammingen von (Kav.   Petersdorff (Lt.)
Capt.)
Petersdorff von (Genlt.)   Petersen (Oberstlt.)
Petri (Capt.)   Pfeifer (Lt.)
Pilz (Country Forest Master)   Plessen von (Gen.Colonel)
Planitz Edler von der (Saxonian   Pohl (Colonel)
Gen. of Inf.)
Polmann (Oberstlt.)   Poschinger Knight von (Maj.)
Pretzell (Capt.)   Pretzsch (Capt.)
Quast von (Gen. of Inf.)   Rakoff (Bulgarian Oberstlt.)
Quirnheim Knight Mertz von (Bav.   Ramdor (sec. Lt.)
Colonel)
Roseneck Nickisch von (Maj.)   Rantzau von (GenMaj.)
Rasch (GenMaj.)   Rath von (Colonel)
Rauch von (Oberstlt.)   Rayle (Oberstlt.)
Reich (Maj.)   Reinhardt (Colonel)
Reinhardt Knight von (Bav. Maj.)   Rentner (Capt.)
Reuss Heinrich von (Colonel)   Reuss Heinrich-Adolf von (Lt.)
Reuter (Maj.)   Rietzschel (Bav. Maj.)
Rifaat Bey (Osman. Maj.)   Risch (Capt.of Reserv.)
Roeder von (Maj.)   Roerdanss (Maj.)
Roedern Count von (State   Roeth (Lt.)
Secretary)
Rohr (Maj. Leader of the Storm   Rolfs (Lt.)
Battl.)
Roon Count von (Gen. Field   Roemer (Professor)
Marshall, Prussian War Min.)

Roeschke (Maj.)
Rumschoettel (GenMaj.)
Rupprecht (Crown Prince of
Bav. Gen. Field Marshall Leader
of Army Group Crown Prince
Rupprecht)
Schaefer von (Oberstlt. Director of
War History of the Army)
Sulicki Klara von, born von
Eberhardt
Schellendorff Bronsart von
(Oberstlt.)
Scheele (Rifleman Jaeg. Battl. 14.)
Schellkopf (Lt.)
Scheuch (Genlt. Prussian
War Min.)
Schippert von (Genlt.)
Schlieffen Count von (Gen. of Kav.
Gen. Field Marshall Chief of Gen.
Staff)
Schmettow Count von Eberhard
(Genlt.)
Schmit (Rifleman 1. / IR. 119)
Schoeler von (Genlt.)
Schoenfelder (Officer substit.
RIR. 230.)
Schroeder von (Admiral)
Schubert von (Gen. of Artill.)
Schulenburg Count von der
(GenMaj.)
Schulenburg-Wolfsburg Count von
der (Colonel)
Schuster (Lt.)
Schwander (Upper Mayor of
Strasburg / Elsass)
Schwerin Count von (Gen. of Inf.)
Seybold (Corporal 3. / Bav. Ers.
Battl. 1)

Ruith Knight von (Maj.)
Runkel von (Genlt.)
Sarrade (French Gen.)

Sulicki Marschall von (Genlt.)

Schaeffer (Commiss. Council)

Schaeffer von (Maj.)

Schell von (Maj.)
Scherer (Capt.)
Schikowski von (sec.Lt.)

Schlueter (Lt.)
Schmidt (Capt.)
Schmidt (Lt.)

Schmiedecke (Genlt.)

Schmitt Konstantin (Capt.)
Schoetti (Bav. Oberstlt.)
Schroeder (Maj.)

Schubert (Bav. Maj.)
Schueller (Capt.)
Schulz von (Lt.)

Schurig (Capt.)

Seldner (sec. Lt.)
Senftleben (Capt.)

Seudel (Capt.)
Sieger (Genlt.)

Soden Baron von (Gen. of Inf.)
Staabs von (Gen. of Inf. Kdr. XXXIX. RK.)
Stadthagen (Colonel)
Stein von (State Secretary)
Stemmler (Rifleman Saxon. IR. 107)
Stetten Baron von (Bav. Gen. of Kav.)
Stuelpnagel von (Gen. of Inf.)
Sunkel (Genlt.)
Sydow von (sec.Lt.)
Tattenbach Count von (Maj.)
Teetzmann (GenMaj.)
Thormann (Factory Owner in Heilig-Blasien/Vogesen
Tieschowa Tieschowitz von (Oberstlt.)
Toost (Capt.)
Tutschek Knight von (Bav. GenMaj.)
Uechtritz und Steinkirch von (GenMaj.)
Umbach (Lt.)
Unger (Professor)
Velten (Lt. of Resev.)
Versen von Lonni (Red Cross Sister)
Vietinghoff called Scheel Baron von (Genlt.)
Vogeley (sec. Lt.)
Wagner (Rifleman 3. /Bav. Ers. Battl. 1.)
Waldersee Count von (Gen. of Kav. Chief of Gen. Staff Gen. Field Marshall)
Wartenberg von (Genlt.)
Watter Baron von (GenMaj.)

Siehr (oberstlt.)
Spranger (Capt.)

Stapf (Maj.)
Stengel Baron von (Oberstlt.)
Stietencron von (Capt.)

Stranz von (Gen. of Inf.)

Stuenzner von (Gen. of Kav.)
Suter von (GenMaj.)
Tann Baron von der (Lt.)
Tappen (Colonel)
Tettenborn von (Sax.Genlt.)
Tippelskirch von (Capt.)

Toepfer (Capt.)

Tuechert (Capt.)
Twickler (Rifleman IR. 78.)

Ulfert (Maj.)

Unger Fritz von (Genlt.)
Uthmann von Genlt.)
Vignau du (Oberstlt.)
Volkmann (Maj.)

Vogel (Colonel)

Waechter von (sec. Lt.)
Wagner (Capt.)

Waldorf (Genlt.)

Wasserfall (Maj.)
Weech von (Oberstlt.)

Weidner (Colonel)

Weizenegger (Colonel)

Wember (War Volunteer R. Hus. R. 9.)

Wencher von (Genlt.)

Westernhagen von (sec.Lt.)

Wetterle (Member of Parlament)

Wicke (Capt.)

Wiedebach-Rostitz von (Kav. Capt.)

Wiese (Corporal 4. / IR. 42.)

Wilhelm I. (King of Prussia, Germ. Kaiser)

Wilhelm II. (King of Prussia, Germ. Kaiser)

Wilhelm (Crown Prince, Gen. of Inf. Kdr. Army Group Germ. Crownprince)

Wrangel Count von (Gen. Field Marshall)

Xylander Knight von (Bav. Gen. of Inf.)

Zech Count von (Bav. GenMaj.)

Zechlin (Oberstlt.)

Ziegler (sec. Lt.)

Zimmermann (sec. Lt.)

Zobeltitz von (Capt.)

Weis (French Gen.)

Wissel von (GenMaj.)

Wist (Maj.)

Werthern Baron von (Maj.)

Westhoven von (Maj.)

Wichura(Gen. of Inf.)

Wittgen von (Colonel)

Wiedner von (Capt.)

Witting (Capt.)

Wolf von (Maj.)

Woellwarth (Colonel)

Wilberg (Capt.)

Wrede (Lt.)

Winter (sec. Lt.)

Wundt (GenMaj.)

Zahn von (Professor)

Zeitz (Capt.)

Zietlow (Genlt.)

Zimpelmann (Oberstlt.)

Zuehlke (Capt.)

Korps-Haupt-Quartier St. Blaise (Heilig-Blasien)

Eberhardt-Bahn im Bau

Unterer Teil der Eberhardt-Bahn (Bahnhof Prinzenwald). Rechts: Endstation der Eberhardt-Bahn auf Chaume de Lusse (900 m)

nach rechts: Gen. d. Inf. v. Eberhardt (Kom. Gen. des XV. RK.); der größte Esel der Tragtierkolonne; Genlt. v. Gynz-Rekowski (Kdr. der 39. RD.).

Märj 1915 in Allarmont im Plainetal

Von links nach rechts: GenOberst Frhr. v. Falkenhausen (Oberbefehlshaber der AA.), Genmaj. Neuber
(Kdr. der 84. Landw J.Br.), Gen. der Inf. v. Eberhardt (Kom. Gen. des XV. RK.)

Genlt. Krause (Kdr. der 30. RD.) mit den Offizieren
des bayer. ErfBatl. 8

Am 18. Märj 1915 auf dem Adlerfelsen nördlich Les Noires Colas im Plainetal
nordöstlich Celles

Von links nach rechts: Rittm. Vahls (Generalstab des XV. RK.); Gen. der Inf. v. Eberhardt (Kom. Gen. des
XV. R.K.); Genmaj. Neuber (Kdr. der 84. Landw JBr.); Oblt. Burckhardt (R.Adj.RJR. 70); GenOberst Frhr.
v. Falkenhausen (Oberbefehlshaber der AA.); Rittm. v. Westenhagen (Adj. des AOK.); Oberst Stabthagen (Kdr.
des RJR. 70); Oblt. der Res. Bornhardt (RJR. 70); Lt. Kettner (Ord.-Off. beim AOK.); Lt. Koch (Ord.-Off.
beim XV. RK.); Prof. Verber (Kraftwagenf. beim AOK.); ganj rechts Gefr. Schäfer (Kraftwagenf. beim XV. R.K.).

Printed in the United States
By Bookmasters